THE u.k. internet starter kit

CONTENTS

INTRODUCTION

The Internet really hit the headlines in a big way in 1994. People started talking about it, national newspapers started featuring articles about it, and those weird-looking addresses full of dots and dashes started popping up at the end of TV shows and adverts. 'Ah yes', everyone said, knowingly. 'Hype – it'll be something different next year.' But something unexpected happened…

Unlike most other objects of media hype in recent years, after the dust has settled millions of people are still using the Internet every day – for entertainment, for business, for leisure, to communicate with others, to learn or research, to buy goods, the list is almost endless. And every day the number of people using the Internet grows by thousands. If these people were not finding it useful, or enjoyable, that number would instead be getting smaller.

These people can't all be computer whiz-kids either, can they? In fact, you don't have to be a technical genius to use the Internet. As long as you're reasonably comfortable with using a PC and Windows, it is no more tricky than anything else that you already use your computer for. What really happened in 1994, even though the Internet has actually been around since the 1960s, was the appearance of new software that made it friendly and easy to use.

But all that's history, and I'm not going to bore you with lengthy history lessons, or throw a lot of impressive but unnecessary jargon at you. The aim of this book is twofold – first, to help you connect your computer to the

Internet and find your way around it, and second, to point you towards the practical, useful, or just plain fun things that the Internet has to offer. To that end, any technical detail that you won't need straight away has been banished to the back of the book. In fact, you may never need all that technical detail at all!

Why Do I Need a UK Guide to the Internet?

In the UK we use the Internet differently from our US counterparts: different companies provide the services we need, charge different prices for them, and give us different options to choose from. And once we're connected, we want to find the information that matters to us, so we need to look in different places to find it. In addition, because we're not from the USA (or France, or Italy, etc), our interests, habits, laws, environment and whole way of life differ enormously. These affect both the way we use the Internet, and what we use it for.

- Most US users have access to free local telephone calls, which means that they can stay connected to the Internet all day long for no extra charge. In the UK we still pay by the minute, and to follow some of the suggestions given in a US guide could end up costing a small fortune! Throughout this book, it's assumed that you want your time on the Internet to have as little impact as possible on the size of your telephone bill.

- As a UK user, you want to find UK information. For example, you want to read UK newspapers and magazines; see local weather forecasts; check local TV listings and sports results; find out what's showing at your nearest cinema; use UK travel agents, hotels, airlines, and trains; plan days out at UK theme parks and museums, and so on.

- Many Internet sites give support, help and advice on any subject you can imagine. Although some US Internet books can point you towards valuable information, they won't tell you where to get the best UK legal or consumer advice, find a job, or discuss financial matters with other UK investors.

- You can now buy almost anything from 'cyberstores' on the Internet. But do you really want to do your shopping in dollars and wait for the goods to be shipped from America when there are plenty of UK shopping sites just a couple of mouse clicks away? In fact, if you want to use the Internet to arrange car insurance, manage your bank account, or book theatre tickets, among other things, you'll have to find the right sites in the UK!

How Is This Book Organised?

This book is split into six major parts to help you find the answers you want quickly and easily.

Part 1 ***Getting Online,*** introduces all the basic concepts and services of the Internet, helps you choose the type of Internet account that suits you best, and tells you what you need to know to get online.

Part 2 ***Finding your Way Around,*** shows you the main services you can use on the Internet, and the software you'll need to access them. All of this software can be found on the CD-ROM in the back of this book (as well as on the Internet itself), and these chapters explain how to set it up and how to use it.

Part 3 ***Using the Internet,*** gives an in-depth guide to using your connection and software to accomplish something on the Internet, such as reading online newspapers and magazines, researching, shopping, planning days out, finding computer software, managing your bank account, or just having heaps of fun.

Part 4 ***The Web – Active and Interactive,*** introduces you to multimedia on the Internet, and leads you to some of the weird, wonderful and exotic locations on the World Wide Web. You'll also learn how to design your own World Wide Web pages and publish them for the rest of the world to see.

The Appendices section includes handy references, lists and glossaries, and a 'JargonBuster Super Reference' to help you decipher what everyone's talking about!

The Directory is a useful collection of contact details for companies that provide access to the Internet, sell computer software and hardware, or offer other computer-related services.

How Should I Use It?

This book is organised in such a way that you can read it from cover to cover if you want to, but you certainly don't have to. Personally, I like books that you can dip into and learn something new from reading just a couple of paragraphs, so don't feel guilty if you like to do that too! You'll find plenty of cross-references to tempt you towards other parts of the book. However, I do have a few suggestions:

- If you haven't yet connected to the Internet and you don't have an Internet account, I recommend that you read the first two parts of the book, which will help you get online and give you all the basic information in a sensible order.
- If you already have an Internet connection, you can cheerfully skip Part 1 and begin at Part 2, which will set you on the road to mastering the Internet's services and software.
- If you've been using the Internet's tools and services for a while and you know the basics, skip about the book all you like. You may still find some things you didn't know in Part 2, but I suggest taking a look at Parts 3 and 4 – you'll find plenty of great sites to visit, together with information and tips to help you get the most out of the Internet, design and publish your own web pages, explore virtual worlds online, and lots more.

Icons & Conventions

Throughout the book I've used a few special features and conventions that make it easier to find your way around. In particular you'll see that chapters are split up into bite-sized chunks with subheadings. If something looks a bit complicated or dull, just skip to the next heading.

You'll also find some icons and text in boxes containing extra information that you may find useful:

A question-and-answer format highlighting questions or problems that may present themselves while you're reading about something or trying it out yourself.

A selection of handy hints, tips and incidental notes that may save you some time, point you in a new direction, or even help you avoid pitfalls.

Explains any technical terms that couldn't be avoided, or any related jargon that you may encounter when dealing with a particular area of the Internet.

Indicates that the software program being mentioned is included on the free CD-ROM that is attached to the inside back cover of this book.

I've also used different type-styles and keyboard conventions to make particular meanings clear, as shown below.

Convention	Description
Bold Type	indicates a new term being encountered, an Internet address, or text that you'll type yourself
Bold-italic Type	means that you'll type this text yourself, but I don't know exactly what it will be. For example, if you have to type the location of a file you want to open, you'll see something like **open *directory/filename***
Ctrl+C	A key-combination, saving frequent mouse excursions to pull-down menus. The keys to press will be separated by'+' signs. This example means press and hold the 'Ctrl' key while pressing 'C' once
File | Open	Means that you should open the software's 'File' menu, and select its 'Open' option. You might see something longer, such as View | Options | General: in this case you'll open the 'View' menu, select the 'Options' entry and then click on something that says 'General' – it may be a button or a tabbed page, but it will always be obvious when you get there!
Enter	Although I've referred to the 'Enter' key throughout, on your keyboard this key might be labelled 'Return' instead
Directories	To users of Windows 95 and later, these are better known as 'folders'. On the Internet (as in MS-DOS and Windows 3x) they're known as 'directories', but the meaning is the same

A Few Basic Assumptions

Finally, I'm assuming that you know how to use a computer and you're reasonably familiar with the different parts of Windows. By that, I mean that you know how to use the mouse, you understand what directories and files are, you're comfortable with using menus and dialogs, and you know how to start programs and switch between windows. If you get stuck, you can usually find the answers in Windows' Help files, but for a solid grounding in how to use your computer and Windows, grab a copy of my book, *The 'What PC?' Guide To Your PC,* also published by Prentice Hall.

1

GETTING ONLINE

In This Part...

1 **Meet the Internet**

2 **How Can I Get Online?**

3 **Connecting to an Access Provider**

4 **Connecting to an Online Service**

1

MEET THE INTERNET

In This Chapter...

- Find out what the Internet really is
- Discover some of the great things you can do on the Net
- Meet the seven most popular areas of the Internet
- Learn what those cryptic addresses are all about

Before you can really get excited at the prospect of 'getting on the Internet', it helps to have some idea of what it really is, what you can use it for, and (I hate to say it) how it works. So let's kick off by looking at how the Internet is organised, and at some of the ways you can use it. I'm also going to introduce most of the technical-sounding stuff you'll need to know in this chapter. It's all quite painless, though, and hopefully this appetiser will leave you hungry for the main course.

What Is the Internet?

This is the obvious first question that everyone asks, but to avoid blinding you with science, let's try and skip through its literal answer as quickly as possible. The technical explanation is that it's a giant, worldwide computer network made up of lots of smaller computer networks. As with any network, these computers are connected to one another so that they can share information. However, unlike most networks the vastness of the Internet means that this information has to be passed around using modems and telephone lines rather than an office full of cables.

But all that's just hardware, and it's probably not making your mouth water. Instead, let's zoom in on that word 'information', the key to the real Internet. The types of information that these computers can share covers an enormous (and ever-expanding) range – pictures, sounds, text, video, applications, music, and much more – making the Internet a true multimedia experience. Anyone can connect their home or office computer to the Internet and gain almost instant access to many millions of files, browse around, or search for some specific item, and grab as much as they want while they're there.

GOOD QUESTION

How big is the Internet?

When it comes to numbers, no one knows. A lot of informed guesswork goes on, but it doesn't look terribly well informed when you compare results. It's safest just to say that millions of computers are serving tens of millions of people, and leave it at that. To be honest, even if I could give you the exact numbers right now, they'd be wrong by lunchtime and wildly inaccurate before *EastEnders* started.

People Power

The other aspect of the real Internet is people. All the information you'll find is put there by real people, often simply because they want to share their knowledge, skills, interests or creations with anyone who's interested. The people themselves may be companies keen to promote their products; organisations such as universities, charities and governments; or individual users like you and me.

Along with people, of course, comes communication, and the Internet is a great communications system. You can exchange messages (email) with other users, as you'll see in Chapter 7, hold conversations or online meetings by typing messages back and forth, or actually send your voice over the Internet using a microphone instead of a telephone (which we'll investigate in Chapter 10). You can take part in any of twenty-eight thousand discussion groups on any subject you'd care to mention (and quite a few more you wouldn't!), and you'll find out how in Chapter 8. Add to this the wealth of human knowledge and experience that lies at its heart, and the Internet is, quite simply, a very big place that makes the world seem much smaller.

What Can I Use It For?

Once you're armed with a connection to the Internet, the possibilities for using it could fill a book. (Well OK, they do fill a book – that's why you picked it up!) Here's just a tiny sample of the things you can do on the Net, all of which you'll be learning about later:

- Control robots and movie cameras on other continents while the live camera footage is beamed straight to your desktop.
- Book a skiing holiday online, and check the snow conditions in your chosen resort with up-to-the-minute pictures.
- Hold conversations with people on the other side of the world by typing on your keyboard, talking into a microphone, or adopting the role of a cartoon character.
- Explore 3D 'virtual reality' worlds, and play games with people visiting the same world.
- Manage your bank account, transfer money, and pay bills at any time of the day or night, or do all your shopping in online supermarkets and stores.

- Read magazines and newspapers online, along with books, dictionaries, encyclopaedias, thesauruses, and every type of reference you could dream of.
- Download the latest versions and updates of your software long before they hit the shops, or be among the first to use brand new 'test editions' of major software titles (known as **beta releases**).
- And a microscopic taste of the rest: Do you need legal advice or a map of the Cotswolds? Are you looking for a new job or an old master? Do you want a picture of your favourite rock star or the price of the latest Jaguar? Do you need a car-insurance quote or a change of diet? You get the idea…

JARGON BUSTER

Download

The act of copying a file from one distant computer across a network of computers and telephone lines to your own hard-disk. Everything you look at on the Net downloads automatically so that you can see it. The opposite term is 'upload' – copying a file from your own disk to a remote computer.

The Magnificent Seven – Internet Services

What you've just read is a general taste of what's on offer on the Net, but all the things you want to do (or get, or see) will be scattered around the world on different computers. In other words, these computers offer the services you want to use. The Internet is made up of a bundle of different services, but here's a quick look at the seven most popular:

- **Email** Email is the oldest and most used of the Internet services with millions of messages whizzing around it every day. Most email messages are just ordinary text, but you can attach almost any type of computer file you want to send along with it (such as a spreadsheet or a small program), and encrypt the message so that no one except the intended recipient will be able to read it.
- **The World Wide Web** This service, often known simply as the Web, has had so much publicity and acclaim that you may think it is the Internet. In fact, it's the Net's new baby, which was born in 1992. It's a very lively,

gurgling baby though, packed with pictures, text, video, music, and information about every subject under the sun. All the pages on the Web are linked together, so that a page you're viewing from a computer in Bristol may lead you to a page in Tokyo, Brisbane or Oslo with a single mouse-click. Many individual users have their own pages on the Web, along with multinational companies, political parties, universities and colleges, football teams, local councils, and so on.

- **Newsgroups** A newsgroup is a discussion group that focuses on one particular subject. The discussion itself takes place through a form of email, but the major difference is that these messages are posted for the whole group to read and respond to. You can join any group you like from a choice of over twenty-eight thousand, with a variety of subjects ranging from spina-bifida support to alien landings, James Bond films to Turkish culture.
- **Chat** This isn't chat as in 'yackety-yak', more like 'clickety-click'. You can hold conversations with one or more persons by typing messages back and forth that instantly appear on the screens of everyone involved. Some recent chat programs allow 'whiteboarding' (drawing pictures and diagrams in collaboration), private online conferences, and control of programs running on someone else's computer.
- **Voice on the Net** This is chat as in 'yackety-yak'. As long as you've got a soundcard in your computer, and a microphone plugged into it, you can talk to anyone in the world just as you do with the telephone (provided they're online and have a soundcard and microphone too). So why not use the telephone? Your Internet connection will be a local call, letting you hold these conversations for as little as 60p per hour. Compare that with the cost of a direct-dialled call to New York (roughly £12.60 per hour) and you've got a pretty good reason!
- **FTP** The computers that make up the Internet hold a combined library of millions of files. The FTP system lets you look inside directories on some of these computers and copy files straight to your hard-disk just as if you were copying files between your own directories.
- **Archie** (Yes, really, Archie!). Copying files from some distant computer to your own using FTP really is as straightforward as I just made it sound. But first you've got to track down the file you want, which, if it exists at all, may exist on only one computer in the whole world. Don't even try – ask Archie instead, he'll usually find it in seconds.

Although many other services exist, these are almost certainly the ones you'll be using most frequently (and you may use nothing but email and the World Wide Web). The services are there if you want them, but you don't have to use them.

Understanding Internet Addresses

So the Internet is big, the computers that form the Internet are counted in millions, and yet somehow all that information manages to get wherever it's supposed to go. But how does that tiny, helpless file find its way from deepest Ohio to your own computer all by itself?

The answer is, in much the same way that an ordinary letter manages to arrive at your house: it has an address attached to it that identifies one single house in the whole world. Every single computer on the Internet has a unique address, called its **IP address**, which consists of four numbers separated by dots, such as 194.72.6.226 (the IP address of my own access provider, BT Internet).

JARGON BUSTER

IP address

'IP' stands for Internet Protocol. IP works with its best friend, TCP (Transmission Control Protocol), to handle the tricky job of sending computer files down telephone lines, and part of this job is knowing which computer is asking for the file and which is sending it. Is it really as exciting as it sounds? Yes, almost exactly. But if you still want to know more about TCP, IP, and protocols in general, skip ahead to the Glossary on page 370.

Domain Names – the Easier Way

Of course, if you need to connect to one of these computers you'll need to know its address. But don't panic! You don't have to remember streams of meaningless numbers, there's an easy way. As well as this numerical IP address, each computer is given a much friendlier **domain name**. Going back to that IP address I mentioned just now, the domain name of that computer is the much more memorable **btinternet.com.** Best of all, most of the Internet programs you'll be using will store these addresses for you so that you can just recall them with a few mouse-clicks.

Talking in dots

If you're ever in that awkward situation where you have to say a domain name out loud, use the word 'dot' to replace the dot itself (as in 'btinternet dot com'). The rule applies to every dot in the address, such as 'bbc dot co dot uk' for bbc.co.uk. This will ensure that you don't sound like a rank outsider.

The function of the domain name is just to make life less complicated for Internet users. The computers themselves still use that numerical IP address. Whenever you want to connect to a computer somewhere on the Internet, you'll type its domain name into your software (or perhaps select it from a list of your favourites). This domain name is sent to another computer called a **domain name server** (DNS). The job of the DNS is to find the 'numbers and dots' IP address of the computer that uses that nickname and send it back to your computer. It might sound cumbersome, but this conversation between computers should happen very quickly. You probably won't be aware that it's happening, but you'd certainly be aware if it stopped happening!

Dissecting Domain Names

Apart from being a lot easier to remember than numbers, domain names can also tell you whose computer you're connected to, what type of organisation it is, and where the computer is located. The 'who' part is usually easy: given an address like **www.channel4.com**, the computer almost certainly belongs to the Channel 4 television company. It's the bits that come after that (known as **top-level domains**) which can be interesting, so here's a few to look out for:

Domain	Used by
.co	a commercial company
.com	until recently a US company; now also used for companies outside the States
.ac	an academic establishment (college, university, etc)
.edu	another college or university domain
.gov	a government agency
.mil	a military establishment
.net	an Internet access provider
.org	an organization (as opposed to a commercial company)

Room for more on top

At the time that I'm writing this book, a new plan has just been announced to add a few more top-level domains to the list.

So in the very near future we'll be seeing large business users with the top-level domain **.firm**, information services using **.info**, consumer retailers using **.store**, and individuals using **.nom**, among others.

US domain names stop at this point (that's one way to tell them apart from UK domain names). Most of the domain names in other countries have an extra dot and a country code tagged on to the end (yes, our domain names are bigger than the US ones – do you think they've spotted that?). For example, you'll see **.uk** for United Kingdom, **.se** for Sweden, **.fr** for France, **.jp** for Japan, and **.fi** for Finland.

Getting Everything to Work Together

At this point you've jumped the last fence on the technical background course, and you're blazing down the final straight. There are just three more elements that should be mentioned – clients, servers and protocols. These are the vital ingredients that, when mixed together, give you access to all the Internet's services.

- The **client** is a software program that you run on your own computer to access a particular service. For example, if you want to send and receive email messages you'll need an email client; if you want to browse on the World Wide Web you'll need a web client. These all look and work in much the same way as any other program you already use on your computer, and you can pick, choose and swap programs until you find the ones you are most comfortable using.
- The **server** is a computer owned by whoever provides your Internet access, but servers work in a similar way to clients. When you're dealing with email, your email client will contact the mail server; when you want to look at a page on the World Wide Web, your web client will ask the web server to fetch it from wherever it is in the world and send it down the line to you.

Protocol

When two computers need to communicate but don't speak the same language, they follow a set of rules called a 'protocol', just as a Czech and a Frenchman who don't speak each other's language may still be able to communicate in Spanish. For example, your email program will talk to the mail server in a language called SMTP (Simple Mail Transport Protocol) whenever you want to send an email message.

- The word **protocols** popped up a couple of pages back – to mere mortals they're dull as ditchwater, but they're the vital link in the chain that makes everything work. These protocols (you won't be surprised to hear) are known by bunches of initial letters like HTTP, SMTP and NNTP.

You may need to know which protocol is which when you're setting up your Internet connection or installing new client programs, but the rest of the time it's all just technical drivel. If you do need to know, you'll find it all explained in the 'JargonBuster Super Reference' in Appendix D.

2

HOW CAN I GET ONLINE?

In This Chapter...

- Read about the different ways to get on the Internet
- Find out what you need to surf the Net
- Get top performance from your modem
- Learn the differences between Online Services and Internet Access Providers
- Get those phone charges sorted out

Congratulations – you've waded through all the technical stuff and emerged unscathed! In this chapter you'll find out about the different ways you can go online and surf the Net, the decisions you'll need to make about how you want to do it, and the pros and cons of the two connection options.

Where Can I Get Internet Access?

There are several ways to get access to the Internet, and at least one of them is available to you immediately:

- **Set up your own Internet connection** This is the option you probably want to take, and the rest of this part of the book is devoted to making it happen. With your own computer connected to the Internet, you can use all its services whenever you want to.
- **Visit a cyber café** These cafés and converted pubs have been springing up all over the place in the last couple of years, and offer coffee, beer, Twiglets – and Internet access. If you're not convinced that the Internet is for you, cyber cafés offer valuable hands-on experience. Expect to pay around £6 per hour, and try to book time in advance (especially at lunch-times, evenings and weekends). Turn to page 403 for a list of UK cyber cafés.
- **Use your account at work** Some companies have an Internet connection to their own internal network to take advantage of its email, research, and long-distance collaboration opportunities. Be warned, though – if you spend your working hours surfing the Net for pleasure, your boss can still find out exactly where you've been, regardless of the care you've taken to cover your tracks!
- **Use your college account** Many universities and colleges provide use of computers with Internet connections for their students. As long as you can avoid doing something as rash as graduating you'll enjoy unlimited free access.

What Do I Need?

That's the first decision taken care of – you want your own private Internet connection. The next step is to consult the checklist and see which of the required bits and pieces you're missing. Actually, it's a very short list: you'll need a telephone line, a computer, a modem, and an Internet access account. Let's look at each one in a little more detail.

Telephone Line

Just an ordinary telephone line, with a socket fairly close to your computer so that you can plug your modem into it. For a pound or two you can buy an adapter to let you plug a telephone and a modem into the same socket, which is a worthwhile investment. If you find yourself spending a lot of time online, you may want to consider installing a second telephone line just for Internet access so that people can still telephone you while you're surfing, but that's a decision for later.

BY THE WAY

Turn off call waiting!

If you have the Call Waiting service on your telephone line, make sure you turn it off every time you go online (by dialling **# 43 #**) and back on again when you've finished (*** 43 #**). Otherwise, an incoming call at the wrong moment could disconnect you and cancel anything you were doing (particularly irritating if you were waiting for a huge file to download and were just seconds from completion!).

Computer

Yes, you knew you needed a computer! But a common misconception is that you've got to have a fast, powerful computer to surf the Net. In fact, almost any computer will be up to the task. I do have a few suggestions that will enrich your online time though:

- Windows 95 has built-in support for Internet connections that make all the setting-up and connecting happen smoothly and simply.
- To hear the Internet's musical offerings and use Voice on the Net software (see page 143) you'll need a soundcard.
- To enjoy the World Wide Web at its graphical, vibrant best, you'll be happiest with at least a 256-colour, 800 x 600 display. On modern computers that's a standard setup, so don't worry if that's all Greek to you!
- Finally, a large hard-disk. It's not vital – you'll have to install a few new programs, but they won't take more than a few megabytes – but you'll find it hard to resist downloading some of the free or inexpensive software you'll find on the Net!

Modem

The modem is the device that converts the information on a computer into sound that can be sent down a telephone line, and converts it back to meaningful information again when it gets to the other end. The most important thing to look at when buying a modem is its speed – how much information it can move around per second. The faster your modem (in theory, at least), the quicker you'll get everything done that you planned to do, cutting your telephone bill and any online charges as a result.

Is a fast modem worth the extra money?

Generally speaking, yes it is. But you've heard the term 'superhighway' used to describe the Internet. Like any highway, there's a lot of people all trying to get to the same place and things can get jammed solid, so while the person with the slow modem is gazing at his screen for some sign of information arriving, the person with the fast modem is doing just the same. But, when everything's running smoothly, a 28.8Kbps modem is streets ahead of a 14.4.

At the moment, the fastest modems shift data around at a maximum speed of 56Kbps (56,000 bits per second). The slowest (and therefore cheapest) modem you'll find is 14.4Kbps, with a 28.8 and a 33.6 sitting in between. A 14.4Kbps modem really is a false economy – if you connect to the Net for more than a few minutes a week at this speed you'll be miserable. I strongly recommend going for either of the 'in-between' speeds, with models starting at around £100, but make sure you check the connection speed offered by your access provider before parting with your cash.

Turbo-charge your modem

Data passing into and out of your computer through the modem is compressed, so make sure you squeeze the most out of it. Find the settings for the serial (COM) port that your modem is plugged into, and change the port speed to at least double your modem's rated speed (e.g. 57,600 for a 28.8Kbps modem).

Finally, on the subject of modems, you can choose between an internal or an external model. Although the external modem is slightly more expensive, I'd go for it every time. It's much easier to install (just plug in the telephone cable, serial cable, and mains plug), and the lights on the front make it easier to tell what's going on.

Internet Access Account

With all the necessary hardware bits and bobs in place, the final thing you need is a way to connect to a computer that's a part of the Internet. There are hundreds of companies in the UK who specialise in selling dial-up links to the Internet via their own computers, so the next step is to choose one of these companies and set up an account with them.

This leads to the final decision you have to make: do you want an account with an **Internet access provider** (often simply referred to as an IAP) or with an **online service?**

Online Services & IAPs – What's the Difference?

The most important thing that access providers and the major online services have in common is that they both let you connect to the Internet. It's the way they do it and what else they have to offer that makes them different, along with their methods of deciding how much you should pay. To round off this chapter, and help you decide which path to follow, let's take a look at the two options and the pros and cons of each.

Online Services

You may have heard of the 'big three' online services: America Online (AOL), CompuServe (CSi), and the Microsoft Network (MSN). In fact, if you buy computer magazines, you're probably snowed under with floppy-disks and CD-ROMs inviting you to sign up to one or other of these. One of the main plus-points of these online services is the speed and ease with which you can sign up: just this one disk and a credit or debit card number is all you need. But it's important not to confuse online services with the Internet itself. An online service is rather like an exclusive club: once you subscribe you'll have access to a range of members-only areas such as discussion forums, chat rooms and file libraries. Although you can 'escape' to the Internet from here, non-members can't get in. You won't find much in the members-only areas that you can't find on the Internet itself, but online services do have the combined benefits of ease of use, online help if you get lost, and a friendly all-in-one program from which you can reach everything you need. Although the Internet certainly isn't the chamber of horrors that some newspapers would have you believe, there's little control over what gets published there; online services carefully filter and control their members-only content, making them the preferred choice for getting the whole family online.

GOOD QUESTION

How 'easy' is it to connect to online services?

I knew you'd ask, so I've just signed up with a major online service (I won't say which). It took 12 minutes from inserting the CD-ROM to officially 'arriving online'. Yes, I know, I've done it before; the point is that the most difficult thing I had to do was read those shiny numbers on my credit card.

Online services probably sound pretty good so far – you get the Internet, and a bit more. So what counts against them? Mainly the price. Most online services charge a low monthly subscription fee, which includes 5 hours online free of charge. This is ideal for a light user, but 5 hours per month can pass in a flash if you plan to surf the World Wide Web or download files. Once your free hours are used up you'll be paying extra for subsequent hours, so the online service could be an expensive option. However, most services offer alternative pricing plans, so try to gauge how much time you're likely to spend online as you use your free first month, and change to a different plan if necessary before the second month begins.

Finally, online services tend to offer Internet access as an 'extra' – when you step out on to the Net itself you may find that the information doesn't travel as quickly as it does on a direct Internet connection.

▶ *If an online service sounds like your preferred method of getting online, you might like to skip ahead to Chapter 4 to find out how to go about choosing one and connecting.*

Internet Access Providers

An Internet access provider gives you access to the Internet, plain and simple. When you dial into your access provider's computer, you'll see some sort of message on the screen that tells you you're connected, but you won't feel the earth move. Instead, you'll start your email program or your web software and start doing whatever it is you want to do.

The IAP account has a number of valuable points in its favour. First, you'll only pay a single monthly charge (plus your telephone bill, of course), with no restrictions or charges for the time you spend online. Second, you'll have far greater flexibility in your choice of software. Most access providers will give you a bundle of programs when you sign up, but you don't have to use them – try some of the programs on the free CD-ROM accompanying this book, or others mentioned in later chapters, until you find the ones that you're most comfortable with.

Choose your email address

Another tempting point about IAPs is that you can usually choose the personalised part of your email address yourself, as long as you can come up with something not already assigned to another subscriber, whereas many online services automatically assign you an email address. If this matters to you, and you think **rob.young@btinternet.com** makes more sense than **ryoung21904@aol.com** or **101355.1436@compuserve.com**, you're probably warming to the idea of an IAP account.

IAPs have their negative side too, of course. Until quite recently, as soon as you'd signed up, your IAP would be vanishing into the distance, clutching your money and giggling insanely at the mess he'd left you in. (My first account took 14 hours of slaving over a hot keyboard before I finally managed to connect!). However, with growing competition among companies eager to part you from your cash, most now send out preconfigured software (all the complicated settings are made for you) so that you can just install it and connect. Many also provide free telephone support in case you get stuck. Sadly, some IAPs still haven't caught on, so you'll have to ask a few searching questions before committing yourself.

▶ *If you like the sound of an IAP account, keep reading! In Chapter 3 you'll learn some of the finer points of choosing an access provider and setting up your Internet connection.*

Any Suggestions?

If you can't decide whether to go for an IAP account or not, let me make a suggestion: go for an online service to start with. It's easy to set up, you'll get (at least) a 30-day free trial, and you can get a taste of the service itself and the Internet. If you decide later that you need the flexibility or economy of an IAP account, you can cancel whenever you like.

GOOD QUESTION

What's the most popular way to get online?

UK users seem to favour online services, the top-three companies being CompuServe, AOL (America On Line) and MSN (Microsoft Network). The top IAP, coming in at number four on this list of favourites, is Demon Internet. But watch out for the newcomer – Virgin Net.

Telephone Calls & Connections

Whether you've chosen to hook up with an IAP or an online service, you'll have to dial into that company's computer every time you want to go online. This means that if you connect for 20 minutes you'll pay for a 20-minute telephone call (although it's your modem using the line, not your telephone). So how much are these telephone calls going to cost?

The good news is that you should always be able to connect through a local telephone number. At the time of writing, British Telecom's local call rate (per minute) is 5p peak rate, 1.7p cheap rate, and 1p at weekends. Add your access number to your 'Friends and Family' list and you'll save a useful 10 per cent. And if your telephone bill is high enough to qualify for the PremierLine scheme you'll be able to knock off another 15 per cent. Prices change, of course, and charges will vary between different telephone companies, so make sure you check these details before relying on them!

Are There Any Other Options?

Yes, indeed. You won't find a cheaper connection than the dial-up accounts we've been talking about, but you can find faster connections. They tend to be the domain of companies and individuals who work extensively on the

Net, and they replace the humble modem. They're also prohibitively expensive for most users, and I'm not going to dwell on them in this book, but since you asked, here's a brief description of each:

- **ISDN line** An ISDN line replaces your modem with a new device called a Terminal Adapter, and gives you a maximum speed of 128Kbps (more than twice that of the fastest modem). Apart from the cost of the Terminal Adapter (between £200 and £500), you'll need to get an ISDN line run out to you from the exchange, and pay a quarterly rental of around £160. Connection charges range from £250 to £600, according to the quantity of 'free' call time you want included in the deal. Call prices themselves are unchanged, and you can use this single line for up to eight devices at the same time (for example, making a telephone call while sending a fax and surfing the Internet).
- **Leased line** This is a mind-bogglingly fast, direct connection to the Internet. A leased line will set you back anything from £7,500 to £250,000 (so don't buy one until you're absolutely sure you need it!) and gives you permanent connection and instant access to the Net.

BY THE WAY

Dig deeper

If you're seriously considering getting an ISDN line, make sure that you thoroughly check the charges of access providers, too – on closer inspection you may find that many providers require a higher monthly subscription for an ISDN connection than for a modem connection.

3

CONNECTING TO AN ACCESS PROVIDER

In This Chapter...

- How to pick the best IAP for your needs
- The six essential questions to ask before subscribing
- Choose what you want your email address to be
- Make sense of all the technical info your IAP gives you

Now that you've made the all-important decisions, this is where things start to happen – after following the instructions in this chapter you'll be online and ready to start exploring the Internet. Right now you're just two steps away from connecting: you need to choose and subscribe to an access provider (IAP), and configure your version of Windows to make the connection. It may look a bit involved at first sight, but remember – you should only have to do it once!

Choosing an Access Provider

OK, it's decision time again! There are countless IAPs in the UK, and more are starting up all the time. You'll find a list of several dozen UK access providers on page 400, and the first step is to whittle this lot down to a shortlist of half-a-dozen or so, using these tips as a guide:

- **Are they local?** You need to know the location of the computer you're dialling into, which is sometimes called a 'node' or a 'PoP' (Point of Presence) – it's the crucial factor in determining whether you should consider an IAP. You must be able to dial-in using a local telephone number! Many IAPs have nodes all over the UK, so you can probably include them on your list. Others may be smaller companies with, perhaps, a single computer in Blackpool. This could be ideal if you live in the Blackpool area, but if you're in Torquay, forget it.
- **Did someone recommend them?** If a particular IAP can offer you local access, and you've heard positive things about them (in terms of reliability of connection, good telephone support, etc), they're definitely worth adding to the shortlist.

The next step is to get on the telephone. Any company that takes itself seriously will be happy to answer your questions, so pick a promising candidate from your shortlist and give them a ring. If you can't get straight answers to the following questions, either press the point harder or cross them off the list (and don't let them blind you with jargon either!).

Asking Questions – Six of the Best

First, check any details from the list of Internet Access Providers, and any that were given to you by another subscriber, to make sure they're accurate and up to date. Then work your way down this list:

1. **What is your monthly subscription fee?** A common price is about £12 including VAT. If this IAP charges more, it's worth asking what else they provide that other companies don't. With many companies you can get a reduction by paying annually.
2. **Do you charge extra for the time I spend online?** The correct answer to this is 'No, we don't'. If they get this one wrong, go no further!
3. **What is your fastest modem connection speed?** If you have a 28.8Kbps modem (see page 32) you don't want to connect at a slower speed. Many companies have upgraded to 33.6Kbps modems, and some even support the very latest 56.6Kbps.
4. **Will you give me a PPP connection?** The two options are PPP (Point to Point Protocol) or SLIP (Serial Line Internet Protocol). You don't want a SLIP connection, but a few companies still use them. A PPP connection is faster, and it's easier to set up (especially in Windows 95 and later).
5. **When is telephone support available?** You'll almost certainly need telephone support sometime, so make sure it'll be available when you're most likely to be using the Internet (for example, during evenings and weekends).
6. **Do you provide preconfigured connection software for my computer?** Many companies will ask you questions about your computer and operating system, and then send you software that's ready to install with all the tricky stuff taken care of. (The software may be on CD-ROM, so be sure to check this if you don't have a CD-ROM drive!) Find out if the connection will be easy to set up on your computer, and whether the technical support telephone line will be able to talk you through the process if you get stuck.

When you've found the access provider of your dreams, you're almost ready to subscribe. But first…

Choosing Your Username

When you start a subscription with an access provider, you'll be identified by your choice of **username** (some companies refer to it as a user ID, logon name or member name). You'll need to quote this when you call the support line with a question, and when you log on to the provider's computer to surf the Internet. More importantly, it forms the unique part of your email address. If you were to start an account with **mycompany.co.uk**, your email address would be *username*@**mycompany.co.uk**, and this is the address you'd give out to friends and colleagues so that they could send you email. As an example, my username is **rob.young** and my IAP is **btinternet.com**, so my email address is **rob.young@btinternet.com.**

Do I have to use my own name?

No, you can use just about anything you want. It'll be easier for you (and other people) to remember if it doesn't contain numbers, but there's nothing to stop you having a username like **jellyfish** or **zapdoodle**, as long as your IAP doesn't already have a zapdoodle on its subscriber list.

The rules on usernames vary a little between providers. They can't contain spaces (in common with any Internet address), but dots, dashes and underscores are usually OK. Most importantly, it must be a username that hasn't already been scooped by another subscriber to your chosen access provider, so think of a second and third choice in case your first is unavailable.

And Now... Subscribe!

It's time to get back on the telephone to your chosen provider and tell them you'd like to subscribe. The provider will set up an account for you, but exactly what happens next will depend on the individual access provider:

- You may receive a disk in the post that's preconfigured for your computer, operating system and account. If so, follow the instructions that accompany it and it ought to be as easy to install as any other program.
- You may receive a disk of software and some documentation that tells you how to install it and how to configure your computer.

You should also receive a wonderfully technical-looking list of IP addresses, domain names and so on, to accompany the software package. Even if your software is preconfigured for quick and easy installation, make sure you hang on to this list for reference – you'll need to enter some of these settings into other software you use in the future. Included on the list will be most (though not necessarily all) of the following items:

- **Local dial-up telephone number** The number your modem will dial to connect to the provider's computer.
- **Username and password** Confirmation of your chosen username, and a personal password. You'll enter both of these into your dial-up software so that you can log on to the provider's computer.
- **Email address** As mentioned above, this will consist of your username and your provider's domain name, looking something like **username@accessprovider.co.uk**.
- **Email account username and password** If you have a POP3 (Post Office Protocol) email account, you'll use these to retrieve your email messages. An SMTP (Simple Mail Transport Protocol) email account will use your normal logon details. (We'll look at these two types of account in Chapter 7.)

JARGON BUSTER

Log on/logon

The first of these is a verb; the second is usually a noun, but you may see a phrase like 'When you logon to the system…' from time to time. Logging on simply means sending your username and password to your access provider's computer so that it can check that you're really entitled to connect to it. Once these details are entered into your software, the logon should happen automatically after dialling.

- **Mail server address** The domain name of the computer you'll connect to when you want to send and receive email. You'll probably have addresses for **SMTP mail server** and **POP3 mail server** – I'll explain these in Chapter 7, but they'll usually both be something like **mail.accessprovider.co.uk.**
- **News server address** The domain name of the computer that handles newsgroup messages, which is usually **news.accessprovider.co.uk.**
- **Domain name server** (DNS) This will be an IP address (you remember those four numbers separated by dots?) for the computer that translates friendly domain names into something that computers can understand and mere mortals can't. You may also be given an **alternative DNS** that your computer will try to connect to if the first one fails.

- **Other bits and pieces** The address of your company's web site in case you want to take a look at it **(www.accessprovider.co.uk)**; the address of your provider's FTP server if it has one **(ftp.accessprovider.co.uk)**; the telephone number and email address of the provider's technical support services.

Now that your account has been set up, and you're the proud owner of a list of technical gobbledegook and a disk of software from your access provider, it's time to get that connection working. Your provider should have included instructions telling you how to install the software, so this should be a pretty painless step. All the same, keep that support-line number handy, just in case! If you need a bit more help, you can head for the back of this book where all the technical stuff is gathered together. If you're using Windows 95, turn to Appendix A; if you're using Windows 3.1, go to Appendix B.

4

CONNECTING TO AN ONLINE SERVICE

In This Chapter...

- Discover the differences between four popular online services
- Follow the simple sign-up routines to get connected
- Start exploring the member-areas and the Internet

Choosing an Online Service

This should be an easy choice to make – not only is the list of online services fairly short, but most offer a free 30-day trial, so you've got nothing to lose by picking one at random. All the same, it's better to make an informed choice if you can, so let's take a slightly closer look at the three most popular online services, CompuServe, America Online and The Microsoft Network, and the UK-only newcomer, Virgin Net.

CompuServe

CompuServe has more than a thousand different areas covering just about every conceivable subject, including finance, news, TV listings, articles from popular magazines, travel information, film and music previews, along with interactive chat rooms. Many retail companies have their own forums offering advice and product support, and business users will probably find more to interest them on CompuServe than the other services. The program used to move around this lot (shown on page 94) is smart and fairly formal, although not quite as easy to get to grips with as America Online. It's also unaccountably slow in use. The UK-specific content is sparse for a company with so many UK users, but CompuServe is trying to improve things in this area. Parents can download a program called Cyber Patrol to restrict kids' access to areas of CompuServe itself or the Internet, and limit the time they can spend online.

America Online

In comparison with CompuServe, America Online (AOL) has a very sunny, friendly and informal feel to it (just take a look at the picture on page 50), making it a good choice for both children and inexperienced computer-users. The content provided is actually very similar to that of CompuServe, but

GOOD QUESTION

Can I control my kid's access to the Internet?

Yes, although you don't have to use an online service in order to control access. There are also many good programs available that you can use with an Internet Access Provider account to restrict access to different areas of the Net, or to particular types of information. You'll learn about those programs in Chapter 14.

there are a couple of differences: the business content, although growing by the day, is still far from comprehensive, but on the plus side you will find plenty of UK content. Parental controls are very good, although there's currently no way to restrict how long your kids stay online. One major bonus is that AOL allows an account-holder to have up to five different member-names (AOL calls them Screen Names), which means that you can have five different email addresses; in the case of families or small businesses, this allows everyone to receive their own personal email. More importantly, perhaps for families, it also means that you have the facility to bar your children's access to specific areas of the service without having to restrict your own use.

The Microsoft Network

The Microsoft Network (or MSN) has a stylish, modern appearance, contrasting massively with CompuServe's formality and AOL's friendliness. It also requires Windows 95 or later in order to run, and a reasonably fast computer. MSN is 'cool', and unashamedly has a US bias, and this follows through to its content, which is geared more towards entertainment than information. The service is split into four main areas – OnStage, Essentials, Communicate and Find. The first of these splits into sub-areas called 'channels', with each channel aimed at users with particular types of interest. Parental controls do exist, but they don't match up to those of CompuServe or AOL – you'll have to grab Junior by the ear and drag him away. Also in contrast with those two services, MSN is an Internet-based service: when you decide to explore the rest of the Net's offerings you should find that the information travels much more speedily than with AOL or CompuServe.

Virgin Net

Virgin is the new kid on the block as far as online services are concerned, and is positioning itself halfway between IAPs and the 'usual' online services. Although a range of online content is included (chiefly information and entertainment rather than business), Virgin's aim is to provide the easiest possible access to the Internet, which includes a 24-hour telephone support line. Like MSN, Virgin Net is an Internet-based service, so you'll notice little difference in speed when you move from the members-only areas to the Net itself. Being a UK-only company, the content that is included is UK-specific, with news, sport, chat rooms, and hundreds of ready-sorted links to places of interest on the Internet. You'll find everything you'll need to sign up with Virgin Net on the free CD-ROM accompanying this book.

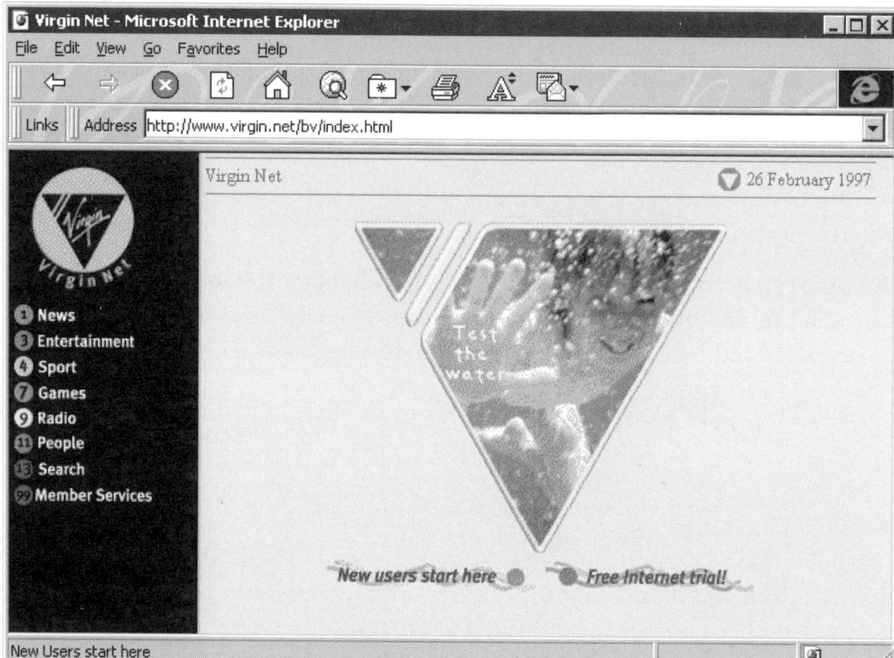

▶ Virgin Net's simple Internet-based service.

How Do I Sign Up?

The first job is to get your hands on the free connection software. These disks are regularly glued to the covers of computer magazines so you may have dozens of them already. If you have, make sure you pick the most recent. If you haven't, either take a trip to your newsagent or phone the services and ask them to send you the correct software for your computer and operating system. You'll find their telephone numbers on page 403.

GOOD QUESTION

What's to stop me using free trials forever?

Don't think that the software manufacturers haven't thought of this scam! The setup routines for most online services are sophisticated enough to recognise your personal details. They'll still allow you to sign up a second time of course, but you're pretty unlikely to get another free trial.

That was the tricky part! Somewhere on the disk you'll be told how to start the program that signs you up, and the whole process will advance in simple steps. The exact routine will vary from one service to another, so I can't tell you exactly what to expect, but here are a few tips to bear in mind:

- Somewhere on the disk packaging you'll find a reference number (perhaps on a small label, or perhaps on the disk itself). Don't lose it! You'll have to enter this into the software to start the sign-up procedure.
- Make sure you've got your credit card or debit card handy. Although you won't be charged for the first 30 days' access, you'll have to enter the card number and its expiry date when you sign up.
- You may be asked to choose a dial-in telephone number from a list covering the whole country. If so, make sure that you choose a local number. (In some cases, the software will work out the best dial-in point for you, based on your own telephone number, alternatively it may use a local-rate 0345 number.)
- After you've entered all the necessary personal details, the program will dial up the service's computer and automatically set up your subscription. Within a minute or two you'll receive a username and password. These are your entry-ticket, so write them down and keep them safe.

BY THE WAY

Don't pass on your password

Keep your password private. Never include it in an email message, don't type it in front of anyone, and make sure you change it at least once a month (you'll find instructions for this online). If possible, use a combination of letters and numbers at least five characters in length. And don't even consider using the word 'password' as your password!

How Do I Use an Online Service?

When you dial-in to your online service and log on using your username and password (which should happen automatically), you won't actually be on the Internet. At the click of a few buttons you can enter chat rooms or join in with other activities and forums, and you'll find plenty of assistance if you get lost, both in help files and online support areas.

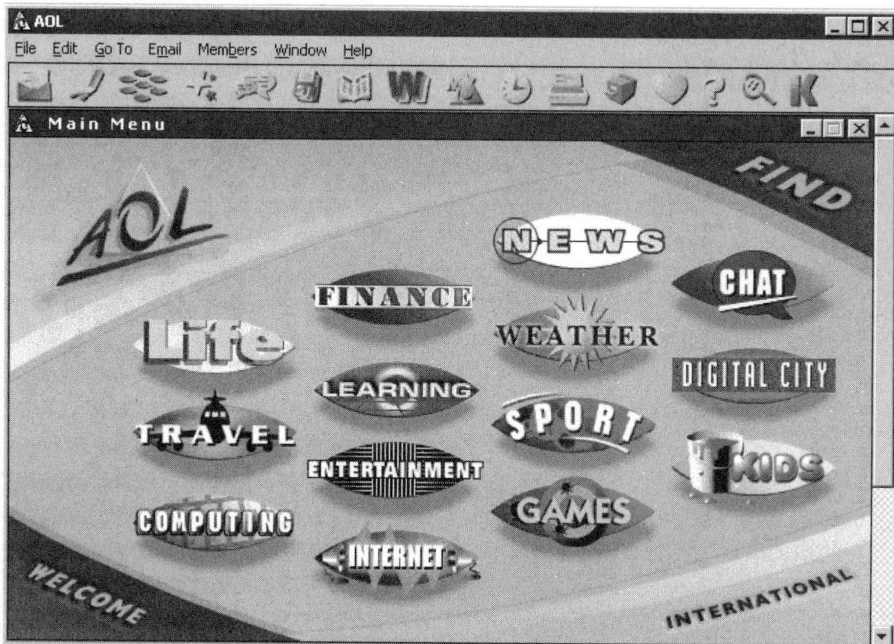

▶The main AOL desktop lets you click on a button to access the Internet or to use one of its own private services.

Access to the Internet itself will be marked as one of the areas you can visit, and you'll probably see a big friendly button marked 'Internet' that will take you straight there. In most cases any extra software needed for Internet access was installed when you signed up, but you may be told that you need to download it yourself. If so, another friendly button will probably appear in front of you and all the tedious spadework will be done for you while you sit back and wait.

Because this is a book about the Internet, I'm not going to dwell on the members-only areas of online services. But once you've clicked that big friendly button you're surfing the same Internet as everyone else, so the rest of the book is just as relevant to you. One of the few differences is in the way that email is handled when it's sent to and from some online service accounts, and you'll learn how to work with email in Chapter 7.

2

FINDING YOUR WAY AROUND

In This Part...

5

EXPLORING THE WORLD WIDE WEB

In This Chapter...

- Discover the amazing World Wide Web
- Learn to use your Web Browser and start surfing
- Keep track of where you've been and where you're going
- Find out what else your multi-talented browser can do

A First Look at the Wonders of the Web

How would you describe television to someone who's never seen it? Somehow you've got to convey its variety, its entertainment value, and its potential as a learning tool. You've got to explain that some of the content is staggeringly good, and some is mindless twaddle, but sometimes the mindless twaddle can be more entertaining than the 'good' stuff. How do you describe a whole amazing new experience?

You wouldn't even try to describe it – you'd switch on the TV set and say 'Just watch!'. To describe the World Wide Web experience on paper isn't as easy – I can't show you the colour or the animation, and although it's interactive, you won't be able to interact with it. Nevertheless, a picture paints a thousand words, so here's the Web equivalent of a few photos of your TV screen.

Paintings at Le Louvre
http://www.paris.org/Musees/Louvre/Treasures/Paintings/

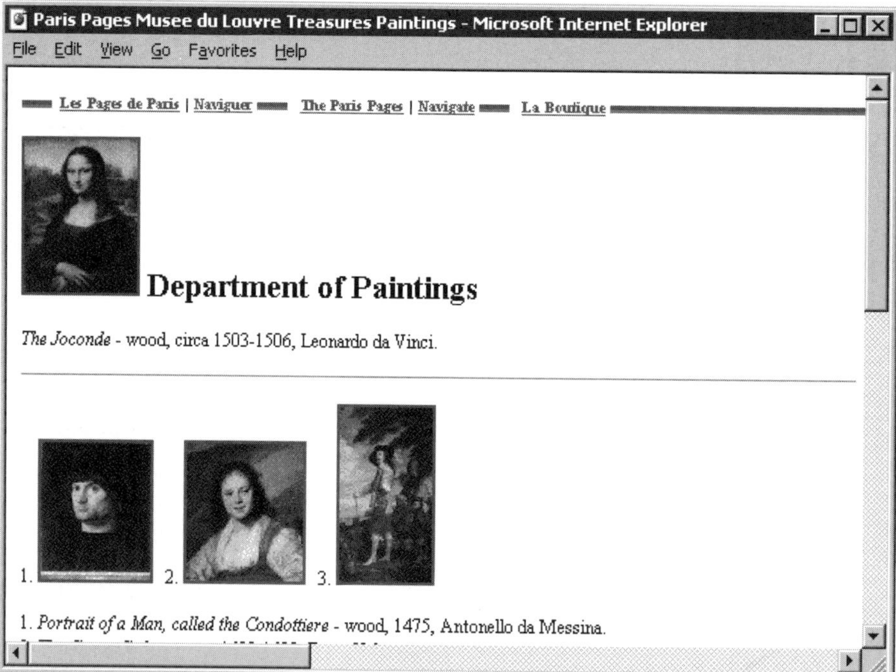

▶ Check out that enigmatic smile while browsing through one of the world's finest galleries. Click on any image to view a larger version and save it to your own hard-disk.

Pepsi World
http://www.pepsi.com/highroad/pworld1a.html

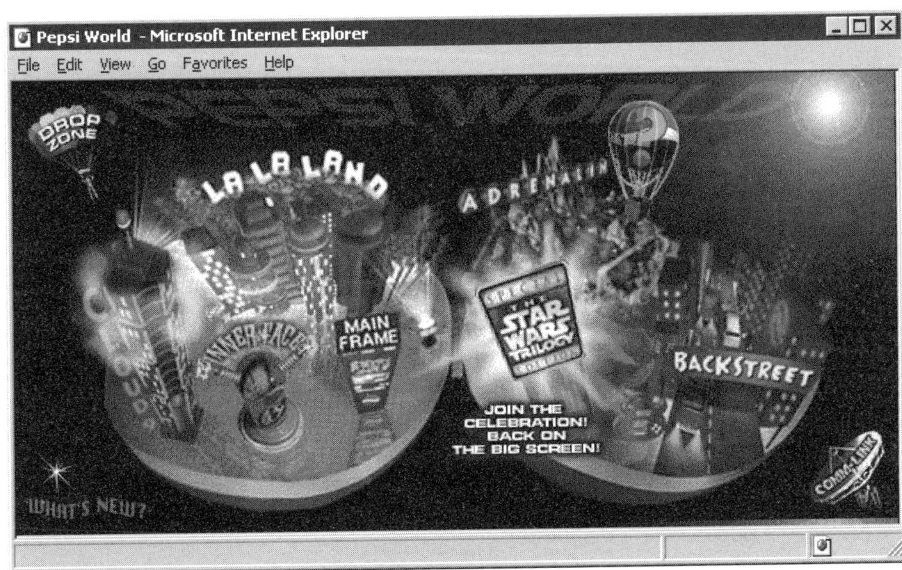

◀ All of the fizz, none of the stickiness. Pepsi's state-of-the-art site bristles with funky sounds, animations, and interactive games. Plus the odd mention of soft drinks, but that's probably to be expected.

The Virtual Frog Dissection Kit
http://george.lbl.gov/ITG.hm.pg.docs/dissect/dissect.html

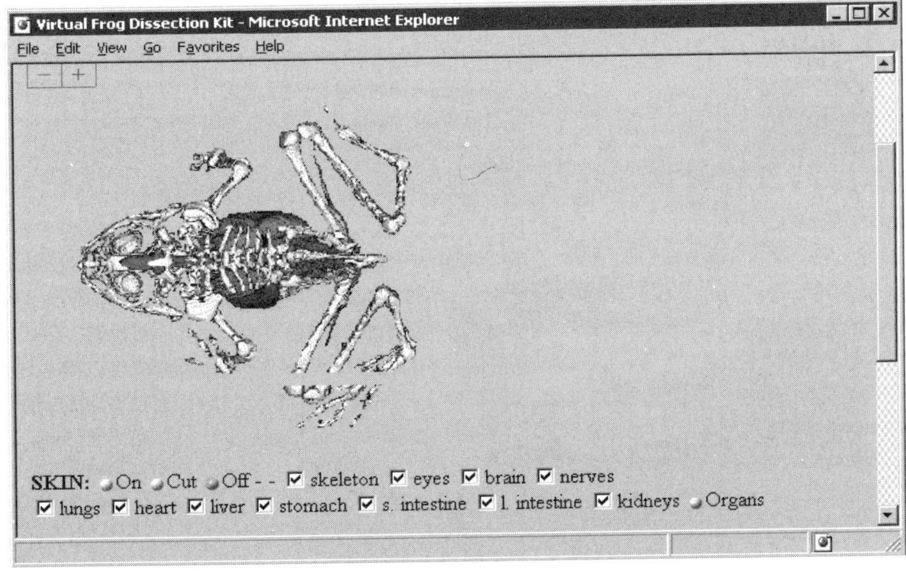

◀ Surprisingly, one of the few frog dissection kits on the Web. In fact this isn't intended to be gruesome – every organ and system can be examined, with detailed information provided, and not a single frog has to croak!

LiveCam at The Epcot Centre
http://www.disney.com/DisneyWorld/cgi-bin/SeeEpcot.cgi

▶ Watch the action at The Epcot Centre or DisneyWorld's Main Street from a live camera feed. Many sites even let you control the camera yourself, as if you were looking through a telescope!

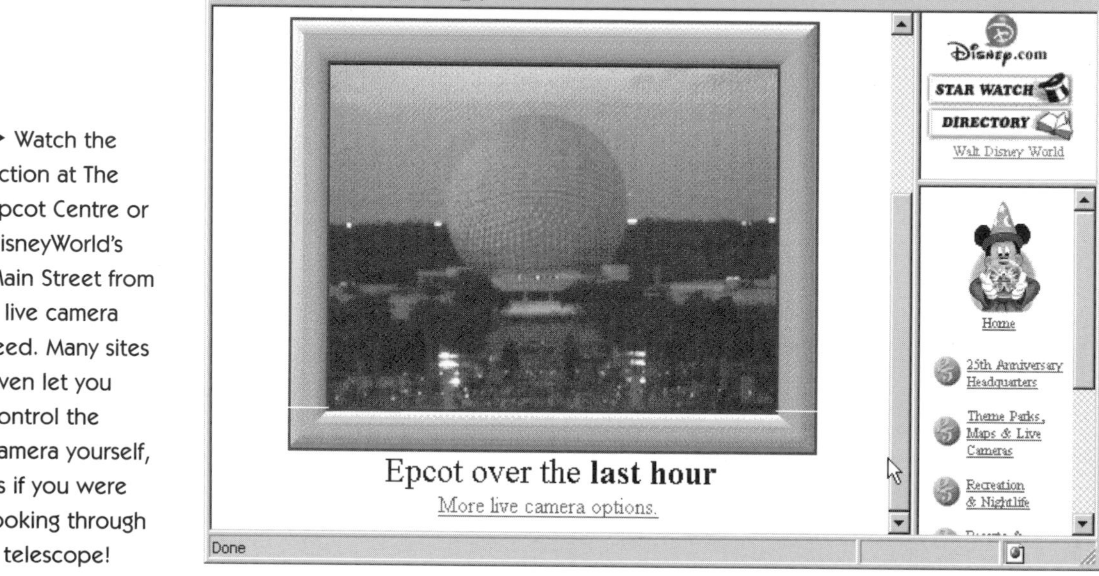

Crepes Demystified
http://desires.com/2.0b3/Food/Crepes/Docs/crepes3.html

▶ Are you mystified by crêpes? Panicked by pancakes? Then just let super chef Paulette Licitra better your batter and unscramble your eggs.

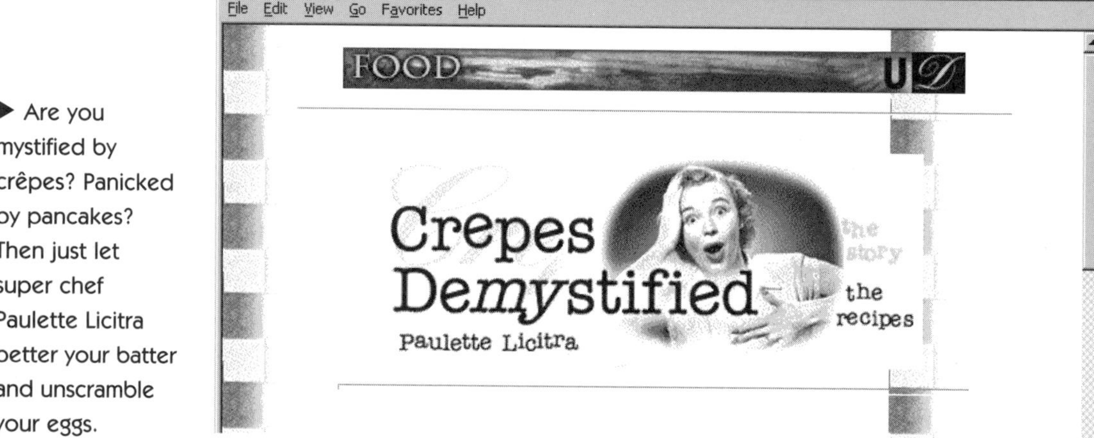

Understanding the Web

The World Wide Web is the jewel in the Internet's crown, and the reason for the 'Internet explosion'. Much of the Web's popularity lies in its simplicity: you don't have to be a computer whiz to use it, you just point and click. The 'pages' you find on the Web contain a scattering of words that are underlined and highlighted in a different colour from the text around them. Just move your mouse-pointer on to one of these words or phrases (you'll see it change into a hand with a pointing finger) and click. Hey presto, another page opens

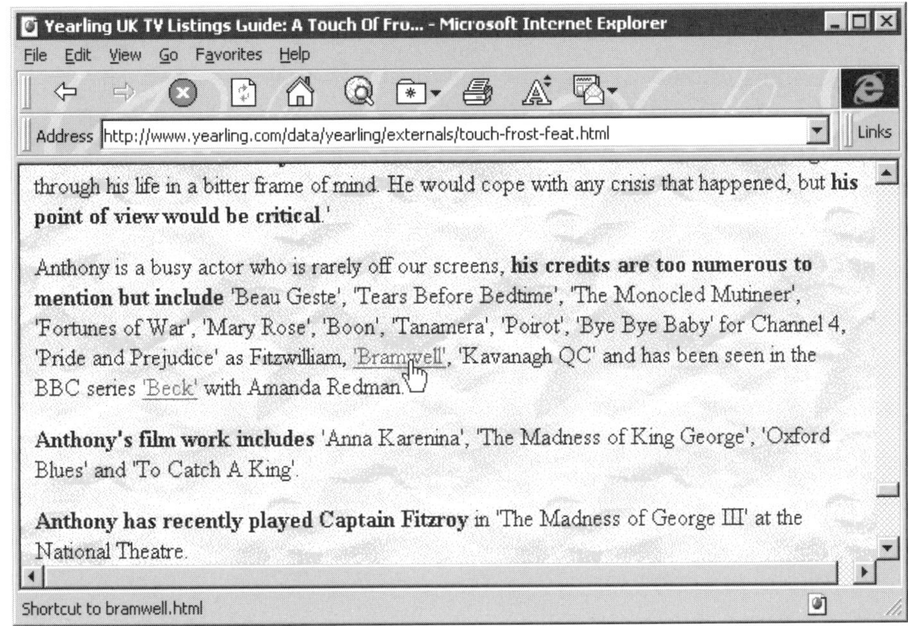

◀ To jump between pages, move the pointer over the coloured hypertext and click to open the related document then just keep clicking for more and more pages.

JARGON BUSTER

Web page

A 'page' is a single document that can be any length, like a document in a word processor. Pages can contain text, graphics, sound and video-clips, together with clever effects and controls made possible by new programming languages such as Java and ActiveX (I'll tell you a bit about those languages in Chapter 22).

The system of clickable text is called **hypertext**, and you've probably already seen it used in Windows help-files and multimedia encyclopaedias as a useful way to make cross-references. The Web takes this system a few stages further on:

- These links aren't restricted to opening a document stored on the same computer: you may see a page from the other side of the world.
- A hypertext link doesn't have to be a word or phrase: it could be a picture that you click on, or be a part of a larger picture, with different parts linking to different pages.
- The link doesn't necessarily open a new web page: it could play a video or a sound, download an application, display a picture, run a program – the list goes on...

The Web is made up of millions and millions of files placed on computers called web servers, so no one person or company actually owns the Web itself. The web servers are owned by many different companies, and they either rent space (or give it away for free!) to anyone who wants to put their own pages on the Web. The pages are created using an easy-to-use, text-based language called **HTML** (HyperText Markup Language), which you'll learn about in chapters 23 and 24.

Once the newly created pages are placed on the web server, anyone who knows their address can take a look at them. This partly explains why the Web became such an overnight success: a simple page can be written in just a few minutes, so a web site can be as up-to-date as its creator wants it to be. Many sites with news or sports pages are updated daily, and some pages may even change every few minutes.

JARGON BUSTER

Web site

Web site is a loose term that refers to the pages belonging to an individual or company. A site could be just a simple single page that your Auntie Ethel wrote to share a particularly tasty fruitcake recipe, or it could be hundreds of complex pages belonging to a large supermarket chain.

What Do I Need?

To view pages from the World Wide Web you'll need a program called a **browser**. In fact, this single program will be the most powerful weapon in your Internet arsenal, and not just because you'll be spending so much time on the Web – you can use this program to handle many of your other Internet-related tasks as well. Although there are many different browsers available, the most capable is Microsoft's **Internet Explorer**.

If you're connected through one of the online services you'll usually be able to use Internet Explorer. Both MSN and CompuServe provide Explorer by default (although you can easily switch to something different if you prefer); both America Online and Virgin Net will allow you to use any browser that takes your fancy.

Internet Explorer is included on the free CD-ROM accompanying this book. If you've recently bought a copy of Windows 95 (or a new computer with Windows 95 already installed on it) you'll find Internet Explorer is included – it may be installed on your system already, or you may have to install it yourself using the **Add/Remove Programs** icon in Windows' Control Panel. It's a rather out-of-date copy, though, so I recommend that you install the later version included in the back of this book.

I use Navigator. Will I understand this chapter?

Netscape Navigator is another popular browser. Netscape's buttons and menus differ from those in Explorer, but both tools were designed to do the same job so the methods are very similar. For simplicity, I'm going to assume that you're using Explorer throughout this book, but you'll find the equivalent Netscape options listed in Appendix C.

Start Browsing

When you open Explorer, the first thing you'll see is your **Start Page**. Unlike a word processor or a paint program, the browser must always display a document, and until you tell it which document you want to look at it will display the document set as its Start Page. By default, Explorer is set to display the first page of Microsoft's Internet site.

For now this is just a matter of idle curiosity – you've just arrived online, and you're eager to explore, so we'll forget about it for a while. But it could start to get irritating later on: every time you start Explorer you'll have to wait for this page to download before you can go anywhere else! In the Customising Your Browser section of Chapter 6, I'll explain how to swap this page for a different one or replace it with a document on your own disk.

BY THE WAY

Start going home

Although Explorer actually calls this page the Start Page, there's a button on the toolbar with the word **Home** beneath it. Wherever you're wandering through the Web and you get lost or you want to stop sampling the delights it has to offer, all you need to do is click the Home button to return to your Start Page anytime you want to.

Anatomy of a Web Page

Now it's time to get acquainted with the basic workings of the browser and with the Web itself. If you look at the Start Page you should be able to see several hypertext links (underlined, coloured text). Move your mouse-pointer on to any link that you think looks interesting and click on it. When you do that, your browser sends a message to the server storing the page that you want. Then, if everything goes according to plan, the server will promptly respond by sending back the requested page so that your browser can display it.

Spend a little time following links to see where they lead. Don't limit yourself to clicking textual links alone, though – many of the pictures and graphics you see on a page will lead somewhere too. Take a look at the page shown in the opposite screenshot from Time Out magazine's site **(http://www.timeout.co.uk)** for a few clues to the type of thing you'll find on a web page.

- **Plain text** Ordinary readable text. Click it all you like – nothing will happen!
- **Hypertext link** A text link to another page. Hypertext links will almost always be underlined, but their text colour will vary from site to site.

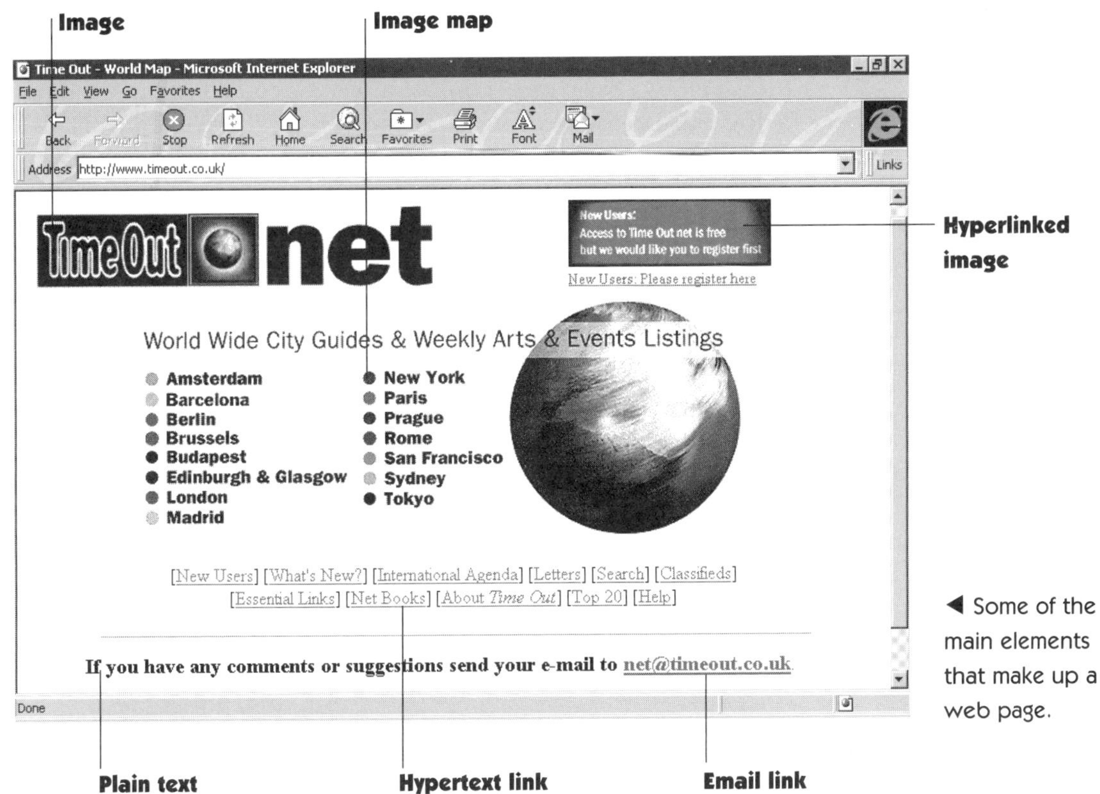

◀ Some of the main elements that make up a web page.

- **Image** A picture or graphic that enhances a web site. Like most pictures, it paints a thousand words, but it won't lead anywhere if you click it.
- **Hyperlinked image** Clicking this image will open a new page. In most cases a hyperlinked image will look no different to an ordinary image, but it may have a box around it that's the same colour as any hypertext links on the page.
- **Image map** An image split up into small chunks, with each chunk leading to a different page. In this case, every city name is linked to its own page listing forthcoming events in that city.
- **Email link** Click on this link and your email program will open so that you can send a message to the web page's author. The author's address will be automatically inserted into the message for you.

Is it an ordinary or linked image?

Watch your mouse-pointer! When you move the pointer on to any link (image or text), it will turn into a hand shape with a pointing finger. In a well-constructed image map, the different areas of the picture itself should make it clear where each link will lead. Finally, keep an eye on the status-bar at the bottom of the browser – as you move over a link of any sort you'll see the name of the linked document or file appear.

Links & Colours

On the Start Page you were viewing, the text you clicked was probably blue. If you go back and have another look you'll see it's changed colour (probably to purple). This is a neat indicator that helps you keep track of pages you've seen before as you flit from one page to another. These links will return to their original colour after a few days, but it's worth noting that writers of web pages can make their own colour choices, so the colours of visited and unvisited links will vary from one site to another.

Charting Your Course on the Web

By now you should be cheerfully clicking links of all descriptions from hypertext to images and skipping from page to page with casual abandon. The problem is, you can only move forwards. If you find yourself heading down a blind alley, how can you retrace your steps in order to head off in a different direction? This is where the browser itself comes to your rescue. So this is a good point to spend some time getting acquainted with the features and functions of its toolbars and menus.

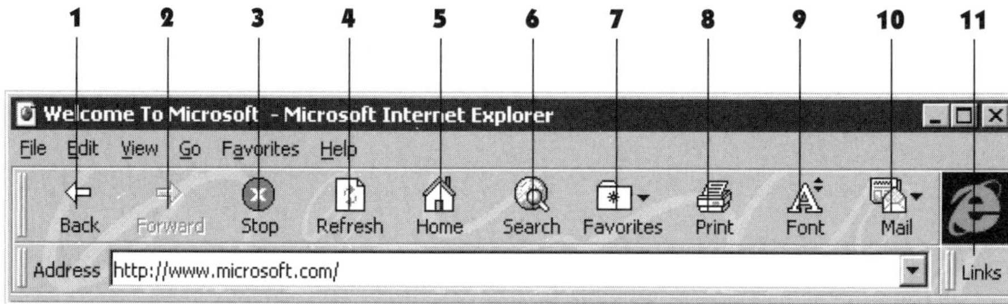

▶ Internet Explorer's button bar and address bar.

1 **Back** Clicking this button will take you back to the last page you looked at. If you keep clicking you can step all the way back to the first page.

2 **Forward** After using the Back button to take a second look at a previously viewed page, the Forward button lets you return to pages you viewed later. This button will be greyed-out if you haven't used the Back button yet.

3 **Stop** Stops the download of a page from the server. This can be useful if a page is taking a long time to appear, or if you clicked a link accidentally.

4 **Refresh** Click this and your browser will start downloading the same page again. See Sometimes Things Go Wrong… on page 68 for reasons why you may need to Refresh.

5 **Home** Opens your Start Page, explained on page 59.

6 **Search** Opens a search site from which you can search for pages by subject or keyword. You'll learn about searching for information in Chapter 12.

7 **Favorites** See Many Happy Returns – Using Favorites, below.

8 **Print** Prints the current page.

9 **Font** Clicking repeatedly enlarges or reduces the size of text on the page. (You can do this in a more controlled way by selecting **View | Fonts**).

10 **Mail** Opens a menu from which you can run your email or newsreader software, or open a blank form to send an email message.

11 **Links** If you click on this word a new button-bar will slide across revealing links to Microsoft's own site and some useful jumping-off points. To hide the Links bar again, click the word 'Address' to its left.

BY THE WAY

Increase your viewing space

You can find all these options on Explorer's menus as well, and most have keyboard shortcuts. If you'd like to see more of the pages themselves in Explorer's window, head off to the **View** menu and click on **Toolbar** to turn it off, this will automatically increase your viewing area.

One useful extra tool is a facility to search the page you're viewing for a particular word or phrase. Open the **Edit** menu, choose **Find (on this page)...** (or press Ctrl+F), and type the word you're looking for.

Many Happy Returns – Using Favorites

One of the most powerful Explorer tools is the **Favorites** system (known as Bookmarks or Hotlists in other browsers). Any time you arrive at a page you think may be useful in the future, you can add its address to your list of Favorites and return to it by opening the menu and clicking the relevant shortcut. To add the current page to the list, click the **Favorites** toolbar button and click **Add to Favorites**. A small dialog will appear giving a suggested title (you can replace this with any title you like to help you recognise it in future). To place the shortcut directly on the menu, click **OK**.

You can also organise your shortcuts into submenus to make them easier to find. Click the **Create in...** button and **New Folder**, then type a name for the folder. Click the folder into which you want to save the new shortcut and click the **OK** button to confirm. (If it ends up in the wrong place, don't worry! Select **Organize Favorites** from the Favorites menu and you'll be able to move, rename and delete folders and shortcuts, and create new folders.)

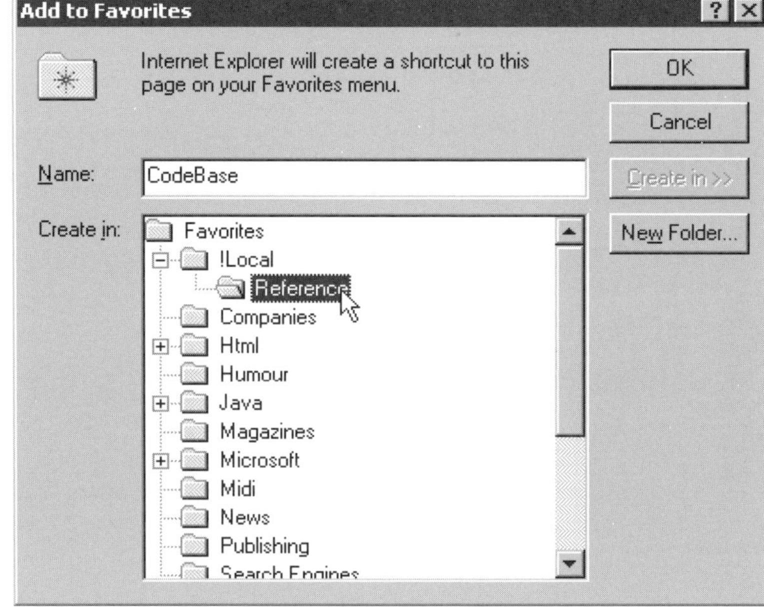

▶ Add a new shortcut to a Favorites submenu by clicking the submenu's folder followed by the OK button.

Retracing Your Steps with History

The History list provides a handy way of finding an elusive site that you visited recently but didn't add to your Favorites list. In fact, there are two lists. If you open the Go menu you'll see a short list of the last six pages you viewed – click one to reopen the page. For a longer list, choose the **Open History Folder** option from the same menu. The History folder lists every page together with its address and the date you last visited it. You can choose how long Explorer should store details of a visited page by clicking your way to **View | Options | Navigation**. Double-click an entry in the History folder to return to that page.

Are you a furtive surfer?

Explorer's History folder can be many things – useful, interesting, nostalgic, to name but a few. It can also be a dead giveaway. Although there's no foolproof way to cover your tracks, clearing the History folder is a sensible move if you'd prefer to keep your web-surfing habits private.

The Address Bar & URLs

Every page on the World Wide Web has its own unique **URL**. URL stands for Uniform Resource Locator, but it's just a convoluted way of saying 'address'. You've seen a few of these already; if you skip back to the beginning of the chapter you'll see the URLs of each web site screenshot.

You'll also notice URLs at work as you move from page to page in Explorer, provided you can see the toolbar (if you can't, go to **View | Toolbar** to switch it on). Every time you open a new page, its URL appears in the address bar below the buttons. You can also type a URL into the address bar yourself – just click once on the address bar to highlight the address currently shown, type the URL of the page you want to open, and press Enter. For example, if you want to look at today's peak-time TV listings, type: **http://www.link-it.com/tv** into the address bar. In a similar way, if you find the URL of a site you'd like to visit in an email message or word processor document, copy it to the clipboard using Ctrl+C, click in the address bar, and paste in the URL by pressing Ctrl+V.

BY THE WAY

Accuracy is everything

URLs are case-sensitive, so make sure you observe any capital letters. Also, in contrast with the directory-paths used in Windows computers, URLs use forward-slashes rather than backslashes. Actually, these don't matter too much – if you forget and use the wrong type, Explorer will know what you mean.

Understanding URLs

You'll come into contact with a lot of URLs on your travels around the Internet, so it's worth knowing what they mean. As an example, let's take the URL for the Network Chart's Top 10 singles page and break it up into its component pieces. The URL is: **http://www.netchart.co.uk/html/topten.htm**

- **http://** This is one of the Internet's many protocols, and it stands for HyperText Transfer Protocol. It's the system used to send web pages around the Internet, so all web page URLs have the http:// prefix.
- **www.netchart.co.uk/** This is the name of the computer on which the required file is stored (often referred to as the host computer). Computers that store web pages are called web servers, and their names usually begin www.
- **html/** This is the directory path to the page you want to open. Just as on your own computer, the path may consist of several directories separated by forward-slashes.
- **topten.htm** This is the name of the file you want. The .htm (or .html) extension indicates that it's a web page, but your browser can handle any number of different file types, as you'll see in Chapters 6 and 13.

GOOD QUESTION

Why don't some URLs contain filenames?

Some URLs finish with a directory name (i.e. **http://www.link-it.com/tv**). When your browser sends this type of URL to a web server, the server will look in the directory for a default file, often called **index.htm**. If a file exists with this name it will be sent back to your browser; if not, you'll receive a hypertext list of all that directory's files.

A little while ago I said your browser was the most powerful tool in your Internet-software armoury, and I wasn't kidding. In later chapters we'll be looking at other Internet services you can use, and I'll point you towards some of the best software to help you use them. But your browser is a multi-talented chap: some of these services can be accessed directly within the browser itself without the need for any other software, and for those that can't, your browser still makes a great jumping-off point.

We've just seen that the World Wide Web service uses a protocol called HTTP, so all your web page URLs will start http://. Here are some of the other prefixes your browser will handle and the results of using them:

Prefix	Result
ftp://	The URL of a library of files on an FTP server. Your browser will display directory and filenames, and allow you to download files. Try typing **ftp://sunsite.doc.ic.ac.uk/computing/systems/ibmpc** into your address bar to visit one of the best software libraries in the UK. For more on FTP, turn to Chapter 9.
gopher://	Gopher was the forerunner of the Web and is now largely ignored, but your browser will still happily access Gopher sites. You'll learn more about this creature in Chapter 11, but you can get a taste from the Definitive Sitcom List at **gopher://info.mcc.ac.uk/11/miscellany/sitcom**.
telnet://	Your browser will start your Telnet program rather than accessing the site itself. We'll have a closer look at Telnet in Chapter 11, but in the meantime, type **telnet://mud.erols.com:5000** into your address bar to take part in a brain-twisting, text-based adventure game called StarGate.
mailto:	Mailto: links crop up a lot on web pages. You can also type them into your address bar to open a blank email form with the email address already inserted. For example, to send me a message type: **mailto:rob.young@btinternet.com**.To find out more about sending and receiving email, turn to Chapter 7.
news:	This will be a link to a particular newsgroup for which your browser will start your newsreader software (unless it has its own built-in newsreader) to display the messages in the group. You'll learn about newsgroups in Chapter 8, but for now try entering **news:news.groups** to see a newsgroup for newcomers to the Internet.
file:///	Using this prefix you can open a local web document, that is, a file on your own hard-disk that has the .htm or .html extension. Browsers can also open many other types of file (such as images with the .gif or .jpg extension), as we'll see in Chapter 13. In Explorer, unlike most other browsers, you can actually leave out this prefix and just type an ordinary file path like **c:\mydirectory\myfile.htm**.

A little less typing

When you type the URL of a web page into your address bar you can leave out the **http://**. Most browsers will assume you're looking for a web page and add that part themselves. Similarly, if you type an address that starts with 'ftp' (such as **ftp.download.com**) or 'gopher' (as in **gopher.micro.umn.edu**) you don't need to type the **ftp:// or gopher://** prefixes either – your browser will know they're not web sites and will use the correct protocol automatically

Sometimes Things Go Wrong...

Things don't always go as smoothly as you'd hope for when you're trying to open a web page. To begin with, the server may not be running and you'll eventually see a message telling you that the operation 'timed out' – in other words, your browser has waited a minute or so for a response from the server and doesn't think anything is going to happen. Another reason for a delay is that although the server is running it may be busy. In this case you may get a similar result, or you may get a part of the page and then everything seems to stop dead. You may be able to get things moving by clicking the **Refresh** button on the browser's toolbar, forcing your browser to request the document again, but be prepared to give up, visit a different web site, and try this one again later.

And then there's the Mysterious Vanishing Page syndrome. Although all web pages contain links, sometimes the pages those links refer to no longer exist and you'll see an error-message instead. The reason is simple: on the perpetually changing landscape of the World Wide Web, pages (and even entire sites) move elsewhere, are renamed, or just disappear. In fact, the average lifespan of a site is a mere 90 days! Anyone putting links to these sites in his own pages has no way of knowing when this happens other than by regularly clicking all the links himself to check them. By the same token, some of the URLs included in this book may be defunct by the time you get to try them. The endless arrivals and departures are a fact of web life, but also a part of its magic.

▶ *So how does anyone find what they're looking for on the Web? Turn to Chapter 12 to find out.*

What Next?

There's much more to the World Wide Web than we've covered in this chapter, but you've seen enough to know what it is and how to move around it. In the next chapter you'll go a stage further, learning how to use other features of Internet Explorer to make your web-surfing faster, easier, and more efficient.

6

MASTERING YOUR WEB BROWSER

In This Chapter...

- ▶ Tricks for easier, faster browsing
- ▶ Discover the power of the mouse's 'other button'
- ▶ Download and save what you find on the Web
- ▶ Learn how to tweak-up the cache and make the most of shortcuts

In Chapter 5 you learnt the basic moves that let you view web pages, store the location of a useful page so that you can revisit it later, and use your browser to access a few of the other Internet services. But there's a lot more to the Web than I could reasonably fit into a single chapter. In fact, there's more to it than I can fit into two chapters! To give you a good head start on the Web, I'm going to linger here a little longer and show you some of the ways in which your browser can power-up your surfing. Later on, in parts 3 and 4, I'll introduce you to some of the 'sideshows' of the Web, such as multimedia, search engines, and online shopping, and I'll show you how to create your own web pages.

Customising Your Browser

Let's start with some browser tips to help you fine-tune your surfing:

- **Customise your Start Page** If you're content to let your browser download a page every time you run it, you can choose what that page should contain; you could perhaps have the latest news stories displayed automatically. Visit **http://home.microsoft.com** and follow the instructions on the page. (If you're using Netscape, go to **http://www.netscape.com/custom/index.html**.)
- **Use a blank Start Page** The problem with the traditional Start Page is that Explorer will try to download it every time you start up, even if you weren't planning to go online. The other option is to use a blank page from your own disk instead. Go to **View | Options | Navigation**, make sure that **Start Page** is shown in the topmost box and type **file://c:\windows\system\blank.htm** in the box labelled Address, then click **OK**.
- **Use a different Start Page** You can use any page on the Web as your Start Page. Click your way to **View | Options | Navigation**, check that **Start Page** is shown in the upper box, and then either type a URL into the **Address** box below, or click the **Use Current** button to set the page you're currently viewing as your Start Page. (You can even create your own Start Page if you want to – I'll explain how to do that in Chapter 24.)
- **Browse faster without images** The actual text on a web page downloads very fast; it's the images that you're often left waiting for, and most pages have at least one image. To skip around the Web faster, you can turn off the display of images, and have them replaced by empty boxes or small

'placeholder' icons on the page. To do this in Explorer, go to **View | Options** and remove the checkmark from **Show pictures** on the **General** tab. (You can also prevent sounds and videos playing automatically, but these are still rarely encountered on the Web.) If you want to view an image on a particular page, click it with the right mouse-button and choose **Show Picture**.

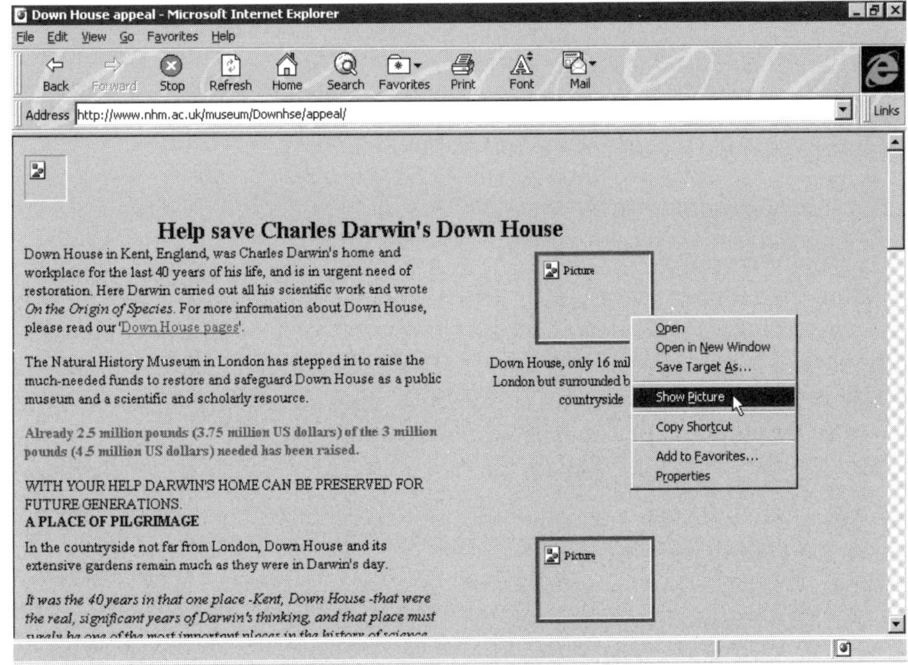

◀ With the automatic display of images turned off, you can right-click the placeholder and choose Show Picture to reveal the missing image.

▶ **Rearrange your Toolbars** The main toolbar and the Address and Links bars have a 'raised' vertical strip to their left. By grabbing the strip with the mouse-pointer you can drag the toolbars around. If you'd like both the Address and Links bars to be permanently displayed, drag one of them downwards into the window and let go. If you'd like a little extra viewing space for pages, drop each bar next to the buttons on the toolbar. You can even hide them completely, or remove the text labels from their icons: go to **View | Options | General** and play with some of the options in the **Toolbars** section of the dialog. Click the **Apply** button to see if you like the changes – that way, the dialog will stay open so that you can change them back again if you want to.

Double-glazing – Opening a New Window

Like most recent applications, web browsers let you open a second window (and a third, and a fourth, as long as your computer has the resources to cope) so that you can run several Web sessions at the same time. There are a few reasons why you may find this useful. If you're searching for a particularly elusive piece of information, you can follow two different paths in the two windows and (perhaps) track it down a little sooner. Or you can view a page in one window while waiting for another page to finish downloading. And here's one that I use all the time: if you find a page full of links to sites you want to visit one by one, open each link in a new window, and then close that window when you've finished – the original window is still waiting patiently for you to try the next link on the list. (It really is a lot quicker than using the Back button or the Favorites menu!) You can close one of these windows without it affecting any of the others – as long as Internet Explorer has at least one window open, it'll keep running.

GOOD QUESTION

Will more windows turbo-charge my surfing?

Yes and no. If you're downloading a web page in each window, you're ultimately downloading exactly the same amount of data as you would if you used one window and opened the pages one at a time (a faster modem is the only way to make this happen any more quickly). However, if you organise things so that one window is always downloading a page while you're reading the page in the other window, it may help.

To open a new window in Internet Explorer, you can use any of the following methods:

- Click on **File | New Window** or press Ctrl+N. The new window will start by showing the same page as your original window.
- Click any link with the right mouse-button and choose **Open in New Window** from the context menu.
- Type a URL into the address box, and then press Shift+Enter.
- Non-mouse fans should press the Tab key repeatedly until the link you want to follow is highlighted, and press Shift+Enter.

Why did it do that?

You may sometimes be innocently clicking links when suddenly a new window opens for a particular page. Web-page authors occasionally add an extra piece of code to make a link open in a new window so that you can still find their original page easily. They can also add a code forcing your browser not to show toolbars or the status-bar in the new window to give a larger viewing area.

Right-click for Easy Surfing

I've already acknowledged the existence of the right mouse-button a couple of times in this chapter – you can open a link in a new window or display an image represented by a placeholder by right-clicking and then selecting the appropriate option from the popup context-menu. The contents of the menu vary according to the type of item you clicked, but always contain a feast of goodies you won't find elsewhere, so don't forget to use it.

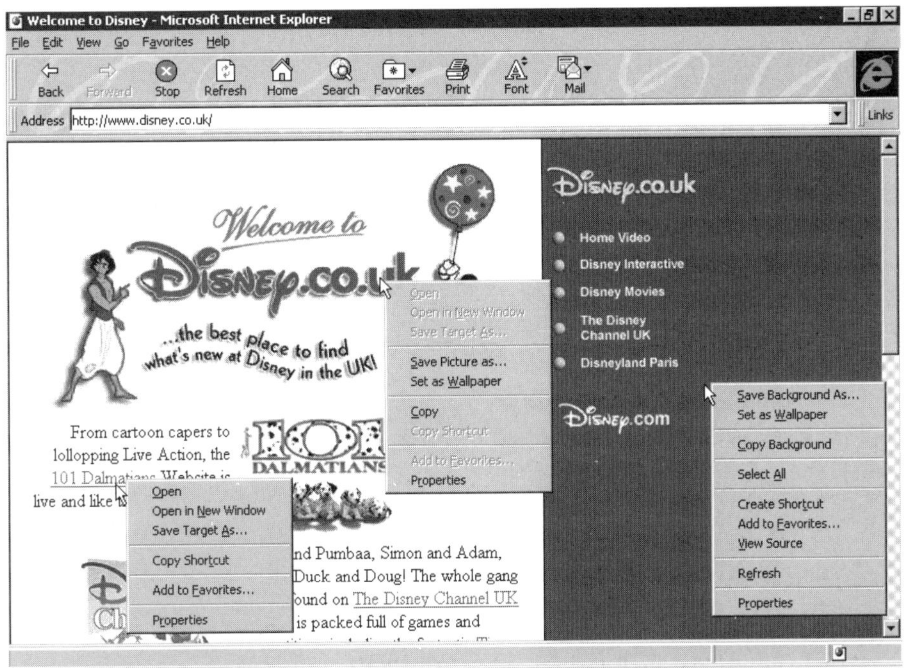

◀ OK, I've cheated here, I admit it! This composite screenshot shows the context menus that appear after right-clicking a link (left), an image (centre) or the page background (right) while using Explorer.

Let's have a closer look at what some of these options do:

Clicking This	Does This
Copy Shortcut	Places the link's URL on the clipboard ready for you to paste into another application.
Add to Favorites...	Places a shortcut to this page on your Favorites menu. If you clicked the page background, the URL of the current page will be saved; if you clicked a link, the URL referred to by the link will be saved.
Set as Wallpaper	Replaces the wallpaper on your desktop with the web page's background. This will remain on your wallpaper list as **Internet Explorer Wallpaper** for you to choose, but each wallpaper you save will replace the last.
Create Shortcut	Places a shortcut to the current page on the desktop. See Using Internet Shortcuts later in this chapter to find out more about these.
Save Target As...	Downloads the file to which the link points and saves it on to your disk, but doesn't display it in the browser window. You'll be prompted to choose a location in which to save the file.
Save Picture As...	Stores the image you clicked to a directory on your hard-disk. You can also drag the image off the page and on to your desktop or a hard-disk directory.

The last two items lead us neatly into a major area of Internet life, and a likely reason you wanted to become a part of it: there's lots of stuff on the Web, and most of that stuff you can grab for your own use. So how do you do it?

Saving Files From the Web

There are two groups of files you can grab from the World Wide Web – those that are a part of the web page itself (such as an image), and those that aren't. The second group is huge, covering applications, sound files, videos, spreadsheets, ZIP files, and a whole lot more. Although the methods of saving any file are straightforward enough, that second group is going to lead us into a few complications, so let's begin with the first.

Saving Page Elements

- **Saving the web page's text** To save the text from the entire page, open the **File** menu and choose **Save File As...** Select **Plain Text** from the **Save as type** list and choose a name and location for the file. Alternatively, if you only need a portion of the text on the page, you can highlight it using the mouse, copy it to the clipboard by pressing Ctrl+C, and then paste it into another application.

- **Saving the web page's source** The source of a web page is the text you see in your browser, plus all the weird codes added by the page's author that make the page display properly. These codes belong to a language called HTML (HyperText Markup Language), which you'll learn about in chapters 23 and 24. To save the HTML source document, follow the same routine as above, but choose **HTML** from the **Save as type** list. (If you just want to have a peep at the source, right-click the web page's background and choose **View Source** from the context menu.)
- **Saving images from the page** As you learnt above, it just takes a right-click on any image to save it to disk (or a drag, if you prefer). You can also save the background, a small image file that the browser tiles to fill the entire viewing area. In addition to the **Set as Wallpaper** option mentioned opposite, you can right-click the background and choose **Save Background As...** to save the image file to the directory of your choice. You can also copy images or the background to the clipboard with a right-click, ready to paste into another application.

Why would I want to save the HMTL source?

As languages go, HTML is a very easy one. It may look a bit daunting on first sight, but the millions of people who've added their own pages to the Web can attest to its simplicity. Most of these people learnt the language by saving the source files of other web pages and then having a look at them later. (Of course, you can also pull bits out to use in your own pages!)

Is that your image, Sir?

Although you can easily copy text and images from someone else's page and use them yourself, remember that copyright laws apply to information on the Internet just as they do to information you find anywhere else. Not that people don't 'recycle' stuff they find on the Web of course, but always consider whose it is and how you're planning to use it.

Saving Other Types of File

Although most of the links you find on web pages will open another page, some will be links to files that you can download (don't worry – it should be obvious, and if it isn't, just hit the Cancel button as soon as you get the chance!). As I mentioned earlier, this is where things get a bit more complicated. Come what may, the file must be downloaded to your own computer before you can do anything with it all, but how you choose to handle the download will depend upon what you want to do with the file itself. The browser may be multi-talented, but it can't display every type of file that exists!

However, what it can do is to launch an **external viewer** to display the file. An external viewer is just a slightly technical way of saying 'another program on your computer'. (You'll find some of the best available viewers on the free CD-ROM in the back of this book, and I'll show you where you can find others on the Web in later chapters.) Two vital elements are required for your browser to be able to do this:

- You must have a program on your disk that can open the type of file you're about to download.
- The browser needs to know which program to use for a particular type of file, and where to find it on your disk.

After you click the link, Internet Explorer will start to download the file it refers to and then show the dialog below. It wants to know what to do with the file when it's finished downloading: do you want to save the file and carry on surfing, or open it immediately using an external viewer?

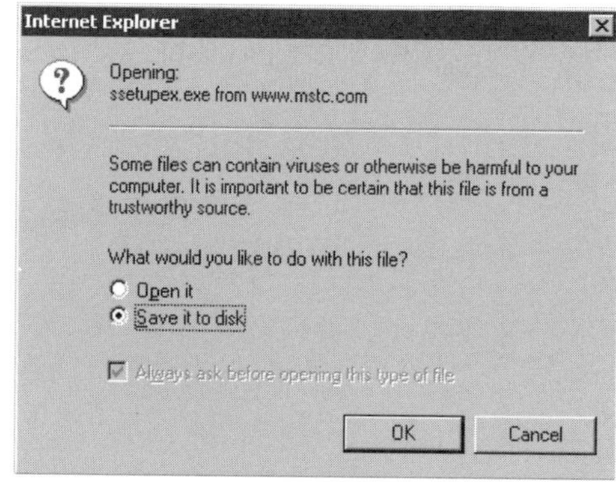

▶ Explorer wants to know whether it should open this file after downloading, or save it to your hard-disk.

- **Save it to disk** If you choose this option, Explorer will present a **Save As** dialog so that you can choose a directory to save the file into, followed by a smaller dialog that will keep you posted on the progress of the download and how much longer it should take. While the file is downloading you can wait, or continue surfing the Web, and there's a handy **Cancel** button you can use if you change your mind halfway through, or if the download seems to be taking too long. The **Save it to disk** option is the best (and safest) option.

- **Open it** For a file that you want to view or play straight away, you can click the **Open it** button. Explorer will then prompt you to choose the program you want to use, so click the **Browse** button in the next dialog to locate and double-click a program that can handle this type of file, and then click **OK**. Explorer will download the file and then launch that program to display the file. After clicking the **Open it** button, you'll see a checkbox below labelled **Always ask before opening this type of file**. If you remove the checkmark from this box, Explorer will always use the program you select whenever you download files of the same type in the future. You can view and edit the settings for different types of file by going to **View | Options | Programs** and clicking the **File Types** button. Click a file type from the list, and click the **Edit** button. If the box beside **Confirm open after download** isn't checked, this type of file will always be opened – you can check this box if you'd like the chance to save this type of file in future. To find out which program will open this type of file, click on either **Play** or **Open** in the **Actions** box, then click **Edit...**

BY THE WAY

Virus alert!

Always run a virus-checker before running any program you've downloaded. Although people get a bit too hysterical about it, there's a small risk that a program may contain a virus. It only takes a few seconds to do and may just save a lot of hassle later. I'll show you where to find a virus-checker in Chapter 13.

Configuring Your Browser – Automatic or Manual?

In the routine above, I've assumed that you do actually have a program on your own system that can play or display the type of file you're downloading. Of course, that won't always be the case. Remember that you can opt to save any file so that you know you've got it safe and sound on your disk, and then go hunting for a suitable player or viewer program afterwards. You can then install the new program in the usual way and use it to open this file.

If you do that, you have three possible options for the future:

1 Every time you come across a file of this type on the Web you can opt to save it, and open it yourself later on in the same way.
2 You can wait until you find another file of this type, click on **Open it** and then direct Explorer to the external viewer that you now possess. If you choose this method, your browser will automatically configure itself to use this viewer for this type of file in future.
3 You can configure Internet Explorer yourself as soon as you've installed the new program so that it knows exactly what to do next time you choose to open this type of file.

I strongly recommend you go for one of the first two options. If you save the file and view it later, you won't be wasting expensive online time looking at something that'll still be there when you disconnect. And if you wait until the next time you find this kind of file, you'll just have to spend a few seconds pointing Explorer to the correct viewer.

If you do want to configure Explorer yourself, you'll need to know about file types, extensions, and the way in which particular file types are associated with a certain program. That's the sort of technical stuff I'm not going to venture into here (you'll find it in my book *The What PC? Guide To Your PC*, also published by Prentice Hall), and it's rarely necessary to configure these settings yourself when your browser makes such a good job of it.

▶ *For more on file types and viewers, skip ahead to Chapter 13. Or turn to Chapter 21 to find some of the best add-ons for viewing the Web's multimedia files.*

Using Internet Shortcuts

We've looked at a few ways that you can go to a particular page on the Web – you can click a link on a page, type a URL into the address bar and press Enter, or select the site from your history list or Favorites. Another method is the **Internet Shortcut**.

An Internet Shortcut is a tiny file that contains only a web page's URL. You can keep these little files on your desktop (or anywhere on your computer's hard-disk) and double-click them to go to the page they point at. In effect, they work in exactly the same way as the links you find on a web page.

Internet shortcuts are my Favorites

If you're using Internet Explorer, you'll find a directory called Favorites on your hard-disk. When you open it, you'll see all the items on your **Favorites** menu. These are all Internet Shortcuts; you can create new shortcuts here, and add subdirectories, all of which will appear on your **Favorites** menu.

The easiest way to create an Internet Shortcut is to click on any link in a web page and (before releasing the mouse-button) drag it to your desktop. You can also create your own shortcuts by hand. Open a text-editor such as Windows' Notepad and type the following:

[InternetShortcut]
URL=*type the URL here*

After the equals sign, type the URL you want this shortcut to point at, such as **http://www.disney.co.uk.** Save the file wherever you like with an appropriate name and the extension **.url**. For instance, you may call this example **Disney Site.url**. You can create Internet Shortcuts that use the other protocols mentioned on page 67, such as a link to a newsgroup, an FTP site, or the email address of someone you contact frequently.

To use an Internet Shortcut, just double-click it. Your browser will start and open the page. If your browser is already running, you can drag and drop a shortcut into its window. You can also copy these shortcuts on to a floppy-disk or attach them to an email message so that someone else can use them.

Browse Faster Using the Cache

If you've spent some time surfing the Web and skipping backwards and forwards between pages, here's a phenomenon you may have noticed: when you return to a page you've seen before (perhaps by clicking the Back button) you don't have to wait – the page appears almost instantly. This is the **disk cache** at work. Every page you view, along with its constituent images, is saved to a directory on your own computer's disk. Most browsers simply call this directory **Cache**, but Internet Explorer uses its own, quite intuitive name, **Temporary Internet Files**. But for brevity I'm just going to refer to it as the Cache Directory.

Every web page that Explorer downloads and displays is also saved into the cache directory, along with images and other items on the page (yes, there can be more to a page than just text and images, as you'll learn in Chapter 22). The cache directory will gradually increase in size until it reaches its maximum allowed size, at which point the oldest files will gradually be removed to make way for more recent ones.

Whenever you click a link or type a URL into the address bar, the browser looks in the cache first to see if it can grab the files it needs from there instead of downloading them from the Web. Not only does this speed things up for you, it also takes some of the strain off the poor old Internet.

Tweaking the Cache Settings

While this isn't a 'must do', it is certainly a 'may want to do'. Explorer will be set up to use the cache by default, so you're reaping the rewards already. But it may be set up to use a much larger chunk of hard-disk space than you really want to sacrifice.

Click your way to **View | Options | Advanced**. On the part of the page labelled **Temporary Internet Files** you'll see two buttons, **View Files...** and **Settings...**. Click the first of these to take a look at the files in the cache. This can be every bit as informative as the History folder, as it gives the names of the files, their original URL, the date on which you last viewed them, and much more. If you click the **Settings...** button you'll see the dialog shown in the next screenshot. Here's a quick description of the controls and what they're for:

- **Check for newer versions of stored pages** Choose when Explorer should look in the cache for a page and when it should download it. If you choose **Every visit to the page**, Explorer will never search the cache, even if you only looked at this page two minutes ago. **Every time you start Internet Explorer** means that if you haven't visited this URL in this Web session, Explorer should download the page; if you have, it will retrieve it from the cache. **Never** means that Explorer will never try to download the page if there's a page in the cache with the same URL, regardless of its age.
- **Amount of disk space to use** When it's first installed, Explorer will pick what it reckons to be a sensible percentage of your hard-disk to hold cached files. If you think that it is too high a percentage drag this slider to the left to reduce the figure.

- **Move Folder** lets you move your **Temporary Internet Files** directory elsewhere. This feature could be useful if you have another external drive with more available free space.
- **Empty Folder** clears all existing files out of the cache, letting you regain some of your disk space.

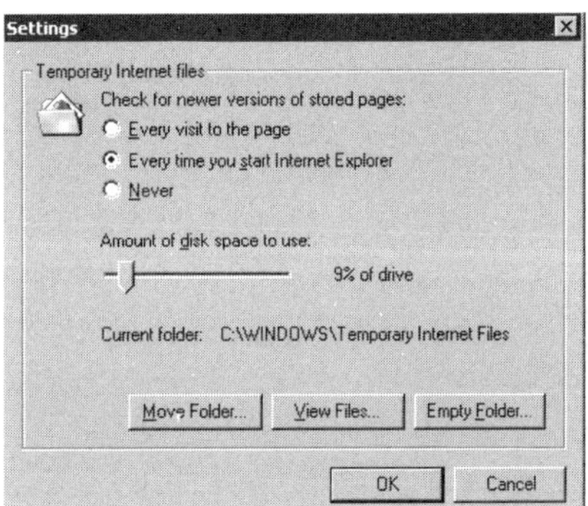

◀ Alter Explorer's use of the disk cache and take a look at the files in the cache directory.

Your files are downloading anyway

Because Explorer uses the files' original names and locations in the cache, you can open it any time you want to and drag files out for your own use. So instead of saving text, source and images from a page as you surf, you could just go to the cache after disconnecting.

Which Option Should I Use?

It depends on the web sites you visit. Sites specialising in news and stock exchange quotes change frequently, so choose **Every visit to the page** to see the latest version. If you visit sites that rarely change, speed things up by selecting **Never** and loading the page from the cache every time. If in doubt, the safe 'middle option' is **Every time you start Internet Explorer** – you'll always see the latest version of the page when you first visit that site but if you return to it later in the same session it will be opened from the cache.

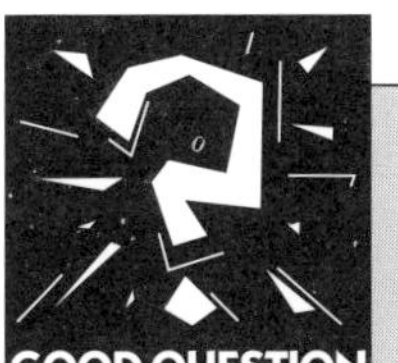

How can I see if the page has changed?

You don't need to go back and change the cache settings. Just click the **Refresh** button on the toolbar (or press F5). This forces Explorer to download and display the current version of the page from the server, and store it in the cache to replace your old copy.

7

EXCHANGING MESSAGES BY EMAIL

In This Chapter...

- What's so great about email anyway?
- Choose and set up your email software
- Send and receive your first email message
- Take the mystery out of sending files by email
- Learn the secret language of the Internet – emoticons & acronyms

Email is the old man of the Internet, and one of the reasons the network was constructed in the first place. It's one of the easiest areas of Net life to use, and one of the most used; for many people, sending and receiving email is their only reason for going online. By the end of this chapter you'll be able to send email messages and computer files to millions of people all over the world (well, perhaps not all of them!) in less time than you can stick a stamp on an envelope.

Why Should I Use Email?

First, it's incredibly cheap. At the time of writing a first-class stamp costs 26p and will get a letter to a single, local (in global terms) address. But for a local telephone call costing 5p you can deliver dozens of email messages to all corners of the world. Second, it's amazingly fast. In some cases your email may be received within just seconds of your sending it. (However, it isn't always quite as fast as that: on occasions, when the network conspires against you, it could take hours.) Third, it's easy to keep copies of the email you send and receive, and to quickly sort and locate individual messages. There's a possible fourth reason, but it should be regarded with some caution. If you agonise for hours over ordinary letter-writing, email should make life easier for you. An inherent feature of email is its informality: spelling, grammar and punctuation are tossed aside in favour of speed and brevity.

Incidentally, if you encounter the phrase 'snail mail', and are bemused by its meaning, it's simply a popular term for ordinary mail sent through the land-based postal service, the implication being that its speed is closer to that of a certain mollusc than email.

Everybody's First Question...

Whenever the subject of email comes up with Internet beginners, the same question is guaranteed to arise within the first minute. So that you can comfortably concentrate on the rest of the chapter, I'll put your mind at ease by answering it straight away. The all-consuming question is: What happens if email arrives for me and I'm not online to receive it?

The answer: email arrives at your access provider's computer (their **mail server**) and waits for you to collect it. In fact, it will wait there for a long time if it has to: most mail servers only delete messages that remain uncollected for several months, but if you take a week's holiday you can safely collect your week's worth of email when you return.

Understanding Email Addresses

There are two easy ways to spot an Internet newbie. The first is that their messages begin 'Dear…' and end 'Yours sincerely'. The second is that they tell you their 'email number'. Don't fall into either trap!

Newbie

You're a 'newbie'! It's OK, I'm not being abusive. It just means that you're new to the Internet. You wouldn't be proud to describe yourself as a newbie, but you may want to do so when appealing for help in a newsgroup, for example, to keep responses as simple as possible.

I'll tell you how to avoid the first pitfall later in the chapter; in the second case, you definitely have an email address (not a number)!

Email addresses consist of three basic elements: a username, an '@' sign, and a domain name. Your username will usually be the name in which your account was set up, and the name that you log on with when you connect. The domain name is the address of your Internet Access Provider or online service. For example, my username is **rob.young**, and my access provider's address is **btinternet.com**, so my complete email address is – **rob.young@btinternet.com**.

Quoting your email address

If for some reason you have to say your email address out loud and don't want to sound like a total newbie, when you are speaking replace the dots in the address with the word 'dot' and the @ sign with the word 'at'. My email address is pronounced 'rob dot young at btinternet dot com'.

Email Addresses & Online Services

The email address of someone using an online service is structured in a similar way, although CompuServe calls the username a 'User ID', and AOL calls it a 'Screen Name'. If you have an account with an IAP, and you want to send email to an AOL member, use the address ***ScreenName*@aol.com**. To send to a member of MSN, use ***username*@msn.com**. CompuServe members' User IDs are in the form 101355,1436 and an email message can't contain commas, so you've got to make a slight adjustment – the comma has to be replaced with a dot. To email the CompuServe member with that User ID, the address would be **101355.1436@compuserve.com**.

Members of online services can also send email out on to the Internet to someone with an IAP account. In fact, members of AOL and MSN can use the email address without making any changes to it. However, if you're a CompuServe member, you'll have to insert the word 'Internet:' (including the colon) before the address. To send me a message, for example, a CompuServe member would use the address **internet:rob.young@btinternet.com**. The word 'internet' isn't case-sensitive, and it doesn't matter if you leave a space after the colon.

If you're a member of an online service, and you want to email another member of the same service, all you need to enter is the username (or User ID, or Screen Name) of the person you want to email.

What Do I Need?

If you have an account with an online service such as CompuServe or AOL, you don't need anything more – the software you use to connect to and navigate the service has built-in email capability. If you have an IAP account, you'll need an email client (geek-speak for 'a program that works with email'). There are many of these to choose from, and your IAP may have provided one when you signed up. There are three major factors to consider when choosing an email program. It should:

- be compatible with the protocols used by your email account (I'll explain that in a moment)
- let you work offline
- let you organise incoming and outgoing messages into separate 'folders'.

Offline

Software that lets you work offline allows you to read and write your messages without being connected to your IAP or online service and clocking up charges. You only need to go online to send your messages and receive any new email. The earliest email had to be written online, which is why speed mattered more than spelling.

Oh dear, you're thinking, more of those protocols again. This isn't too tough though. There are two main protocols used to move email around: **SMTP** (Simple Mail Transport Protocol) and **POP3** (Post Office Protocol, which is currently at its third version). SMTP is the protocol used to send email messages to the server, and POP3 is (usually) the protocol used by the server to deliver messages to you. What you need to know is whether you have a POP3 email account – your IAP should have made that quite clear when you signed up. There are several dull, technical reasons why a POP3 account is better than an SMTP-only account, but what you care about right now is that you'll have a far wider range of email software available to choose from.

If you do have a POP3 account, the most popular email clients on the Internet are:

- **Internet Mail & News** Despite the rather pedestrian name (and it's soon to be renamed 'Outlook Express'), I highly recommend this package for users of the Internet Explorer browser. This package gives you email and newsgroup programs which integrate themselves with the browser very neatly. In fact, when Internet Explorer was installed on your system (see page 59), these should have been installed along with it. You can check for newer versions at **http://www.microsoft.com/ie/download**.

- **Pegasus Mail** An excellent free program that you can download from **http://www.let.rug.nl/pegasus/ftp.html**.
- **Eudora Light** This is 'postcard-ware' (it's basically free, but the author would like a picture-postcard of your home town as payment). You can download it from **http://www.eudora.com**, or install an evaluation version of its big brother, Eudora Pro, from the free CD-ROM accompanying this book.

What about Microsoft Exchange?

Exchange (also known as Windows Messaging) is included in recent versions of Windows, but I don't recommend using it; it's bloated, slow, and unfriendly. However, if you have Microsoft Outlook (also included in Office 97) I suggest you try that and see how you get on. It's not perfect, but it is quicker and easier to use.

If you don't have a POP3 account:

- **Tetrix Reader Plug** This is simple and neat, and doubles as a newsreader program. Type the following URL into your browser's address bar and press Enter to start the download:

  ftp://sunsite.cnlab-switch.ch/mirror/winsite/win3/winsock/trp110.zip

If you use the Netscape Navigator browser, you already have a built-in email client. Open the **Window** menu and click on **Netscape Mail** to compose, send, receive and read email messages.

Setting Up Your Email Program

Before you can start to send and receive email, your software needs to know a bit about you and your email account. This simply involves filling in the blanks on a setup page using some of the information given to you by your access provider (see page 43). The first time you start the program it should prompt you to enter this information, but it's worth knowing where to find it in case you ever need to change it in the future. (If you use Windows 95, some Internet programs will store these details in the Registry when you enter them, letting other programs set themselves up automatically).

- In **Eudora**, go to **Tools | Options**. Click the icons in the left pane to open the various option pages. The settings you're concerned with at this point are scattered over the first five pages. On the **Sending Mail** page, remove the checkmark from the **Immediate Send** box.
- In **Pegasus**, click **Tools | Options**. Click on **General Settings** and **Network Configuration** in turn to fill in the details.
- In **Internet Mail**, choose **Mail | Options** and click the **Server** tab.

In the first two programs especially, you'll find a bewildering array of checkboxes and options. Ignore them! Just fill in personal details about your email address, POP3 account name and password, SMTP and POP3 mail server addresses, and so on. We'll look at some of the other options later in this chapter. For now, though, they're set at sensible defaults, so leave them this way until you're sure you want to change something.

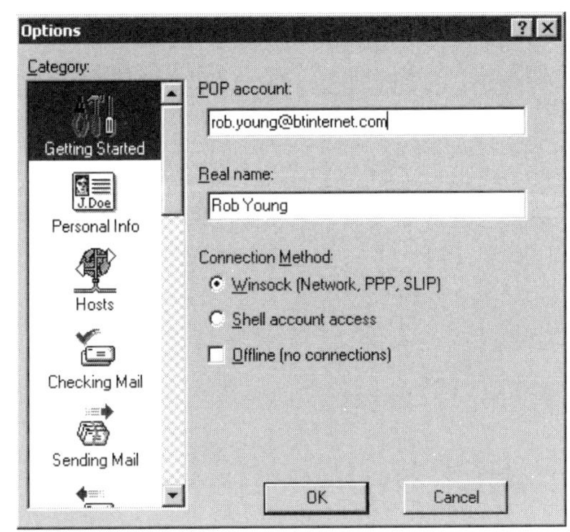

◀ Entering personal email account details into Eudora Light.

Sending an Email Message

You probably feel an overwhelming temptation to email everyone you know and tell them you've 'joined the club', but hold that thought for a moment. Start by sending a message to yourself instead – that way you can check that everything's working, and learn what to do when you receive a message as well.

Fire up your email program or your online service's software and click the button that opens a message window. In Eudora and Pegasus, the button shows a pen and paper; in Internet Mail, click the envelope icon with a 'sparkle' in the corner.

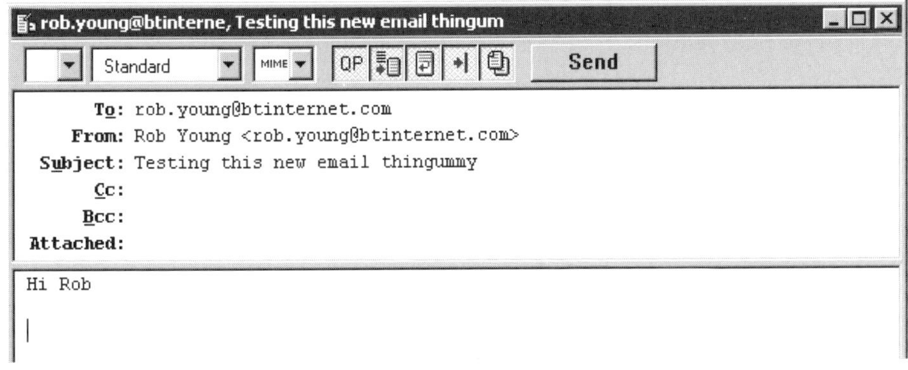

◀ Eudora Light's mail message window.

Although all of these email programs look a little different, the important features are the same:

To: Type the email address of the person to whom you want to send the message.

CC: Carbon copy. If you want to send the message to several people, type one address in the To field and the rest in the CC field. Using this method, all recipients will know who else received a copy of the message.

BCC: Blind Carbon Copy. If you want to send the same message to several people and you don't want any of them to know who else is getting a copy, place their addresses in this field instead of the CC field.

From: You'll rarely see this in the message window, and the email software will enter your email address automatically from the information you entered when you set up the program. This tells the recipient who to reply to.

Subject: Enter a short description of your message. In some email programs you can send a message with a blank subject line, but avoid doing this. Although most people will open any email they receive (even if the subject is blank), this entry really comes into its own when the recipient is looking for this message again in six months time.

Attached: Lists the names of any computer files you want to send to the recipient along with the message. You'll learn about attaching files later in this chapter.

Below these fields is the area in which you type the message itself. Because you're going to send this message to yourself, type your own email address into the **To** field, and anything you like in the **Subject** field (just to get into the habit!), and then write yourself a welcoming message.

Now you need to send the message. Once again, the programs differ here, but look for a button marked **Send**. Some programs will send email immediately, and try to log on to your service to do so; others add mail to a 'queue' of messages to be sent all together when you're ready to do so. You may even have two Send buttons with a choice of Send Now or Send Later. Pegasus and Internet Mail score highly for ease of use in this department: messages you write are automatically queued, and you can click a single button that will send all mail in the queue and retrieve any incoming mail in a single operation. If you have to make a choice on an Options page about how the program should send mail, always choose to queue/send later.

If you're not sure how your program handles all this, just take a deep breath and click the Send button. (You'll have to go online first, but your email program may start your connection automatically when you click Send.) If the message really is being sent, something on the screen should tell you so. If nothing seems to be happening, look for a button or menu-option that says something like **Send Mail Now** or **Send Queued Mail**.

BY THE WAY

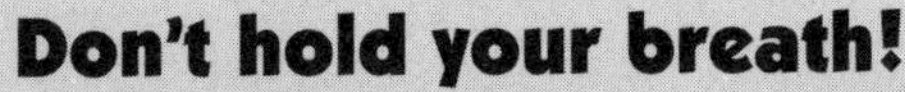

Don't hold your breath!

If your program sends and receives mail in a single operation, the email you're posting to yourself may come back to you instantly. On the other hand, it may not. Email messages usually take a few minutes to get to where they're going, and can take hours (or even days in the very worst cases).

I've Got New Mail!

You really feel you've arrived on the Internet when you receive your first message, but how do you know there are messages waiting for you? Unfortunately, you don't – your email program has to go and look. With an online service account, you'll see an on-screen indication that new mail is waiting after you log on, and you can retrieve it by clicking the obvious button. With an IAP account, if you're using one of the email programs already mentioned, you'll have a button labelled **Check for new mail**, or you may have the more useful combined **Send & Receive All Mail** button.

Most email programs use an Inbox/Outbox system: email waiting to be sent is placed in the Outbox, and new mail will arrive in the Inbox. When new mail arrives, all you'll see is a single entry giving the subject line of the message and the name of the sender (although some programs give a wealth of information including dates and times of sending and receiving the message, its size, and the number of attached files). To read the message, double-click this entry.

▶ When you log on to CompuServe a message at the bottom of the screen informs you of new messages. Click the envelope-button to retrieve them.

Now you can decide what to do with the message. You can delete it and it will remain visible in the program's Inbox or main folder until you do. You should also be able to print it on to paper. Good email programs allow you to create named folders to store and organise your messages (you may, for example, want to create a Business and a Personal folder), and you can move or copy messages from the Inbox to any of these folders. You may also be able to save a message as a separate file on to your hard-disk or a floppy-disk.

BY THE WAY

The dubious automation feature

Each of the programs mentioned here can be set to check for mail automatically at regular intervals (usually entered in minutes), and give an audible or visual prompt when new mail arrives. Useful as it sounds, this is a feature best suited to busy offices with a leased line connection (until the UK catches up with the many countries in which local telephone calls are free).

Replying & Forwarding

One of the things you're most likely to do with an incoming message is send a reply, and this is even easier than sending a brand new message. With the message open (or highlighted in your Inbox) click on the program's **Reply** button. A new message window will open with the sender's email address already inserted and the entire message copied. Copying the original message in this way is known as **quoting**, and it's standard practice in email. The program should insert a greater-than sign (>) at the beginning of each line, and you can delete any part of the original message that you don't need to include in your reply.

What's the point of quoting in replies?

The main reason is that it helps the recipient to remember what it is you're replying to. For example, if someone sends you a list of questions you can type the answer after each quoted question, saving the recipient the need to refer back to his previous message. Remember that the aim of quoting is not to build up a message containing your entire conversation, though – remove anything being quoted a second time (>>), and cut the rest down to the bare memory-jogging essentials.

The Reply button also inserts the word **Re:** to the beginning of the subject line, indicating to the recipient that it's a response to an earlier message. Although you have the facility to change the subject line of a reply, it's often best not to change it – many email programs have search and sort facilities that can group messages according to subject (among other things) making it easy to track an earlier email 'conversation' that you've long since forgotten about.

Another useful facility is that you can also send a copy of a received message to someone else, and you'll probably have a **Forward** button on the toolbar that does this job. Simply enter the recipient's email address and any additional message you want to include, then click the Send button. Just as in new messages, you can include **CC** or **BCC** addresses when replying or forwarding.

Forward messages usually have **Fwd**: inserted at the start of the subject line.

Getting Attached – Sending Files Via Email

Ordinary email messages are plain text (7-bit ASCII) files, and have a size limit of 64Kb. While 64Kb is an awful lot of text, it's a pretty small measure in terms of other types of computer file you may want to send with a message. And most other types of file are **binary** (8-bit) files, so you'd expect your email program to collapse. Until recently it would do just that and many people still delight in telling you that attaching binary files to email messages is dodgy. However, most modern email programs are much more capable: you choose the file or files you want to attach, your emailer converts them to ASCII ready to be sent, and the recipient's emailer converts them back again at the other end. In most cases it really should be as simple as that. The only blot on the landscape is that there are several methods used to do it, and both sender and recipient must be using the same method.

> BY THE WAY
>
> **It may be text to you...**
>
> Remember that a text file is just that – plain ASCII text. A formatted document created on a word-processor may look like ordinary text but it needs to be encoded to be sent as an attachment. The acid test is: Will the file look the same if you open it in a text-editor such as Windows Notepad? If not, it's a binary file and must be encoded.

- **UUencode** The original (rather messy) conversion system for PCs. The file is converted into ASCII and, if necessary, broken up into chunks to get around the email size restriction. It looks like pure gobbledegook until converted back by a **UUdecoder**.
- **MIME** A modern successor to UUencoding, now also used on the Web for transferring files. It can identify the type of file you're sending and act appropriately, and the whole system works unaided at both ends.
- **BinHex** A conversion system mostly used on Macintosh computers, similar to UUencoding.
- **Online Services** Online services have their own systems that allow an attachment to be sent from one AOL member to another, or from one

CompuServe member to another, and so on. Sending attachments between CompuServe and the Internet raises problems, though, and you may prefer to try a different method (I'll come to those in a moment).

GOOD QUESTION

Which method should I use?

Provided you're not sending to or from an online service, use MIME. If your email program can't handle MIME, replace it with one that can. If you have a choice of methods on your Options page, set MIME as the default. Only use a different system if your recipient doesn't have a MIME-compatible email program (and refuses to do the sensible thing!).

If you know that your software and that of your recipient both use the same system, attaching files is simple: look for a toolbar button with a paperclip symbol and click it (in Internet Mail and Pegasus you'll find the button in the New Message window itself). You can then browse your computer's directories to find and double-click any files you want to attach; the software will handle the rest.

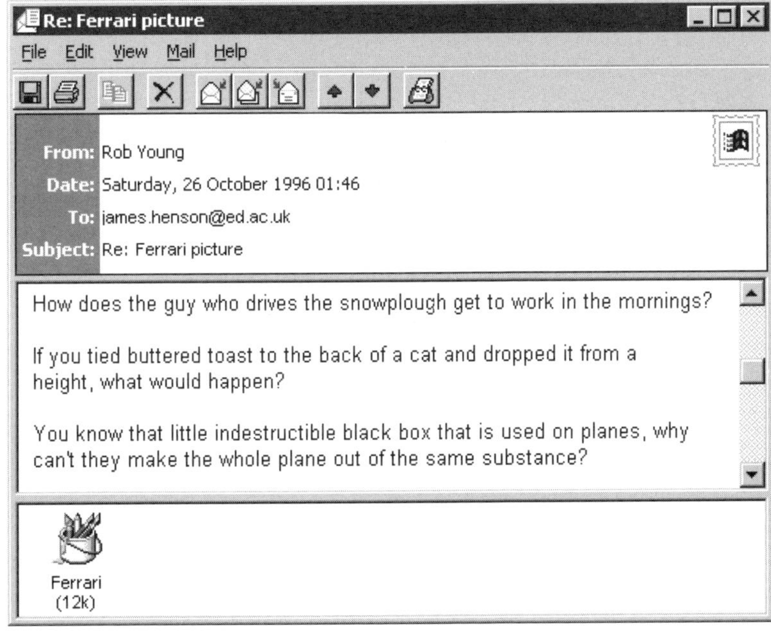

◀ Attachments in Internet Mail appear as file icons. Right-click the icon to open or save the attached file, or drag it to your desktop.

Receiving attachments in incoming email should be just as simple and transparent, especially if your email program recognises both MIME'd and UUencoded attachments, as many do. Eudora, for example, will decode attachments and put them in a directory called Attach; Internet Mail will show an attached file as an icon at the end of the message itself.

Although sending and receiving email attachments should usually be straightforward, there are a couple of situations that could present problems, so let's examine those briefly.

Sending between Online Services & the Internet

For AOL and MSN users there's no problem at all – both services use MIME and handle it all without raising much of a sweat. For CompuServe users it's a different story – attaching pure text files presents no problem, but binary files must be UUencoded and must not total more than 50Kb. To be honest, it's a lot easier to avoid attaching files in messages to and from CompuServe. Many people have two or more email accounts, and one of those may be more 'attachment-capable'. Alternatively, if your access provider gives you space on its web server, upload the file as if it were part of your web page (more about that word 'upload' on page 346) and send an email telling the recipient the URL of the file. This is a more reliable method to use for *any* file over about 100Kb. Email isn't really built to handle large attachments.

Attachments that Use a Different Conversion Method

Although you've got the whole attachment business sorted out, and you're happily MIME-ing files to all and sundry, you may still receive a UUencoded file from someone else, or need to UUencode a file for someone who doesn't have MIME. Even if your email software can't handle the conversion for you, there are utilities available that you can use to do the job yourself. Two of the best (both of which handle MIME and UUencode as well as several other methods) are WinPack and ESS-Code. You'll find WinPack on the CD-ROM with this book, and you can look for a later version at:

http://www.retrospect.com/winpacki.htm

and ESS-Code can be directly downloaded by typing the following into your browser's address bar:

http://tucows.cableinet.net/files/ecd75w95.zip

An emotional attachment

If there's someone special in your life and they also think the Net is the best thing since sliced bread, why not use the Web to show them just how much you care. Send them a kiss, a card, or even a proposal as an email attachment. Turn to **It Must Be Love** in Chapter 18 to find out how.

What Else Should I Know About Email?

Like most simple tools, email software has grown to offer a lot more than the basic requirements of writing, sending, receiving, and reading. Once you feel comfortable using the program you've chosen, spend a little time reading the manual or Help files to see what else it offers. (Remember that you can keep sending yourself test-messages to find out if or how an option works.) Here's a selection of options and issues worth knowing about.

Address Books

An address book is simply a list of names and email addresses. Instead of typing the recipient's address into a new message, you can click the Address Book button and double-click the name of the intended recipient to have the address inserted for you. You may be able to add new addresses to the book by clicking on a message you've received and selecting an **Add to address book** option. Many programs will allow you to create multiple address books, or to group addresses into different categories, for speedy access.

A similar option is the **address group** (known by different names in different software). You can send the same message to all the addresses listed in a

How can I find someone's email address?

Believe it or not, the only truly reliable way to get the email address of a business or an individual is to ask them! But there are, however, search facilities on the World Wide Web that can find people rather than places, and you'll learn where to find them and how to use them in Chapter 12.

group by simply double-clicking the group's name. This is an option worth investigating if you need to send an identical memo or newsletter to all the members of a team or club.

Signatures

An email 'signature' is a personal touch to round off an email message. You'll find a **Signature** option on one of your program's menus that provides a blank space for you to enter whatever text you choose, and this will automatically be added to the end of all the messages you write.
A signature commonly gives your name, and may also include the URL of your web site if you have one, your job description and company if you're sending business mail, and (very often) a quotation or witticism. However, try to resist getting carried away with this – eight lines is an absolute maximum for a signature.

Emoticons & Acronyms

Emoticons, otherwise known as 'smilies', are little expressive faces made from standard keyboard characters used to convey feelings or to prevent a comment being misunderstood in email messages, newsgroup postings and text-chat. As an example, you may put <g> (meaning 'grin') at the end of a line to say to the reader: 'Don't take that too seriously, I'm just kidding'. Here's a little bundle of the more useful or amusing emoticons. (If you haven't come across emoticons before, look at them sideways!)

Symbol	Meaning
:-)	Happy
:-(	Sad
:-))	Very happy
:-((	Very sad
;-)	Wink
>:-)	Evil grin
:-D	Laughing
:'-)	Crying
:-O	Surprised
:-&	Tongue-tied
:-l	Unamused
:-ll	Angry
X-)	Cross-eyed

Symbol	Meaning
:-#)	Has a moustache
:-)>	Has a beard
(-)	Needs a haircut
(:-)	Bald
:-)X	Wears a bow-tie
8-)	Wears glasses
:^)	Has a broken nose/nose put out of joint
:-W	Speaks with forked tongue
:-?	Smokes a pipe
:-Q	Smokes cigarettes
*-)	Drunk or stoned
<:-)	Idiot
=:-)	Punk rocker

Communicate or confuse?

You can really go to town on these emoticons, and you could turn just about any phrase you like into an acronym. Just because you know that IJBMS stands for 'I just burnt my sausages' doesn't mean that anyone else does! Similarly, an emoticon meant to indicate that you're an angry, cross-eyed punk rocker with a beard may just look like you've sat on the keyboard.

Acronyms came about as a result of Internet users having to compose their email while online and clocking up charges. Although messages are now mostly composed offline, these acronyms have become a part of accepted email style, and have been given new life by the emergence of online text-chat, which you'll learn about in Chapter 10.

In fact, most of these aren't acronyms at all, but they fall under the banner of TLAs (Three Letter Acronyms). And before you say "Ah but...", no, they don't all consist of three letters either.

Symbol	Meaning
AFAIK	As far as I know
BCNU	Be seeing you
BST	But seriously though
BTW	By the way
FAQ	Frequently asked question(s)
FWIW	For what it's worth
FYI	For your information
GAL	Get a life
IMO	In my opinion
IMHO	In my humble opinion
IMNSHO	In my not-so-humble opinion
IOW	In other words

Symbol	Meaning
KISS	Keep it simple, stupid
L8R	Later (or See you later)
LOL	Laughs out loud
OAO	Over and out
OIC	Oh I see
OTOH	On the other hand
OTT	Over the top
PITA	Pain in the a~!!
ROFL	Rolls on the floor laughing
RTFM	Read the f*%£?!# manual
TIA	Thanks in advance
TNX	Thanks

Another common requirement in email and newsgroup messages is to emphasise particular words or phrases, since the usual methods (bold or italic text, or underlining) aren't available. This is done by surrounding the text with asterisks (*never*) or underscores (_never_).

Undelivered Email

If an email message can't be delivered it will be 'bounced' straight back to you, along with an automatically generated message telling you what went wrong. If the address you typed doesn't exist, or you made a mistake, the message should come back within seconds or minutes. In some cases a message may be returned to you after several days, which usually indicates that the problem lies in delivering the message at the other end. If this happens, just send the message again. If the problem persists, try altering the address so that it looks like this:

[SMTP:*username@domain*]

(including those square brackets) or send a message addressed to **postmaster@*domain*** (using the domain of the person you were trying to contact) asking if there's a problem with email delivery and quoting the email address you were trying to send to.

Other Email Bits & Pieces

Filtering

Modern email programs offer filtering options (sometimes known as 'Rules') that let you decide how to handle certain types of incoming email. For example, you may choose to have all messages from a particular person moved to a special folder as soon as they arrive.

Formatting

The latest email programs allow you to add formatting to your email as if it were a word-processor document, choosing fonts, colours, layout styles, and even background pictures. The problem with formatting is that your recipient must have the same software as you, or he'll just receive a message with the formatting codes placed in a meaningless attached file. This is almost always an option to ignore, unless you're an AOL user sending to another AOL user.

Delete on receipt

As soon as you collect your email it should be deleted from your access provider's mail server. This is because your provider won't give you unlimited space for email on the server: when your mailbox is full, mail will just be bounced back to the sender. Your email software may give you an option to delete retrieved messages, but it will usually be switched on by default. (Of course, this means that you can only retrieve a message once, so think carefully before deleting a message from your own system!)

Yes, it's electronic mail but...

It's not supposed to look like a letter. You don't need to put the date or the recipient's postal address at the top, or use any conventional letter-writing formalities. On some occasions you may want to include your own postal address and telephone number, but only do this when the recipient needs to know them.

Writing style

Don't start with 'Dear …' and end with 'Yours sincerely'. You could send a message that starts 'Hi Rob', or 'Hello Rob' if you really want some sort of salutation, or you could just start 'Rob,'. But it's perfectly acceptable and not regarded as rude just to get straight into the message. Similarly you could sign off with 'Regards' or 'Best wishes', but there's no need to put anything at all but your name. (You could find it a hard habit to break – I know I do – but don't think people rude when they do it!)

Email Netiquette

The term 'netiquette' is an abbreviation of 'Internet etiquette' – a set of unwritten rules about behaviour on the Internet. In simple terms, they boil down to 'Don't waste Internet resources' and 'Don't be rude', but here are a few specific pointers to keep in mind when dealing with email:

- Reply promptly. Because email is quick and easy, it's generally expected that a reply will arrive within a day or two, even if it's just to confirm receipt. Try to keep unanswered messages in your Inbox and move answered messages elsewhere so that you can see at a glance what's waiting to be dealt with.
- DON'T SHOUT! LEAVING THE CAPS LOCK KEY SWITCHED ON IS REGARDED AS 'SHOUTING', AND CAN PROMPT SOME ANGRY RESPONSES. IT DOESN'T LOOK AT ALL FRIENDLY, DOES IT?
- Don't forward someone's private email without their permission.
- Don't put anything in an email message that you wouldn't mind seeing on the nine o'clock news! Anyone can forward your email to a national newspaper, your boss, your parents, and so on, so there may be times when a telephone call is preferable.

8

NEWSGROUPS – THE HUMAN ENCYCLOPAEDIA

In This Chapter...

- What are newsgroups all about?
- Choose a newsreader & download a list of available newsgroups
- Start reading (& writing) the news
- Send & receive binary files with news articles
- Mailing lists – have your news delivered by email

News, as we generally think of it, is a collection of topical events, the latest political embarrassments, showbusiness gossip, and so on. All of that, and much more, can be found on the Internet, but it's not what the Net calls 'news'. The newsgroups we're talking about here are more formally known as **Usenet discussion groups**; there are more than twenty-eight thousand of them (and they're increasing all the time) covering subjects as diverse as accommodation and zebrafish.

Newsgroup discussions take place using email messages (known as **articles** or **postings**), but instead of addressing articles to an individual's email address they're addressed to a particular group. Anyone choosing to access this group can read the messages, post replies, start new topics of conversation, or ask questions relating to the subject covered by the group.

How Does It Work?

Your access provider has a computer called a **news server** that holds articles from thousands of newsgroups that form part of the Usenet system. This collection of articles will be regularly updated (perhaps daily, or perhaps as often as every few minutes) to include the latest postings to the groups. Using a program called a **newsreader**, you can read articles in as many of these groups as you want to, and post your own articles in much the same way that you compose and send your own email messages. Messages that you post will be added to the server's listings almost immediately, and will gradually trickle out to news servers around the world (the speed with which they appear depends on how often all the other servers update themselves).

GOOD QUESTION

My IAP doesn't subscribe, how can I find it?

If you're looking for a group dedicated to tortoise farming and your IAP doesn't seem to have one, use your browser to search the lists of newsgroup names at the following web sites, using the keyword 'tortoise'. If you find a promising group, ask your IAP to subscribe to it.

http://www.nova.edu/Inter-Links/usenet.html
http://www.magmacom.com/~leisen/master_list.html

Although there are currently more than twenty-eight thousand groups, you won't find every group available from your access provider. Storage space on any computer is a limited commodity so providers have to compromise. In addition, many providers are now taking a moral stance against groups involving pornography and software piracy (among others) and these are unlikely to be available. But if you really needed access to a group concerned with grape-growing in Argentina (and one existed), most reasonable providers will subscribe to it if you ask nicely. If a suitable newsgroup doesn't exist, and you think the world is itching to discuss the Argentine grape with you, you could even talk to your IAP about setting up the newsgroup yourself in the 'alt' hierarchy (more about that below).

Newsgroup Names

Newsgroup names look a lot like the domain names we met in earlier chapters – words separated by dots. Reading the names from left to right, they begin with a top-level category name and gradually become more specific. Let's start with a few of these top-level names:

comp Computer related groups such as **comp.windows.news**
rec Recreational/sports groups like **rec.arts.books.tolkien**
sci Science-related groups such as **sci.bio.paleontology**
misc Just about anything – items for sale, education, investments, you name it
soc Social-issues groups such as **soc.genealogy.nordic**
talk Discussions about controversial topics such as **talk.atheism** or **talk.politics.guns**
uk UK-only groups covering a wide range of subjects including politics, small ads, sport

BY THE WAY

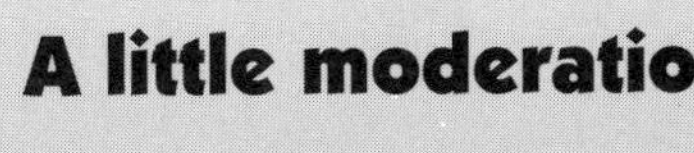

Some newsgroups are moderated, meaning that the creator of the group (or someone else appointed to run it) reads all the messages and decides which to post. The aim is to keep the topics of discussion on course, but they often tend to weed out deliberately argumentative or abusive messages too.

One of the largest collections of groups comes under a completely different top-level heading – **alt**. The alt groups are not an official part of the Usenet service, but are still available from almost all service providers. Because almost anyone can set up a group in the alt hierarchy they're sometimes regarded as anarchic or somehow 'naughty', but in truth, their sole difference is that their creators chose to bypass all the red-tape involved in the Usenet process. Here's a taste of the breadth of coverage you'll find in the alt hierarchy:

alt.culture.kuwait	**alt.education.disabled**
alt.fan.david-bowie	**alt.games.dominoes**
alt.ketchup	**alt.paranormal.crop-circles**
alt.windows95	**alt.support.spina-bifida**

What Do I Need?

You need two things: a program called a **newsreader** and a little bit of patience. We'll come to the second of those in a moment; first let's sort out the newsreader. These come in two flavours. First, there's the **online newsreader**; you don't want one of those, as reading and posting articles all takes place while connected and clocking up charges. Second is the **offline newsreader**, which is definitely the type you want, but offline readers also vary. Some offline readers automatically download all the unread articles in your chosen group so that you can read them and compose replies offline; the problem is that in a popular group you may have to wait for several hundred articles to download, many of which you won't be interested in. The second (and by far the best) type of offline reader just downloads the **headers** of the articles (the subject-line, date, author and size). You can select the articles you want to read based on this information, and then reconnect to have them downloaded.

If you don't already have a good offline newsreader, here are my recommendations:

- **Internet Mail & News** As mentioned in the previous chapter, this integrates nicely with Microsoft's Internet Explorer browser, and also gives you an email client. In fact, if you've installed Internet Explorer from the free CD-ROM accompanying this book you should already have this installed. If you need to, you can download the pair from

http:// www.microsoft.com/ie/download. (By the time you read this, the package may have been renamed 'Outlook Express'.)

- **Agent** or **Free Agent** A popular newsreader available in two versions – one is free, the other you'll have to pay for (guess which is which!). Free Agent is included on the CD-ROM with this book. Point your browser at **http:// www.forteinc.com** for the extra features built into Agent.
- **Oui** You'll have to pay for this if you choose to use it for longer than 30 days, but it's a superb (and unusually attractive) program that can also handle email. Visit **http:// www.dvorak.com** for this one.

BY THE WAY

Attention, Netscape user!

If you use the Netscape Navigator browser you have a built-in newsreader – just click **Window | Netscape News**. You can read messages offline, but you have to select and download the messages you want to read while online and save them. It's rather clumsy, but its integration with the browser may convince you that you can live with it.

Having got your hands on one of these, the setting up is fairly simple. The program should prompt you for the information it needs the first time you run it, which will include your name, email address, and the domain name of your news server (usually **news.*accessprovider.co.uk***). You'll probably see other options and settings, but don't change anything just yet.

Now switch on your own personal patience circuits! Before you can go much further, your newsreader has to connect to the server and download a list of the newsgroups you can access. How long this takes will depend upon the number of groups available, the speed of your modem, and whether you strike lucky first time and get a good connection. It may take only 2 or 3 minutes, or it may take 15 or more.

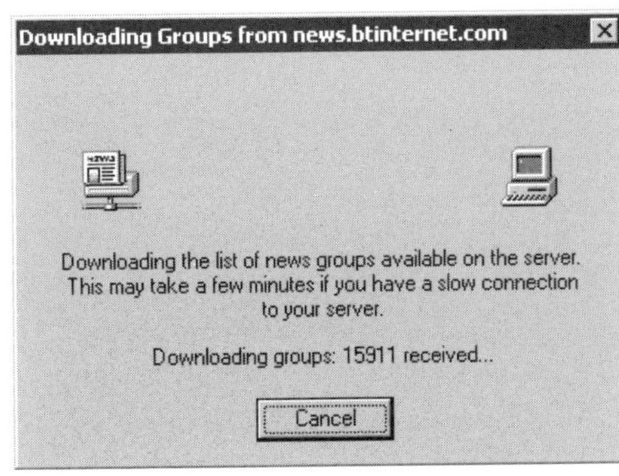

◀ While your newsreader downloads a list of groups, you'll have to sit tight and count to 10 – lots of times!

That was the bad news. The good news is that you'll only need to download the group list once, as long as you don't decide later that you want to use a different newsreader. In future, when your newsreader connects to the server to download new articles, it will automatically fetch the names of any new groups that have been created and add them to the list.

BY THE WAY

Newsgroups & online services

To access newsgroups in AOL, use the keyword **newsgroups**; in CompuServe, use the Go word **usenet**. When you look at the list of groups your online service provides, many may be missing (such as the entire 'alt' hierarchy). In many cases you can access these, but you need to 'switch on' access to them yourself. For example, AOL has an Expert Add function for this. Check the Help files for details, or contact the service's support line.

Subscribing to Newsgroups

Before you can start reading and posting articles, you need to subscribe to the groups that interest you. ('Subscribing' is the term for letting your newsreader know which groups to download headers from – there are no subscription fees!) Although you can scroll your way through the thousands of groups in the list, it's easier to search for a word you'd expect to find in the group's name. In Internet News, click the button with the newspaper symbol on the toolbar (or press Ctrl+W), and type a keyword into the box above the list; in Agent, click the toolbar button with the torch symbol and type a word into the dialog box.

BY THE WAY

Choose Your News

If you want to subscribe to a group that your access provider doesn't (and won't) subscribe to, you may be able to access it through one of the public-access news servers instead. Visit **http://www.jammed.com/~newzbot** for a list of public servers. There are no lists of the groups covered by each server; you'll have to configure your newsreader to connect to it, download a list of groups, and see if the group you want is there.

To subscribe to a newsgroup in Internet News, click its name, and click the **Subscribe** button. When you've subscribed to all the groups you want, click **OK**. In Agent right-click a newsgroup's name and click **Subscribe**.

▶ *If you need to find out whether a newsgroup exists on a particular topic, or you want to search the newsgroups for information, turn to Searching the Newsgroups in Chapter 12 to find out how to do it.*

Reading the News

When you've chosen the groups to which you want to subscribe, you're ready to download the headers from one of the groups. In Internet News, click the drop-down box in the toolbar and click the name of one of the groups you've chosen. The program will connect to your news server and download the headers from articles in the selected group (shown in the next screenshot). By default, Internet News will download 300 headers at a time (as long as there are that many articles in the group!), but you can change this figure by going to the **News** menu, selecting **Options** and changing the figure shown at the top of the **Read** tab.

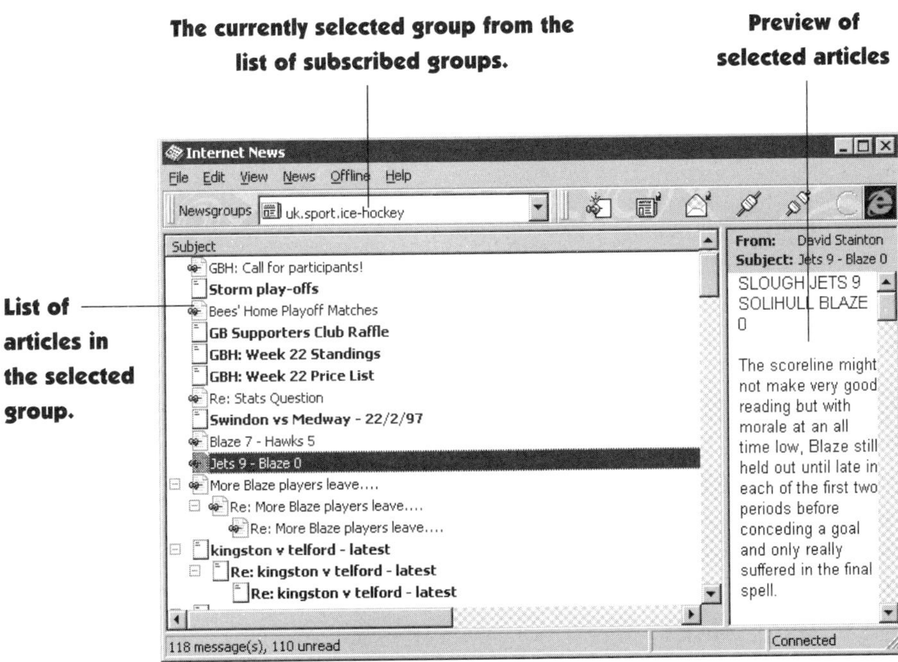

◀ Internet News.

In Agent, click on **Group | Show | Subscribed Groups** (or click the large button marked **All Groups** until it says **Subscribed Groups**). You'll see the list of newsgroups you subscribed to, and you can double-click one to download its headers. Agent will present a dialog asking if you want to collect all the headers, or just a sample of 50. Some popular newsgroups have several thousand articles, so it's best to start with a sample just to get a flavour of the group first. Change the figure if you want to, and then click the button marked **Sample Message Headers**.

To download and read an article immediately in the preview window, click the header once in Internet News, or double-click it in Agent.

Usually you'll want to download articles to read offline, and Internet News makes this easy: just tell it which articles you want. If you want to grab every article in the group, click the **Download All** button. If you just want selected articles, either right-click each article separately and choose **Mark Message for Download**, or hold the Ctrl key while clicking all the required articles and then right-click on any of them and choose **Mark Message for Download**. Beside the headers for messages you've marked there will be a little green arrow indicator so that you can see what you've chosen. You can now select another group to download headers for, and mark those in the same way.

When you've finished marking the articles you want in all groups, click the **Post and Download** button. Internet News will download the marked articles in any groups, and send any articles you wrote yourself that are waiting in the Outbox. Downloaded articles will be indicated by a green thumb-tack icon beside the header.

GOOD QUESTION

Why can't I download some of the articles?

Although the headers are displayed, you may find that some of the articles are no longer available. Older articles have to be deleted to make room for new ones. In the most popular groups, receiving several hundred messages per day, articles may vanish within a matter of days, so if you see some articles that you are definitely interested in, download them straightaway.

Agent (and most other newsreaders) use similar methods. To mark a message for download in Agent, highlight it and press M, or right-click it and choose **Mark for Retrieval**. Once you've marked all the articles you want to download, click the toolbar button with the blue arrow and thunderbolt symbol and Agent will then fetch them for you and mark them with a little 'page' icon.

Threads – Following a Conversation

Although a newsgroup is dedicated to one subject, there may be dozens (or even hundreds!) of different conversations going on. Fortunately all newsgroup articles have a subject-line just like email messages, so all messages with the same subject-line will be part of the same conversation, or in newsgroup-speak, the same **thread**. Most newsreaders let you choose how you want to sort the list of articles (by date or by sender, for example), but the best way to view them is by thread so that articles from one conversation are listed together.

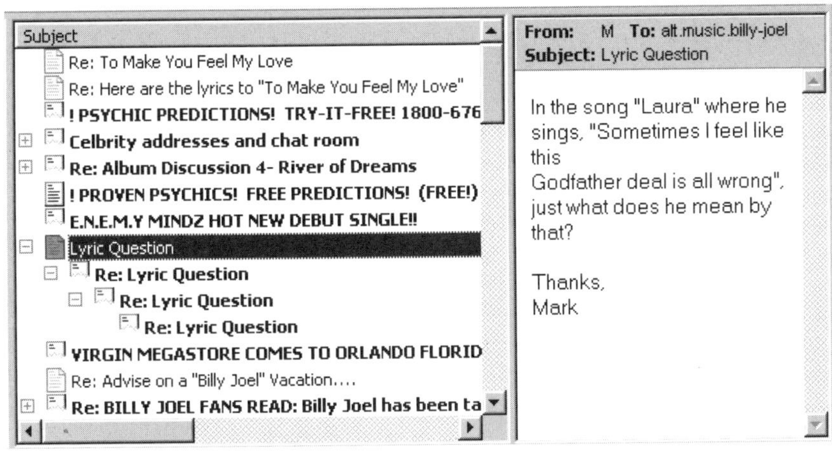

◀ Click the '+' icon to reveal the rest of the thread, or the '-' icon to hide it.

So how do threads work? When you post a brand new message to a newsgroup, you're starting a new thread. If someone posts a reply, their newsreader will insert the word **Re:** in the subject-line (just as in email replies). Your newsreader gathers together the original message and all replies (including replies to replies) and sorts them by date. The original message will have a little '+' icon beside it indicating that it's the beginning of a thread, and you can click this to reveal the other articles in the thread.

Why is it nothing to do with the subject line?

Some threads go on and on for months and may eventually have nothing to do with the article that started it all, despite the subject line. All it takes is for someone to raise a slightly different point in a reply, and someone else to pick up on it in their reply, for the entire thread to veer on to a whole new course.

Marking Messages

In most newsreaders, as soon as you open an article to read it, the article will be marked as **Read**. (In Internet News the read articles turn from bold type to normal; in Agent they turn from red to black.) You can also mark a message as Read even if you haven't read it, or mark an entire thread as Read (perhaps you read the first couple of articles and decided everyone was talking rubbish). In modern newsreaders this just acts as a useful way to remember what you've read and what you haven't – you can just as easily delete messages you've read if you don't want to read them again.

If you want it save it!

Modern newsreaders automatically store the list of downloaded headers, and all downloaded articles, but they'll eventually delete them before they swallow up too much of your hard-disk. If there are particular articles you want to keep for future reference, you can usually save them to a special folder, or to any directory on your hard-disk. You should also be able to print an article, or copy it to the clipboard to be pasted into another application.

Older newsreaders don't store the headers: they download them, display them, and then forget them again when you move to a different newsgroup or log off. All they know is which messages are marked as Read. Next time you open this newsgroup, the unread headers will be downloaded, so it makes sense to mark as Read any headers that you're definitely not interested in so that they're not continually being downloaded. (You can even mark every message in the group as Read so that you'll only see any newer messages that appear).

Pure Gobbledegook – ROT13

Once in a while, you may come across a message that looks a bit like the one shown in the next screenshot – they could be words, but they don't seem to mean anything. Yes, it may be a transcript of a Party Political Broadcast, but it's more likely that it's been encrypted with **ROT13**.

Why encrypt a message with ROT13 at all?

ROT13 is used to prevent anyone from accidentally reading a message that may offend or disgust them. In other words, if you see a message like this, you can decide for yourself whether you really want to read it. But don't say I didn't warn you – it could be pretty nasty.

ROT13 stands for Rotated 13, and it's a pretty simple encryption system: every letter is replaced with the one 13 steps along in the alphabet, so E becomes R, H becomes U, and so on. Simple (or rather, 'fvzcyr'.) But working it out that way could start to lose its novelty value after a while. Most newsreaders have a menu option called **Unscramble ROT13** that will do it for you (and you may be able to use the same option to scramble your own messages.)

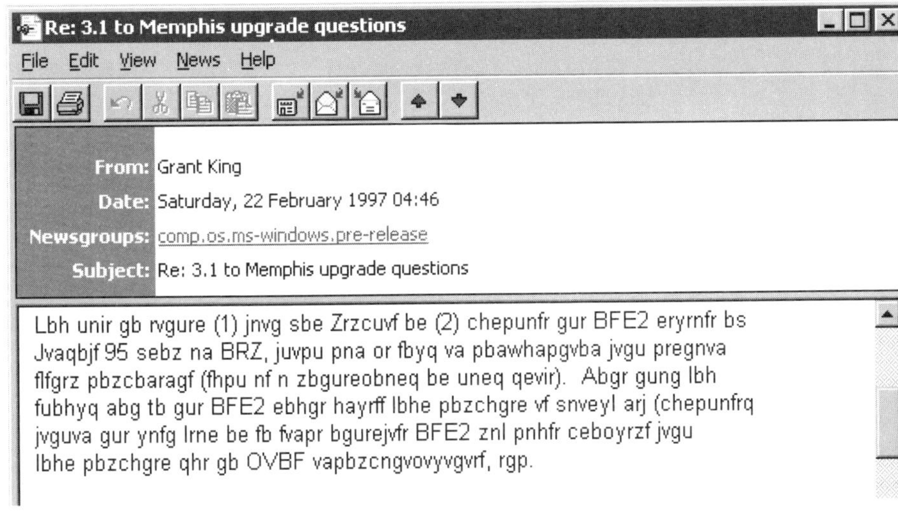

◀ A ROT13-encrypted message in Internet News. (No, this one isn't offensive, just a bit dull. I've encrypted it as an example).

Posting Articles to Newsgroups

It's a funny old language really. Newsgroup messages work just like email: the only difference is that the address you use is the name of a newsgroup, not an email address. But even though you send an email message, you post a newsgroup article. Don't ask why, just accept it!

Although just reading articles can be very addictive, sooner or later you'll want to get involved. There are various ways to post articles, and they're common to just about every newsreader you'll come across. In the following list I'll take Microsoft's Internet News as an example, but if you're using something different you'll still have all the same options (although their names will vary).

BY THE WAY

Test the water first

Before posting an article to a 'proper' newsgroup where everyone can see it, you will probably want to send a test message first as you did with your email program in the previous chapter. You can send a message to **alt.test**, but it's worth checking to see if your access provider has its own 'test' group. You may even get a reply from another newcomer. Remember to be patient – allow at least a few minutes before checking the group to see if your message is listed.

- To reply to a message you're reading, click the **Reply to Group** button, or right-click the header and choose **Reply to Newsgroup**. (In many newsreaders, a reply is called a **Follow-up.**) A new message window will open with the name of the group already entered, and the same subject-line as the message you were reading. Type your message and click the **Post Message** button (or press Alt+S).
- To reply to the author of the article privately by email, click the **Reply to Author** button and follow the routine above. In this case the article won't be posted to the newsgroup.
- To reply to the newsgroup *and* send a copy of your reply to the author by email, go to **News | Reply to Newsgroup and Author**. Once again the routine is the same as above.

▶ To create a new message (and start a new thread), click the **New Message** button (or press Ctrl+N). A new message window will open with the currently selected newsgroup shown. To send to a different newsgroup, or to more than one group, click the newspaper icon beside the name to add and remove groups from the list. Enter a title for the article on the Subject line, and then write your message. Click **Post Message** to send.

In keeping with email, any replies to newsgroup articles automatically **quote** the original article (see page 95). Make sure you delete any of the original article that doesn't need to be included. Remember that newsreaders list earlier messages in the thread in a well-organised fashion, so most people will have already read the message you're replying to.

BY THE WAY

Don't change the subject!

When replying to an existing thread, you must not change the subject line at all! If just one character is different, newsreaders will regard it as the start of a new thread and won't group it with the other articles in the thread, so your reply might be overlooked by the very people who would find it most interesting.

Attachments & Newsgroup Articles

At the risk of being boring, let me just say again: newsgroup articles and email messages are so similar even their mother couldn't tell them apart. A case in point is that you can send and receive computer files as part of a newsgroup article just as you can with email. So I'm going to assume that you've read the section on attachments in the previous chapter, beginning on page 96.

In most newsreaders, attaching a binary file to an article is a simple case of clicking a button marked **Attach File** (often marked with a paperclip icon), browsing your directories for the file you want to send, and double-clicking it – your newsreader should do the rest. At the moment, the UUencode system tends to prevail in the newsgroups, but MIME is becoming more recognised as people replace their newsreaders for newer, MIME-capable programs.

Most modern newsreaders will also decode any attachments in an article you open: these may automatically be saved to a directory on your computer, or you may have to click a button on the toolbar (as in Agent) to view them. Internet News displays attachments as an icon at the bottom of the window. On occasion, an attached file may be split into several messages due to its size (known as a **multi-part attachment**) and the subject lines for each message will include additions like [1/3], [2/3] and [3/3] to number the parts of a three-part file. If you try to open any one of these, many newsreaders will realise that the file isn't complete, automatically download the other two as well, and piece them together. In the remaining few programs, you'll have to select all three parts in advance.

GOOD QUESTION

How will I know there's an attachment?

Newsreaders show the number of lines in an article as part of the header information in the list. Even a long text-only article should keep to within about sixty lines. An attached picture or sound file will usually range from about two hundred up into the thousands. Only newsgroups that have the word 'binaries' somewhere in their name should have articles that include attachments, so you'll probably be expecting to find a few if you're in one of these groups.

If you have a problem with attachments at all, it'll be when you open an article with an attached file that uses a format your newsreader can't handle (not all newsreaders can decode both UUencode and MIME files). In this case you'll see line upon line of textual gibberish in the article. Unlike ROT13-encrypted articles, these characters will be in an endless stream, and will often use more symbols than letters and numbers. In this case you'll need to decode the attachment yourself by saving the message on to your own disk, and using one of the programs mentioned on page 98.

Newsgroup Netiquette & Jargon

Newsgroups are pretty hot on netiquette – the 'rules' you should follow when using them – and Usenet has invented its own brand of weird language to go with some of these.

- It's good practice to lurk a while when you visit a new group (especially as a newcomer to newsgroups). What's 'lurking'? Reading newsgroup articles without posting any yourself. Get an idea of the tone of the group, the reactions of its participants to beginners' questions, and the types of topics they cover.
- Before diving in and asking a question in the group, read the FAQ. This stands for Frequently Asked Question(s), and it's an article that tells you more about the group, its topics, and other related groups. Many groups post an FAQ every few weeks, but if you don't see an article with 'FAQ' in its header, send a short message asking if someone could post it.
- Don't post 'test' articles to any newsgroup that doesn't have the word 'test' in its name.
- Don't post articles containing attachments to any newsgroup that doesn't have the word 'binaries' in its name. This is out of respect for people whose newsreaders give them no choice but to download every article and who don't expect to spend 5 minutes downloading an attachment they don't want.
- Don't spam! Spamming is a lovely term for sending the same article to dozens of different newsgroups, regardless of whether it's relevant. These messages are usually advertising mailshots, get-rich-quick schemes, and similar stuff that no one finds remotely interesting. The risk is greater than just being ignored though, you could be mail-bombed – many people will take great delight in sending you thousands of email messages to teach you a lesson! So, why 'spamming'? Monty Python fans may remember a sketch about a certain brand of tinned meat – try asking for a copy of the script in **alt.fan.monty-python**!
- When replying to an article requesting information, or an answer to a question, it's good practice to also send the author a copy by email, in case your newsgroup reply doesn't get noticed. By the same token, if someone asks for answers by email, post your answer to the group as well – it may be of interest to others.
- Don't rise to flame bait! Some people delight in starting arguments, and deliberately post provocative articles. Personal attacks in newsgroups are known as 'flames', and on occasions these can get so out of hand that the whole group descends into a 'flame war', with little else going on but personal abuse.

Mailing Lists – More Discussions

You may feel that a choice of up to 28,000 discussion groups is enough, and I wouldn't disagree. But let's round off this chapter with a look at a different system that can add another few thousand to that total – **mailing lists**.

A mailing list is like a newsgroup that arrives by email: once you've subscribed, all the messages from the group are automatically delivered to your mailbox for you to download when you like. In most cases, you can opt to receive a digest version that gives a single, large daily or weekly message rather than a constant stream of separate ones. To subscribe to a mailing list takes a single email message, as does unsubscribing.

BY THE WAY

Mailbox mayhem

Be wary of mailing lists – if you like the general idea, start by subscribing to one and see how things go. Popular lists generate a huge amount of email, and it's not a good idea to be subscribed to half a dozen of those while you're still finding your feet or you'll be drowned in a deluge of email!

Mailing lists come in many shapes and forms, but the two primary systems are **LISTSERV** and **MajorDomo**. Like most mailing list systems, these are automatic, and are run by a program on a computer which reads the email you send to subscribe and adds your email address to its list. For automatic lists, your email message must be constructed in a certain way.

LISTSERV Mailing Lists

LISTSERV is one of the major automated systems, and requests for information and subscriptions are made by sending an email message to one of the computers on the LISTSERV system. All LISTSERV computers are linked together, so it doesn't matter which one you use for requests; if you don't know of any other, send your messages to **listserv@listserv.net**. The request message you send needs nothing in the **Subject** line, although if your email program insists you enter something, just type a dot. The message itself must contain nothing but the request (so make sure you turn off your email program's Signature option!).

To Do This	Type This Request in Your Email Message
Subscribe to a list	SUB *listname your name*
Unsubscribe to a list	SIGNOFF *listname*
Get information about a list	INFO *listname*
Receive the digest version of a list	SET *listname* DIGEST
Get a list of request commands	HELP
Find all the lists on this system	LIST
Find all LISTSERV lists in existence	LISTS GLOBAL

Be a bit wary of that last option – the message you'll receive containing a list of all the mailing lists available will be about half a megabyte in size! Most LISTSERV lists can also be read using your newsreader – you'll find them in the **bit.listserv** hierarchy.

To send messages to a list you've subscribed to, you'll need to know which computer runs that list (the sitename, which should be in the details that are returned to you). You can then take part in the discussion by sending messages to ***listname@sitename***. Make sure you don't get these two addresses confused. The first address I gave above is only for making requests and queries about lists, and this second address is only for messages that you intend every subscriber to read. If you send your requests to the second address, a copy will be sent to everyone on the list, but the request itself won't be processed!

BY THE WAY

If you're going on holiday for a while and won't be able to download your email, consider unsubscribing from your mailing lists for the period that you're away. Otherwise you may be faced with an overwhelming barrage of email when you log on after your holiday!

MajorDomo Mailing Lists

The MajorDomo system is similar to LISTSERV, but each computer on the system is independent so you need to know which computer handles the list you're interested in (the **sitename**). Then send an email message to **majordomo@*sitename*** containing one of the following requests:

To Do This	Type This Request in your Email Message
Subscribe to a list	subscribe *listname*
Unsubscribe to a list	unsubscribe *listname*
Find all lists on that computer	list

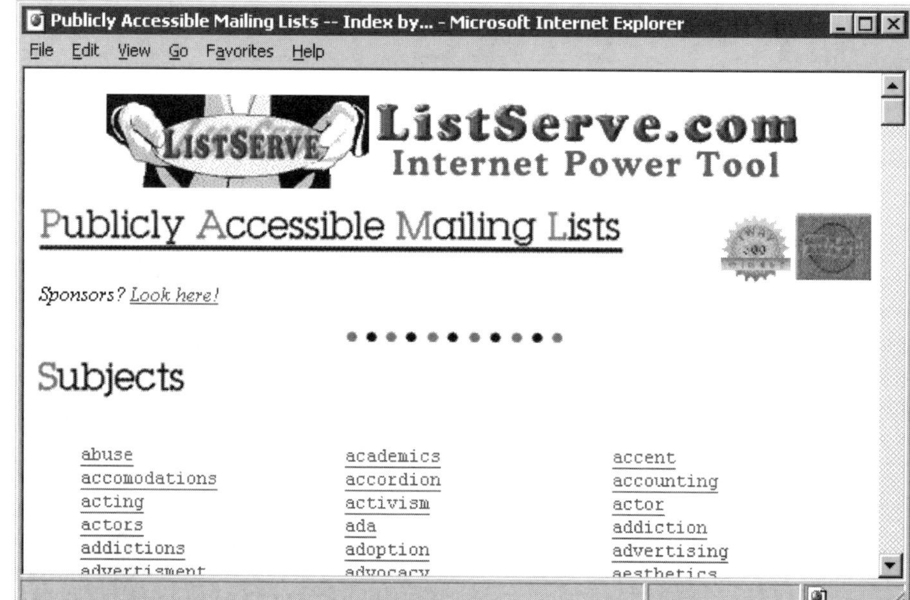

▶ Pick one of hundreds of subjects to choose from thousands of lists.

There May Be an Easier Way...

I mentioned a moment ago that you can get a flavour of some of the LISTSERV lists before subscribing by using your newsreader. Many mailing lists also have their own page on the World Wide Web giving information about the list, and a simple form you can fill in online if you want to subscribe. To find lists of mailing lists on the Web, use your browser to go to **http:// www.liszt.com** (where you can search for a mailing list by typing in a keyword) or **http:// www.neosoft.com/internet/paml/bysubj.html** (where you can choose a subject from a list of hundreds, as shown in the screenshot above).

GRABBING THE GOODIES WITH FTP

In This Chapter...

- It sounds horrible! What is FTP?
- FTPing using your Web browser
- Setting up & using a 'real' FTP program
- Getting into private & anonymous FTP sites
- How to find the files you want

FTP – a bunch of initials. Why did they have to do that? The Web is the Web, email is email. Why couldn't this be called 'Dave' or something? Perhaps then you wouldn't feel like skipping this chapter. FTP really deserves a much simpler name – it's one of the easiest Internet services to use, and if you've been surfing the Web you know something about using it already. So don't be fooled by the name, come on in and meet 'Dave'!

What Is FTP?

Imagine you're in a room full of computers with huge hard-disks. You can root around, grab any files you want, and take them home with you. If that sounds good, you'll like FTP – that's what it's for. FTP stands for File Transfer Protocol, and it works in a similar way to Windows Explorer or File Manager. You can open directories by clicking them, browse around, and click on any file to copy it to somewhere else. There's just one difference: on your own computer you may copy a file from one directory to another, or to a floppy-disk, but FTP copies the file to a different computer – your own.

We've already looked at links to files on the World Wide Web in Chapter 6. What you didn't realise is that you were already using FTP just by clicking these links and letting the file download. Some of the files are stored on a web server, others are stored on an FTP server, but you don't need to know what the main job of the computer is: you click the link, the file is sent, end of story. (If you're interested, move your mouse-pointer on to the link and look at your browser's status-bar to see where the link points. If the address starts with **ftp://** you'll know it's an FTP site. It could be worth knowing, as you'll learn in a moment.)

I can't connect to the site. What's wrong?

It could be closed, or it could be very busy. Some FTP sites put a limit on the number of people that can visit at once, and others don't allow anonymous logins during business hours, so try again later. It's good netiquette to avoid accessing FTP sites during their local business hours (some knowledge of time zones is helpful here!), and you'll usually get a much faster service too. Of course, you may just have typed the address wrongly – always a good place to start!

Using Your Browser for FTP

FTP addresses look a lot like web addresses: they begin with the name of the computer, and continue with the directory path to the file you want. To use your browser to visit an FTP site, you'll usually need to prefix the whole thing with **ftp://** (the only exception is when the name of the computer starts with 'ftp', but you can still use the prefix in these cases if you prefer). To get acquainted with FTP using the browser, let's visit an FTP site. Start up your browser, type **ftp://sunsite.doc.ic.ac.uk** into the address bar, and press Enter.

Once you're connected to the site, you'll see a dull grey background with a plain black welcoming message. (This is how the whole World Wide Web looked until a couple of years ago!) Scroll downwards in the window and a list of blue hypertext links will come into view. In true Web style, the blue text is clickable and will lead somewhere else. To the left of each hypertext entry you'll see either **Directory** or a set of figures. The word Directory indicates that this is a link to another directory (like clicking a folder icon in Windows); the figures show that the entry links to a file and give its size. Further to the left you'll see the date and time that the file was placed on the computer. On some FTP sites, you may see friendly icons next to the hypertext links – a folder icon for a directory, and a page icon for a file.

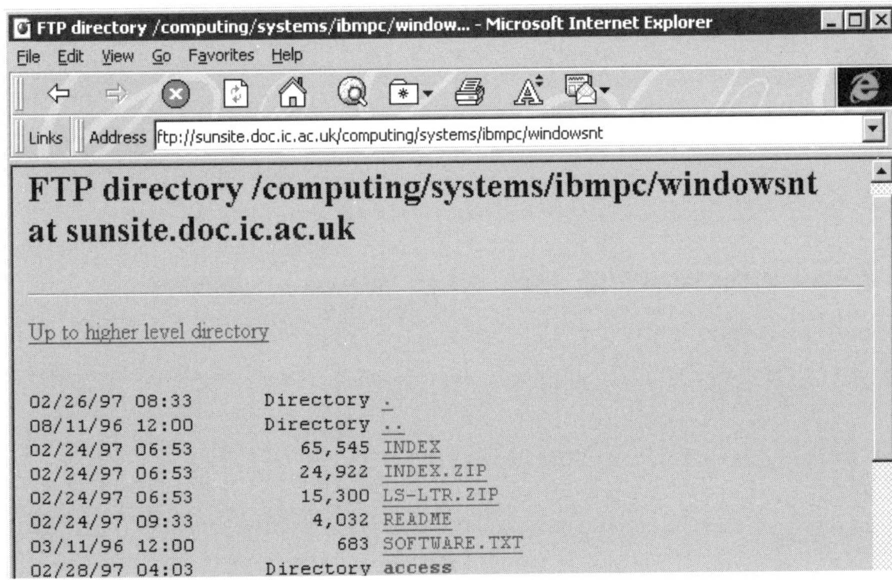

◀ One-click browsing through an FTP site using Internet Explorer.

To get to the directory shown in the screenshot, click on the directory entry **computing**. Explorer will display the contents of the **computing** directory and you can then click on the **systems** directory, followed by **ibmpc**, and then **windowsnt**. From here, you could click on another directory to open it, or click on one of the files to start downloading it. To go back to the **ibmpc** directory you just left, click the text at the top of the list that reads **Up to higher level directory**, alternatively click the second entry in the list that just consists of two dots.

BY THE WAY

Avoiding the scenic route

If you know exactly where you need to go, don't waste time clicking your way through all the directories. For example, to get to the windowsnt directory in the example, type **ftp://sunsite.doc.ic.ac.uk/computing/systems/ibmpc/windowsnt** into the address bar. Better still, if you know the name of the file you want to download from this directory, add ***/filename*** on the end. Explorer will connect and start downloading the file, but won't waste time showing you the FTP directory.

Keep a look out for files called **Index**. These will tell you something about the site you're visiting, and give a list of all the files on the site or in the current directory (depending on the individual site – some give more detail than others). As you can see in the screenshot, there are two Index files. One is a text file that you could read on any word processor or in your browser's window; the other is a compressed version of the same file (indicated by its **.zip** extension and much smaller size) and needs a program like WinZip to decompress it, which you'll learn about in Chapter 13. It's well worth grabbing Index files to read offline; they usually include a brief description of each file to supplement the rather cryptic filenames you see listed on the screen.

Private Sites & Anonymous Sites

To gain access to any FTP site you have to log in, just as you do when you connect to your IAP or online service. Some of these sites are private, and you'll need a username and password to get access. For example, a company may allow you access to their site in order to upload information or files rather than sending them by email. If you create your own web site and upload the files by FTP, you'll have a username and password to prevent anyone else having access to your directory and tampering with your web pages.

Heading straight for the pub

Many anonymous sites will give free access only to certain areas; some directories will be 'roped off' and you won't be allowed into them. Keep a look out for a directory called pub, which will contain all the files and subdirectories available to anonymous visitors.

Many other sites are accessible to the public, and anyone can log on and delve in. These are known as anonymous sites, because the system doesn't need to find out who you are before letting you in. To access these sites, you'll log in with the username **anonymous** and give your email address as the password. Using your browser, this is handled automatically and you won't be prompted to enter anything. Using an FTP program, as you'll learn in a moment, you just click a box labelled **Anonymous** to have the details entered for you.

Why would I want to upload files?

If you've logged in anonymously you won't be able to upload files. The main time you'll want to do this is when you've created your own web site, and have to copy the files to your access provider's web server. You'll learn more about doing that in Chapter 25.

Using a 'Real' FTP Program

So if the browser can cope with FTP, why would you want to use anything different? Quite simply, a 'real' FTP program is custom-built for the job. With a few minutes' practice, it's actually easier and friendlier to use, and it can usually connect to an FTP site faster than your browser can, speeding up the transfer of files that you download. It also gives you more information about the progress of downloads from FTP sites than your browser does. Finally, it will let you upload files as well as download them, which, at the moment, browsers can't do.

You'll need to grab a copy of an FTP program, and three of the best are listed below and included on the free CD-ROM. For the rest of this chapter I'm going to assume you're using WS_FTP, but don't worry if you're not.

What about the Windows 95 FTP program?

Can you use the FTP program that lives in your Windows directory? The literal answer is yes, you can. But it's like nailing jelly to the ceiling. It's an MS-DOS program with an unfriendly set of commands, and takes a lot of very precise typing. I'd give it a miss.

All three programs look very similar and have almost identical features.

- **WS_FTP** One of the most popular programs, despite the dull name. You can find updates and the fully fledged WS_FTP Professional at **http://www.ipswitch.com.**

- **FTP Explorer** A neat program for Windows 95 and later, found at **http://www.ftpx.com.**

- **CuteFTP** No more cuddly than the others, but every bit as good. If you choose to use this program for longer than 30 days, head for **http://www.cuteftp.com** to register it.

Setting up WS_FTP couldn't be easier: when you first start it up, you'll be asked to enter your email address, and that's it. The program will open and you'll see the Session Properties dialog, pictured in the next screenshot. WS_FTP comes with a list of FTP sites all ready to go, so you can just choose one of those from the **Profile Name** box and the program will try to connect you. If there's a particular site you want to visit that's not on the list, you'll have to set up a Session Profile for it first. This will be saved so that you can use it again in the future (rather like Internet Explorer's **Favorites** menu). Click the **New** button and follow these steps:

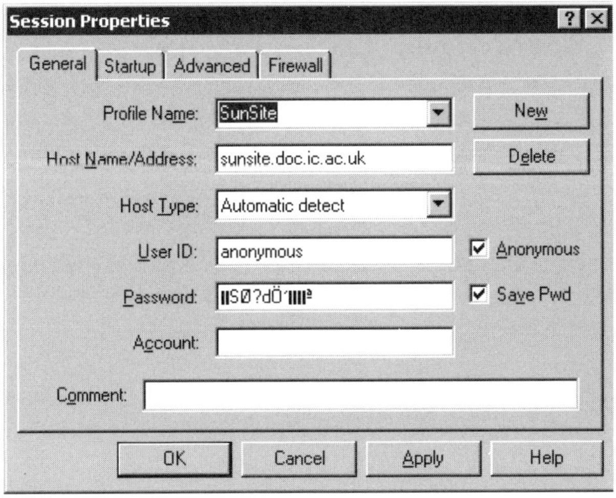

1 In the **Profile Name** box, type any name that will help you recognise the connection to this FTP site in future.

2 Type the name of the computer you want to connect to in the **Host Name/Address** box.

3 If you know the **Host Type**, enter it in the appropriate box. If not, ignore this and let WS_FTP work it out for you. (I've never needed to change this setting!)

4 If you're connecting to an anonymous FTP site, click the **Anonymous** box to place a checkmark in it. If you're going to a private site, type your username in the **User ID** box.

5 If you're visiting a private site, type your password in the **Password** box. Check the **Save Pwd** box if you don't want to enter your password manually every time you visit this site (but remember that anyone else using your computer will be able to log on just as easily if the password is saved!).

6 Click the **Startup** tab. In the box labelled **Initial Remote Host Directory,** type the path to the directory you want to start in when connected (if you know the whereabouts of the file you want). Taking the example from earlier in this chapter, you'd enter **/computing/systems/ibmpc/windowsnt** (and don't forget that very first forward slash).

7 In the box marked **Initial Local Directory**, you can type the path to a directory on your own computer that you want any files to be downloaded into. This directory will be selected for downloads every time you connect to this site.

8 Click **OK**, and WS_FTP will save these settings for future use and try to connect to the site.

◀ Creating a Session Profile that will connect you to an FTP site in WS_FTP.

> **BY THE WAY**
>
> ## FTP and the online services
>
> The major online services will also let you transfer files by FTP. When using America Online, use the keyword **ftp**; in CompuServe, use the Go word **ftp**. In either program you can click on the big **Internet** button on the main desktop and choose FTP from the next menu.

When WS_FTP has connected to the site, you'll see the window shown in the next screenshot. The directories and files on your own computer are listed on the left, and those of the computer you're connected to are listed on the right. You can move through the directories on the remote computer by double-clicking the yellow folder icons or, if you know the path to the directory you want to open, click on the **ChgDir** (Change Directory) button and type it in to get there more quickly.

▶ Double-click a directory to open it, or click a file followed by the left-pointing arrow to download it.

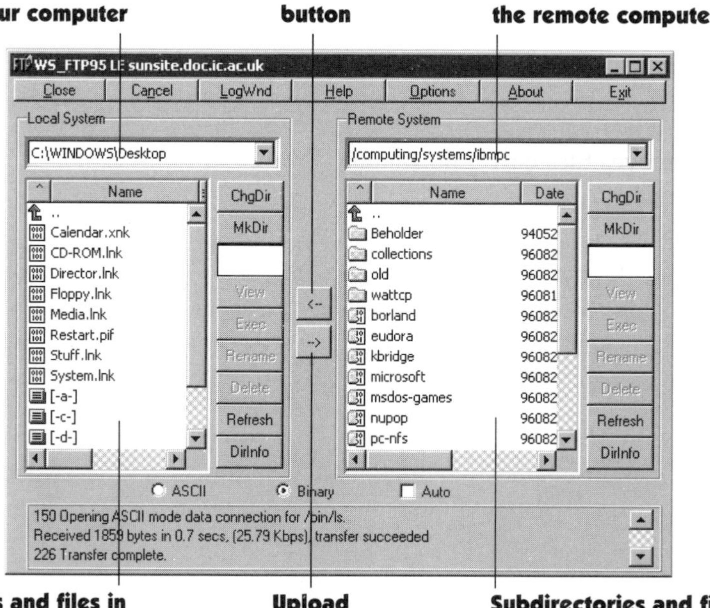

The buttons you'll use most of the time are the **View** and <— buttons. If you want to read the Index file you find in most directories, for example, click it once, then click the **View** button and the file will be opened in Windows Notepad. To download a file to your own computer, click it once, and then click the <— button. The file will be copied to the directory shown in the left-hand side of the window. (If you want to download several files, hold Ctrl while you click each file you want, and then click the <— button; they'll be downloaded one at a time.)

BY THE WAY

Choosing the correct file type

Below the directory and file lists are three buttons labelled **ASCII**, **Binary** and **Auto**. Binary will be selected by default. ASCII can only be used to download plain text files, and the Auto setting will try to determine whether a file is ASCII or Binary. But any file will download with the Binary setting, and although a plain-text file will download a little more slowly this way, text files are usually so small that the difference is negligible.

Apart from the **ChgDir** button mentioned earlier, there are buttons marked **MkDir** and **RmDir** (create a new directory or remove an empty one), **Delete** (which removes files only) and **Rename**. You can use these to navigate your own computer's hard-disk and create, delete and rename files and directories. On the remote system you won't be able to tamper with files and directories in this way unless you've connected to a private site by entering a recognised username and password.

Finding the Stuff You Want

The trick with FTP is to actually locate what you're looking for. There may be dozens of directories, all containing more directories, and the structure may not always be as intuitive as the way you structure your own hard-disk. Let's look at several things you may want to do, and come up with some solutions.

- If you know the name and location of the file you want, type it into your browser's address bar, or type the path into WS_FTP's **Initial Host Remote Directory** mentioned on page 129 and look for the file when the directory's contents are shown.

- If you know the location of the file you want, but not its name, visit that directory and either View or download one of the Index files, which should give a short description of each file in that directory.

- If you don't know the location of the file (or the location you were given is wrong), but you know its name, there are several options. One is to see if it's listed in an Index file, another is to use an Archie search (you'll meet Archie in Chapter 11). A third possibility is to use your browser to visit FTP Search at **http://ftpsearch.ntnu.no/ftpsearch** (pictured in the next screenshot). Type the name of the file into the **Search for** box and click the **Search** button. (If FTP Search doesn't do the trick, a similar search at **http://www.snoopie.com/pquery.html** could yield different results.)

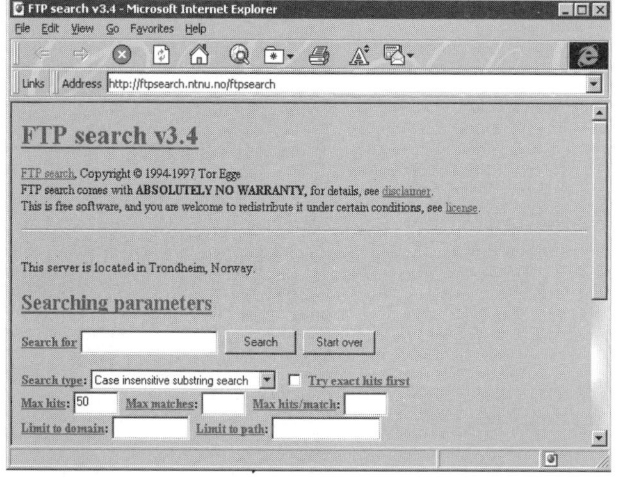

▶ Track down elusive files using the FTP search page.

- If you're only searching for general stuff, it's fun just browsing through directories until you find something interesting. Directory names tend to become more specific as you dig deeper. For example, if you're looking for email programs, start in the pub directory, and from there you may find a computing directory, which will lead you to software, then Internet, then email. If the pub directory has an Index or Readme file, grab that first – it may contain a listing of all its subdirectories and an explanation of what each contains.

- *Another, often better way to find a file is to run an Archie search. What's that all about? Skip ahead to Chapter 11 to find out.*

10

CHAT & TALK WITHOUT MOVING YOUR LIPS

In This Chapter...

- ▶ Chat, talk and VON – what's it all about?
- ▶ Using online services' chat rooms
- ▶ Take part in IRC chat sessions on the Internet
- ▶ Spice up your chat sessions with cartoon characters
- ▶ Cut your phone bill using Talk & Voice on the Net

Chat *and* talk? Am I losing my marbles? No, I'm not (or at least if I am, you couldn't count this as evidence). In Internet-speak, chatting and talking are two different things, but what they have in common is their immediacy: you can hold conversations with people from all over the world at a speed almost comparable with talking on the telephone. In most cases, you won't know who these people are, and you may never 'meet' them again.

Reactions to this area of cyberspace vary considerably. Many people find it exciting or addictive, to the point of spending hours every day 'chatting'. Many more find it inane, frustrating, or offensive. Quite simply, these services bring Internet users into the closest possible contact with each other, and are used by many to meet members of the opposite sex. However unsatisfying you imagine cybersex to be, it's very real, and all potential 'chatters' should be aware of its existence before taking part. That said, chatting and talking can also be sociable and fun, practical and informative – to a large extent, the choice is yours.

What Are Chatting & Talking?

Chatting means holding live conversations with others by typing on your keyboard. You type a line or two of text into a small window and press Enter, and the text is almost instantly visible to everyone else taking part. They can then respond by typing their own messages, and you'll almost instantly see their responses on your screen. Chatting usually takes place in a **chat room**, which may contain just two or three people, or as many as fifty.

GOOD QUESTION

Doesn't everyone talk at once in a chat room?

Sometimes, yes. Sometimes no one seems to talk at all. Sometimes there are two or three conversations going on between little groups of people, with all the messages appearing in the same window, and things can get a bit confusing. But although there may be 35 people in a room, many are just 'listening' rather than joining in.

Talk is a little different. Although the method of sending messages to and fro is the same, 'talk' usually takes place between just two people, and in a more structured way. Using a talk program, you'd usually enter the email address of the person you want to talk to, and if that person is online (and willing to talk to you!) the conversation begins. To cloud the issue a bit, chat programs also allow two people to enter a private room and 'talk', and many talk programs will allow more people to join in with your conversation if you allow them to enter.

As you can tell, the boundary between chat and talk is a bit smudged. Making things even more complicated is the recent arrival of **Voice on the Net** (VON), by which people can really talk to each other using microphones. Most talk programs support VON, and it's slowly being added to chat as well. Actually this isn't all as confusing as it sounds; let's take them one at a time to see how each works.

Chat & the Online Services

One of the major reasons for the early popularity of online services was their built-in, easy-to-use chat systems. The major online services put a lot of effort into improving their chat facilities, and also now offer parental controls that can bar access from certain chat areas. As a measure of how seriously they regard these facilities, online services regularly enlist celebrity guest speakers to host chat sessions and answer questions. The simplicity of these chat areas makes them a good introduction to the workings of chat, even if you have an IAP account, so we'll look at the online services' offerings first.

Both AOL and CompuServe have a large button on their desktops marked Chat that will take you to the chat rooms, or you can use the Go or Keyword 'chat'. In CompuServe this will lead to a short menu from which you can choose the General or the Adult chat forum. Click the forum of your choice and you can use the buttons on the left to switch between chat, file and

BY THE WAY

Make CompuServe chat your Favourite

Like many areas of CompuServe, the chat forums will take about five minutes to load the first time you access them. Make sure you add the forum to your list of Favourite Places when you arrive, as this will shave a few valuable minutes off your subsequent visits.

message areas. The list of chat rooms shows how many people are in each room, and the Who's Here tab behind it gives a list of CompuServe members currently chatting and the rooms they're in. To enter a chat room, click its name and then choose Participate or Observe (depending on how adventurous you're feeling!).

In AOL you'll see a menu allowing you to choose between UK and US chat. Choose either, and you'll be launched into a chat room called the New Members Lobby (although you can leave this if you choose to). You'll also see a list of chat rooms. To enter a room, double-click its name in the list. In both AOL and CompuServe you can leave a chat room by closing its window.

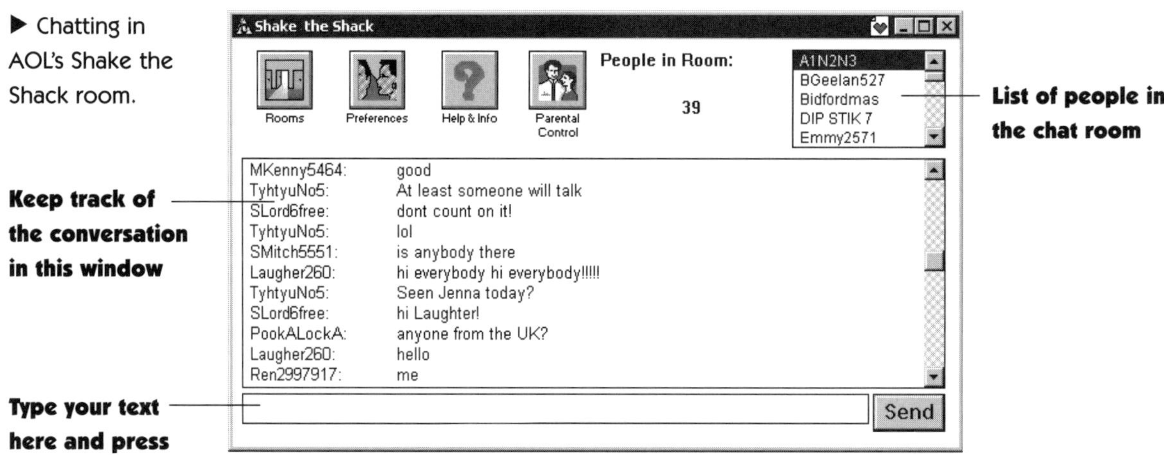

▶ Chatting in AOL's Shake the Shack room.

Once inside a chat room you can watch the conversations unfold in the upper portion of the window, or participate by typing text into the space at the bottom and pressing Enter. (Don't type your username before each line – the chat program displays that automatically.) AOL shows a list of the people in the room in the top-right corner; in CompuServe, click on the **Who's Here** button for a similar list. Some members fill in a Member Profile giving details such as age, location and interests, which can shed some light on the people you're chatting to. In AOL, double-click the name in the **People In Room** list and click the **Get Info** button; in CompuServe, click **Who's Here**, click on a name, then select **Member Profile**.

If you're of a shy disposition, you'll probably have a great time with chat. When no one can see you (and you can easily escape if you feel foolish!) you can pretend to be anyone you like. In fact, the adoption of a whole new persona is part of the fun for many users. But if you really don't want to get involved, it can still be very entertaining just to 'lurk' and watch.

You can also invite someone to 'talk' privately. In AOL, double-click the name of the person you want to talk to in the **People In Room** list, click the **Message** button and type a short message (such as 'Do you want to talk?'). If the person accepts, a small window will open in which you can type messages back and forth. In CompuServe, click the Private Chat button.

Chatting on the Internet

The Internet has its own chat system called Internet Relay Chat, or **IRC**. Like all the other Internet services, you'll need to grab another piece of software to use it. One of the best, and the easiest to use, is **mIRC** from **http://www.mirc.co.uk** and included on the free CD-ROM with this book. The first time you run mIRC, you'll see the dialog shown in the following screenshot into which you can enter the few details needed by the program.

Enter your name and email address in the appropriate spaces, and choose a nickname (or 'handle') by which you'll be known in chat sessions.
A nickname can be anything you choose: it may give an indication of your hobby or job, or a clue to your (adopted?) personality, or it may just be meaningless gibberish, but it can't be more than nine characters in length. Finally, choose a UK server from the list and click **OK**.

◀ Fill in three boxes, choose a server, and you're ready to start chatting.

Now you're ready to connect and start chatting. Make sure you're connected to your service provider first (mIRC won't start the connection for you), and then click the thunderbolt-button at the extreme left of the toolbar. As soon as you're connected, you'll see a small dialog box listing a collection of channels that mIRC's author thought you may like to try. You could double-click one of these to enter that channel, but now is a good time to use one of the many IRC commands. Close the little list of channels, type **/list** in the box at the bottom of the main window, and then press Enter. A second window will open to display all the channels available on the server you chose (shown in the next screenshot). There could be several hundred channels, so this may take a few seconds. Beside each channel's name you'll see a figure indicating how many people are on that channel at the moment, and a brief description of the channel's current subject of discussion. Choose a channel, and double-click its list-entry to enter.

JARGON BUSTER

Channels

In the weird world of Internet Relay Chat (IRC), the regular users have evolved their own jargon as a type of shorthand. It is based heavily on the language used in CB radio. To the 'newbie' it can all be rather daunting, so as a starter to understand what's going on – remember that a 'channel' is the term for a chat room.

Some long-time IRC users can be a bit scathing towards newcomers, so it's best to choose a beginners' channel while you take your first faltering steps. Good channels to start with are **#beginners**, **#mirc** (for mIRC users), **#irchelp** or **#ircnewbies**. You may see some more channel names that refer to help, beginners or newbies – try to pick a channel that has at least half-a-dozen people in it already so that you won't feel too conspicuous!

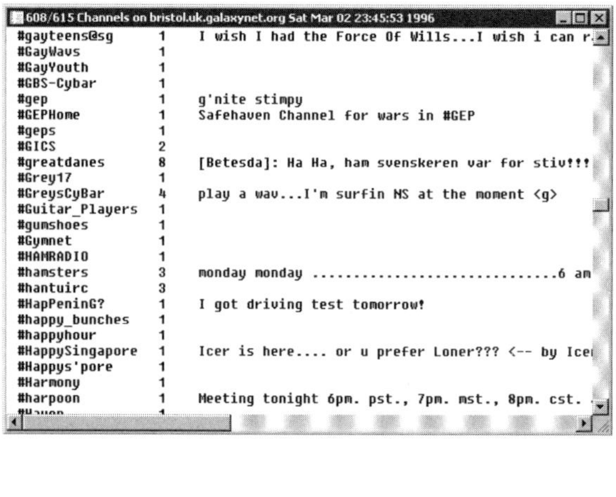

608/615 Channels on bristol.uk.galaxynet.org Sat Mar 02 23:45:53 1996

#gayteens@sg	1	I wish I had the Force Of Wills...I wish i can r
#GayWavs	1	
#GayYouth	1	
#GBS-Cybar	1	
#gep	1	g'nite stimpy
#GEPHome	1	Safehaven Channel for wars in #GEP
#geps	1	
#GICS	2	
#greatdanes	8	[Betesda]: Ha Ha, ham svenskeren var for stiv!!!
#Grey17	1	
#GreysCyBar	4	play a wav...I'm surfin NS at the moment <g>
#Guitar_Players	1	
#gumshoes	1	
#Gymnet	1	
#HAMRADIO	1	
#hamsters	3	monday monday ....6 am
#hantuirc	3	
#HapPeninG?	1	I got driving test tomorrow!
#happy_bunches	1	
#happyhour	1	
#HappySingapore	1	Icer is here.... or u prefer Loner??? <-- by Ice
#Happys'pore	1	
#Harmony	1	
#harpoon	1	Meeting tonight 6pm. pst., 7pm. mst., 8pm. cst.
[illegible]	1	

▶ The complete channel listing from GalaxyNet's Bristol server. Choose any channel from 615 possibles!

When a channel window opens, you'll see your nickname listed among the channel's other occupants on the right, with the conversation taking place on the left. As soon as you enter the channel, your arrival will be broadcast to everyone else (you'll see this happen when others arrive and leave) and you may receive an automated Welcome message, or someone may even say Hello. To join in with the chat, just start typing into the textbox at the bottom and press Enter to send. If you want to leave a channel, type the command **/leave** and press Enter.

How can I start chatting without 'butting in'?

Whenever you arrive in a channel there's likely to be a conversation going on. If no one brings you into the chat, it's a good idea to 'lurk' for a few moments to see what it's all about, but it's quite acceptable to type something like **Hi everyone, how's it going?** and you'll usually get a friendly response from someone. If you don't, follow the conversation and try to interject with something useful.

IRC Commands – Chat Like a Pro

The IRC system has a huge number of commands that you can learn and put to good use if you're really keen, and mIRC includes a general IRC help-file explaining how they work. You certainly don't need to know all of them (and mIRC has toolbar buttons that replace a few), but once you feel comfortable with the system you can experiment with new ones. Here's a few of the most useful to get you started.

Type This	To Do This
/help	Get general help on IRC
/list	List all the channels available on the server you are connected to
/list -min *n*	List all the channels with at least n people in them (replace *n* with a figure)
/join *#channel*	Enter a channel. Replace ***channel*** with the name of your chosen channel
/leave *#channel*	Leave the specified channel (or the channel in the current window if no channel is specified)
/quit message	Finish your IRC session and display a message to the channel if you enter one (see below)
/away message	Tell other occupants you're temporarily away from your computer, giving a message
/away	With no message, means that you're no longer away
/whois *nickname*	Get information about the specified nickname in the main window

So what are those messages? When you quit, you may want to explain why you're leaving, by entering a command like **/quit Got to go shopping. See you later!** Similarly, if you suddenly have to leave your keyboard, you could type **/away Call of nature. BRB** to indicate that you'll be back in a minute if anyone tries to speak to you. (BRB is a common shorthand for 'Be right back' – turn to page 101 for a few more of these.) When you return, just type **/away** to turn off this message again.

If you need more help than mIRC's help file provides, the newsgroups provide an ideal place to ask questions (and are more likely to get positive responses than questions asked in an IRC channel). You'll find a large **alt,irc** hierarchy, along with an **alt.mirc** group.

BY THE WAY

An easy way to make a fool of yourself

Try to remember that all commands start with a forward-slash. If you type the command without the slash it will be displayed to all the participants in your channel, and everyone will quickly identify you for the 'newbie' that you are and have a good giggle at your expense.

You can also 'talk' privately to any of the participants in a channel. If you want to start a private talk with someone called Zebedee, type the command **/query Zebedee Can I talk to you in private?** (of course, the message you tag on the end is up to you). Zebedee will have the opportunity to accept or decline the talk: if he or she accepts, a separate window will open in which the two of you can exchange private messages.

BY THE WAY

Easy window management

You can keep windows open in mIRC as long as you want to. The program places each new window on a taskbar so that you can switch between open channels and lists to your heart's content. Many people even keep several 'chats' going at once in this way!

Starting Your Own IRC Channel

If you always connect to the same server, and always use the **/list** command to get a list of channels, you may notice that the number of channels varies. Channels are dynamic – anyone can create a new one, and when the last person leaves that channel it ceases to exist. The steps below show you how to create your own channel:

1 Pick a channel name that doesn't already exist and enter it. To create a channel called Skylight, type **/join #Skylight**.

2 To put yourself in charge of this channel you have to promote yourself to channel-operator status. Do this by typing **/op *nickname*** (entering your own nickname). As operator, your nickname will be displayed with an '@' prefix to indicate your status to anyone who enters your channel.

3 Now set a topic that will be displayed in the channel list and (with luck!) attract some passers-by. Type **/topic** followed by a description of what your channel would be discussing if there was someone else to discuss it with. As people join your channel and the discussion moves to different areas, use the **/topic** command to update the description.

As channel operator you are all-powerful: you can invite people into your channel using **/invite** followed by their nickname and the name of your channel (for example, **/invite Zebedee #Skylight**), and you also have the ability to kick someone out if their conduct is offensive or disruptive using **/kick #Skylight Zebedee.**

When you tire of all this heady power stuff you can use the **/op** command to promote other visitors to channel-operator status if you wish to.

BY THE WAY

Get the picture?

Many people frequent the same IRC channels, so you may start to recognise a few regulars. (It's not unknown for people to fall in love, get engaged, and even hold a wedding ceremony on IRC!) If you'd like to see what these folk look like, head off to the IRC Picture Gallery on the Web at **http://www.powertech.no/IRCGallery** to see if their pictures are there. And while you're about it, why not add your own?

Chatting Can Be Comical!

Simple though it is, chatting can be very addictive. But it's still plain text, and in Internet-land that just won't do. The latest thing is graphical chat software in which you choose a cartoon character called an **avatar** to represent yourself. These programs offer you a list of avatars to choose from, and some even let you create your own. The following screenshot shows one of the most popular graphical chat programs, **Microsoft Chat** (which also supports ordinary textual chat if those avatars get on your nerves!). You can download **Microsoft Chat** from **http://www.microsoft.com/ie/comichat/default.htm**.

BY THE WAY

Turn'off your avatar

Microsoft has set up its own chat rooms, but you can also connect to the usual IRC channels, and Chat will assign other occupants an avatar so that you can still take part using avatars rather than plain text. However, if you do connect to an IRC channel, go to Chat's **View | Options | Settings** page and check the box beside **Don't send graphics information**, or the rest of the channel will see some strange stuff alongside your typed text!

▶ Microsoft's visual Chat program lets you choose an avatar, and you can also select different emotions to match your text.

If you get a taste for this type of more animated chat, this program is just the tip of a whole new iceberg. On the free CD-ROM accompanying this book, you'll find details of programs that you can use to access sites on the World Wide Web that use avatars and virtual reality to combine chat with the exploration of 3D worlds. In fact, some of these worlds are so amazing, you won't even want to stop and chat!

Finally, on the subject of chat, a word about personal security – never give out personal details other than your name, age, sex, and email address. After chatting with someone for a while, it's very easy to forget that you really know nothing about them but what they've told you (and that may not be strictly true!).

Voice on the Net – Talk Really Is Cheap!

The sort of chat we've looked at so far is 'unplanned' – you arrive in a channel or chat room and chat to whoever happens to be there. If you get on well enough, you may want to invite someone else to have a private chat (or 'talk') in a separate window. But what if there's someone in particular you want to talk to? Until recently, your options were limited: you could agree to meet in a chat room at a certain time and take it from there, or you could pick up the telephone.

But the latest 'big thing' on the Internet is **VON** (Voice on the Net). VON is the Internet equivalent of a telephone: you start the program, choose an email address to 'dial', and start talking. But in this case, talking really means talking. You can hold live conversations with anyone in the world by speaking into a microphone, and hear their responses through your speakers or a headset.

BY THE WAY

Will they be online?

You can only talk to someone else if they're online and have their VON software running. Many US users have access to free local telephone calls and can stay online all day, but if you want to contact another UK user you may still have to arrange to be online at a pre-specified time.

So how does VON differ from an ordinary telephone conversation? First and foremost, the cost – because you're only dialling in to your local access provider, you're only paying for a local telephone call even though you may be speaking to someone in Australia. But it's the extra goodies that VON programs offer that make them valuable. Depending on the program you use, you can send computer files back and forth, hold conferences, use a whiteboard to draw sketches and diagrams, and you can even take control of programs on the other party's computer. Recent programs have made the fabled 'video phone' a reality at last – admittedly the pictures are small, rather jerky (especially with a slow modem) and a bit blurred, but finally you can see and be seen while you talk!

Sounds Good – What's the Catch?

The downside is that the other party must also be online to receive the 'call', so you'll both pay telephone charges; however, even added together these could amount to less than 10 per cent of a conventional international call charge. In fact, there are already systems that allow you to dial someone's telephone number rather than email address, making it possible to make these cheap international calls to someone who doesn't even have their own Internet account!

A second catch (at the moment) is that you must be using the same program as the person you want to talk to. If you talk to a lot of people, you may need several different programs that do the same job just because they all use different programs. Fortunately, some of these programs are free, so it's probably easiest to pick a free one and then convince your friends to grab a copy themselves! Don't fret, before long, the various software companies involved will probably get their acts together on this as they have with the other Internet services.

What Do I Need?

Unlike the other services you use on the Net, VON programs have some definite hardware requirements. To begin with, you'll need a soundcard. It doesn't need to be a flashy, expensive card since the quality of these voice calls isn't high, but look out for a **full-duplex** card. You need a reasonably fast computer too (at least a 486DX, but preferably a Pentium) with a bare minimum of 8Mb RAM. And you'll need a microphone and speakers plugged into your soundcard; the quality of these doesn't matter too much and any computer-peripherals store can supply them very cheaply.

Full-duplex

There are two choices: full-duplex and half-duplex. A full-duplex card can record your voice while playing the incoming voice so that you can both talk at the same time if you want to (ideal for arguments, for example!). With a half-duplex card you can either talk or listen, but not both – you'd normally switch off your microphone after speaking as an indication you'd finished (rather like saying 'Over' on a walkie-talkie).

Next there's your Internet connection and modem to consider. You could get by with a 14.4Kbps connection, but you'll get much better results from a 28.8Kbps modem, and most access providers now support this speed. Finally, of course, you need the software. There are many different programs to choose from, some of which are aimed more at business use than personal, but here's a brief selection, all of which you'll find on the free CD-ROM:

- **PowWow** A very friendly, free program from Tribal Voice, which we'll look at in a moment. You can download this from **http://www.tribal.com**.
- **PowWow For Kids** A version of PowWow for children up to 13 years, with great security features that filter out profanity and warn the child when they try to contact an adult or when an adult requests a chat. However, the child will need a personal email address, rather than sharing yours. **Visit http://www.tribal.com/kids.htm** for details and download.
- **NetMeeting** Microsoft's free VON program aimed largely at business users, but (seemingly) used more by personal talkaholics. NetMeeting supports video, voice, and multi-user conferences, and you can use programs on the other person's computer by remote control. This can be installed along with Internet Explorer from the free CD-ROM accompanying this book, or you can download it as a separate item from **http://www.microsoft.com/netmeeting**.

- **Web Phone** A multi-talented, and very stylish, VON program based on a mobile-phone design with features such as video, text-chat and answerphone, as well as four separate voice lines. You'll need to 'activate' the evaluation copy (an unusual way of saying 'pay for') to unlock some of its smartest features by visiting **http://www.itelco.com**. Although inexpensive, Web Phone is targeted more at the business user than NetMeeting or (particularly) PowWow.

▶ **Internet Phone** A true VON program in that it has no 'text-talk' or whiteboard facilities, so it will be no good to you without soundcard, microphone and speakers. Until you pay for your copy, your talk time will be limited. You can register the evaluation copy by pointing your browser at **http://www.vocaltec.com**.

BY THE WAY

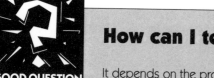

Don't be out when the call comes in!

To get the most from any chat, talk or VON program, make sure you run it every time you go online; if you don't, it's like leaving your telephone permanently off the hook – no one will be able to contact you! Even if you just plan to do a bit of web-surfing, run the program and then minimise it. If someone wants to talk, a dialog will appear to ask if you'd like to accept.

Start Talking

As usual, most VON programs have similar features, although their names and toolbar-buttons vary. It's probably an inescapable fact of life that the most popular VON programs are the free ones, so let's take a look at Tribal Voice's **PowWow** as a representative example.

When you first run PowWow you'll be prompted to enter your name, email address and a choice of password. The program will then dial up and register these in the main PowWow database and you're ready to start. Click the **Connect** button at the left of the toolbar and type in the email address of the PowWow user you want to contact. To save their details to the Address Book

GOOD QUESTION

How can I tell who's online and available?

It depends on the program. In some programs you can't – you have to send a request and see if you get a response. In other programs, such as NetMeeting and Internet Phone, as soon as you connect you'll see a list of users currently online; take your courage in both hands and double-click one!

for future use, fill in their name or nickname and click **Add**. Make sure you're connected to your IAP and click the **Connect** button. If the other person is online and running PowWow (and willing to speak to you, of course!) the main window will split into two and you'll see their reply. Just as in any Chat program, you simply type your side of the conversation and press Enter.

To speak to someone using your microphone, click the **Voice** button. Although PowWow lets you text-chat with up to seven people, you'll only be able to have a voice conversation with one at a time. Here's a brief run-down of features you'll find in PowWow (and most other VON programs):

- Transfer files by clicking the Send File button and choosing a file to send. You can continue to talk while the file is being transferred.
- Set up an Answering Machine message that will be sent to anyone trying to contact you when you're unavailable. Some programs (such as Web Phone) can also record messages left by anyone trying to contact you.
- Send a picture of yourself to the other user by entering its location in PowWow's setup page. Most programs can send images to be displayed on the other user's screen without interrupting the conversation.
- Click the **Whiteboard** button to collaborate in drawing pictures using a similar set of tools to those found in Window Paint.
- Host a conference with up to 50 people taking part in text-chat.
- If you have your own web site, you can add a PowWow link to your page to tell visitors that you're online and available to chat. This is an unusual feature, but Internet Phone users have a similar option. Visitors to the page can click the link to start their own software and invite you to talk.
- Stuck for someone to call? Click the **White Pages** button in PowWow and your web browser will open the main Tribal Voice page. Click a button to see a list of users currently online, then click one of the names to request a chat.
- Punctuate your chat with WAV audio files by clicking the **Sound** button. PowWow comes with its own set of sound files such as 'Applause', 'Hi', 'Cool' and 'Bye', and lets you choose between a male or female voice. Provided the same sound file is on the other person's system too, you'll both hear it.

11

EXTRA TOOLS & UTILITIES

In This Chapter...

- Research & exploration with Gopher
- Play adventure games by remote control with Telnet
- Let Archie take the strain of finding elusive files on the Internet
- Find information about people & companies using Whois & Finger
- Iron out connection problems with Ping

Since the Internet's popularity explosion in 1994, the main attractions for newcomers to the Net have been the World Wide Web and email, with newsgroups and chat close behind. Of course, you don't have to use any part of the Internet you're not interested in, but there's plenty more treasure to be found if you like digging around. In this chapter, we'll take a look at some of the backwaters of the Internet, and a few extra utilities that one day could come in handy.

Searching Gopherspace

I'm going to tell you this up front – you probably won't like Gopher. However, a few years ago you'd have loved it. Until that time, the Internet was an unfriendly place that had to be navigated with complicated text commands, and Gopher came along to solve everyone's problems by grouping everything on to a series of menus. Clicking a menu entry could lead to another menu on another computer somewhere in the world, or it could lead to a file or document. It was a great leap forward, and was heralded as the future of the Internet. So what happened? The World Wide Web came along, and few people wanted to use a menu-driven system any more, whether it had a cute name or not.

JARGON BUSTER

Gopherspace

The Gopher system consists of many computers around the world acting as Gopher servers (just as there are web servers, FTP servers, news servers, and so on). When you look at a document from a web server, you're using the World Wide Web. Connect to a Gopher server, and you're said to be in 'Gopherspace'.

Nowadays you won't find many Gopher sites on the Internet; most have become web sites instead. And for any that you do come across, your web browser can access them without needing any outside help. But although links to Gopher sites are not plentiful on the Web, there are still many useful documents stored on Gopher servers, and the easiest way to find them is to use a dedicated Gopher program. One of the best is **WSGopher** from **http://www.mstc.com**, which is included on the free CD-ROM accompanying this book.

Once you've installed WSGopher, it's easy to set up – there's nothing to do at all! I would make two suggestions, though. Before you do anything at all, select **Edit | Fonts** and choose a smaller font for the first three items on the list. Next, click your way to **Edit | Preferences | Home View** and choose any window layout that shows bookmarks (you'll understand that as soon as you see the **Home View** page). As soon as WSGopher has connected to your Home site (a Gopher server listed in **Edit | Preferences | Home Gopher**) you'll see a list of directories containing links to menus and files in the Directory List. Click on the '+' sign to expand a directory and see its subdirectories, or click on any directory to see its contents in the Document List window, and then double-click a document to download and open it.

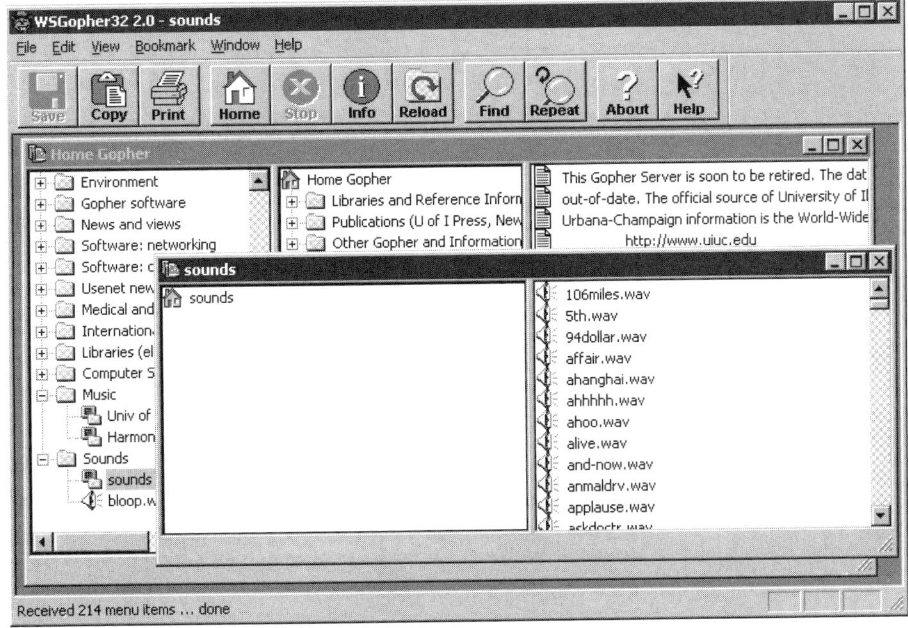

◀ Use WSGopher's supplied bookmarks to find your way to some of the best Gopher sites.

WSGopher has its own bookmarks system that works like Internet Explorer's Favorites menu. Best of all, the program's author has thoughtfully supplied a ready-sorted bundle of bookmarks, but you'll only see these if you chose the window-layout I suggested a moment ago. These are a great place to start: expand one of the bookmark directories and double-click on any of the entries. An excellent site to try is **Gopher Jewels**, which is listed in the **Gopher services** directory. If you find any sites that you'd like to add to the bookmarks list, right-click them, choose **Add**, and select a Category in which to store the bookmark (or create a new Category by typing a name for it and clicking **Create** followed by **OK**).

Is Gopherspace as exciting as the WWW?

No, by comparison it's like watching paint dry. Although you can find sound and picture files for downloading, Gopher is still a text-based system. However, it can be extremely useful for research purposes – many of the remaining Gopher sites belong to universities, libraries, government departments, and other organisations which choose to publish their information widely in a simple form.

Taking Control with Telnet

Telnet is yet another rather dull way to get at information on the Internet, and it's another service that's been overshadowed by the World Wide Web. The reasoning is: if you want to do it, and it can be done on the Web, why would you choose the difficult way instead? But, like Gopher, there are places you can get to only by Telnetting there, and some of them hold a few surprises.

Telnet is a system that lets you use programs running on another computer, or explore their files and databases. To do this, you'll need a Telnet program. If you use Windows 95 you already have a good Telnet program: click **Run** on the Start Menu, type **telnet** and press Enter. I'm going to assume you're using the Windows offering, but you'll find a smarter and friendlier Telnet program, NetTerm, from **http://starbase.neosoft.com/zkrr~01** on the CD-ROM.

Read the rules

All Telnet sites are different, and what you see after connecting will vary from a plain text display to a lavish graphical interface – you take pot luck. For the same reason, the commands you use will vary too, so it pays to read any helpful notices you can find when you arrive. If all else fails, try typing **help** followed by Enter.

There are several ways that you can connect to a Telnet site: if you click a Telnet link on a web page, your browser will automatically start your Telnet program to connect to it (if it can't locate a Telnet program, the browser will ask you to specify its exact location). Similarly, you could type the URL of the Telnet site you want to visit into your browser's address bar, prefixing it with **telnet://**. Finally, you can start the Telnet program yourself; click on **Connect | Remote System**, and then type the site's address into the **Host Name** box and click the **Connect** button. When you've finished a Telnet session and are ready to log off, try typing the commands **quit** or **exit** followed by Enter. If you don't get a response, go to the **Connect** menu and choose **Disconnect**.

If you want to give Telnet a go, use your web browser to visit the HYTELNET site at **http://library.usask.ca/hytelnet/**. Click the **Other Resources** link or either of the **Library Catalogs** links to see a list of Telnet sites you can try. At a few of the Telnet sites you'll have to log in using an account name and give a password, but many of these sites still allow public access so HYTELNET will usually tell you the account name and password to use.

Telnet & the online services

Both America Online and CompuServe have built-in Telnet support. In both cases, the Go or Keyword is telnet. If you're a Virgin Net or MSN subscriber you'll need to use Windows 95's Telnet program or install a separate program such as NetTerm.

Fantasy & Adventure by Remote Control

One of the few reasons for Telnet's continuing survival is a type of role-playing game called a MUD (short for Multi-User Dungeon). You'll also come across MUCKs, MUSHs, MOOs and a few more, but to the non-purist they all mean much the same. These are usually science fiction or adventure games where the program gives you information like You are in a large room with a door to the West. In front of you is a table. On the table is a book. You control the action yourself by typing commands such as **get book**.
These games are very popular and could keep you online for days. A good

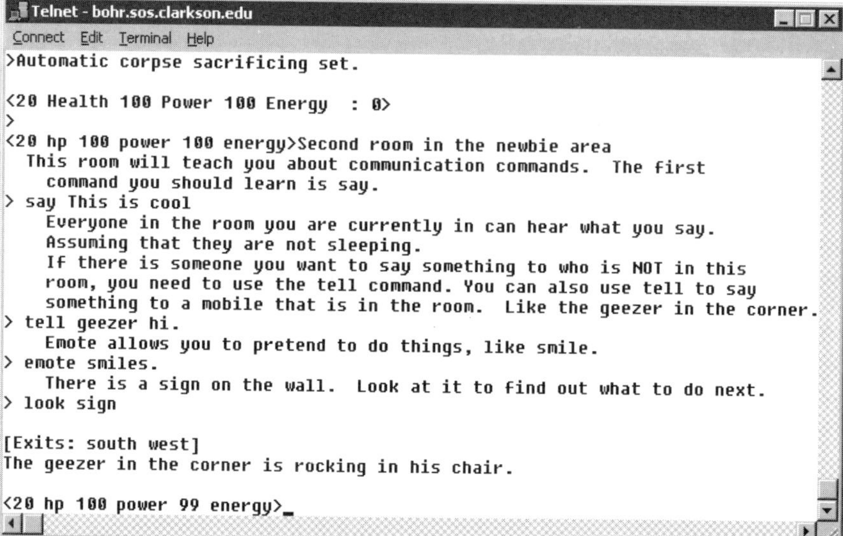

▶ Role-playing MUD games – the most popular use of Telnet.

MUD for beginners can be found at **bohr.sos.clarkson.edu:9000/**. It takes you through the game's commands step by step, so take time to read the text at the beginning. If you fancy trying some more of these, point your browser at **http://www.teleport.com/~morpheus/mudlist.html** for a huge hypertext list.

Finding Files with Archie

Once you've found the file you want, downloading it with FTP is a simple job of clicking one button, as you learnt in Chapter 9. And exploring the directories of FTP servers can lead you to some weird and wonderful files. The puzzle with FTP is how to find the particular file you need without spending hours searching computers, and this is where **Archie** can help.

Why is it called Archie?

The Archie system stores a list (or 'archive') of the files it finds, and Archie is just 'archive' minus the 'v'. But Archie also happens to be a famous cartoon character, so two later search systems were named 'Veronica' and 'Jughead' – characters from the same cartoon show. (Even Internet-geeks have a sense of humour!)

The Archie system consists of a bunch of computers around the world which regularly examine the contents of FTP servers and store a list of the files they find. Using an Archie program, you can connect to one of these computers and ask it to search its list for a particular file name. Two of the best programs, both of which are free for personal use, are:

- **WSArchie** This program works hand in hand with your FTP program to make downloading quick and easy. You can grab a copy of WSArchie from **http://dspace.dial.pipex.com/town/square/cc83**.
- **fpArchie** Going one step further, fpArchie doesn't need a separate FTP program: if it locates the file you want, it can download it for you. You can install fpArchie from the free CD-ROM accompanying this book, or visit its web page at **http://www.euronet.nl/~petert/fpware**.

Setting up these programs is a quick job. If you opted for WSArchie, go to **Option | Ftp Setup**, and tell the program where to find your FTP program (click the **Browse** button to locate and double-click the program). In fpArchie, go to **View | Options** and click the **FTP** tab. Fill in your email address and, if you wish, enter a directory to which all downloaded files should be saved. (Turn to Downloading – Choose Your Directory on page 184 for a suggested way of organising your directories.)

To find a file using one of these Archie programs, go to the **Search For** (or **Name & Location**) tab, and type the name of the file you want to look for. If you know the exact name of the file, you can speed up the search by selecting **Exact** (or **the exact name**). If you only know a part of the filename, type it in and select **Substring** (or **a part of the name**). For example, if you're looking for a program called ABC101.EXE, but you think it may have been

BY THE WAY

Not all Archie servers are the same

Although all Archie computers in the system do much the same job, some find files that others don't. If you run a search and get no results, click WSArchie's Archie Server tab (or fpArchie's Servers tab), and choose a different server to search from the drop-down list. You may find that you can't connect to a particular server at all if you were unlucky enough to choose a busy time.

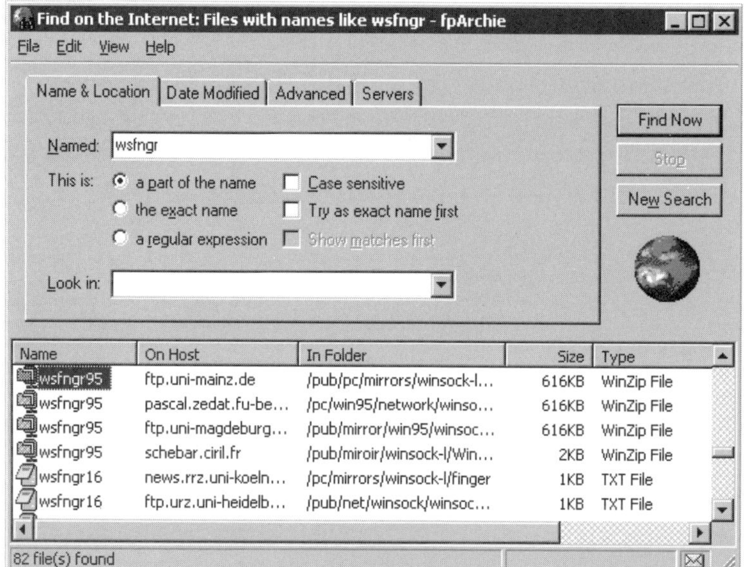

▶ Using fpArchie to search for files containing the characters 'wsfngr'.

replaced by a newer version called ABC102.EXE, just enter ABC10.

If either program finds any files matching the text you entered, you'll see the filenames displayed in the main window, together with their sizes, and details of the FTP server on which each file was found. If one of the files listed is the one you want, just right-click on the filename and choose **Retrieve** – as long as the FTP server isn't too busy, the program will automatically handle the download for you. If the file you want is listed as being available on several different FTP servers, you'll usually get the quickest download time by choosing the FTP server that is geographically closest to you.

BY THE WAY

Archie on the Web

If you really don't want another program just to handle the occasional search for a file, you can find Archie on the World Wide Web too. Go to **http://src.doc.ic.ac.uk/archieplexform.html** and type the name of the file you're looking for using similar options to those covered here. If the search is successful you'll see a page of hypertext links to all the files that match the text you entered – just click one to download it.

Quickfire Extras

For this last little batch of utilities I'm going to move into 'quickfire mode'. The odds are that you'll never want to use these programs unless you like to experiment with software and you're not put off by technical gibberish like 'IP address' and 'name server'. If that doesn't sound like you, skip this section by all means!

Shareware

Shareware is a popular method of selling software on the Internet. You can download the program and try it out for a while, but if you choose to continue using it beyond a specified period you should register it (in other words, pay for it). Shareware has become a generalised term encompassing nagware, crippleware, and others, which you'll learn about in Chapter 13.

Using Your Finger

Finger is a program that may be able to give you some information about an Internet user if you know their logon username and domain name. Of course, if you know that, you probably know their email address too, and you could get the information pretty easily by asking them for it. However, some people set up a special file to provide instant access to certain information (a business may provide product details, for example) that you can retrieve by fingering them. To finger someone, just enter ***username@domain*** and click **OK**. There are many Finger programs available with varying features, but the most popular is WSFinger, a shareware program that can be downloaded from **http://www.biddeford.com/~jobrien**.

Give 'em a Ping

Ping is a little utility used to test a connection by sending a short message to a chosen computer to see if it responds and, if it does, how quickly. This can be handy for two purposes. First, if you're not sure whether your own connection to your IAP is working, start your Ping program and type in the domain name of any computer (such as **www.btinternet.com** or **ftp.tcp.com**). Second, if you're trying to connect to a particular site and it's not responding, try Pinging it instead. The program will send out several short messages, and

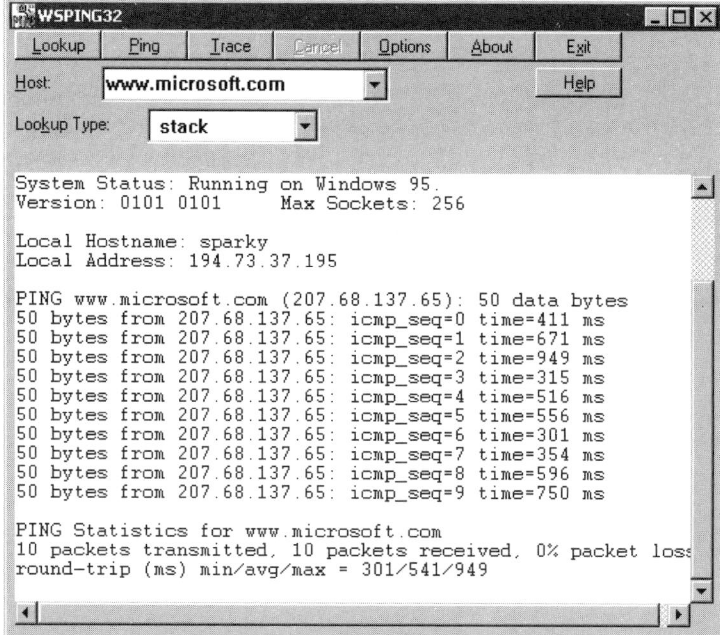

▶ Using Ping to test and time an Internet connection.

the results will show whether the Ping was successful and tell you how long the computer took to respond.

Windows 95 users already have a Ping program – open the Start Menu, choose **Run**, and type **ping** followed by an Internet address (for example, **ping www.microsoft.com**). A good (and free) Ping program is WSPing, which is available from **http://www.csra.net/~junodj** and included on the free CD accompanying this book. Type the name of the computer whose connection you want to test into the **Host** box, and click the **Ping** button. WSPing has a couple more tricks up its sleeve. Type an address into the **Host** box as above, and click the **Trace** button. The program will show you all the computers in the chain linking you to that computer, and the time each takes to respond. Apart from its initial novelty value, if a link in this chain has failed, you'll see straight away why you're unable to connect. (Windows 95 users have this facility too – follow the same routine as you did for Ping, but replace the word **ping** in the command with **tracert**.) Finally, Ping can also translate between domain names (such as www.microsoft.com) and IP addresses (such as 207.68.137.65). Type either into the **Host** box, and click the **Lookup** button.

◀ A quick and simple Whois search can give a comprehensive set of contact information on a business or name.

Whois...?

In theory at least, a Whois program will tell you someone's email address. In reality, it probably won't, since the Whois service lists about 1 per cent of Internet users, but it can give you some useful information about businesses on the Internet. The neatest Whois program around is WinWhois96 by Steven Doyle, which you can install from the free CD accompanying this book. As soon as you start WinWhois, a small textbox will open into which you can type the name to search for. You can start further searches by clicking the 'paper' icon on the toolbar, or selecting **File | New**.

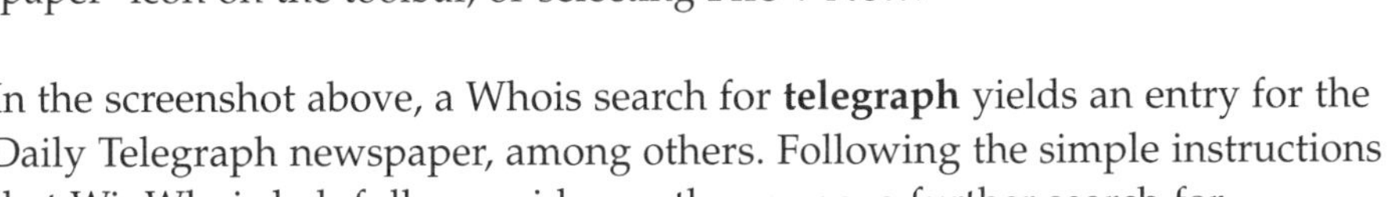

In the screenshot above, a Whois search for **telegraph** yields an entry for the Daily Telegraph newspaper, among others. Following the simple instructions that WinWhois helpfully provides on the screen, a further search for **!DAILYTELEGRAPH-DOM** gives the postal address, telephone number, and a contact name and email address.

3

USING THE INTERNET

In This Part...

12

FINDING STUFF ON THE INTERNET

In This Chapter...

- Finding Web sites using search engines & directories
- Power-searching with Internet Explorer
- Locate people, companies & services using white pages & Yellow Pages
- Track down newsgroups of interest, & useful articles
- Check out the best (& worst!) that the Web has to offer

Now that your connection is sweetly humming along, your software is installed, and you know how to use it, you're ready to start surfing the Internet. And almost immediately you'll hit a predicament: how on earth can you find what you're looking for? As you probably guessed, the Internet is one jump ahead of you on that score, and there's no shortage of tools to point you towards web sites, email addresses, businesses and people. Choosing the best tool to use will depend largely on the type of information you want to find, but don't panic – these search tools are ridiculously easy to use, and you'll probably use several of them regularly. And, yet again, all you need is your trusty browser.

Finding a Search Site

Anything you can find on the World Wide Web you can find a link to at one of the Web's search sites. Although finding a search site on the Web is easy (especially as I'm about to tell you where the most popular ones are!), picking the one that's going to give the best results is never an exact science. Essentially, there are two types of sites available: **search engines** and **directories**:

- Search engines are indexes of World Wide Web sites, which are usually built automatically by a program called a spider, a robot, a worm, or something equally appetising (the AltaVista search engine uses a program it endearingly calls Scooter). These programs constantly scour the Web, and return with information about a page's location, title and contents, which is then added to an index. To search for a certain type of information, just type in keywords and the search engine will display a list of sites containing those words.
- Directories are hand-built lists of pages sorted into categories. Although you can search directories using a keyword search, it's often as easy to click on a category, and then click your way through the ever-more-specific sub-categories until you find the subject you're interested in.

As a result of their automation, search engines have the benefit of being about as up-to-date in their indexes as it's possible to be. The downside is that if you search for **pancake recipe** in a search engine, the resulting list of pages won't all necessarily contain recipes for pancakes – some may just be pages in which the words 'pancake' and 'recipe' both happen to appear. However, the robot-programs used by the search engines all vary in the ways they gather their information, so you'll quite likely get results using one engine that you didn't get using another.

Directories don't have this problem because they list the subject of a page rather than the words it contains, but you won't always find the newest sites this way – sites tend to be listed in directories when their authors submit them for inclusion.

GOOD QUESTION

Which search site is the best?

There really isn't a 'best'. To some degree it's a matter of preference, and you'll probably find a couple that you favour, perhaps for the way they present their results. Yahoo! is an incredibly useful directory that's certainly worth adding to your Favorites menu. Of the rest, I find myself using Excite more than any other, but don't just take my word for it – try a few!

Here's a short list of popular search engines and directories to get you started. When you arrive at one of these, it's worth adding it to Internet Explorer's **Favorites** menu so that you can get back again whenever you need to without a lot of typing.

Search Site	URL
AltaVista	http://www.altavista.digital.com
Excite	http://www.excite.com
HotBot	http://www.hotbot.com
Infoseek	http://www.infoseek.com
Lycos	http://www.lycos.com
SavvySearch	http://www.cs.colostate.edu/~dreiling/smartform.html
WebCrawler	http://www.webcrawler.com
Yahoo! UK & Ireland	http://www.yahoo.co.uk

Using a Search Engine

For this example I'll pick Excite, but most search engines work in the same way, and also look much the same. Indeed, directories such as Yahoo and Infoseek can be used like this if you enjoy the simplicity of keyword searches.

When you arrive at Excite you'll see a page like the one shown in the next screenshot. For the simplest sort of search, type a single word into the textbox, and click on **Search**. If you want to search for something that can't be encapsulated in a single word, it's worth reading the instructions – you'll probably see a link on the page marked Help or Search Tips or something similar – but there are a few tricks you can use that most search engines will understand (and those that don't will generally just ignore them):

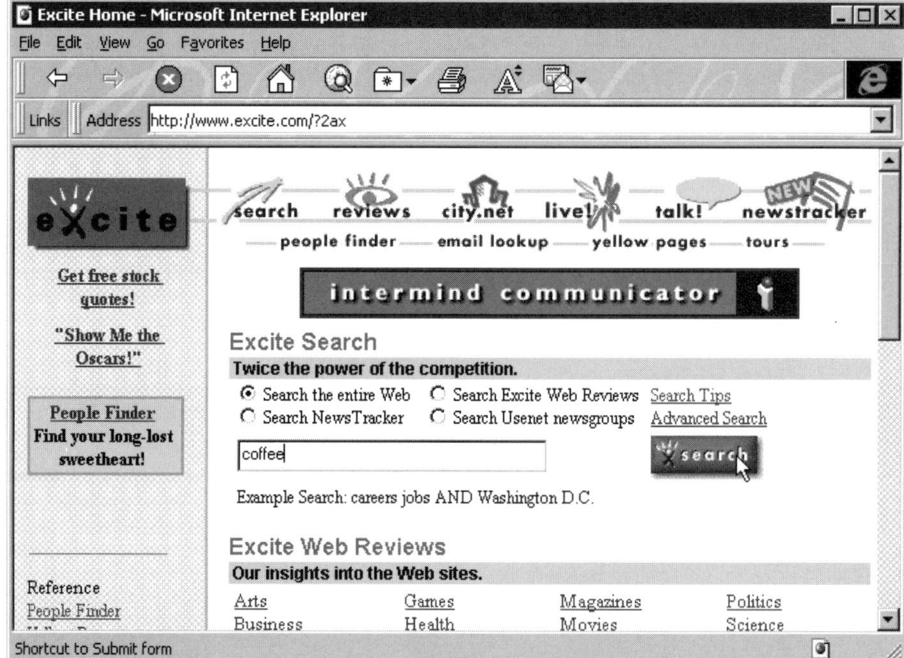

▶ Type a keyword into the search engine's textbox and click Search.

- If you enter several keywords, it is a good idea to type them in descending order of importance. For example, if you wanted to find pictures of dolphins, type **dolphin pictures**. The list will then present good links to dolphin sites before the rather more general links to sites which only contain pictures.
- Use capital letters only if you expect to find capital letters. Searching for **PARIS** may find very little, but searching for **Paris** should find a lot. If you don't mind whether the word is found capitalised or not, use lower case only (**paris**).

- To find a particular phrase, enclose it in "quote marks". For example, a search for **"hot dog"** would find only pages containing this phrase and ignore pages that just contain one word or the other.
- Prefix a word with a '+' sign if it must be included, and with a '-' sign if it must be excluded. For example, if you're an economist searching for banking information, you could enter **bank -river** to ensure that you didn't find documents about river banks. Similarly, you could enter **+printer inkjet -laser** if you wanted to find pages about printers, preferably including inkjet printers, but definitely not mentioning laser printers.

After entering the text you want to search for and clicking the **Search** button, your browser will send the information off to the engine, and within a few seconds you should see a new page like the one pictured below listing the sites that matched your search criteria. I used the keyword **coffee**, and Excite has found 272,017 different pages. It's worth remembering that when some search engines say they've found pages about coffee, they've really found pages that contain the word 'coffee' somewhere within the page's text. Many of these pages may be about something entirely different.

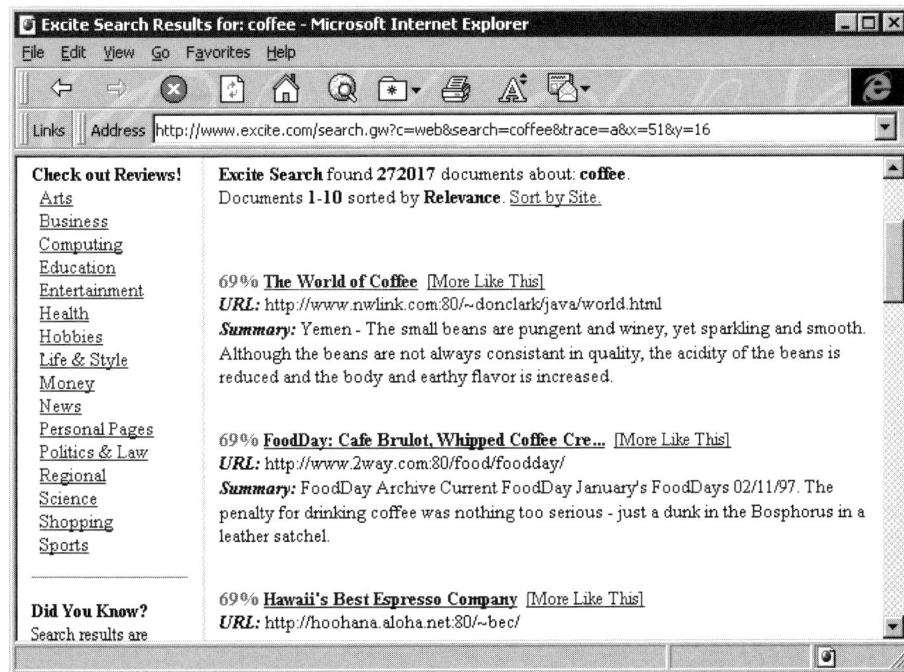

◀ A search for 'coffee' finds more than enough results to keep me up all night!

Of course, you won't find all 272,017 pages listed here. Instead you'll see links to the 10 most relevant pages, with a few words quoted from the beginning of each. At the bottom of the page you'll find a button that will lead you to the next 10 on the list, and so on. In true Web style, these are all hypertext links – click the link to open any page that sounds promising. If the page fails to live up to that promise, use your browser's **Back** button to return to the search results and try a different one.

BY THE WAY

Save your search for later

When the search results appear, you can add this page to Internet Explorer's **Favorites** menu. Not only is the URL of the search site stored, so are the keywords you entered for the search. It's a handy option to remember if you don't have time to visit all the pages found in the search straight away.

Most search engines give the pages a score for relevancy, and these are worth keeping an eye on. In many cases, a page scoring below about 70 per cent is unlikely to give much information. If you can't find what you want using one search engine, always try another; because their methods are different, their results can vary dramatically.

▶ *A search engine may be able to find a program for you by name (such as* ***WSFinger****), but it may not be as successful if you enter a filename (such as* ***WSFNGR.ZIP****). To find a file by name, try using one of the FTP search engines mentioned on page 132, or use an Archie search, as explained on page 154.*

Searching the Web Directories

Top of the league of web directories is Yahoo, which now has a particularly relevant 'UK & Ireland' site at **http://www.yahoo.co.uk**. When you first arrive at the Yahoo site, you'll see a search-engine style textbox into which you can type keywords if you prefer to do your search that way. However, you'll also see a collection of hypertext links below that, and these are the key to the directory system. Starting from a choice of broad categories on this page, you can then dig more deeply into the system to find links to more specific information.

For example, click on the **Computers and Internet** link. On the next page, you'll see the list of sub-categories, which includes **Graphics**, **Hardware**, **Multimedia**, **Training**, and many more subjects. Click on the **Multimedia** link, and you'll see another list of multimedia-related categories. Below this list of categories, you'll see another list: these are links to multimedia-related sites rather than more Yahoo categories. To find out more about multimedia, you can click one of these to visit that site; to find out more about an area of multimedia such as sound, video or virtual reality, you can click that category in the upper list.

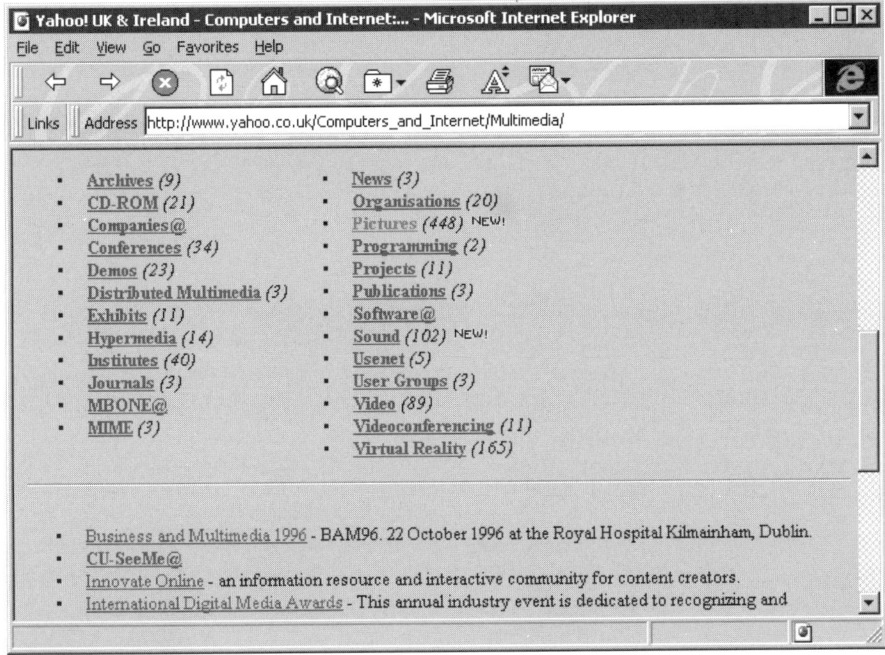

◀ Choose a more specific Yahoo category from the upper list, or a direct link to a web site from the lower.

BY THE WAY

One for the kids

The Internet is teeming with web sites for children, and Yahoo has a sister-site called **Yahooligans at http://www.yahooligans.com**. The format is the same as Yahoo's main site, but all the links lead to pages for, or by, kids.

The layout is pretty easy to follow when you've browsed around for a few minutes, but Yahoo has simplified it further by using bold and plain text to help you identify where you're going. Bold text means that this is a link to another Yahoo category; plain text indicates that it's a link to a page elsewhere on the Web that contains the sort of information you've been searching for. Beside most of the bold category-links, you'll also see a number in brackets, such as **Pictures (448)**. This number tells you how many links you'll find in that category.

Why do some categories finish with an @ sign?

The '@' sign indicates a cross-reference to a different main category. For example, click on **Companies@** and you'll be moving from the Computers and Internet heading to the **Business and Economy** heading. You'll find links to multimedia companies here, but other categories will be more related to business matters than to computing.

Easy Web-searching with Internet Explorer

To reach a search site quickly in Internet Explorer, click the **Search** button on the toolbar. Clicking this button will open the search engine at Microsoft, but you can change this default. Click on Internet Explorer's **View** menu, select **Options** and click the **Navigation** tab. From the drop-down list beside **Page** choose **Search Page**. Next, double-click inside the box marked Address to highlight the text already there, and type in the URL of the page you'd like to use instead. Click **OK**, and you've reprogrammed your Search button!

BY THE WAY

Instead of clicking the **Search** button and waiting for the search page to load, try this quicker method offered by Explorer. In the address bar, type a question mark, followed by two keywords you want to search for, such as **?motor racing**, and press Enter. You'll be taken immediately to the search-results page. If you want to search for only one keyword, you'll need to enter it twice (e.g. **?squirrels squirrels**).

Finding People on the Internet

Finding people on the Internet is a bit of a black art – after all, there are in excess of forty million users, and few would bother to 'register' their details even if there were an established directory. In addition, of course, if you move your access account to a different online service or IAP, your email address will change too (more on that in Chapter 15). It's all a bit hit and miss, but let's look at a few possibilities.

Flick Through the White Pages

In the UK, the term Yellow Pages is synonymous with finding businesses. White pages is a type of directory listing people (what we usually call a telephone book), and the Internet has a few 'white pages' directories that may turn up trumps. Some of these rely on people submitting their details voluntarily; others take the more crafty approach of searching newsgroups and adding the email addresses of anyone posting an article. Searching white pages is just like using any other search engine.

- **Bigfoot** at **http://bigfoot.co.uk**. Don't be fooled by the URL – the search engine itself is in the USA, but this is the directory most likely to find the email address of a UK Internet user.
- **Four11** at **http://www.four11.com**. The biggest and most popular 'people locator' in the USA, which searches the Internet for email addresses and accepts individual submissions. Details may include a user's hobbies, postal address and telephone number, but most entries are from the USA.
- **Infospace** at **http://www.infospace.com/info/people.htm**. Another US service, again unlikely to produce an email address for anyone living outside the USA.

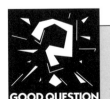

GOOD QUESTION

Are there any other white pages I can search?

Head off to **http://www.yahoo.com/Reference/White_Pages** for links to other white pages. You could also try The Directory Of Directories at **http://www.procd.com/hl/direct.htm**, which could help you find someone if you know something about their hobbies, interests, or occupation.

If you really want to find an address and are prepared to wait a little while for a result, you may find someone you're looking for at the American college MIT (Massachusetts Institute of Technology), which regularly scans Usenet archives to extract names and email addresses. Send an email message to **mail-server@rtfm.mit.edu**, with the text **send usenet-addresses/*name*** as the body of the message (remembering not to add your email signature on the end). Provided that the person you're trying to trace has posted a message to a newsgroup in the past, you should, in theory, receive a reply containing the email address. As an example, it should be possible to retrieve my email address by sending the message: **send usenet-addresses/Rob Young**. (It's worth remembering that this will work only if the person has posted an article to Usenet using their own name; some users frequent the type of newsgroup in which it's common to post your messages under an alias.)

GOOD QUESTION

Can I find the email addresses of the famous?

If they've ever posted an article to a newsgroup you may just get lucky, although you may get a list of dozens and dozens of Hugh Grants or Jennifer Anistons (of Friends fame). One site to try that keeps a handy list of popular celebs is simply called Celebrity Email Addresses. For obvious reasons there are no guarantees of accuracy, but if you fancy emailing John Travolta, Bob Hoskins, or Madonna (among others), head off to the much visited site at **http://oscar.teclink.net/~chip1120/email.html**. You might even get yourself a famous penpal!

Back to the Search Engines

Some of the popular search engines mentioned earlier in this chapter also have 'people-finder' options. If you visit Lycos, you can click the **People Find** button to search for someone's email address. Excite has buttons marked **People Finder** (for addresses and telephone numbers) and **Email Lookup** (for email addresses). In Infoseek, click the arrow button on the drop-down list box and choose **Email Addresses**, then type someone's name into the textbox.

▶ *Although the only truly reliable way of finding someone's email address is to ask, you could try using Whois (covered on page 159) as a last resort.*

Yellow Pages – Searching for Businesses

Just as there are white pages on the Net, there are Yellow Pages. The difference is that businesses want to be found to the extent that they'll pay to be listed, so these searches will almost always yield results. Two of the most useful search engines for UK businesses are Yell (the Yellow Pages we all know and love, in its online incarnation), and Freepages.

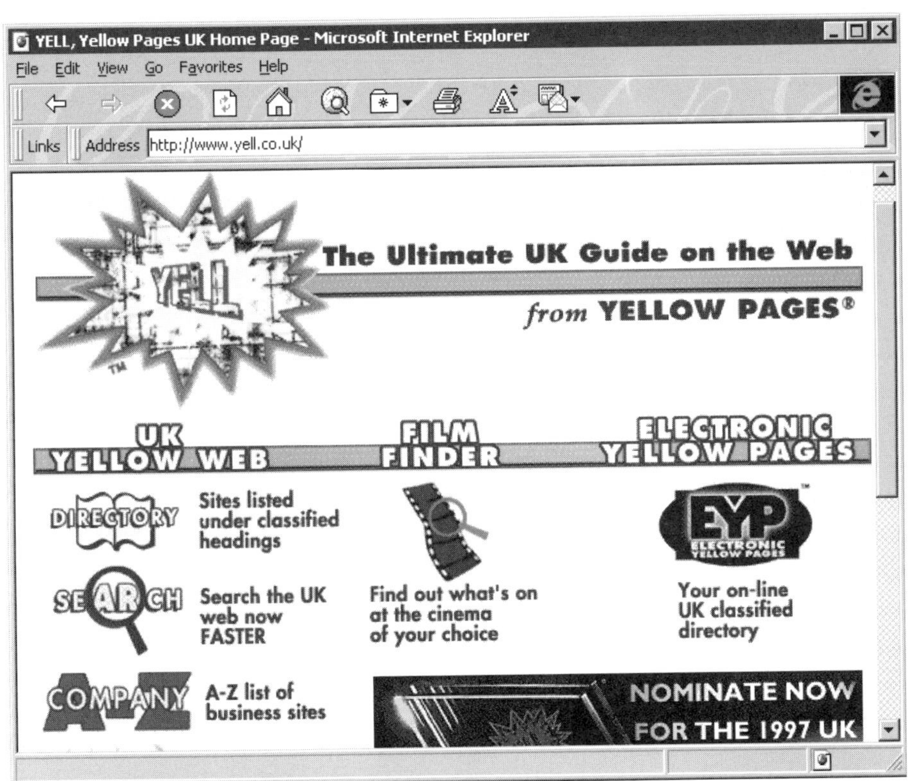

◀ The (bright) Yellow Pages online is the ideal place to find the web sites and contact details of UK companies, and to take your pick of the flicks.

Yell, at **http://www.yell.co.uk**, is an ideal place to begin a search for a UK company. Click one of the icons on the left to look for a company's web site by category or in an alphabetical list. There's also a search engine dedicated to finding UK web sites. The EYP link on the right takes you to an automated search of the Electronic Yellow Pages: enter a company's location, and either a Business Type or Company Name, to start the search. The results mirror those you'd expect to find in the paper version. As a bonus, click the centre icon to find out what films are showing at almost any cinema in the country.

Guesswork is good

If you can't trace the URL of a company's web site, try typing a few guesses into your browser's address bar. Most companies use their own name as their domain name, so if you're looking for a company called Dodgy Goods plc, try **www.dodgygoods.com** or **www.dodgygoods.co.uk**. If you look at the company URLs given in the next few chapters, you'll see how likely this is to get a result.

The Freepages site, located at **http://www.freepages.co.uk**, is dedicated to finding companies' addresses and telephone numbers, and works in a slightly different way from Yell. Begin by entering a town or city in which the company is based. On the next page, confirm the county listed is correct. Finally, on the third page, choose a category of business to search for from the drop-down list box. The search will return a list of all the businesses of that type in your chosen area. This is a great way to search if, for example, you need a plumber and you're currently too damp to care which plumber it is.

If you haven't found the company yet, it's either American or it doesn't want to be found! To search for US companies, head off to Excite at **http://www.excite.com** and click the **Yellow Pages** button. Enter a company name and category description, together with location details if known, and click the Search button. If the category you have chosen doesn't match an Excite category, you'll be given a list of similar categories to choose from. You can also try **http://www.companiesonline.com**, a new addition to the Lycos search engine family. If you're looking for financial or performance-related information about a company, visit Infoseek and select **Company Profiles** from the drop-down list to search through almost fifty thousand US companies. Finally, of course, there's the good old workhorse, Yahoo. Visit **http://www.yahoo.co.uk/Business_and_Economy/Companies** and you'll be presented with a list of over a hundred categories. The sites you'll find in Yahoo's categories cover the UK and Ireland as well as America and beyond.

Searching the Newsgroups

There's more value to searching Usenet newsgroups than there appears at first. For example, with so many thousands of groups to choose from, a quick search for the keywords that sum up your favourite topic could help you determine the most suitable newsgroup to subscribe to. Or perhaps you need a quick answer to a technical question – it's almost certainly been answered in a newsgroup article.

One of the best sites to use for newsgroup searches is Deja News at **http://www.dejanews.com**, which looks just like any other search engine you've come across in this chapter, except that there's a choice of two textboxes for keywords. If you're looking for a newsgroup, enter a keyword into the lower of the two to find groups that discuss the subject you want. If you're looking for individual articles, use the upper textbox. The search results list 20 articles at a time (with the usual button at the end of the page to fetch the next 20), and include authors' details and the names of the newsgroups in which the articles were found. Click on one of the articles to read it and you'll find a handy button-bar added to the page that lets you view the topic's thread, read the next or previous article, and post replies to the newsgroup or the article's author by email.

BY THE WAY

Stick to what you know

If you search Deja News for newsgroups, you can click any newsgroup you find on the results list to read its articles. But, although it's possible, it's not the easiest way to navigate a newsgroup – you'll find it simpler to run your newsreader program and read the articles from the chosen group with that instead.

The great value of Deja News is that articles are available here long after they were first posted to Usenet. The only possible fly in the ointment is that the group you want may not be covered. If it isn't, head for Infoseek's search engine and choose **Usenet** from the drop-down list.

Surf's Up! Now, Where Shall I Go?

All dressed up and nowhere to surf? The sheer unpredictability of the World Wide Web will almost certainly tempt you at times, even if there's nothing in particular you need to do. For those moments when you've just got to surf, here's a list of sites that give you somewhere worth surfing to. (The official term for these is 'cool' sites. On the Web, you have to aspire to being cool!)

- **Cool Site Of The Day** A single cool site every day. And every day the entire universe goes to visit the lucky recipient of the title. You'll also find The Still Cool Archive, The Cool-O-Meter, and Cool Site Of The Year. Bucket-loads of cool, and you'll find it all at **http://cool.infi.net.**
- **Top 50 UK Web Sites** Links sorted into 26 categories such as Jobs, Finance, Jokes, Autos, ShowBiz and Travel. The sites are sorted by how many visits they get, although there's a fair sprinkling of 'dead' links (links to sites that no longer exist). Head for **http://www.100hot.com**.
- **PC Magazine's Top 100 Web Sites** Top sites chosen by the magazine's editors, and sorted into five categories: Commerce, Computing, Entertainment, News and Reference. Go to **http://www.zdnet.com/~pcmag/special/web100** for this one.
- **Weekly Hot 100** A simple list of sites numbered 1 to 50 according to how many visitors (or 'hits') each site has had in the last week. You'll find a huge variety of stuff here, but they must all be good, mustn't they? Skip off to **http://www.top50.co.uk**.
- **Jacob Richman's Hot Sites** Twenty-eight categories of useful links sniffed out and sorted by Jacob himself, including Humour, Education, Law and Music. Although he has no greater claim to fame than any other web surfer, Jacob has a keen eye for good sites, and a well-organised collection of links. Find this at **http://www.jr.co.il/hotsites/hotsites.htm**.

BY THE WAY

Finding more cool sites

Back to those search engines again. At Lycos you can click a Top 5% button to find recommended sites; Excite has a Web Reviews button. You can also try a keyword search in any search engine for cool sites or best web sites. Or skip ahead to Chapter 21 for some sites that make cool use of multimedia.

The World Wide Web is an art form, and like any form of art, some people can do it and some people can't. Depending on your viewpoint, bad art can be far more entertaining than good art: there are countless web sites out there which, far from being cool, have been caught with their trousers around their ankles. If you've overdosed on cool, try these as an antidote:

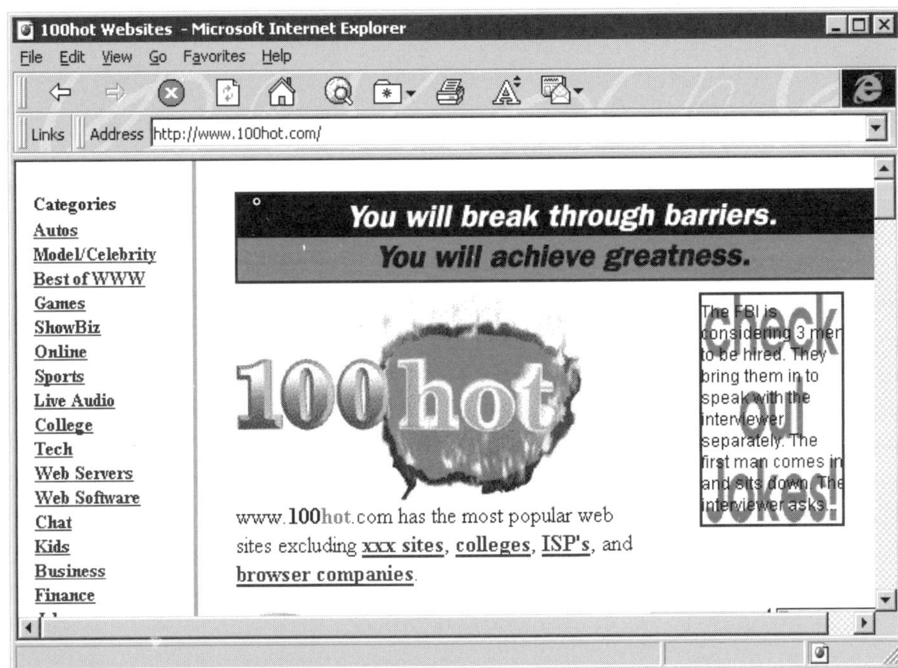

◀ 100 hot web sites – if you've used Yahoo, you'll know exactly what to do with those categories on the left.

- **The Worst Of The Web** Click on the large image to take a trip through the current 'worst sites', accompanied with comments from your three cartoon hosts. Alternatively, follow the links below the image to see previous award-winners in this category. Visit **http://www.worstoftheweb.com** for this 'bland bombshell'.
- **Mirsky's Worst Of The Web** A famous site, sadly now closed, but you can still visit Mirsky's past winners, take the Drunk Browsing Test and surf through the Nicknames Page. You'll find Mirsky's at **http://mirsky.com/wow**.
- **The World Wide Web Hall Of Shame** Links to some of the best 'dead flies' that litter the Web, replete with introductory comments, at **http://www.rt66.com/smcinnis/hos**.

13

SHAKING THE SOFTWARE TREE

In This Chapter...

- ▶ Unravel the mysteries of shareware, nagware and postcard-ware
- ▶ Explore the top software collections on the Web
- ▶ Organise your directories & simplify your life
- ▶ Dealing with compressed archives
- ▶ Installing & un-installing software

The Internet is knee-deep in software, and much of it is free. I've already pointed you towards some of the best Internet programs and utilities, but these are just the tip of the software iceberg; you can find just about any type of file you want, from screensavers to word processors, icons to personal organisers. And with just a single click, you can download and start using them immediately.

The Internet is reckoned to be the software supply-line of the future. Within a few years, we'll be purchasing and downloading all our software over the Internet, and programs will automatically update themselves when newer versions and improvements become available. One bonus of this is that software should become much cheaper by removing the middleman and the need for flashy packaging. The downside, as you're sure to discover pretty soon, is that you'll spend all the savings you make on ever-larger hard-disks to hold all these goodies!

Shareware, Freeware, Everyware

Every piece of software you find on the Internet is something-ware, and the two terms you'll come across the most are **freeware** and **shareware**. Freeware is easily explained – it's free! If you like it, you keep it, no questions asked. However, there are usually a few limitations: the author will usually retain copyright, and you won't be allowed to sell copies to anyone.

GOOD QUESTION

Why is freeware free? Doesn't it work?

Freeware is often as good as an equivalent product you'd pay for. For many programmers, the reward comes in knowing that their creation is being used and appreciated. On a more fundamental level, perhaps, the administration involved in collecting money from all over the world takes up a lot of time that could be more enjoyably spent programming something else!

Shareware is an economical method of selling software that bypasses packaging, advertising and distribution costs, resulting in a much cheaper product for us and a much easier life for its author. The most important benefit of the shareware concept is that you get the opportunity to try out the software before you buy it, but the understanding is that you should pay for it if you continue to use it beyond the specified trial period (known as **registering** the software). In return for registering, you'll normally receive the latest version, and you may be entitled to free upgrades as they become available. Apart from shareware and freeware, there are a few more terms you'll come across in reference to software.

Term	Meaning
Postcard-ware	Instead of paying for the software, you send the author a picture-postcard of your home town.
Nagware	A type of shareware program that nags you to register it by regularly displaying a little 'Buy Me' dialog that has to be clicked to make it go away. Only money can stop it doing that.
Crippleware	The software is crippled in some way that prevents you making full use of it until you pay, usually by removing the options to save or print anything you create with it. Sometimes more formally referred to as save-disabled.
Time-limited	You have full use of the program for a set period (usually 30 days) after which the software won't run until you enter a valid registration number.
Alpha versions	These are very early versions of a program which may (or may not) be unreliable, but are released to anyone willing to try them. The author hopes that you'll report any problems you find so that they can be fixed. Unless you're a very experienced computer-user, avoid any software labelled as an alpha.
Beta versions	Later, and usually more stable, versions of a program than alphas, but still not regarded as a saleable product. You may prefer to wait a little longer for the finished article.

Most of the software you download will include several text files that you can read in a text-editor such as Windows Notepad or any word processor. Keep a lookout for a file called **Readme.txt** or **Register.txt** that will tell you about any limitations of use, provide installation details, and explain where and how to register the software.

Where Can I Find Software?

The best places to find software are all on the World Wide Web. If you're feeling adventurous, you could visit an anonymous FTP site (see page 126) and root around its directories and Index files, but that's not the easiest way to go about it. (OK, adventurers, go to the Imperial College site at **src.doc.ic.ac.uk** for oodles of software, a fast response, and very informative Index files.) Most of the software sites on the Web use a directory layout from which you select the type of software you're looking for, browse through a list of software-titles and descriptions, and click a link to start downloading the file you want. (For more on downloading files with your browser, skip back to page 78).

JARGON BUSTER

Mirror site

The most popular web sites are those that give something away, and software sites are top of that list. If everyone had to visit the same site, that server would slow to a crawl and no one would be able to download anything. So exactly the same collection of files is placed on other servers around the world to spread the load, and these are called mirrors. When you get a choice of sites to download, you'll usually get the quickest results by choosing the site that is geographically closest to you.

Here's a quickfire list of some of the best software sites that you can find on the Web:

- **Tucows** The definitive site when you want to find Internet applications for Windows. Tucows has mirror sites all over the world, but visit **http://tucows.cableinet.net** for a good, responsive connection in the UK – and a few pictures of cows.
- **Shareware.com** One of the best sites for software of all types, located at **http://www.shareware.com**. It has a keyword search facility to help you track down a particular program by name, or a type of program.
- **Windows95.com** An excellent site providing all kinds of software for Windows 95 and later, found at **http://www.windows95.com**.
- **Software Warehouse** Possibly the latest shareware source on the Web, with thousands upon thousands of software products, some by very well-known software companies. Searching is easy, and there are good descriptions of each item. You'll find this at **http://www4.zdnet.com/wsources/content/current/warehous.html**

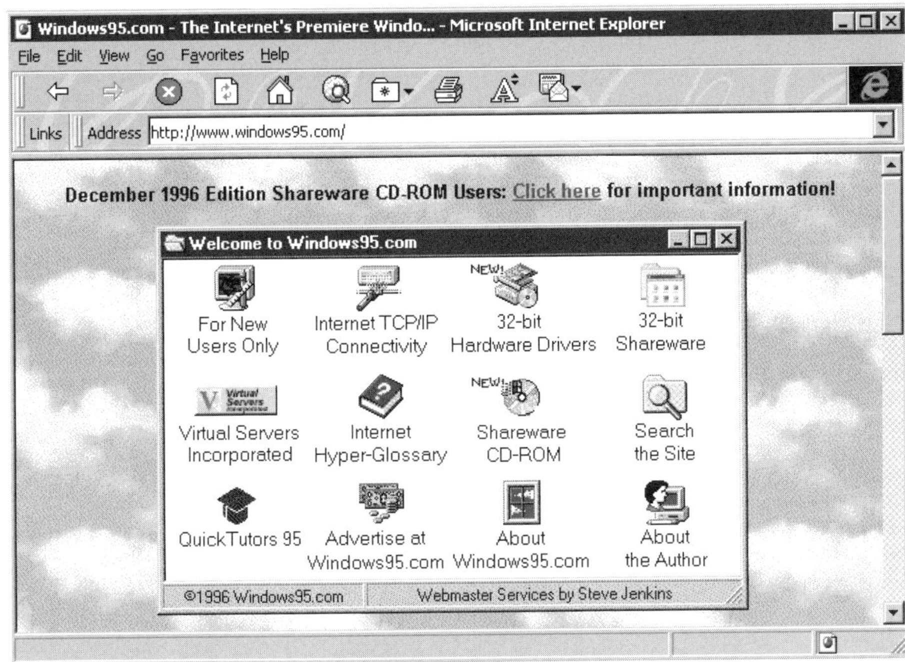

◀ Navigate the **Windows95.com** site by clicking icons instead of dull hypertext links.

Apart from directories of software (and you'll find links to more of those on the free CD accompanying this book), there are a number of other avenues worth exploring. If you visit **http://www.yahoo.com/Computers_and_Internet/Software/Shareware** you'll find a long list of links to shareware pages, most of which are accompanied by useful descriptions. Or go to one of the search engines mentioned in the previous chapter and use the keyword **software** or **shareware**. If there's a particular type of program you're looking for, such as an appointments calendar, try searching for **freeware shareware +calendar**.

BY THE WAY

Shareware news by email

If you want to keep up with the latest shareware releases, hop over to **http://www.shareware.com/SW/Subscribe/?swd**, type your email address into the box, and click the **Subscribe** button. Every week you'll receive an email message listing the most popular downloads at Shareware.com and details of the latest arrivals.

Downloading – Choose Your Directory

If you plan to download a lot of software, it helps to create a few directories first to keep things organised. So I'm going to pile straight in and make a suggestion that works well for me. First, create a new directory on your hard-disk and call it **Internet**. Then open that directory and create three subdirectories called **Download**, **Temp** and **Store**. You may want to choose different names for the directories, but here's how they're used:

Internet Simply a handy container for the other three directories.

Download When you click a file to download in your browser and choose to save it to disk, the browser will ask you to choose a directory to save into. Choose this directory. When you've used this directory once, it will automatically be offered to you for future downloads.

Temp Almost all of the programs you download will be in compressed archives (I'll explain those in a moment). In some cases, before you can start to install the software it has to be un-compressed, and the Temp folder provides somewhere to put those un-compressed files. As soon as the software has been installed you can delete the contents of the Temp folder.

Store You may want to keep some of the compressed files you download, perhaps as safety copies or to give to someone else later. Move them from Download into this directory when you've finished un-compressing and installing them so that you'll know they've been dealt with.

If you download files by FTP, as discussed in Chapter 9, you can enter the path to the Download directory in WS_FTP's **Initial Download Directory** box when you create a new session profile, saving you the need to click around in the left-hand window before you start to download a file. The Store directory is a good place to keep Index files from FTP sites you expect to find useful in future.

What Are Compressed Archives?

If you wanted to send several small packages to someone through the post, you'd probably put them all in a box and send that for simplicity. An archive works in a similar way – it's a type of file that contains other files, making them easy to move around on the Internet. Most of the software you download will consist of several files, including the program itself, a Help file, text files that tell you how to register, and so on. Downloading a single archive that contains the whole package is far simpler than downloading a dozen separate files one at a time. Before you can use the files in the archive they have to be extracted from it.

Most archives are also compressed. Using clever software trickery, files can be squeezed into these archives so that they take up much less space – sometimes only a few per cent of their original size – which means that downloading an archive will be a vastly quicker job than individually downloading its constituent files. When you extract the files from the archive, they'll automatically be un-compressed at the same time.

There are a few different types of archive, but all are very easy to handle, and you'll be able to recognise them by their icons, shown in the screenshot below.

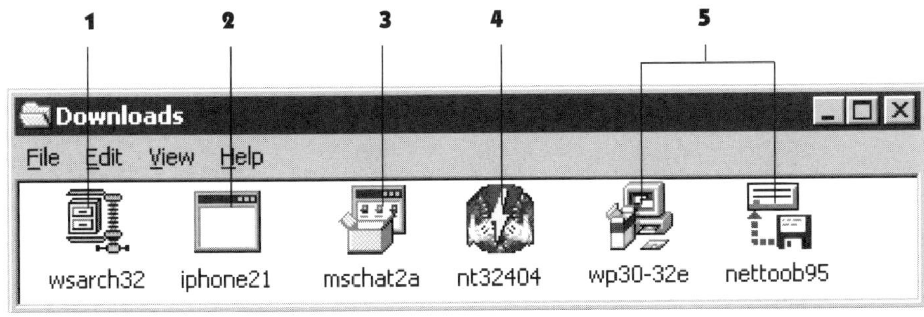

◀ Archive files are easy to recognise by their icons.

1 A ZIP archive – these files have the file extension **.zip**. You'll come across a lot of these, and they may contain just one file or many. You'll need a special program to extract the files from a ZIP archive, and the best of the lot is called WinZip (shown in the next screenshot). You'll find this on the CD-ROM accompanying this book, or you can download it yourself from **http://www.winzip.com**. It's very easy to use, and includes good Help files, so I won't explain it all here.
2 This is an MS-DOS self-extracting archive with the extension **.exe**. Copy this file into your Temp directory, double-click it, and its contents will automatically be extracted and placed in the same directory.

3,4,5 These are all types of self-extracting archive, also with the **.exe** extension, but they're even easier than **2**. Double-click the file's icon, and everything should happen automatically. The files will be extracted, the setup program will run to install the software, and the program should then delete the extracted files to clean up any mess it made.

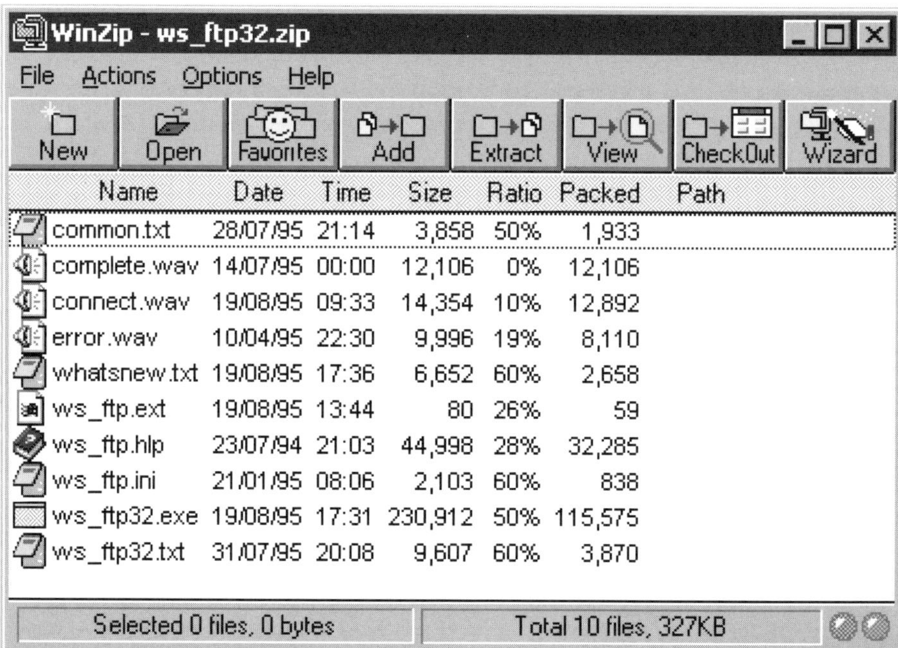

▶ View and extract the contents of an archive using WinZip.

GOOD QUESTION

What is a 'file extension'

A group of three (or sometimes more) characters at the end of a filename, preceded by a dot. For the file **readme.txt** the extension is **.txt**. The extension tells you and your computer what type of file it is, which determines what type of program is needed to open that file.

There are several other types of archive, and they'll get a mention later in the chapter, but almost every piece of software you download will either be a **.zip** or an **.exe** archive. However, archive files don't just contain programs –

you may find a collection of pictures or icons gathered into an archive, or word-processor documents, sound and video clips, etc – their portability and smaller size makes them the favourite way to transfer all types of file over the Internet.

Installing Your New Program

Before you start to install any software you've downloaded, your first job should be to check it for viruses, and we'll discuss those further in a moment. What you do next depends on the type of file you downloaded. If it's a ZIP file, use WinZip to extract its contents to your Temp directory; if it's an MS-DOS self-extracting file, copy it to your Temp directory and double-click it. Next, have a look in your Temp directory for a file called **install.exe** or **setup.exe**. If you see one of these, double-click it and follow any onscreen instructions to install the software. If you can't see one of these files, the software probably doesn't have an automatic setup program. Create a new directory somewhere, move the files into it, and create a shortcut to the program on your Start Menu or in Program Manager for easy access. With the new program installed, you can delete all those extracted files in your Temp directory.

BY THE WAY

Close programs first

Before you install any new software, it's a good idea to close any programs you're running (some setup programs remind you to do this). Sometimes the setup program needs to alter existing files on your computer while installing the software, and if another program is running it may not be able to do so.

The other types of self-extracting archives just need a double-click. Usually their setup program will run automatically and you can just follow the instructions to complete the installation. On occasions, though, you may find one of these that just extracts all the files and leaves you the job of finding the **install** or **setup** file, and of deleting the extracted files afterwards.

What if you don't like the software and want to un-install it? If the software had its own setup program that installed it for you, the same program can usually un-install it too – look in its directory for a file called uninstall.exe and double-click it. If there isn't one, run the install or setup program again to see if there's a button marked Uninstall (if there isn't, click Cancel). Failing that, Windows may be able to un-install it for you. Open Control Panel, double-click **Add/Remove Programs** and see if this program is on the list; if it is, select it and click the **Add/Remove** button to un-install it. If you simply created a new directory and copied the program files into it, you can delete the directory and its contents, and then also remove any shortcuts you added.

Scanning for Viruses

The risk from viruses on the Internet is pretty small and far less significant than some of the hysterical chatter would have you believe. And if you are unfortunate enough to get a virus on your computer, it won't necessarily be harmful – some viruses are jokey little things that do no more than make your computer go beep once a year. But there are others that can make a nasty mess of your system by trashing your files, swallowing your disk space, and filling your memory, and these are definitely best avoided. Fortunately they're also easily avoided.

GOOD QUESTION

What is a virus?

A virus is a small piece of code maliciously inserted into an ordinary program. When the program is run, the virus immediately starts running too, and begins to do whatever it was programmed to do. Most viruses can replicate themselves and often invade other programs.

There are two popular virus-checking programs widely in use, and both can be downloaded from the Internet.

- McAfee VirusScan, available from **http://www.mcafee.com**
- Norton AntiVirus from **http://www.symantec.com/avcenter/index.html**.

Which of these you choose doesn't really matter, but you must remember to regularly update it – about every couple of months. This will ensure you're protected from the latest viruses.

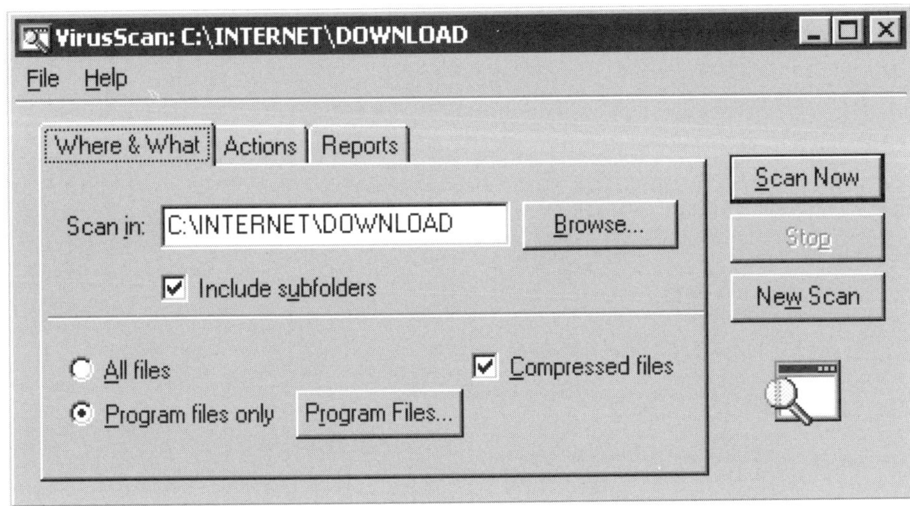

◀ McAfee VirusScan – a simple but effective virus checker.

So, what sort of files should you scan for viruses? The answer is any file with an **.exe** extension, including self-extracting archives. After extracting files from a ZIP archive, always virus-check any .exe files it contained before you run them. You should also check any documents containing little 'macro' programs. Files that are simply displayed by a program (such as a picture, video, or text file) are safe. Virus-checking software will tell you if a file contains a virus, and can usually 'kill' any it finds at the click of a button. If you're unsure whether a particular file constitutes a risk, virus-check it – it only takes a few seconds.

What Are All Those File Types?

So far we've only looked at downloading programs from the Net, but you'll find many different types of file there – documents, sounds, videos, images, and a lot more. Clicking a link to any file will download it regardless of what type of file it is, and your browser will ask you whether you want to open it immediately or save it to disk to look at later (as we discussed in Chapter 6). But first you'll need to be able to recognise these different types of file by their extension and make sure you've got a program that can display them. The list of computer file extensions is endless, and I'd be crazy to try to list all of them, but here's a brief description of the file extensions you're likely to find on the Net. Some of these can be displayed or played by your browser itself, and many are compatible with programs included with Windows.

File Extension	Description of File Type
.arc, .arj	Two older types of compressed archive, similar to ZIP files
.au, .aif, .aiff, .snd, .aifc	A type of sound file used by Apple Mac computers. Internet Explorer will play these files itself
.avi	A Video For Windows file. Windows Media Player will play these once they're downloaded
.bmp, .pcx	Bitmap files. View these in Windows Paint or Paintbrush.
.doc	A Microsoft Word document. If you don't have Word you can use Windows 95's WordPad (although you may lose some of the document's formatting) or search **www.microsoft.com** for a viewer called WordView
.flc, .fli, .aas	Animation files. Once downloaded, Windows Media Player should handle these
.gif, .jpg, .jpeg, .jpe, .jfif	Image files often used on web pages, and displayed by your browser
.gz, .gzip	Another less common type of compressed archive
.htm, .html	World Wide Web documents (better known as 'pages')
.mid, .rmi	MIDI files, a type of compact sound file. Windows Media Player can play these after you've downloaded them
.mov, .qt	A QuickTime movie file
.mpg, .mpeg, .mpe	An MPEG video
.mp2	An MPEG audio file
.pdf	Portable Document Format. A hypertext document similar to web pages that can be read only by Adobe Acrobat
.ra, .ram	A RealAudio sound file
.rtf	A Rich Text Format document that can be read by almost any Windows word-processor
.tar	Yet another type of compressed archive
.txt, .text	A plain text file. Your browser should display these, or you can read them in Windows Notepad or any word processor
.uue	A UUencoded file (see page 96)
.wav	A Windows wave audio sound. Your browser should automatically play these, or you can use Media Player or Sound Recorder
.wri	A Windows Write document. Most Windows word-processors will display these if you don't have a copy of Write
.wrl	A VRML (virtual reality) 3D object. (We'll look at virtual reality in Chapter 21)

You'll notice that some of these files have two slightly different extensions (such as **.htm** and **.html**, or **.jpg** and **.jpeg**). This is simply because MS-DOS and Windows 3.11 can't work with four-character extensions, so shorter versions are used instead. The file types are exactly the same.

The Top Five – Complete Your Software Arsenal

A few of the file types listed in the table opposite can't be viewed or played by any program included with Windows – you'll need to find a separate program if you download files of these types. Without further ado, here are my top-five recommended accessories and viewers which, between them, will leave you ready for almost anything the Internet can throw at you.

- **WinZip** from **http://www.winzip.com**. Apart from handling ZIP files, WinZip will extract files from almost any type of compressed archive, and can also decode UUencode or MIME attachments sometimes included in email messages and newsgroup articles. Don't even stop to think about it – you need this program as soon as you hit the Net!
- **LView Pro** from **http://www.lview.com**. A fast and easy image-file viewer that supports all the popular file formats, as well as some of the not-so-popular ones. LView can also create contact sheets containing multiple images, or display them one at a time as a slideshow.
- **RealAudio Player** from **http://www.realaudio.com**. RealAudio is a streaming audio format. Many web sites now have RealAudio sound, and some radio stations use it to transmit live over the Internet. This type of program is known as a **plug-in** because it automatically 'plugs itself into' your browser and waits invisibly in the background until it's needed.

GOOD QUESTION

Streaming

On your surfing trips you'll come across the terms 'streaming audio' and 'streaming video'. Streaming means that the file will start to play almost as soon as you click the link to it; you can watch or listen to it while it downloads instead of having to wait until the download has finished.

- **Net Toob** from **http://www.nettoob.com**. A live streaming MPEG video player which you can also use to play MPEG videos you've already downloaded or found elsewhere. MPEG is the most popular video format on the Internet, and Net Toob handles it better than anything else around. As if that wasn't enough, it can also play most of the other video and sound formats mentioned in the table opposite!

- **Acrobat Reader** from **http://www.adobe.com**. PDF is a popular format for text-based documents such as help files, magazines, and research literature. Documents can include embedded images and fonts, together with hyperlinks to help you navigate long documents easily.

Some of the other types of file we've covered in this chapter can be played in a Windows program, but you have to wait for the file to download, and then find and double-click it, which rather spoils the surfing experience. In Chapter 21, we'll look further at some of the other multimedia plug-ins and viewers you can add to your system that add the necessary capabilities to your browser.

14

SAFETY ON THE INTERNET

In This Chapter...

- Keep your kids safe on the Internet
- The truth about credit-card security on the Net
- Active content on the World Wide Web
- Are cookies really dangerous?
- Email – privacy & encryption

Safety, or the lack of it, is a much-hyped area of Internet life. According to many press articles, as soon as you go online you're going to be faced with a barrage of pornography, your credit-card number will be stolen, your personal email messages will be published far and wide, and your children will be at the mercy of paedophile rings.

Of course, articles like these make good news stories and are much more interesting than 'Child surfs Internet and sees no pornography', for example. In this chapter we'll sort out what the risks actually are, and what you can do to minimise them.

Will My Kids Be Safe on the Internet?

The Internet has its fair share of sex and smut, just as it has motoring, cookery, sports, films, and so on. I'm not going to pretend that your kids can't come into contact with explicit images and language, but there are two important points to note. First, you're no more likely to stumble upon pornography while looking for a sports site than you are to stumble upon film reviews or recipes. If you want to find that sort of content, you have to go looking for it. Second, most of the sexually explicit sites on the World Wide Web are private – to get inside you need a credit card. Nevertheless, there are dangers on the Net, and given unrestricted freedom, your kids may come into contact with unsuitable material.

GOOD QUESTION

What sort of material could my kids find?

On the Web, the front pages of those private sites are accessible to all, and some contain images and language designed to titillate, and to part you from your cash. The Web's search engines are another risk – enter the wrong keywords (or the right keywords, depending on your viewpoint) and you'll be presented with direct links to explicit sites accompanied by colourful descriptions.

However, these are not good reasons to deny children access to the Internet. Quite simply, the Internet is a fact of life that isn't going to go away, and will feature more strongly in our children's lives than it does in ours. More and more schools are recognising this, and promoting use of the Internet in homework and class projects. The wealth of web sites created by and for children is a great indicator of their active participation in the growth of the Net. Rather than depriving children of this incredible resource, let's look at a few ground rules you should agree with your kids, and some simple measures you can take to make sure that their use of the Internet is both enjoyable and safe.

Establish Some Ground Rules

One way to protect your kids is to surf the Internet with them, or to make a point of discussing their online experiences, the services they use, and the web sites they like to visit. Sometimes it's easier said than done of course – for example, the average teenage boy or girl jealously guards their privacy, and any benevolent parental interest and active involvement can easily be misconstrued as 'prying'. The following rules were taken from the excellent kids' site, Yahooligans! (find their site at **http://www.yahooligans.com**). Read through these with your kids, and make sure they understand the importance of sticking to them.

1. I will not give out personal information such as my address, telephone number, parents' work address/telephone number, or the name and location of my school without my parents' permission.

2. I will tell my parents right away if I come across any information that makes me feel uncomfortable.

3. I will never agree to get together with someone I 'meet' online without first checking with my parents. If my parents agree to the meeting, I will be sure that it is in a public place and bring my mother or father along.

4. I will never send a person my picture or anything else without first checking with my parents.

5. I will not respond to any messages that are mean or in any way make me feel uncomfortable. It is not my fault if I get a message like that. If I do I will tell my parents right away so that they can contact the service provider.

6. I will talk with my parents so that we can set up rules for going online. We will decide upon the time of day that I can be online, the length of time I can be online, and appropriate areas for me to visit. I will not access other areas or break these rules without their permission.

More information for parents

You'll find the document from which these rules were taken at **http://www.yahooligans.com/docs/safety**. For more information, and links to other sites providing similar tips for parents, go to **http://www.safekids.com** or **http://www.larrysworld.com**.

If you're ever concerned about the web sites your children may be visiting, remember that you can open Internet Explorer's History folder to see a list of all recently accessed pages, as explained on page 65. For a clearer picture, click on **View | Details** and then **Last Visited** to sort by date and time.

Finally, there are two Internet services that are definitely not suitable places for children to visit unsupervised: newsgroups and IRC chat channels. Many access providers refuse to carry certain newsgroups, such as the alt.sex and alt.binaries.pictures hierarchies, but articles in some quite innocent newsgroups may contain views or language you wouldn't want your kids to read. The same goes for IRC. As I mentioned in Chapter 10, many chat channels are sexual in nature, and often in name too. But the type of people trying to make contact with children through IRC won't limit themselves to those channels. I suggest that if you have young kids in the house, you don't have an IRC program installed on your computer.

Is any type of chat safe for kids?

Online services' general chat rooms are moderated (controlled by a representative of the service) to keep things friendly – I especially recommend AOL in that department. If you access the net through an IAP, give your children a copy of **PowWow For Kids** (see page 145).

Get a Little Extra Help

If all this seems a bit too much to handle on your own, don't worry! There are many software programs around that can take over some of the supervision for you. Let's start with one you're probably using already –

Internet Explorer. Although Explorer's security is far from watertight, and applies to World Wide Web sites only, it's well worth investigating.

Open Internet Explorer and click on **View | Options | Security**. Click the button marked **Settings...** and enter the same password into both boxes, then click **OK**. You'll see a page like the one shown in the screenshot below. On the first tab, labelled **Ratings**, select one of the four categories and drag the slider to the left or right to choose the level of content you feel is suitable for users to access. For example, for young children you may wish to leave the slider for each category fully to the left.

Next click the **General** tab and you'll see two checkboxes at the top of the page. The first of these, **Users can see sites that have no rating**, is best left empty (unchecked) – this ensures that users will be barred from any site that hasn't been rated by the RSACi (Recreational Software Advisory Council for the Internet). You may want to check the second box, marked **Supervisor can type a password to allow users to view restricted content**; you can then view any site, regardless of content, by typing your password when prompted. Click **OK** to confirm these settings, and you'll be returned to the main Security page. Click on **Enable Ratings** and enter your password, and your security settings will take effect. Any time you want to turn them off, return to the Security page, click **Disable Ratings** and enter your password. You'll need to use this password whenever you want to alter Internet Explorer's security settings, or view restricted sites yourself, so don't forget it!

Although Internet Explorer's ratings system is quite good, it gives no control over other Internet services such as chat, email or newsgroups, and you may find that your kids are barred from many web sites simply because they have no official RSACi rating. To find out more about the RSACi, visit **http://www.rsac.org**.

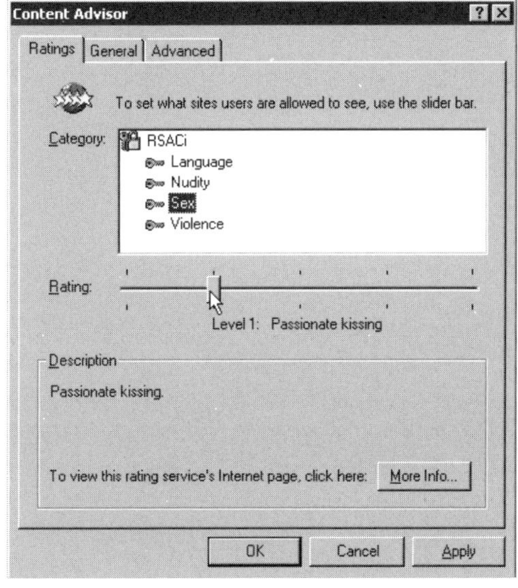

◀ You can use Internet Explorer's built-in ratings system to control access to web sites.

BY THE WAY

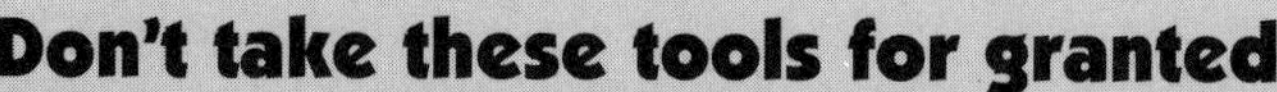

Don't take these tools for granted

While ratings systems and 'babysitter' programs are useful tools for preventing access, bear in mind that a curious or technology-minded child could still find ways to override them. It isn't easy to do it, but these are the same kids that remind us how to set the video-recorder!

To balance maximum access with maximum security, you need a program that can identify the actual content about to be viewed, rather than the name of the page or site. There are many such programs available, but here's a shortlist of the most respected:

- **Net Nanny** from **http://www.netnanny.com/home.html**
- **CYBERsitter** from **http://www.solidoak.com/cysitter.htm**
- **SurfWatch** from **http://www.surfwatch.com**
- **Cyber Patrol** from **http://www.cyberpatrol.com**

I'm going to stick my neck out on this one, and recommend Net Nanny. (Actually I'm not sticking it out too far – you can install the program from the free CD accompanying this book, try it out for 45 days, and then just switch to another if you don't like it.)

The power of this program lies in the fact that it doesn't work solely with Internet programs – it has the capacity to bar access to documents viewed using any program on your computer. When you start your computer, Net Nanny runs invisibly in the background and watches for particular words or phrases. If they appear, Net Nanny instantly replaces them with X's, and threatens to shut down the program in 30 seconds unless you enter a valid password. The words in question may appear in email messages, web pages or chat rooms, they may be in files on floppy-disks or CD-ROMs, or they may form the name of a file. You can add words, phrases, applications and web sites to Net Nanny's list, and download regularly updated lists of restricted sites.

For added parental reassurance, Net Nanny also keeps a record of any attempts to access restricted sites, as do many other programs.

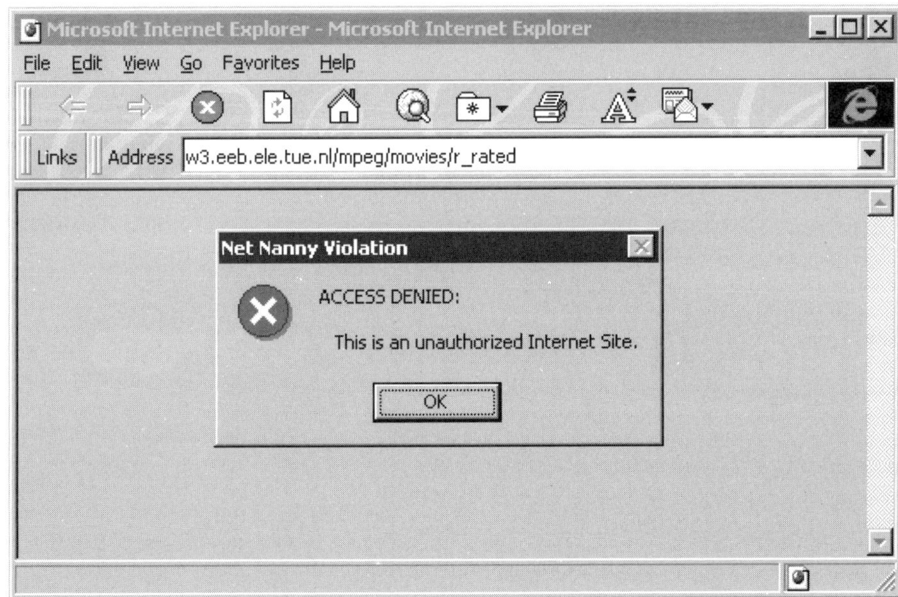

◀ Net Nanny says NO.

Is it Safe to Use My Credit Card on the Net?

Another popular Internet myth is that credit-card transactions are risky because your card number can be stolen. Just consider how you use your credit or debit card in the 'real world'. How many people get to see your card number during a normal week? Do you always ask for the carbon paper after signing for a credit card purchase? The truth is, card numbers are easy to steal. It takes a lot more effort and technical know-how to steal numbers on the Internet, and a single card number isn't valuable enough to warrant the effort.

Making the computer-hacker's job more difficult, browsers can now encrypt the data they send, and most of the web sites at which you can use your credit card run on secure servers that have their own built-in encryption. So when you visit one of these secure sites, enter your card number, and click the button to send it, your number will appear as gibberish to any computer-hacker. In fact, credit-card companies actually regard online transactions as being the safest kind.

▶ *If you're ready for an online spending spree, skip ahead to Chapter 18 to find out how and where to shop on the World Wide Web.*

How can I tell when I visit a secure web site?

In Internet Explorer, look for a little padlock symbol in the lower right corner of the browser. In Netscape's lower left corner you'll see a key symbol; when the key isn't split into two pieces, the site is secure. More and more shopping sites are becoming secure all the time, and those that aren't usually give alternative payment methods, but even an insecure site presents a smaller risk than a restaurant or petrol-station transaction.

Protection From (Over) Active Web Pages

A new piece of jargon has recently been added to the language of the World Wide Web: active content. This term covers various types of small programs that can be included in web pages to provide interactivity and animation. The results of active content are that the Web is better able to function as a productivity tool, and the ride is now so good you won't want to get off.

There are several programming languages used to create this active content, with names such as Java, VBScript and JavaScript. You can learn more about these in Chapter 22, and I'll point you towards some sites where you can sample them for yourself. The language we're interested in right now is called **ActiveX**. This is an extremely powerful and capable language, but its capability means that it can be used to write programs that get into mischief when they run on your computer. At present, ActiveX programs can only run in Internet Explorer, and Explorer also gives you all the options you need to be able to control what's going on.

ActiveX programs are usually referred to as 'controls' by Internet Explorer, or sometimes, more vaguely, just as 'objects'.

Explorer's default settings are going to be fine for most users, but I'll quickly tell you where they are and what they mean. Start Internet Explorer, click on **View | Options** followed by the **Security** tab. You'll see a section at the bottom of the page marked **Active content** containing four checkboxes. You can check and uncheck the lower three boxes to determine whether Explorer will run particular types of program, or remove the checkmark from the upper box (marked **Allow downloading of active content**) to prevent any type of program, animation or sound file from running. Unless you're worried about the effects of active content (and you really have no reason to be) you can leave all four boxes checked.

Next click the button marked **Safety Level...** and you'll see the dialog shown in the screenshot to the right which lets you choose a security level. If you choose **High**, Explorer will not run any controls it doesn't recognise. The **Medium** setting will give you the choice of viewing or ignoring any unrecognised controls. Don't even consider selecting **None** – however minimal a risk may be, there should never be a time in your life when you don't want protection from it!

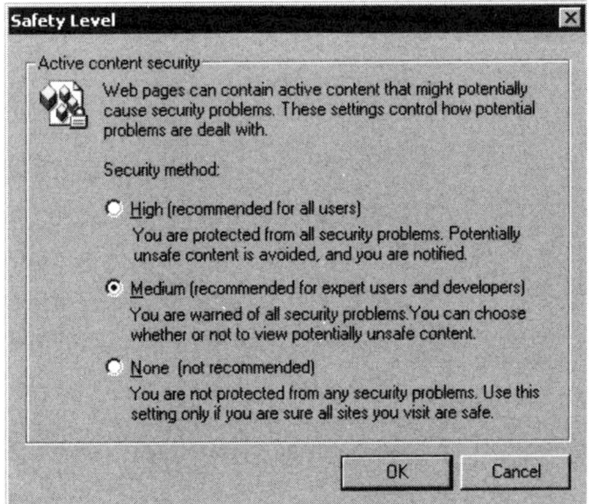

◀ Click an option to choose how Internet Explorer handles active content in web pages.

So how does Explorer know when a control is 'safe'? It uses a system of **publisher certificates**. These certificates are granted to companies by particular authorities, and are automatically installed on your computer when you visit a certified site. When Explorer finds a control on a web page, it searches for a certificate that says the control is from a trustworthy company. If it doesn't find one, it will either not run the control, or it will notify you and ask whether or not you want to run it anyway (depending whether you selected **High** or **Medium** in the **Safety Level** dialog). You can view details of these certificates by going to **View | Options | Security** and clicking the **Sites...** or **Publishers...** buttons.

JARGON BUSTER

Code-signing and Authenticode

Code-signing is a term for the technology that makes this whole certification business work, allowing software writers to put a recognised 'signature' into their controls. The certification system also checks and verifies the authenticity of secure web sites. Authenticode is a trademark for the same technology.

Cookies – Are They Safe to Eat?

They sound cute and harmless, but what are they? They're small text files that are stored on your computer's hard-disk when you visit certain web sites. To look at them, open your Windows directory, and then open the Cookies directory you find inside – you can double-click any of these cookies to read its contents in Notepad.

Cookies can serve several uses to the creator of a web site, and some can even benefit visitors like you and me. A cookie may contain a unique code that identifies you, saving the need to enter a name and password when you visit, and perhaps allowing you to access restricted areas of a site. They're also often used by online shopping sites as a sort of 'supermarket trolley' that keeps track of the purchases you select until you're ready to pay and leave. Sites that rely heavily on displaying banner advertisements for their income may track 'click-throughs', keeping a log of the path you follow through the site and the pages that you decide to visit. Knowing a bit about your interests helps enable the site to target you with the type of adverts most likely to grab your attention.

Do all Cookies have Practical Uses?

No. You may visit a personal site that asks you to enter your name, which it then stores in a cookie. On every future visit, you'll see a message like 'Hello Rob, you've visited this page four times'. It's pointless, but it's still harmless. So, are they safe? Yes, they are. Cookies are often misunderstood – they can't be used to read any other data from your hard-disk, to find out what software you've installed, or to pass on personal information. When you visit a web site, the page doesn't 'search' your hard-disk for a cookie; instead, your browser sends the cookie containing the URL of the site as you click the link.

The wider question is whether you want anyone using your hard-disk as a type of mini-database in this way – it's a point of principle rather than safety. If you want to join the anti-cookie ranks, Internet Explorer can help. Click on **View | Options | Advanced**, and check the box beside **Warn before accepting "cookies"**. Every time a site tries to store a cookie on your disk you'll be given the choice of accepting or rejecting it. However, be warned – some sites just won't let you in if you won't eat the cookie! A more practical method is to delete the entire contents of your Cookies directory once you've finished surfing for the day.

How Private Is My Email?

The words 'email' and 'private' don't go together well. I'm not saying that the world and his dog are going to read every message you send, but email can get you into trouble (and people have got into very deep water from using email where a telephone call or a quiet chat would have been wiser). If you're concerned about who could read it, don't write it.

The most obvious problem is that your 'private' messages can be easily forwarded or redirected, or the recipient could simply fail to delete an incriminating message after reading it. But apart from existing on your computer and the recipient's computer, however briefly, the message also spends time on your access provider's mail server and that of the recipient's access provider. Will the message really be deleted from both? And what if the administrator of one of these systems decides to run a backup while your message is waiting to be delivered?

If you have no option other than to use email to exchange messages of a confidential and sensitive nature, you may want to consider using **encryption** to scramble them. Messages are encrypted and decrypted using two codes called keys that you type into the encryption software. One is your private key, the other is a public key that you'd hand out to anyone who needed to use it, or perhaps post on the Internet. If someone wanted to send you an encrypted message, they'd use your freely available public key to encrypt it, and then send it off as usual. The message can only be decoded using your private key, and only you have access to that key. Likewise, if you wanted to send someone else a private message, you'd use his public key to encrypt it.

Need more encryption information?

The most popular encryption program is called PGP (Pretty Good Privacy). Although unbreakable, it isn't easy to use and you may want an extra program that sits on top and puts a 'friendlier face' on it. Go to **http://www.yahoo.com/Computers_and_Internet/Security_and_Encryption** to learn more about the system and the available software.

15

FAQ – QUESTIONS & ANSWERS

In This Chapter...

- Having trouble connecting to a Web site?
- How you can keep your email address for life
- Combat junk email
- Remain anonymous as you surf the Net
- Internet addiction – fact or fallacy?

Shifting once again into quickfire mode, this chapter contains a collection of answers to recurring questions, as well as problem fixes and pointers to more sites offering useful information.

Why Do I Have to Start My Connection Manually?

This is a question that sometimes crops up for users of Windows 95 and later. Windows uses a system called Dial-Up Networking (DUN) to handle your Internet connection, and, in theory, whenever you start an Internet program and try to access a web site, send email, or whatever, the DUN connection will kick in and automatically connect you.

32-bit and 16-bit programs

This is technical stuff that it's best not to get into. Suffice to say that 32-bit programs are newer and built to run on Windows 95 and later, while 16-bit programs were designed for Windows 3.1. Many programs are available in both 16-bit and 32-bit versions so that you can choose the one that will run on your system.

The trouble is, this only works with 32-bit programs. When you try to do the same with a 16-bit Internet program, it fails. In some cases you may be able to find a more recent, 32-bit version of the program, but a few programs, such as Pegasus Mail, are still only available in 16-bit form.

Why Is the Web So Slow Today?

There could be several reasons. It may be to do with the time you connect. The Internet is used most extensively in the USA so the Net is at its quietest (and therefore its speediest) while the USA is sleeping. Although it isn't a cheap time to connect, you'll normally get a faster response by going online in the morning than the evening. If you're having trouble with a particular site, you can sometimes get things moving by clicking the link again, or, if the page started to download and then stopped, clicking the **Stop** button on the toolbar followed by the **Refresh** button. But if everything seems unreasonably slow, try logging off and then logging back on again – this often seems to result in a faster connection.

Why Can't I Open This URL?

When you click a link to a web page, type in a URL, or even select an entry on your Favorites list, you may not be able to open the page. Either you'll see a plain grey page with the stark heading 'Not Found', a friendlier-looking page that says essentially the same thing, or a dialog from Internet Explorer like the one shown in the next screenshot. So what went wrong?

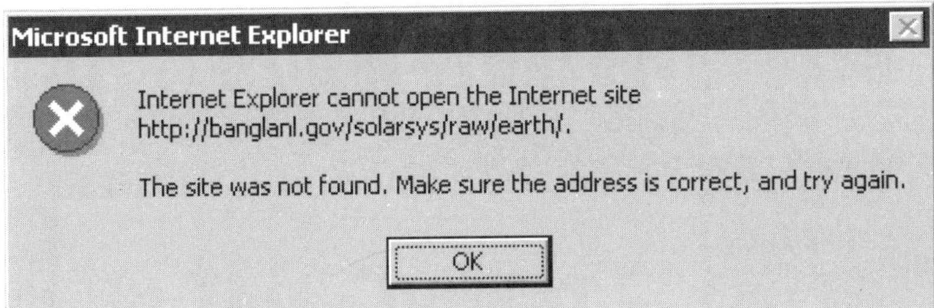

◀ This dialog usually indicates a problem with the domain name in the URL.

Let's take an imaginary URL as an example: **http://someplace.co.uk/food/fruit/peaches/Stones.htm**. If you see one of the 'Not Found' pages, try exchanging that capital 'S' in 'Stones' for a small 's' and pressing Enter (web URLs don't often use capital letters). Failing that, try changing that **.htm** extension to **.html**. If that doesn't work either, it is likely that the document no longer exists. Try deleting **Stones.htm** from the address bar and pressing Enter again, and gradually work your way back, deleting **peaches/** next, and then **fruit/** until you find a document on that site. It may contain a link to the (now retitled) page you were looking for. If you see the dialog shown above instead, it suggests that the domain name (the bit following **http://**) is wrong, which is likely to be a typing error. In the screenshot there should be a dot after **bang**. Check the spelling and press Enter.

GOOD QUESTION

What if the URL isn't in the address bar?

If Internet Explorer can't find the domain and shows the 'site was not found' dialog, it won't place the URL into the address bar if you clicked a link on the page. You can get around this by right-clicking the link, selecting Copy Shortcut, and then pasting it into the address bar to edit.

Connection Crash! Have I Lost the File?

Usually the answer is yes. In the normal scheme of things, you can't reconnect and just grab that portion of the file that you missed. (You can minimise the chances of being disconnected by turning off Call Waiting, though!) But you may be in luck. There are programs such as GetRight from **http://www.headlightsw.com** (also on the free CD accompanying this book) that can retrieve the missing piece of the file for you in some circumstances. It all depends on whether the web server you were downloading from supports partial requests – you won't know until you try, but if you've got 95 per cent of an 8-megabyte file, it's got to be worth looking into!

If I Leave My IAP, Will I Lose My Email Address?

Yes you will, and this can be a real pain. If you use email a lot, it's worth hanging on to that first account for a while as you pass out your new email address to everyone and give things a chance to settle down. But there are a couple of things you can do to ensure that your email address will never change.

The first of these is quick, simple and free. Skip along to Bigfoot (the email lookup site mentioned in Chapter 12) at **http://www.bigfoot.com/Profile/Profile_join.htm**. Type your current email address into the box and click on **Join**, then fill in your details and select a password. You can then choose a brand new email address, which will have **@bigfoot.com** tagged on the end. From now on, give this new email address to everyone, and Bigfoot will automatically redirect your email to the address you entered. If you move to a different IAP, just return to Bigfoot, type in your password, and change the email address to which Bigfoot should send

BY THE WAY

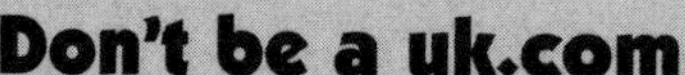

Don't be a uk.com

There are companies offering unusual domains that mix a country suffix with **.com**. Don't pay for one of these – it may become very expensive, or simply cease to be recognised by the Internet at large. Stick to the standard top-level domains listed on page 25, or one of the new suffixes, **.firm**, **.store**, **.web**, **.arts**, **.rec**, **.info** and **.nom**.

your email. (As an example, you can email me at **rob.young@bigfoot.com** and Bigfoot will automatically redirect the message to my current IAP account.)

A more expensive, but flashier, way to go is to buy your own domain name (such as ***myname*.co.uk** or ***myname*.com**). Some service providers will set up a domain name for you (for an additional charge), or you can go direct to Nominet, the organisation that handles the registration of **.uk** domains, at **http://www.nic.uk**. At the time of writing, your own domain name will cost £40+VAT per year. If you register direct with Nominet, your IAP should set up an account for you using that domain (although not all IAPs will do this, so always check first!). And if you ever change to a different IAP, you can take this domain name with you, email address and all, just by contacting Nominet and informing it of the change.

How Can I Stop All This Junk Email Arriving?

You mean you don't want to learn how to become a millionaire overnight simply by posting five letters? The trouble is these offers arrive every day. In most cases you have to download them, which costs money, and you have to sift through to find the messages that matter, which takes valuable time. Pretty soon you'll be poor again, so it's best to nip this in the bud.
Here are three possible solutions, although none is guaranteed to work:

- Enrol a few friends to 'mail-bomb' the guilty company's mail server. The problems with this technique are that it isn't very 'Internet-friendly', it adds to your costs and inconvenience, and there's a chance that all this email will be bounced straight back to you!
- Send the company an email threatening to invoice for your time and expense in retrieving their garbage.
- Send an email to the company's access provider explaining what's happening, and request that it enforces the small-print in its contract with the company that prohibits this abuse of the email system.

Want to Know More about Junk Email?

Stop Junk Email is an excellent site offering clear, practical advice, a wealth of useful information to help you avoid becoming a victim, and examples to help you fight back. Point your browser at **http://www.mcs.com/~jcr/junkemail.html**.

Another possible solution, again not guaranteed to work, comes from those useful folk at Bigfoot (mentioned earlier in this chapter). After registering your email address with Bigfoot and receiving (almost) instant confirmation by email, go back and select the **Edit Profile** link. You'll see a simple page like the one shown in the next screenshot: just check the box, enter your email address, and click the button, and Bigfoot will send your details to the Direct Marketing Association asking for your address to be removed from its lists. And it's free!

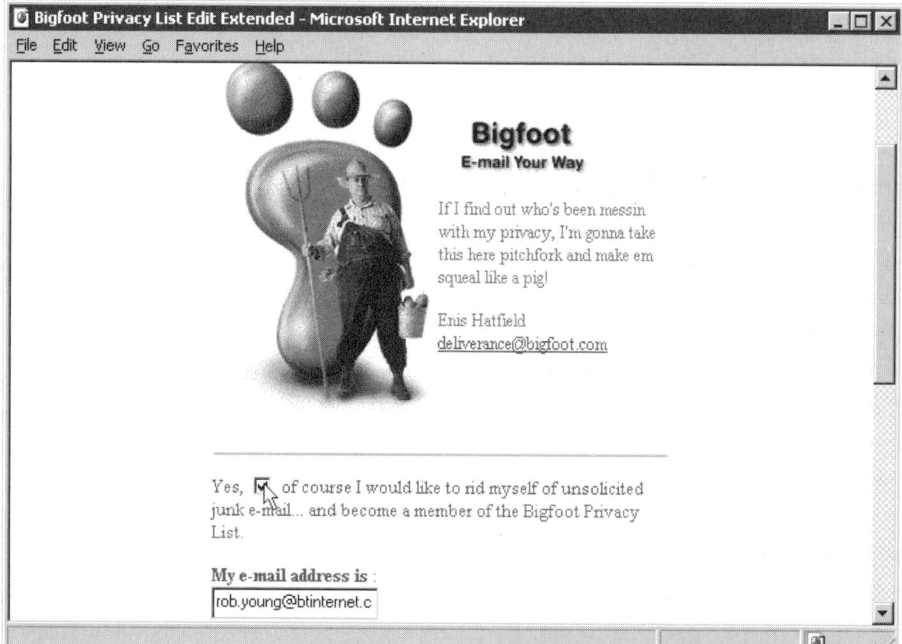

▶ Visit Bigfoot and take a large step towards ridding yourself of junk email.

If you're after a more sure-fire method, you should go for what should be a superb email program called Re:PLY from the folk who brought you CYBERsitter (see page 198).

At the time of writing, the program isn't complete and appears unlikely to be shareware. It's also a more expensive option than other email software, but the program has the ability to 'kill' email from any unwanted source without your ever knowing it arrived, which you may feel is worth something extra. Skip along to their site at **http://www.solidoak.com/reply.htm** to find more information.

Can I Be Anonymous on the Internet?

There may be many non-criminal reasons why you'd want to surf the Internet in anonymity, and it isn't difficult to do. The best way to completely hide your identity is to take out an account with an IAP or online service using an account name (or username) that's nothing like your own. You'll also have to ask your IAP to turn off finger access for your account (we met Finger in Chapter 11). The only way someone could learn your true identity would be to persuade your access provider to disclose it.

If you want to send untraceable email messages and newsgroup articles, you can use an **anonymous remailer**. Following the instructions, send your message to the remailer, which will remove your personal details and send it on to its final destination. Any replies will come back to you via the remailer, but the sender won't know who you are. Although the job they do seems simple, remailers can be tricky to use – they all need their own brand of special commands. You can find out more about the remailers and their instructions at **http://electron.rutgers.edu/~gambino/anon_servers/anon.html**, and you'll find another useful site at **http://noahs-place.com/anon.html**. If you find it all a bit baffling, a program called Private Idaho (from **http://www.eskimo.com/~joelm/pi.html**) may be able to simplify things for you.

BY THE WAY

Anonymity NOT guaranteed!

Anonymous remailers are viewed with (understandable) suspicion by the police and other law-enforcement agencies. Faced with the threat of prosecution, as many have been, the remailer's administrator may swiftly elect to surrender his records rather than get involved in a legal wrangle.

Could Someone Be Forging My Email?

Yes, they could. It doesn't happen very often, but it's easy to do. Every time you send an email message, your name and email address are attached to its header. When the recipient retrieves his email, these details are displayed so that he can see who the message is from. But how does your email program know what details to enter? When you installed your email software and filled in those little boxes on its options page, you told it! So, of course, if you go back to that options page and enter something different, those are the details that will go out with your email. Therefore it's entirely possible that someone could attach your name and email address to a message they send from their computer, and it would be difficult (although not impossible) to trace it back to them. Actually, it's a wonder that email forgery hasn't become a major pastime on the Net, because there's nothing you can do to prevent its happening other than to be careful what you say in chat rooms and newsgroups, and avoid riling anyone.

How Can I Get Maximum Viewing Space?

The easy way is to go to Explorer's **View** menu and click on **Toolbar** and **Status Bar** to remove the checkmarks. You'll still be able to see the menu-bar, so all the options you need are within fairly easy reach of the mouse. But you've also got Explorer's title-bar at the top of the screen, and Windows' Taskbar at the bottom, taking up space. Here's a little-known trick that allows full-screen browsing with Explorer.

Create a new shortcut to Internet Explorer somewhere handy. (The easiest way to do this is to find the file called **iexplore.exe** and just drag it on to your desktop.) Right-click the shortcut, choose **Properties** and click the **Shortcut** tab. In the box labelled **Target**, type a space after the text 'iexplore.exe', and then type **-k**. Press **OK** to confirm. Double-click this new shortcut, and Explorer will open in **kiosk** mode, with the entire screen devoted to the web pages themselves. Of course, this means you'll need to know a few keyboard shortcuts, so here they are:

This Keystroke	Does This
Ctrl+O	Displays a 'File Open' dialog into which you can type a URL that you want to visit
Esc	Cancels the download of the current page
Backspace	Mimics the Back button, to reopen the last page you viewed
Shift+Backspace	Mimics the Forward button
Ctrl+N	Displays the current page in a new, normal Explorer window
F5	Refreshes the current page or active frame
Alt+F4	Closes Explorer when you've finished
Alt+Tab	Switches to a different program hiding behind Explorer's window

How can I get my Favorites in kiosk?

To get at your Favorites in kiosk mode follow these simple commands. Press Ctrl+Esc to open the Start menu, and click on **Run**. Type **favorites** and press Enter. Your Favorites directory will open and you can double-click entries or drag-and-drop them into Explorer's window to open them.

Does Internet Addiction Really Exist?

Yes it does, although as yet it isn't taken that seriously. The Internet is an extremely powerful medium, and it can act as a sort of 'surrogate reality'. Although the World Wide Web is undoubtedly the coolest area of the Net, and it's easy to lose track of time while surfing around it, the most addictive areas are always chat rooms and newsgroups. The immediacy of these areas can be compelling, and many people spend hours every day reading and replying to articles, or typing messages back and forth, at the expense of their work, family life, and health (not to mention the cost involved in spending this much time online).

I'm not going to start handing out advice on beating addiction – as someone who can resist anything except temptation, I'm hardly qualified! But, at the risk of leading you further astray, you can find more information online: two of the best pages for information and links are at **http://www.cmhc.com/guide/iad.htm** and **http://www.addictions.com/internet.htm**. You'll also find a short but useful page at **http://www.wespsych.com/interadd.html**.

Which Sites Should I Download From?

A major conundrum when you're about to download a large file is that some web sites are just too helpful! You arrive at the download page, and they offer you a dozen different links to the same file. Which one should you choose? Here's a couple of rules worth following. First, discount any links pointing to FTP sites if you can – your browser often takes longer to connect to them, and downloading tends to be slower and less reliable. Second, choose the HTTP link that's geographically closest to you (ideally marked as a UK or European site).

Of course, there's no guarantee that you've found the best link using this method. And even if you have got a fast link, you'll still be sitting there wondering if a different one may have been quicker still! For such times, there's a nifty little utility called Dipstick, from **http://www.klever.net/kin/dipstick.html** and also included on the free CD accompanying this book, that's worth keeping handy. Drag the links into Dipstick's window and it will test the speed of each, and then give you a button to click to begin downloading from the site that gave the fastest response.

16

THE WEB – YOUR COMPLETE ENTERTAINMENT GUIDE

In This Chapter...

- Use electronic TV & radio guides
- See the latest movies, & book tickets online
- Find out what's on in towns & cities around the UK
- Book hotels, holidays, flights & cars
- Check travel timetables & traffic conditions
- Giggles, games & gambling online

It's a paper world. It doesn't matter what you want to do, 9 times out of 10 you have to consult a piece of paper before you can do it. Want to watch TV? Book a holiday? See what's on at your local cinema or theatre? Plan a trip or a day out? If you do any of those things, you've probably got a mountain of guides, catalogues, brochures and local newspapers, and many of them are probably out of date! So let's go paperless…

Use Online TV & Radio Listings

No more scrabbling around to see which of those 28 Sunday supplements contains the TV listings this week – just hit the Web instead! Visit Events Online's TV page at **http://www.eventsonline.co.uk/cgi-eol/tv.cgi** for the fastest and most comprehensive guide to seven days of television programmes. Choose the five channels you want from the drop-down lists (or select **Ignore** if you want less than five), click the option-button beside the appropriate day, and then click the **Get TV Listings** button. When the list appears, you can click on a programme's entry to see a brief description. You can save the list to your own disk to read offline by selecting **File | Save As**.

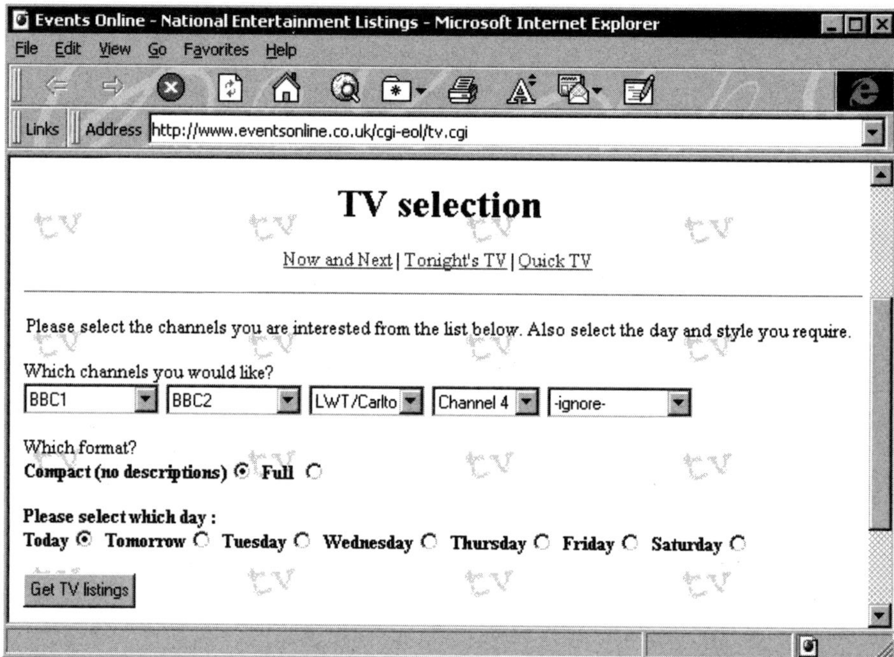

▶ Quick and easy TV listings from Events Online.

Events Online is one of the UK's most popular sites – it's a sort of 'one-stop shop', as you'll learn later in this chapter – and it can get pretty busy. If you can't connect to it, or it won't show you the listings, don't despair: head off to **http://www.link-it.com/tv** where you'll find listings for peak-time viewing.

Where can I get satellite TV listings?

Visit the Satellite Times at **http://www.s-times.demon.co.uk** to find schedules for more than eighty satellite channels available in the UK, plus features and reviews. Or check out Sky's own site at **http://www.sky.co.uk**, and the Discovery Channel at **http://www.discovery.com**.

You'd expect good old Auntie Beeb to have her own web site, and indeed she does. Point your browser at **http://www.bbc.co.uk/schedules/prog_by_day.html**, pick a day, and then choose a BBC TV channel or one of the BBC's five national radio stations for a complete programme listing together with short descriptions. This is a huge site, and many popular BBC programmes have their own mini-sites within it. You'll find links to some of these on the free CD accompanying this book, or you can head off to **http://www.bbc.co.uk/index/progs.html** and select one of the categories such as Drama, Films, Entertainment, or Natural History.

Need a few more TV and radio links?

- **http://www.dananeda.demon.co.uk/marklard** A little lunacy from the Radio 1 Breakfast Show.
- **http://www.ctw.org** Despite the appalling title (Children's Television Workshop), this Sesame Street site brilliantly combines fun and education for young children, although a little parental help may be necessary.
- **http://www.yahoo.co.uk/Regional/Countries/United_Kingdom/News_and_Media/Radio/Stations** Links to the web sites of more than eighty local radio stations.
- **http://www.channel4.com** A well designed and stylish site for Channel 4, complete with full programme listings and an easy-to-navigate set of buttons.

BY THE WAY

Soap heaven

Need to catch up with your favourite UK soap operas? Head for **http://www.geocities.com/TelevisionCity/2533** for the latest news and plot developments. You'll even find 'spoiler' pages of future plot-lines here, but they're easily avoided if you prefer the suspense!

▶ *You don't necessarily need a radio to listen to the radio – this is the Internet after all, and anything's possible.* *Skip ahead to page 292 to find out more.*

Want to Take in a Movie?

The Web can tell you just about everything you want to know about films and cinemas (except for the price of the popcorn), and the site to check out is MovieWeb at **http://movieweb.com/movie/movie.html**. Here you'll find an alphabetical list of films going back to 1995 with cast information and plot synopses, pictures and posters, and a lot more. MovieWeb gets previews of

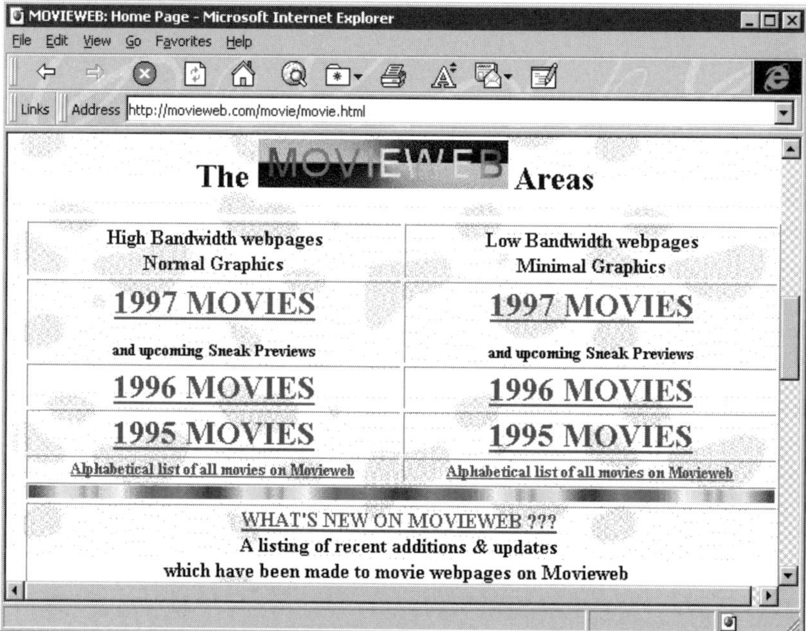

▶ Video previews of the latest films at MovieWeb.

new films long before they hit the cinema, and you can view these online in QuickTime format (you'll find out more about QuickTime in Chapter 21). And if you're not sure what's worth seeing, the weekly Top 25 box-office charts should point you in the right direction.

Once you've chosen the film you'd like to see, it's time to find out which local cinema is showing it. To do that, head off to Yell's site (see page 173) and click the **Film Finder** link. Or maybe you were looking for older films to buy on video? If so, get your credit-card details ready and visit The Zone at **http://www.thezone.co.uk**. (If you haven't bought anything online before, skip ahead to Chapter 18 to see how it all works.)

If you're a real film addict, it's worth visiting the UK Internet Movie Database at **http://uk.imdb.com/a2z**. This site isn't as up-to-the-minute as MovieWeb and you won't find any previews here, but you will find quotes, reviews, news and plenty of fun stuff.

How About a Night at the Opera?

Or if not at the opera, perhaps a ballet, an ice show, a pantomime, a kids show, or the latest Andrew Lloyd Webber musical. Make your way to What's On Stage at **http://www.whatson.com/stage** (shown in the next screenshot) and search for live entertainment in your area. You can select a single region or the whole of the UK, and choose one of 17 categories of stage-show if you're looking for something in particular. You can even confine your search to particular dates, or use keywords.

BY THE WAY

Finding more culture

UK Calling (at **http://www.uk-calling.co.uk/frame.html**) is a very attractive site with extensive listings in eight categories including Classical Music, Art Galleries, Dance, Theatre, and Leisure Breaks. Or visit Events Online (**http://www.eventsonline.co.uk**) and click a category, or browse by event type or venue.

When you've found a show you'd like to see, you can usually book tickets online. Click the **Tickets** button, fill in the form, and you should receive email confirmation within three days.

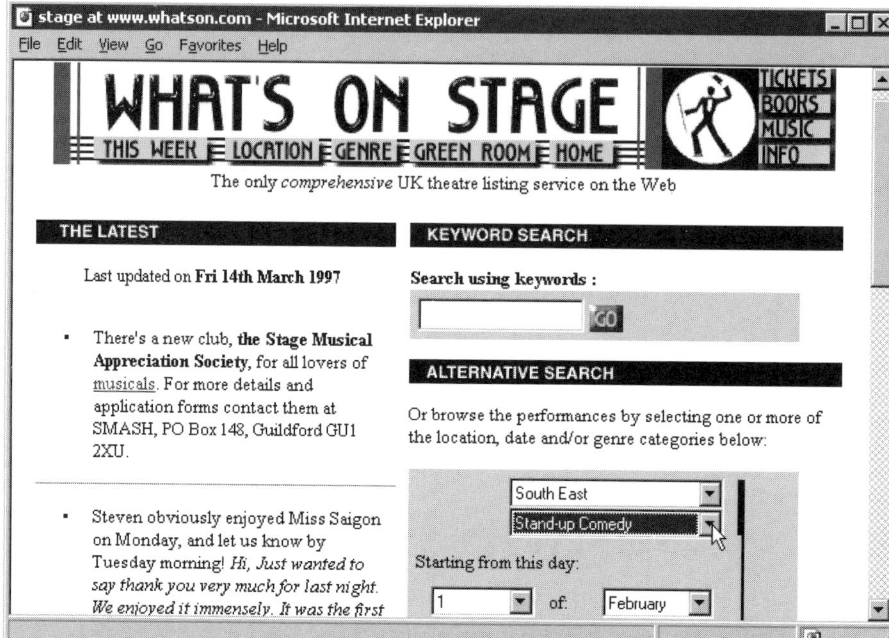

▶ Click on Location or Genre, or run a search for the best stage-shows.

Get Away for the Weekend

If you're going to book to see a show, why not make a weekend of it? To find somewhere to stay, check out Expotel at **http://www.expotel.co.uk/expotel**. You can choose between several search options such as a region of the UK or the name of a hotel, or you can just click **Show me all the hotels in the UK** and then pick a town or city from the list to see what's available. Every hotel listing gives prices and facilities, and **First Choice** and **Second Choice** buttons: choose two hotels and set one as your first choice and one as your second, and then click the **Book hotel choices** button to fill in the online booking form.

BY THE WAY

Insecure, but keen to help

The Expotel booking form isn't a 'secure' site (see page 199 for information on what makes a site secure). If you don't want to enter your credit-card details, you can send Expotel a fax instead, or just leave that section blank to have them telephone you on receipt of your booking request.

If you can't find what you're looking for at Expotel, try the UK Hotel & Guest House Directory at **http://www.s-h-systems.co.uk/shs.html**. This uses handy clickable maps to pinpoint a location (along with ordinary hypertext links for the geographically-challenged!), and gives all the necessary information about each hotel. Booking isn't quite as nifty here: you send an email, which is delivered to the hotel as a fax, and they should then get in touch with you to confirm the details.

Where to Go, What to Do

So you've got tickets to a show, and booked a hotel, but what will you do with the rest of the weekend? Once again, the Web leaps in to help – try one of these sites:

- **Open World** More than eight hundred heritage attractions, museums, theatres and restaurants, with clickable maps, plenty of pictures, and its own search engine. You can even search for accommodation based on price range! Go to **http://www.openworld.co.uk/britain**.
- **UK Guide** A smaller but growing site, sadly missing a search engine, but well worth clicking around. A much-needed Eating Out section should be online soon. Head for **http://www.uk-guide.com**.
- **Events Online** A popular site, probably as much for its clarity and simplicity as its content. Click one of the friendly, coloured categories such as Music, Arts, Stage or Kids. You'll find this at **http://www.eventsonline.co.uk**.
- **UK Calling** A beautifully-designed and stylish site with nationwide entertainment information organised into categories such as Classical and Contemporary Music, Dance, Art Galleries and Leisure Breaks. Visit **http://www.uk-calling.co.uk/frame.html**

And don't forget our old pal Yahoo! Point your browser at **http://www.yahoo.co.uk/Regional/Countries/United_Kingdom/Cities_and_Towns** for a list of hundreds of cities, towns and villages. The entries for a town can be a bit of a mixed bag – all types of local information may be listed here, from tourist attractions and restaurants to butchers and council offices. If you're looking for something particular, such as a zoo or a theme park, visit Yahoo's front page (**http://www.yahoo.co.uk**) and use a keyword search.

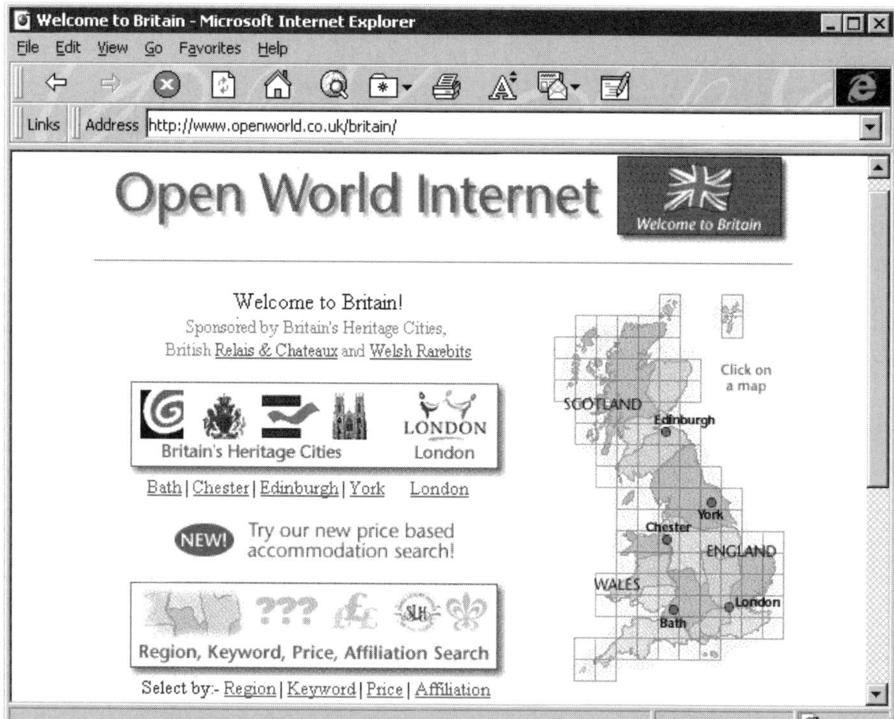

▶ Open World is a great starting point for holidays and short breaks in the UK.

BY THE WAY

Want to play a round?

What better way to relax than to hit a little ball very hard and then go looking for it? If you're tired of looking in all the usual places, visit **http://www.golfweb.com/europe** and try a change of course.

Getting from A to B

Finally, let's sort out those travel arrangements. For this, there's one magical web site that handles the lot – the UK Online All-In-One page at **http://www.ukonline.co.uk/UKOnline/Travel/contents.html**. From here, you can access dozens of European and international airlines and airports and check flight information; find the departure and arrival times of trains and National Express coaches; and book seats on planes, trains and buses. If that isn't enough, you can hire a car from one of four companies (or visit Hertz at **http://www.hertz.com/index.html**), check the latest news on motorways, London traffic and the underground, or look at the World Ski Report.

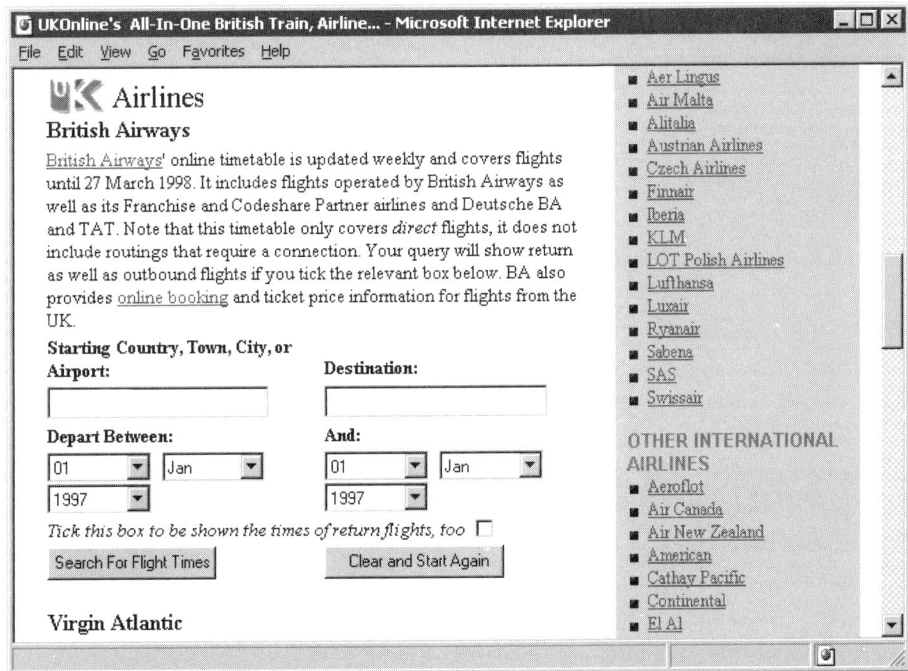

◀ A tiny slice of UK Online's incredible resource for travellers.

Book Your Holiday on the Web

If you want to journey further afield, the Internet has to be the ideal place to start. With a few clicks you can book flights and accommodation, read city guides, swot up on culture and currency, and check local events. Here's a taste of some of the best sites:

- **Internet Travel Network** at **http://www.itn.net.** Enter itinerary details to check pricing and availability, book hotels and hire-cars. Instead of entering your credit-card number, choose a travel agent and you'll be contacted for the final reservation details.
- **World Travel Guide** at **http://travelguide.attistel.co.uk/start.html**. Don't even consider going abroad without coming here first. Every useful piece of information you could ever need is on this site.

- **Thomas Cook** at **http://www.thomascook.com**. A mine of useful information including currency conversion, special offers, and links to other sites.
- **Eurostar** at **http://www.eurostar.com/eurostar**. Fare and timetable information for passenger services through the Channel Tunnel, as well as online reservations.
- **Internet Travel Service** at **http://www.itsnet.co.uk**. Links to sites offering information about every aspect of travel you could imagine, including Health, Self-Catering, Insurance, Ferries, Cycling Holidays, Travel Agents – the list is almost endless.

To find general 'What's On?' information in the major cities of the world, a couple of useful starting points are Excite's CityNet (**http://www.city.net**), and Time Out magazine (**http://www.timeout.co.uk**). The Time Out site requires you to register by entering your name, address, email address, and some extra fact-finding information. However, it is free and it doesn't know whether you're telling the truth!

BY THE WAY

Let's talk travel

For people who have permanently itchy feet, or who just enjoy travelling vicariously, Usenet is a useful source of travel information and real-life experiences. Check out the **alt.travel** and **rec.travel.marketplace** newsgroups, and take a look at the rest of the **rec.travel** hierarchy.

▶ *Need to find maps of towns and cities in the UK and elsewhere? Skip ahead to page 265.*

Amuse the Kids (& Yourself!) Online

Once you've discovered the Web, you've got a whole new world of entertainment at your fingertips. The effort that people put into creating some of these sites is stunning, and they do it for no particular reward. There's no 'licence fee' to pay, and you won't get interrupted by advertisements every 15 minutes!

Entertainment Sites for Kids

The best children's sites are the ones that take a little education and add a sugar-coating of fun and interactivity, and the USA is leagues ahead of the UK in this department. In fact, UK kids' sites are thin on the ground, and good sites are probably still a year or two away. Point your kids at **http://www.yahooligans.com** for a mass of links to tried and trusted web pages.

Of course, you may not be convinced that the Internet is a safe or worthwhile place for kids. Prepare to be persuaded! Fire up your browser and visit **http://www.bonus.com**, shown in the following screenshot. As soon as you arrive, the 'worthwhile' element should be obvious: there are more than five hundred activities for kids, including games and puzzles, animations, interactive adventures and scientific explorations. The entire site is colourful, stylish, and easy to navigate. But apart from the incredible content you'll find, this site illustrates the sense of responsibility increasingly found on the Web – you're kids are locked in and they can't escape! Whenever you visit this site, a second browser window automatically opens, minus toolbars and menus, to display the pages; your children can move around this site to their hearts' content, but the only way to access a different site is to return to the original window and choose a Favorites item or type a URL into the address bar.

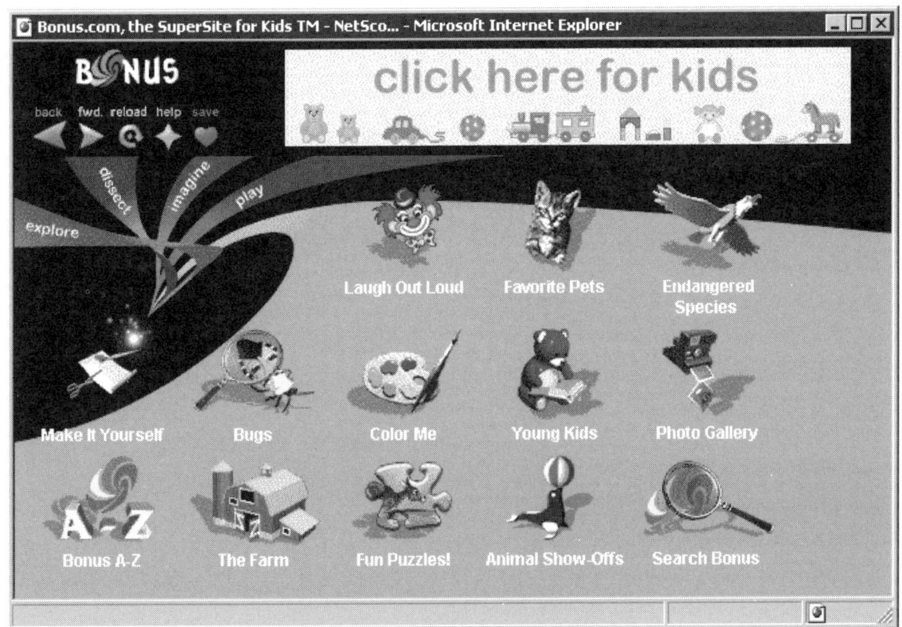

◀ Bonus.com, one of the most absorbing sites on the Web. But give your kids a go too!

Another site that knows how to keep kids entertained, not surprisingly, is Disney, at **http://www.disney.co.uk**. Although the content here is clearly tilted towards the latest cinema and video releases, there's no big sell. Instead, you'll find games and activities that cleverly tie in with the films, with plenty of favourite cartoon characters, animated story-books, and a very friendly 'kids-club' feel. You can also find out more about the various Disney resorts, and watch live camera broadcasts from Main Street.

BY THE WAY

Spin a yarn for the Web

Do you have a budding young novelist in the family? Point your mini-authors at KidPub (**http://www.kidpub.org/kidpub**) where they can have endless fun by submitting their own stories and they can also enjoy themselves (or suss out the competition!) by reading other children's creations online.

The sheer novelty value of surfing the Internet can be enough to keep kids amused for hours at a stretch (if your telephone bill can stand it!), and a particular branch of Web-based entertainment – the online scavenger hunt – also makes a great starting point for learning how the Net works. Working from a set of clues, the goal is to track down pictures, pages and information on the Internet, like a treasure hunt at a kids' party. In fact, scavenger hunts are also popular with adults (especially the ones that pay cash prizes!), and often lead you to explore areas of the Internet that you'd studiously avoided, such as Gopher or Telnet. For a list of current scavenger hunts, head off to **http://www.yahoo.co.uk/Entertainment/Contests_Surveys_Polls /Scavenger_Hunts**.

Play Online Games with Other Web-surfers

If you like computer games, the Web is exactly what you've been waiting for. Forget Minesweeper and Solitaire – Yahoo offers 38 different categories of online games at **http://www.yahoo.co.uk/Recreation/Games/ Internet_Games/Interactive_Web_Games**. Some of these are single-user games in which you play against the clock, solve a brain-teaser, or try to beat someone else's highest score; others are multi-user games in which you play against anyone else that happens to be visiting the same site at the same time.

If you're stuck for somewhere to start, here are a few suggestions:

- **Gameshows** at **http://www.gameshows.com**. From the creator of the TV show Jeopardy, here are two nifty word games called 'Out Of Order' and 'Strike A Match'. Before you can play, a few files have to be installed on your hard-disk (it happens automatically and only takes a minute or two), and you can then pit your wits against those of other visitors to the site.
- **Casino Royale** at **http://www.funscape.com**. If you like a gamble, visit this site and play poker, blackjack, roulette, slot machines and more. However, it really is a gamble – you can win real money, you can lose real money, and you'll have to pay real money to open an account before you start!
- **Entertainment & Games** at **http://tucows.cableinet.net/fun95.html**. Tucows is an excellent source of Internet software, and this page will point you towards dozens of online games such as backgammon, chess, trivia quizzes, and arcade shoot-em-ups. Download the software from this page, and then follow the instructions to visit the web sites where all the action takes place.

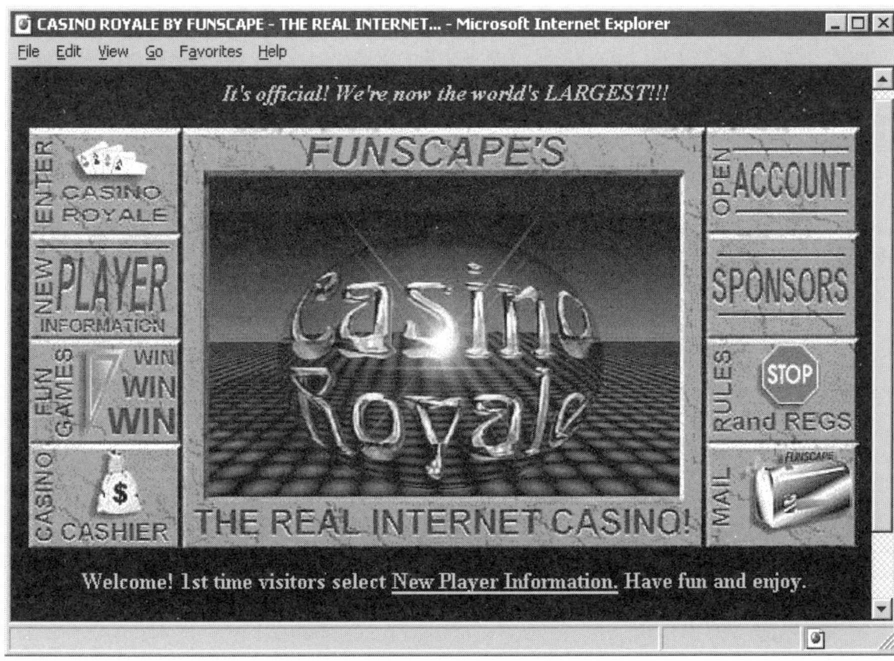

◀ Looking for a new way to spend money on the Internet? Casino Royale has the answer!

BY THE WAY

Looking for single-user games?

If you're in the mood for some solitary game-playing you should wait no longer and visit Karl Hörnell's site at **http://www.tdb.uu.se/~karl** for a collection of beautifully crafted games including Mastermind, IceBlox, and RubikCube.

Gags & Giggles Galore

The World Wide Web has a seemingly endless store of joke pages, cartoons, comic strips and comedy sites. For instance, a great TV page called UK Laughter Links (**http://www.netlink.co.uk/users/tucker/comedy/link.html**) is entirely devoted to comedy shows such as Men Behaving Badly and Fawlty Towers. If you're a fan of sci-fi fantasy writer Terry Pratchett, you can find a page of hilarious quotes at **http://www.lspace.org/pqf/index.html**. For reams of jokes and one-liners, try Darin's Humor Archive (**http://www.ugcs.caltech.edu/~darinh/humor.shtml**) or the Imagine Jokes Board (**http://www.imagineos.com/jokes**).

If you're a cartoon fan, your first stop should be the 10 Laughs A Day site at **http://obryan.com/10Laughs**. As the name suggests, this site delivers 10 new cartoons every day, following regular themes such as pets and business on Mondays, and politics and depraved on Fridays. And, if you haven't spent all your money at Casino Royale, you can spend the remainder on a T-shirt or mug bearing your favourite cartoon.

As usual, Yahoo can lead you to 'funnies' of all descriptions. Just head for **http://www.yahoo.co.uk/Entertainment/Humor_Jokes_and_Fun.**

Whatever flavour of humour you prefer, you'll find another generous helping on Usenet. A couple of self-explanatory newsgroups are **alt.binaries.pictures.cartoons** and **rec.arts.comics.strips**, and there are many more lurking in the **rec.humor**, **alt.humor** and **alt.jokes** hierarchies.

17

ONLINE NEWS & CURRENT AFFAIRS

In This Chapter...

- Daily news & weather on the Internet
- Track investment performance & personal finances
- Create your own personalised news pages
- Custom news stories sent straight to your desktop
- Party politics & government online

Everybody in the world wants news of one sort or another – there's plenty of it and it's being made all the time. But where traditional newspapers can print no more than two or three editions per day, Internet news services can be updated hour-by-hour, or even minute-by-minute. In this chapter you'll find some of the best sources of UK and world news, learn how to build your own tailor-made news service, and meet the revolutionary Internet technology that's about to make your paperboy redundant!

Read Your Newspaper on the Web

Unexpectedly, it's the broadsheets that have made it to the Internet first, and they've made a surprisingly good job of combining content, style, and usability. If you find the paper versions of *The Times* and the *Daily Telegraph* a bit stuffy, their online versions are going to come as a revelation.

Let's take *The Times* (at **http://www.the-times.co.uk**) as an example. As soon as you arrive at the site's front page you're faced with clear icons that take you to *The Times* 'newspaper' itself (shown in the next screenshot), the *Sunday Times*, the Education supplements, and the *Interactive Times*. The latest news stories are easy to find: selecting the link to *The Times* presents summaries of the major stories in several categories, with hypertext links to

▶ Click any hypertext headline at *The Times* to read the complete article.

the related articles if you'd like more detail, plus TV and weather. In true newspaper style, you'll also find links to classified ads, cartoons, crosswords and puzzles, and more hypertext-linked news summaries by visiting the *Interactive Times*.

So, it's all there, and it's easy to navigate. But what makes it better than an ordinary paper version? In a word – storage! Both *The Times*, and my own personal favourite online newspaper, *The Electronic Telegraph* (at **http://www.telegraph.co.uk**), are building ever-expanding databases of news articles. With a quick keyword search you can retrace the path of a news story you missed, track down articles on a particular subject, or find out what made headline news on any particular day. And, of course, it's a lot easier to save and store useful articles on your own hard-disk for future reference than it is to keep a stack of newspaper clippings!

BY THE WAY

Information swapping

Although access is usually free, when you first visit many online newspapers and magazines you'll have to fill in one of those infamous registration forms, giving your name and address, and a few other details. Provided you're honest (nudge, wink), this provides useful marketing information for the publishers, which they regard as a fair exchange for the information they're giving you.

Let's Talk About the Weather

The weather is officially the most popular topic of conversation in the UK. Probably because we have so much of it. And the Internet has a solution to that centuries-old problem: what can you do when there's no one around to listen? Just start up your newsreader and head for **alt.talk.weather** or **uk.sci.weather**.

However, to become a real authority on the subject you need to know what the weather's going to do next. One option is to consult the online newspapers mentioned above, but a better one is to head for **http://weather.yahoo.com/Regional/United_Kingdom.html**. On this page you'll find a hypertext list of almost every town in the UK – click on the appropriate town to see a five-day local weather forecast. (You may want to add the forecast page to Internet Explorer's **Favorites** menu or create a shortcut to it on your desktop for quick access.)

For more weather facts including shipping forecasts and meteorological data, visit the Met Office site at **http://www.meto.govt.uk/sec3/sec3.html**.

BY THE WAY

You will meet a tall dark stranger

Yes, the Net has horoscopes too! One of the best known is Jonathon Cainer's Zodiac Forecasts at **http://www.bubble.com/webstars/main.htm**. Or, for a more humorous approach to your celestial future, visit **http://www.xmission.com/~mustard/cosmo.html**.

Play the Money Markets Online

There's little that can't be done on the Internet, but a few things cost money, and share-dealing is one of them. Because the sort of information you're looking for is worth money, you'll have to whip out your credit card and cross palms with silver before you can trade. Nevertheless, there's no shortage of companies on the Internet holding their palms out expectantly, and one of the better known is Electronic Share Information (ESI) at **http://www.esi.co.uk**. Alternatively, nip along to The Share Centre at **http://www.share.co.uk** – this is a good, easy-to-follow site for new investors, which offers plenty of straightforward help and explanations of the financial world. (Oddly, you can buy classical-music CDs here too!)

For information on more wide-ranging money matters, the place to be is MoneyWorld (**http://www.moneyworld.co.uk**). This is a huge and popular site covering every aspect of personal finance you can imagine – homebuying and mortgages, PEPs, unit and investment trusts, and company performance, to name but a few. You can read the London closing-business report, check the FTSE 100 and 250, view regularly updated world prices, and consult the glossary to find out what everyone's talking about. And if MoneyWorld doesn't have the information you're looking for, you'll find links to other financial services and organisations in the UK and abroad.

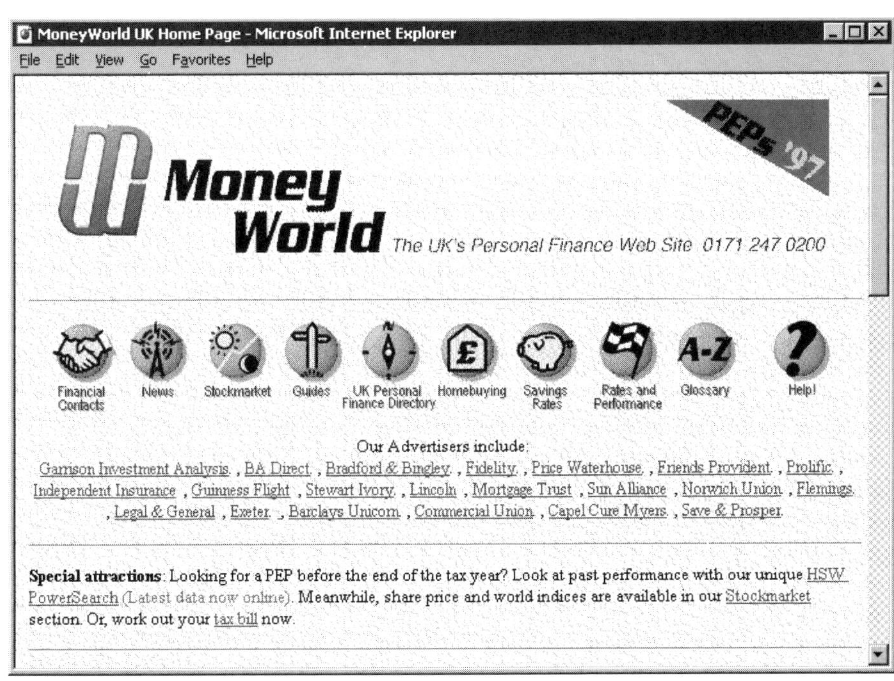

◀ MoneyWorld makes an excellent starting place for all things financial.

BY THE WAY

Money talks

Usenet has several newsgroups for people wanting to give or receive a little financial advice. A good starting point is **uk.finance**. For more international input, try **misc.invest** and **misc.invest.stocks**, and have a look at the **clari.biz.stocks** hierarchy.

Online newspapers such as *The Electronic Telegraph*, mentioned earlier in this chapter, also provide city news and prices just like their disposable counterparts, but if you need in-depth analysis, you can also find the major finance publications on the Web:

- *The Financial Times* at **http://www.ft.com**.
- *The Wall Street Journal* at **http://www.wsj.com**.
- *The Economist* at **http://www.economist.com**.

BY THE WAY

Financial scandals

The financial world has caught a few hands in a few tills in recent years. To find out more about financial scandals and the owners of those unfortunate hands, hurry along to **http://www.ex.ac.uk/~RDavies/arian/scandals.html**. There are also some fascinating insights into insider trading, bribery, and fraud in general.

▶ *As a daily part of financial life, many banks now have the facility to let you run your bank account online, check your account balances, and pay bills. Turn to page 253 to find out more.*

Create Your Own Custom News Page

You probably buy a newspaper every day, and perhaps a weekly or monthly trade journal of some sort too. But do how often do you actually read them all from cover to cover? The chances are that you glance at the headlines or the contents page, read the articles that particularly interest you, and ignore the rest. Wouldn't it be great if there was one publication you could buy that gave you just the stories that specifically appealed to you, and left out everything else? Well there is. In fact, there are quite a few, and as an added bonus you don't even have to pay for them!

The 'personal page' is a recent arrival to the Web, but a growing number of online publications are building the option into their sites. If you find a trade journal that covers one of your hobbies or interests, take a quick look around the site to see if it offers the 'personal page' service, or send an email to ask if it's in the pipeline.

BY THE WAY

The best of Times

The Times Internet Edition (page 230) lets you create a personal news page by choosing the types of business, arts, national and world news that interest you. Click the **Interactive Times** icon, then **Personal Times**, and check the boxes to specify your particular preferences.

One of the best non-specialist services is provided by Yahoo, the web-search chaps, and it takes only a couple of minutes to set it up. Find it at **http://edit.my.yahoo.com/config/login**, and click the **Start Your Own** button. On the next page, click the button to say that you're not a US resident. Then fill in a registration form as Yahoo needs to assign you a unique username and password to personalise your page. When you come to choose these, make sure you pick something that's easy to remember.

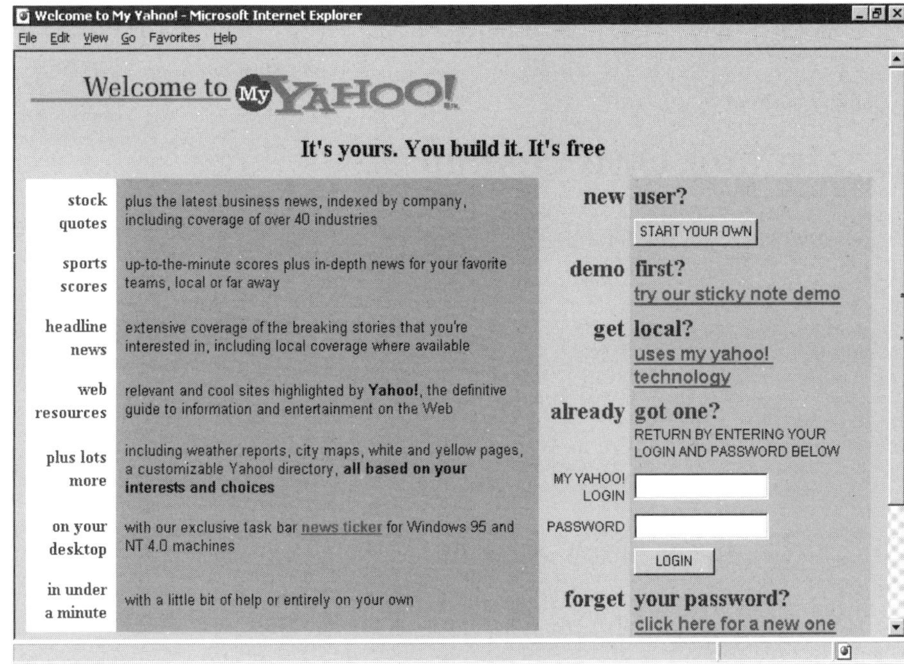

◀ Login at My Yahoo and read your own customised news pages.

As soon as you've filled in the registration form you can start to build your own page by checking boxes in categories covering entertainment, news, sports, and leisure activities; then click the button to confirm your choices. From now on, whenever you visit the main My Yahoo page at **http://my.yahoo.com** you'll see your personal page. Your browser should store and send your username and password to save you the bother of entering it every time, but make sure you keep a note of it somewhere, just in case!

▶ *After setting up a personal page at Yahoo or elsewhere, why not make it your Internet Explorer start-page?* *To find out how, skip back to page 72.*

Hot News Delivered Straight to Your Desktop!

In the hurly-burly of modern life, the personal news page is a great time saver, but you still have to visit the web site to read it. By today's technological standards, that's much too inconvenient! Instead, the news should come to you, and it should do so without even being asked.

The latest Internet innovation is 'push technology', a system that's expected to be at the heart of future Net development. In a nutshell, any type of information you can find on the Web can be sent straight to your desktop – text, pictures, sounds, video, etc – without the need for surfing and searching. You simply install the software, set a few preferences, and then sit back and watch as your personalised content streams down the line to you. Although the technology is in its infancy, you can already receive regularly updated world news, sports results, weather, share prices, and leisure information.

JARGON BUSTER

Push technology

This term is also known as 'server push'. Instead of your computer 'pulling' the information from the Web when you ask for it (client pull), the Web literally 'pushes' the information you have requested down the line to you and it also automatically keeps it updated.

The main program on everyone's lips for personalised news is called the PointCast Network (shown in the next screenshot), and you can download it free of charge from **http://www.pointcast.com**. At the time of writing, its main drawback is its heavy US content, but the company is working hard at providing localised coverage. Getting up and running with PointCast is quick and easy – just follow these steps:

1 After you've installed the software, click the **Personalize PointCast** button that appears, and fill in a few personal details. You'll also have to select the method you use to connect to the Internet.

2 Next you'll see a set of tabbed pages. These are PointCast's channels, following a television metaphor. On the first page you can select up to eight channels to follow from a list of categories such as news, weather, sports

and lifestyle. Clicking the other tabs lets you fine-tune the content to be included in each channel.

3 Finally, click **OK**, and PointCast will automatically download and display the information you selected. You can move between channels using the buttons on the left of the screen, and click on tabs and stories to view them on the right.

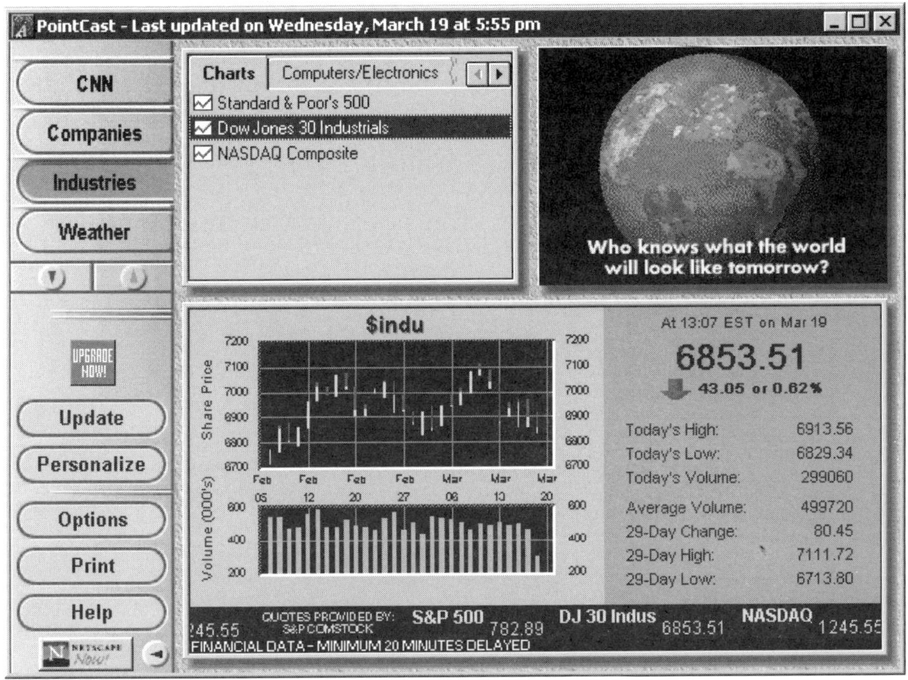

◀ Dynamic news on your desktop, courtesy of the PointCast Network.

Why is the PointCast service free?

PointCast makes its money through advertising, and a small area of the PointCast viewer is entirely devoted to displaying ads. The software has an extra channel called Internet and a built-in browser, and works on the assumption that you'll be so tempted by an advertisement that you'll click on it to visit that company's web site.

You can change the content to be downloaded, and add or remove channels any time you want to by clicking the **Personalize** button to return to those tabbed pages. Selecting the **Options** button lets you choose whether PointCast should dial-up and retrieve information automatically at regular intervals: you can set the frequency of these updates, or (as a more practical method for UK users) bypass the automation and just click **Update** when you want to download the latest batch of news. By default, PointCast also sets itself as your screensaver – make sure you read about this in its Help file!

If you're less than enthralled at the prospect of US content, Yahoo offers its own alternative. After setting up your My Yahoo personal page (as described on page 235), click the **News Ticker** link to download and install Yahoo's own software. This is a small program, which attaches itself to the Windows taskbar or the title-bars of your applications, and scrolls the contents of your personal page through its compact viewing area.

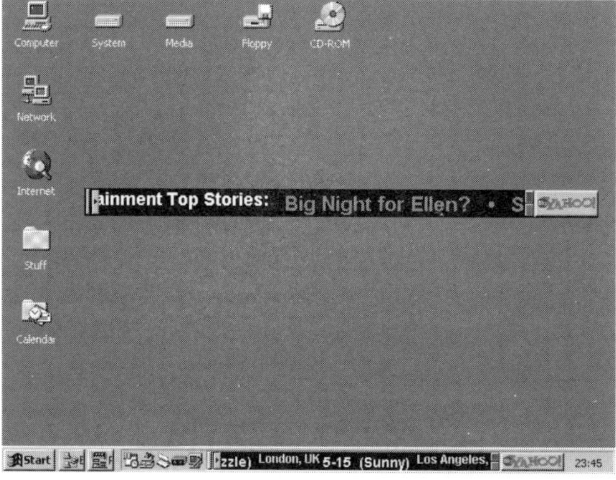

▶ Yahoo's neat News Ticker sits in the taskbar or title-bar, or can be 'glued' to your desktop.

In a similar way to PointCast, the News Ticker can be set to regularly grab updates by itself. If you see a headline that looks interesting you can click it to open your browser and download the related story, and (of course) you can type the relevant keywords into the ticker to start a Yahoo search.

BY THE WAY

All-in-one news & weather

If you prefer to find your news, weather and sports information all neatly located in one place, trot along to **http://www.yahoo.co.uk/headlines** and choose news headlines or summaries in several categories together with UK, Irish and worldwide weather forecasts.

Chart Hits & Bestsellers

Want to take a look at the UK albums and singles charts? The law of averages says you do – Dotmusic, at **http://www.dotmusic.co.uk**, is one of the most successful UK sites on the Web. Along with these charts and other information about the music scene, you'll find the Indie singles and albums charts, dance, R&B and club charts, and the US Airplay chart. While you're there, watch out for the little basket icons – if a CD you want to buy has one of these symbols beside it, you can click to add it to your 'shopping basket', and pay at the checkout when you're ready to leave.

Your bank account isn't running the same risks of being emptied at the Publishers Weekly Bestseller Lists (**http://www.bookwire.com/PW/bsl/bestseller-index.html**), but you'll find useful lists of the current bestsellers sorted into the categories hardback and paperback, fiction or non-fiction, children's, religious, computer, and audio books. For more general information and reviews, the main Bookwire site makes an ideal starting point – head for the home page at **http://www.bookwire.com**.

▶ *Skip ahead to the next chapter to discover more about the ins and outs of shopping online.*

Politics & Politicians on the Internet

Whether you want to explore 10 Downing Street, delve into Government archives, read press releases and speeches, or check electoral and constituency information, the Internet has all the resources you need. But let's start with the obvious: if you're interested in politics, the first place you'll want to visit is your own party's web site, so consult the table below.

Political Party	Web Site URL
Conservative Party	http://www.conservative-party.org.uk
Green Party	http://www.gn.apc.org/greenparty
Labour Party	http://www.labour.org.uk
Liberal Democratic Party	http://www.libdems.org.uk
Monster Raving Loony Party	http://www.raving-loony.pv.org
Plaid Cymru	http://www.wales.com/political-party/plaid-cymru/englishindex.html
Scottish National Party	http://www.snp.org.uk

If you're more interested in the real workings of the Government, head for the Government Information Office at **http://www.open.gov.uk**. This is a huge site containing thousands of documents and articles, but there are several choices of index to help you find your way through it. The easiest method is probably to click on **Functional Index** and scroll through the alphabetical list looking for keywords relating to the subjects you want. Another well organised and informative site is the Central Office of Information at **http://www.coi.gov.uk/coi/depts/deptlist.html**, which provides a comprehensive hypertext list of the many Government departments on the Web.

Until recently, one of the few ways to get a look around 10 Downing Street was to become a politician – rather a high price to pay when one look is probably enough. Thanks to the wonders of the Web, you can tramp around to your heart's content at **http://www.number-10.gov.uk**, and read a selection of speeches, interviews and press releases while you're there. Or jump on a virtual bus to **http://www.parliament.uk** to tour the House of Commons and the House of Lords, and search through the parliamentary archives. Another revealing site is the Register of MPs' Interests published by *The Guardian* (**http://www.guardian.co.uk/interests/index.html**).

BY THE WAY

An Eye on the Internet

For a more satirical view of politics, try that infamous Establishment-knocker Private Eye at **http://www.compulink.co.uk/~private-eye**, or **Scallywag** at **http://www.xs4all.nl/~emags/scallywag/index.html**.

For all the government departments and official bodies on the Web, one of the most useful and informative sites I've come across is actually unofficial. The Main British Politics Page (**http://www.keele.ac.uk/depts/po/table/brit/brit.htm**), shown in the screenshot opposite, is a veritable goldmine that includes local and national electoral information, constituency lists and analyses, local government details, and a useful Basic Information section. There are even lists of MPs' personal web pages and email addresses!

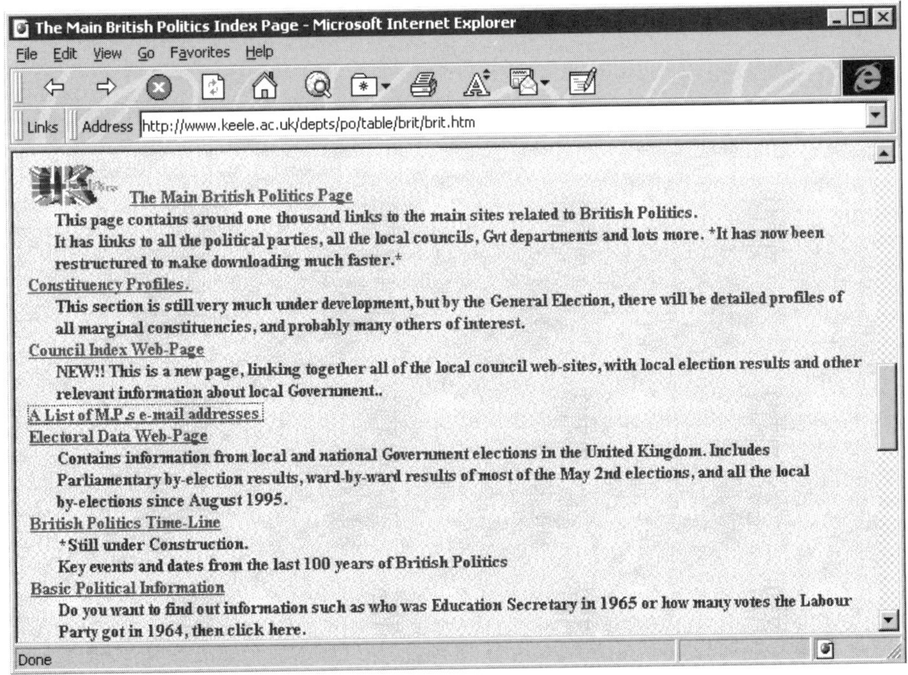

◀ A massive resource of local and national political data at the Main British Politics Page.

Oil the Wheels of Government Yourself!

The newsgroups provide one of the few resources available that allow you to discuss your political opinions with people from all over the world. They could even act as a springboard for launching pressure groups and petitions, or organising online 'conferences' using programs like NetMeeting and PowWow. The three major political newsgroups in the UK are **alt.politics.british**, **alt.politics.europe.misc** and **uk.gov.local**, but you'll find many more under the **uk.politics** hierarchy. Or try filtering your list of groups by entering **politic** to find related groups in other Usenet hierarchies.

Why don't UK politicians answer questions?

It's just possible that they've learnt a lesson or two from the infamously 'foot in mouth' US Senator Dan Quayle! As a welcome dose of light relief from the trials and tribulations of everyday politics, read the 'Wisdom' of Dan Quayle at **http://www.concentric.net/~salisar/quayle.html**.

An alternative to the newsgroups is UK Citizens Online Democracy, a recent newcomer to the Web, at **http://www.democracy.org.uk**. This is a discussion site that works in a very similar way to the Usenet groups: you can post your own messages by email, and follow discussion threads by clicking on hypertext links. The major difference between this site and the political newsgroups is that UK politicians actually take part in the discussions. In the words of the site itself: 'We hope it will become a place to make things happen – an exciting new interface between the public and politicians.'

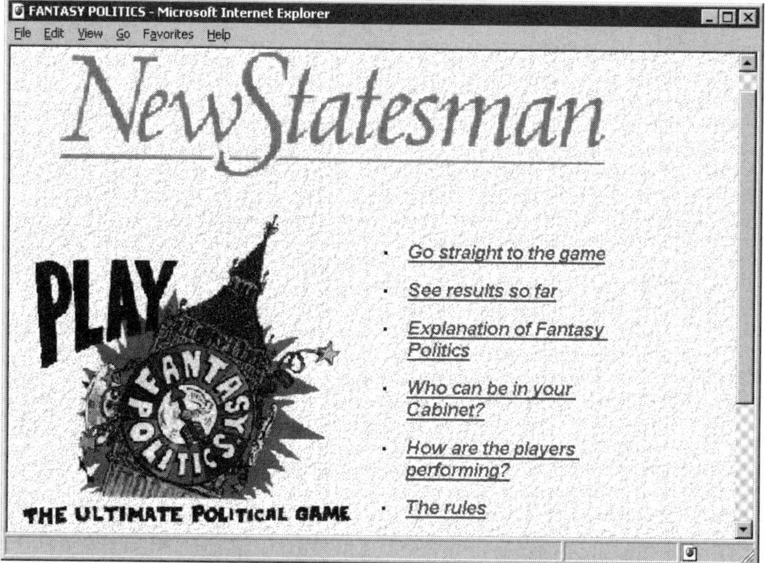

▶ Play Fantasy Politics, and prove that you really do know best!

The best way to make things happen, of course, is to take control of the country's political system. Unfortunately, if you don't manage to do it straight away, you've got to wait five years before you can have another crack at it. The good news is that in the spirit of the popular Fantasy Football League, you can now play Fantasy Politics at **http://www.election-uk.com**.

The rules are simple: after registering, just head for the main game page and pick your dream cabinet from drop-down lists of politicians, ex-politicians and celebrities. Some of the options seem a bit strange (for example, you may feel that Tiffany from EastEnders is a good candidate for Social Security, or you could choose to put Eric Cantona in Defence), but there's some serious thought behind the game, and there's even a prize at the end of it!

18

STAY HOME & GO CYBER-SHOPPING

In This Chapter...

- Learn how to buy goods online
- Visit shopping malls to find the big High Street names
- Buy your groceries on the Web
- Online banking, books, loans, wine & more
- Cyber-romance – kisses, cards & flowers

The Internet connection is starting to look like the Swiss army knife of the twenty-first century. In the last few chapters we've seen how the Net has tools to replace the telephone, answerphone, radio, television, newspapers and magazines, fax machine, and a fair bit more. Granted, there's no tool for getting stones out of horses' hooves, but they're probably working on it.

And now, with the recent arrival of secure transmission on the Internet, you can use your credit card at thousands of online 'cyberstores' to buy anything from a car to a... well, a Swiss army knife. It's quick, it's easy, and in this chapter I'll show you how to do it, and point you towards some of the best stores in cyberspace.

Are These the Stores of the Future?

So will we be doing all our shopping in cyberspace at the turn of the millennium? Definitely not. Let's face it – shopping is fun! Online shopping sites cover the Web, but they haven't really taken off because people like their shopping the way it is. To buy an item without speaking to a cashier, or a voice on the end of the telephone, is a curiously unsatisfying feeling.

That's bad news for the online stores, but it's good news for humanity. The much-vaunted prophecy that we'll live our entire lives hunched in front of computer screens is obviously nonsense – there are few purchases you'd want to make without first seeing, touching and testing the goods. The main use of online shopping is for small, cheap items such as books, videos, CDs and software – the type of item you don't need to see before buying.

GOOD QUESTION

Are cyberstores cheap?

You'll occasionally find a special offer in a cyberstore, but goods are generally a little more expensive than in high-street stores – you're paying a small premium for the convenience of not having to go out of your way to shop, in the same way that you're prepared to pay a little more for a pint of milk from your local corner shop.

And there's more good news: the cyberstores know they've got a fight on their hands! So you can bet your boots that they're putting a lot of effort into making their services as simple, reliable, and quick as they possibly can.

How Do I Buy Stuff Online?

In almost any cyberstore you visit, the routine will be pretty much the same. The names of the options and buttons will vary, but most online stores use a readily accepted 'shopping' metaphor that involves placing items in a basket or trolley and then going to the checkout to pay.

As a typical example of online shopping, follow me through a quick spending spree at theZone (**http://www.thezone.co.uk**), which is a popular UK cyberstore offering videos and chart CDs.

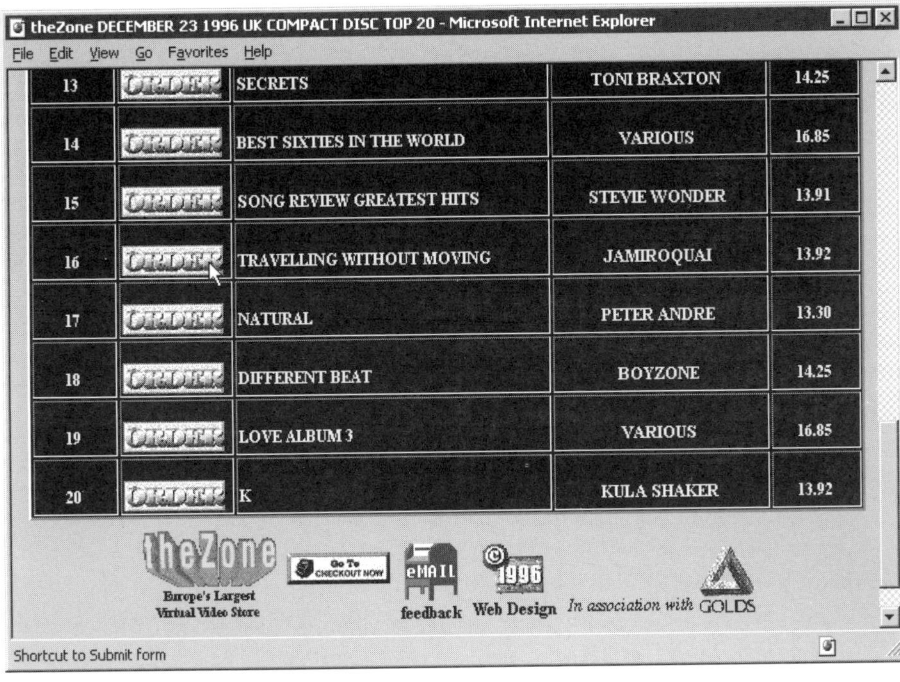

◀ Step one: choose a product you want to buy.

From theZone's front page I choose the link to the best-selling music CDs, arriving at the page shown above. Every item has a silver **Order** button beside it, so I click the button beside the CD I want to buy.

At the bottom of the page is a small white button marked **Go To Checkout Now**: at any point in my shopping trip, I could click that button to go and pay.

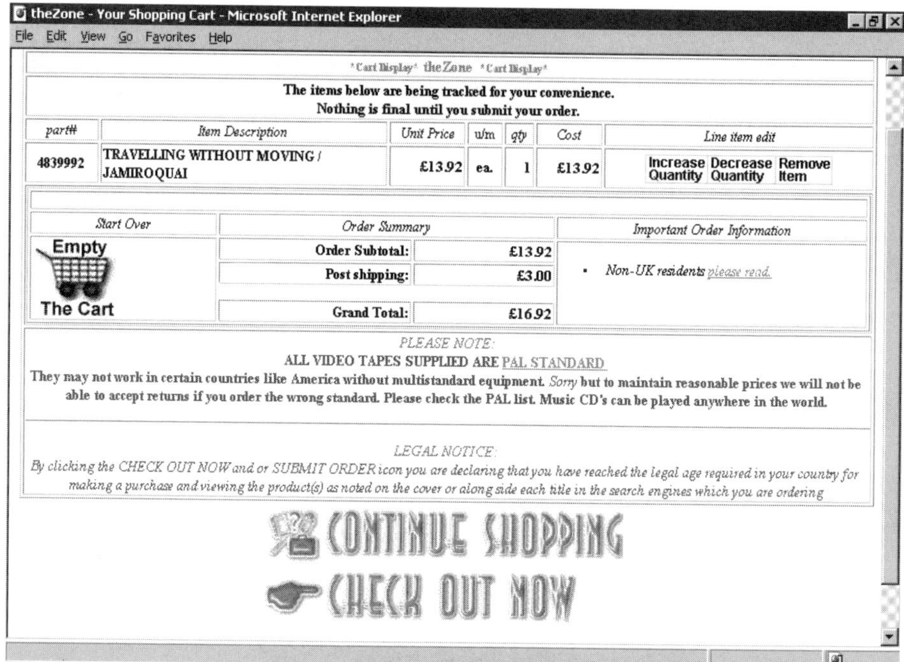

▶ Step two: verify the item and quantity, and decide what to do next.

Clicking the **Order** button takes me to another page, which shows all the items I've placed in my 'shopping cart' – in this case just a single CD so far. There are buttons that will let me increase or decrease the quantity of any item, or remove it from the list if I've had a change of heart. There's also a cute **Empty The Cart** icon in case I want to start all over again. I don't, so I take a quick look at the total price and choose where to go next: should I **Continue Shopping** or **Check Out Now**? Throwing caution to the wind, I **Continue Shopping**.

A few minutes later I'm back here again. I was duly returned to the CD page, from which I followed a link to the video charts and clicked another order button. My shopping cart now boasts two items and I'm ready to pay up and leave, so this time I click **Check Out Now**.

This leads to a page offering a choice of payment methods. The first, and by far the simplest, is to pay by credit card through a secure server. If your browser doesn't support this (Internet Explorer and Netscape both do), you should choose the non-secure system or, if you prefer, order by telephone, fax or email.

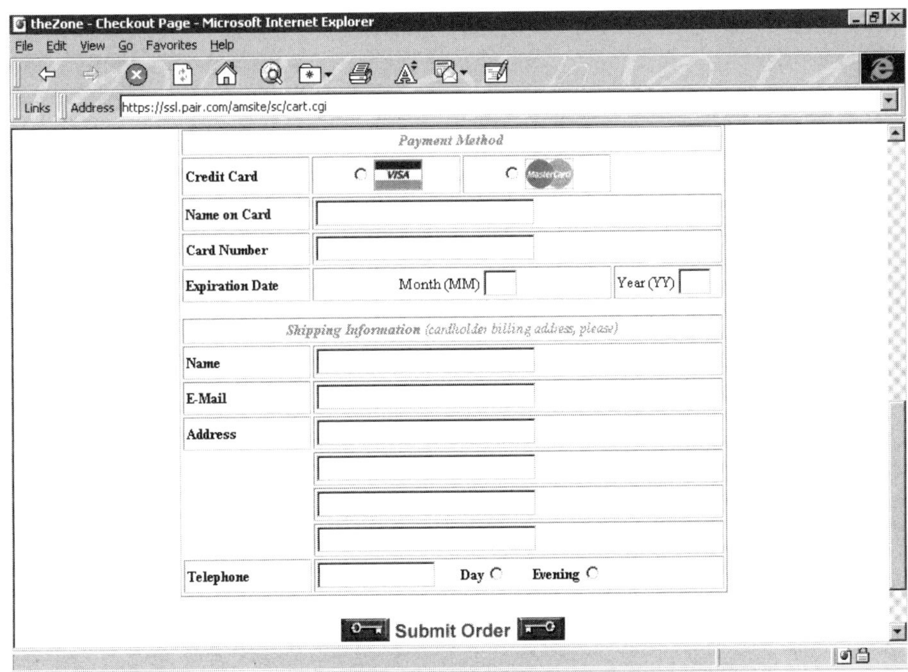

◀ Step three: fill in the details and submit the order.

Choosing the first payment method leads to the site's 'checkout', shown in the screenshot above. (Notice Internet Explorer's padlock symbol in the lower right corner indicating that this is a secure site – see page 200.) The upper part of the page allows me to check through the order again before paying. Then it's just a simple case of filling in personal and credit- or debit-card details.

The final step, which commits me to the transaction, is to click on **Submit Order**. At this point, all these details are passed to theZone and one last page appears giving me a reference number for the order and an email address to contact in case of queries; I click on **File | Save File As...** to save this page to my own disk in case I need to refer to it later. Exhausted, I search for the shop's cafeteria, but it doesn't seem to have one.

▶ *Worried about the security aspects of online shopping? Even the credit-card companies themselves regard this as the safest way to use your card – turn to page 199 to find out more.*

What do you think?

Your opinions are worth money to a lot of companies (that's why you have to fill in forms to access some of the online shops and services). If you head off to **http://www.questions.net** and fill in the questionnaire you can receive entries in a sweepstake and points that you can trade for online goods, or donate to charity.

Take a Tour of the Shopping Malls

Where do you go when you want to find the biggest selection of shops and merchandise quickly and easily? A shopping centre, of course! The theory behind shopping centres in your local town translates perfectly to the Internet – not only are all your favourite shops within easy reach, but while you're there you could be tempted to do a spot of 'window shopping'. You've probably guessed, from the generic name shopping malls, that most of these are US centres. Elsewhere in cyberspace it makes little difference which part of the world you're looking at, but online shopping tends to be different; for example, you may not want to wait so much longer for transatlantic delivery. So, for this section, I'm going to be blatantly British! Actually, one of the first shopping sites to hit the Internet was a UK site

Shopping all over the world

If you can't get what you want from the sites in this chapter, the trusty Yahoo has a mammoth page of worldwide shopping sites at **http://www.yahoo.co.uk/Business_and_Economy/Companies/Shopping_Centers/Online_Shopping**.

called BarclaySquare. It's still there, (and growing), at **http://www.itl.net/barclaysquare**. This is a virtual shopping centre on three levels: when you arrive at the site, you can visit Nightingale Plaza, Eagle Boulevard, or Flamingo Walk (shown in the next screenshot), and navigate by clicking the store you want to visit on the floor plan. If you prefer, you can head straight for your favourite store by selecting it from a list on the front page.

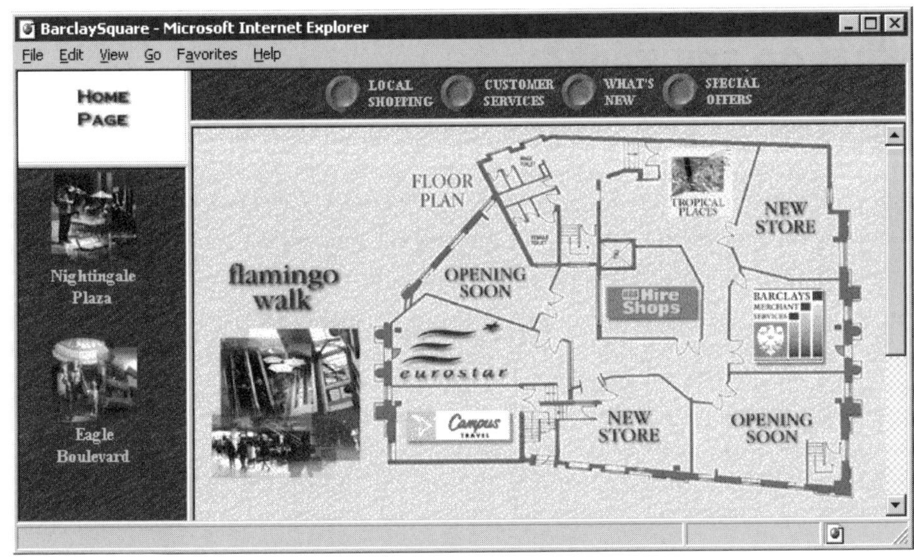

◀ The cash till rang in BarclaySquare.

The site is hosted by Barclays Bank, which gives it the pulling-power to attract some big high-street names such as Argos, Debenhams, Toys 'R' Us, Sun Alliance and Victoria Wine. The site is secure, well-designed and easy to navigate. Its one drawback is that if you're looking for a particular item, it isn't always easy to find when browsing through store-names. If you'd like to find stores by selecting product categories, here's a couple of good centres:

- **The UK Shopping City** at **http://mailgate.ukshops.co.uk:8000.** Choose from categories including Art, Fashion, Motoring and Sport.
- **Shops On The Net** at **http://www.shopsonthenet.co.uk**. Select a product category from a drop-down list of more than forty. The list also usefully tells you how many stores are available in each category.

BY THE WAY

Search for a store

Some items are hard to find wherever you go. If you need to find a particular product, such as a cricket bat, try using your favourite search engine, entering something like **+cricket +shopping online** (substituting the word **shopping** with **buy** if that doesn't yield results).

Groceries in Cyberspace

Ever the innovator, the Tesco superstore chain is adding a new dimension to Internet shopping: one of the first online supermarkets! At the time of writing, this is a trial service with only three Tesco branches taking part, but it seems a racing certainty that the entire country will soon be covered, particularly as other supermarket chains begin to catch on to the idea. You can visit the superstore at **http://www.tesco.co.uk** and take a look at the system for yourself, even if your local store isn't one of the featured three, by clicking the button marked **Guest**.

The service is simple to use. Starting from a choice of store departments (shown in the next screenshot), you work your way through to more specific categories and click the products you want to order. These are then added to your 'trolley' and you can select the quantity and change the pack size as you require. After selecting all of the products you want to purchase from the various departments, head for the checkout to take care of the payment and delivery details.

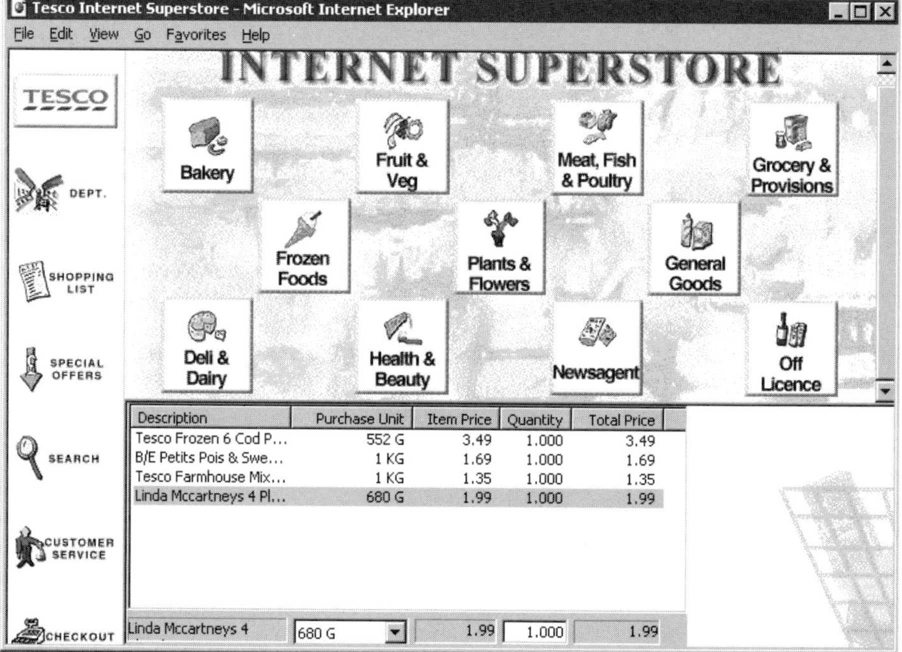

▶ Tesco's technically advanced but easy-to-use online supermarket.

Used in the way I've just described, the navigation can be slow. However, the site has two tricks that can really speed things along. The first is a Search facility – always needed, but all-too-rarely found on large shopping sites. The second is a clever Shopping List feature: by creating a list of the items you buy regularly, you have a basis for all your future visits that you can alter as necessary on each occasion.

Have a Wander Down the High Street

Away from the organised aisles of supermarkets and shopping malls, the Internet has thousands of individual shops gamely vying for your attention. So let's venture out into the fresh air of the global village to see what's what.

History in a box

If you don't already own one, you can buy an 'exclusively boxed specimen-sized' piece of the Tower of London by visiting **http://www.toweroflondon.co.uk**. You could buy several and use the boxes to build your own tower!

How about a new car? CarSource (**http://www.carsource.co.uk**) offers a free service to private buyers and will give you a quote. Or, if you're in the market for a used motor, search the database of more than nine thousand 'previously owned' vehicles. Or you could submit your details to CarSource and they'll try to track it down for you. Alternatively, nip into Car Shop (**http://www.carshop.co.uk**) where you can buy or sell a car, get a valuation, and even carry out an HPI title check. Perhaps you need a loan to buy your dream machine. If so, the Abbey National (**http://www.abbeynational.co.uk**) should give you the information you need, and you can use their handy loan calculator to work out what it's going to cost. Finally, you'll need car insurance, and CarQuote may be able to help you out: visit **http://www.carquote.co.uk**, fill in the details, and CarQuote will submit them to 10 insurance companies on your behalf. You should receive individual replies by email, but you'll have to follow them up yourself. One of the popular insurance companies that doesn't appear on CarQuote's list is Direct Line at **http://www.directline.co.uk**.

Are there any shopping newsgroups?

Not shopping, exactly, but there are certainly small ads and trading groups. You'll find the most useful groups in the **uk.adverts** hierarchy and the extensive **biz** hierarchy. If that's not enough, you should find a few extras by filtering your newsgroup list with the word **marketplace**.

Next, a brief stop at the stylish Wine Cellar. You can find this wonderful, friendly site at **http://www.winecellar.co.uk** and browse through various tempting categories such as Wine, Champagne, Beer and Cider, with a dazzling array from around the world. You can also top up with soft drinks and choose from a wide range of fine cigars. Wine Cellar isn't a secure site, so a slightly different ordering system is used. After choosing your goods and clicking the **Review and Order** button you can select a suitable time when the company will telephone you for your credit-card details.

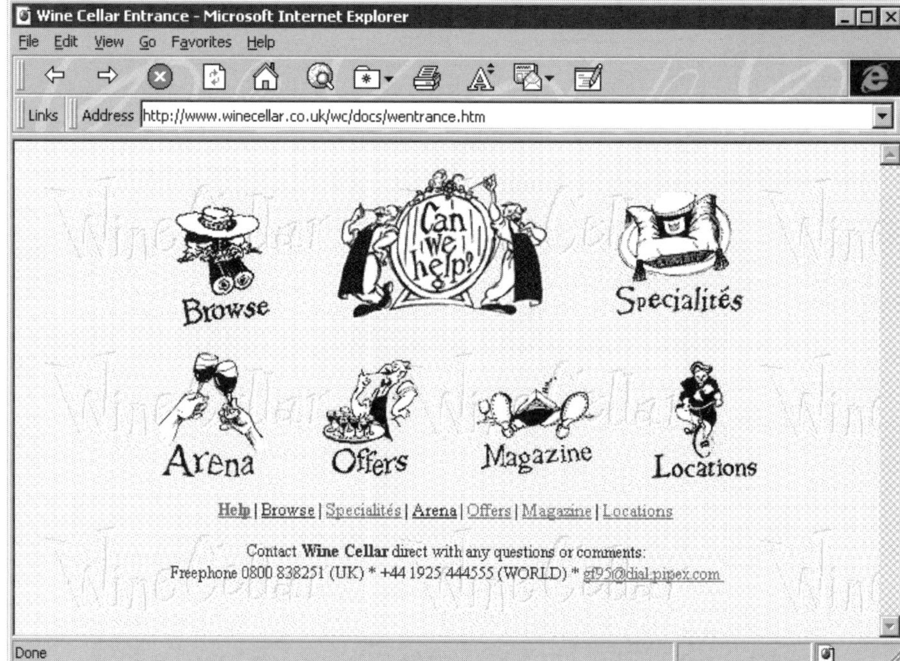

▶ The Wine Cellar – so good you can almost smell the corks!

Not content with simply selling, the Wine Cellar offers some nice extras. Click the **Magazine** icon, for example, and you'll find a range of interesting recipes with suggested accompanying wines. And for real wine aficionados there's a newsgroup-style message centre in the **Arena** where you can follow discussions, ask questions and receive (possibly rather slurred) answers.

After a nice meal and a crate of Beaujolais, you'll probably want to settle down with a good book. Visit the Internet Bookshop at **http://www.bookshop.co.uk**, and search by title, author or subject. The first time you buy, you'll need to set up an account by entering your email address and choosing a password. Or check out Online Originals (**http://www.onlineoriginals.com**), a site which publishes original works in email form only. Read synopses and samples on the web site, and if you find something you like, you can pay around £4 to have the complete text sent to you by email.

BY THE WAY

Classic literature online

If your reading tastes include authors like Somerset Maugham, Daniel Defoe, Oscar Wilde and Arthur Conan Doyle, visit Project Gutenberg at **ftp://sunsite.unc.edu/pub/docs/books/gutenberg/index.html**, which is a site that publishes out-of-copyright works in electronic format.

After all this spending, it's probably about time to check your bank balance and settle your credit-card bill. No, don't get up – you can do that online too! Two of the UK's biggest banks, Barclays (**http://www.barclays.co.uk**) and NatWest (**http://www.natwest.co.uk**) should both be offering online banking to their account-holders by mid-1997, allowing you to transfer funds, pay bills and check balances at any hour of the day or night.

It Must Be Love...

Here's a branch of Internet shopping that romantics won't be able to resist – show someone how much you care by filling their email box with virtual kisses, cards and poetry. For more romance than you can shake a stick at, visit Aphrodite's Love Palace at **http://www.purple.co.uk/purplet/love**.

Kisses are in the form of WAV (audio) files, and cards use graphics, so it pays to choose carefully if the love of your life has a slow Internet connection. You can also order chocolates, take a tour of the Virtual Palace, and test your romance quotient with the online quiz. And if that cyber-kiss hits the spot, why not follow it up with a virtual proposal?

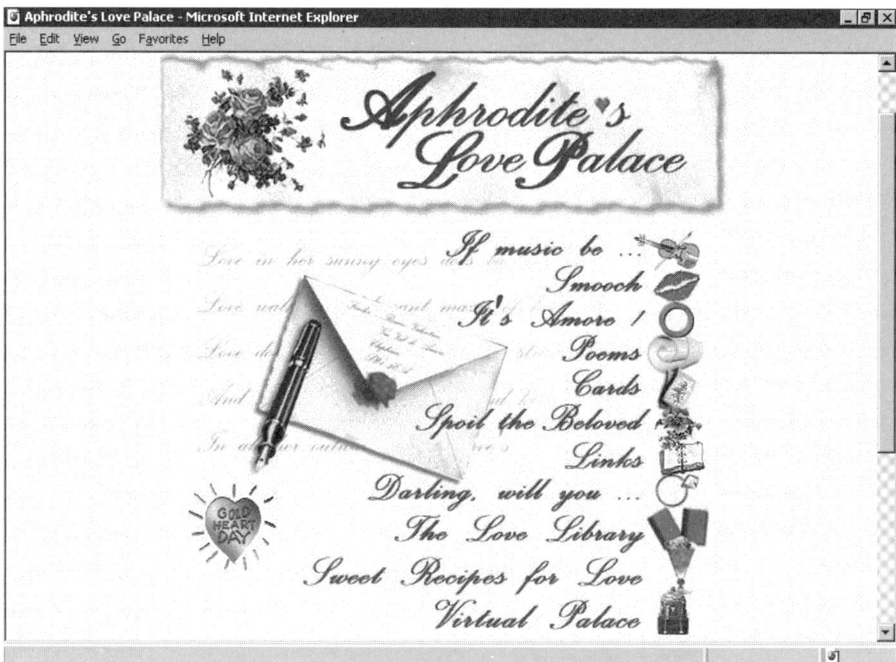

▶ Aphrodite's – the ultimate romance site for lovers with fast connections.

Virtual cards are all the rage on the Internet as more and more people take to email as an alternative to the post. A couple of free 'all-purpose' card shops are 1 Virtual Place at **http://www.1virtualplace.com/card-shop** and Awesome Cyber-Cards at **http://www.marlo.com/card.htm**, or try Bell's Virtual Christmas Cards (**http://www.bell.ca/cards**), which come complete with music and animation. My personal favourite is the Energizer postcard page at **http://www.energizer.com/postcard/haremail.html**, which has a range of cards for all occasions featuring the Energizer bunny. The animations are superb, and they just keep going… and going… and going…

If you'd like to try a few more of these 'gift shops', you'll find a useful collection of links at **http://ns1.inet.net/~jerryz/virtual.htm**.

Online lunar-cy

Have you ever promised someone the moon? Now you can put your money where your mouth is. Visit the MoonShop at **http://www.moonshop.com**, hand over about thirty dollars to the official Lunar Embassy, and you'll receive documentary title to your lunar property and its mineral rights. Getting planning permission for it could be more tricky, of course!

In the time-honoured traditions of romance, you won't be taken seriously if you don't send flowers. Head back to BarclaySquare (see page 248) and you can visit the Interflora store, browse through the catalogue, and place your order online, complete with accompanying message.

But it isn't always possible to 'say it with flowers' – the average bouquet has a limited vocabulary. For those sentiments that only a hand-crafted voodoo doll can truly express, Virtual Design has the answer at **http://www.virtual-design.com/cgi-bin/Voodoo.pl**. To the sound of jungle drums, you can use pins, a candle and a machete to mutilate the doll to your own requirements – inducing yelps and screams as you do so – and then enter the email address of your intended recipient. You'll also have to enter your own email address so that you can receive any response. This site definitely demands a weird sense of humour, but if you have that, you won't be able to keep away!

To finish on a more positive note, let's assume those virtual kisses and proposals did the trick, and a wedding is imminent. Head along to Wedding Bells at **http://www.weddingbells.com/international** to find out what's involved. This is a US site, so you may prefer not to buy goods here, but the other resources are valuable and free: you'll find an Idea Pool, wedding facts and figures, a selection of toasts for worried speech-makers, gift suggestions, wedding etiquette and style advice, and a whole lot more to 'virtually' guarantee a successful day.

19

RESEARCH & WORK ON THE INTERNET

In This Chapter...

- Use online dictionaries, encyclopaedias & more
- Search for specialist research material at Wired Source
- Locate online maps, atlases & city guides
- Find pictures, videos & information about the entire Universe
- Online schools, universities & study tools

Whatever you do in your daily life, the Internet can help. It can provide you with vital reference and research materials; supply information about complementary or competing companies; enable you to work or study from home; and put you in touch with other users working in a similar field. And if your daily life leaves you too much time for aimless surfing, the Internet can even help you find a job!

Look it up Online

I'm not going to pretend that you'll be using 'lookup' references on the Internet a great deal. In the UK, where a local telephone call still costs money, going online every time you need to check the spelling of a word or find a synonym is hardly an economical pastime. More than likely your word processor has a built-in spellchecker and thesaurus; you may have a CD-ROM-based multimedia encyclopaedia too. But it's a safe bet that the Internet outweighs your book and CD-ROM collections, so here are some of the resources you can call on when you need to.

Material gains

If you need more reference materials than those given here and on the free CD accompanying this book, point your browser at **http://www.yahoo.co.uk/Reference** for a characteristically comprehensive set of reference categories.

Encyclopaedias

The words 'online encyclopaedia' sound a bit odd. After all, the Internet itself is the ultimate encyclopaedia, so why would you search its contents for a smaller version? A search engine will provide a greater number and variety of links to information than any encyclopaedia. So the only time you're likely to want an online encyclopaedia is when you need concise, comprehensive information on a subject quickly, and the only contender is the Encyclopaedia Britannica's online incarnation at **http://www.eb.com**.

The Britannica site itself is excellent – you'll find an Image Tour, a word game, Random Article feature, news and current events articles, Birthday

Lookup, and masses more. As for the reason you visited in the first place, the search facilities are fast and powerful: you can enter a keyword or phrase, or even type a question in standard English. The search engine will then give you the information intelligently; if it believes it's answered your question, it will display the relevant article, or the portion of an article that seems to contain the answer. As with keyword searches, you'll also find more links to related articles to help you dig deeper.

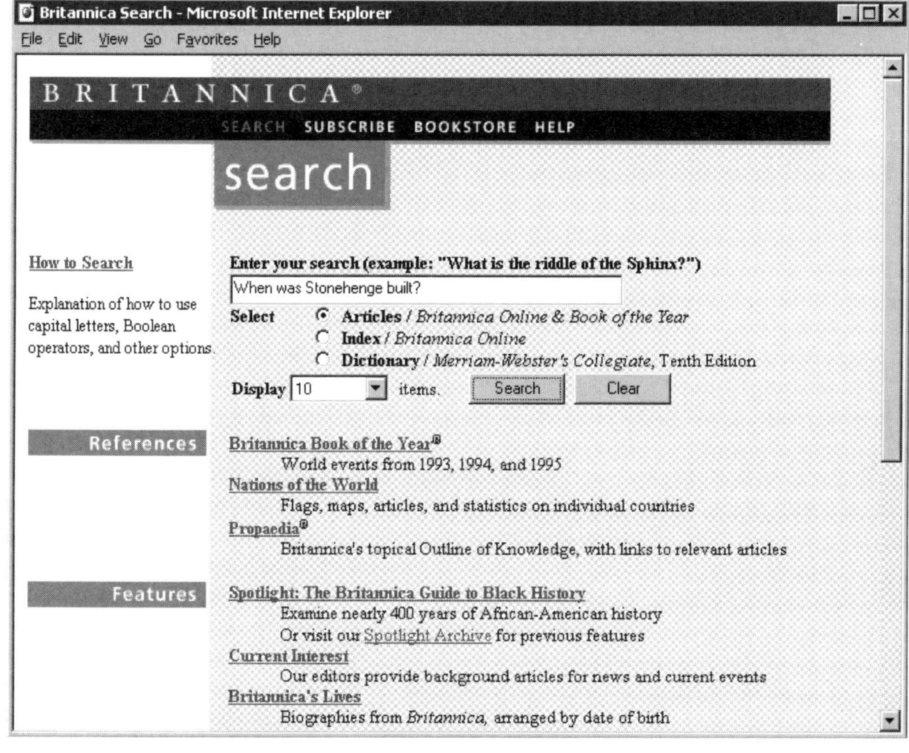

◀ Britannica – as seen by someone who has survived the sign-up procedure.

Being unique, Britannica is a subscription service. It comes at a price not far removed from that of your entire Internet access: $14.95 per month, or $150 per year. You can sign up for a seven-day trial by clicking the **Free Trial** icon, but the process is very convoluted. You'll have to fill in a form, choose and remember a password, and wait for email acceptance. This email contains a username that you'll also have to remember. You have 24 hours to reply to this message, or you'll have to start all over again. Once you've received a response to your reply, you can return to Britannica and give it a whirl.

BY THE WAY

Encyclopaedia for the kids

Kids and teenagers can find a good reference site at **http://www.adventure.com/library/encyclopedia**. This encyclopaedia allows keyword searches, browsing through its nine categories, or a trawl through its entire list of entries. Although it's a US site with an obviously US slant, the information is well presented and could make all the difference to school projects or homework.

Dictionaries

Dictionaries of all types abound on the Internet. One of the best spelling and definition 'lookups' is Webster's (subtly retitled WWWebster's for the Web) at **http://www.m-w.com/netdict.htm**. Enter a keyword, and its pronunciation and definition will appear. If you're not sure of the spelling, just get as close as you can and WWWebster's will suggest some alternatives. A great all-rounder is the OneLook Dictionaries site at **http://www.onelook.com**. This

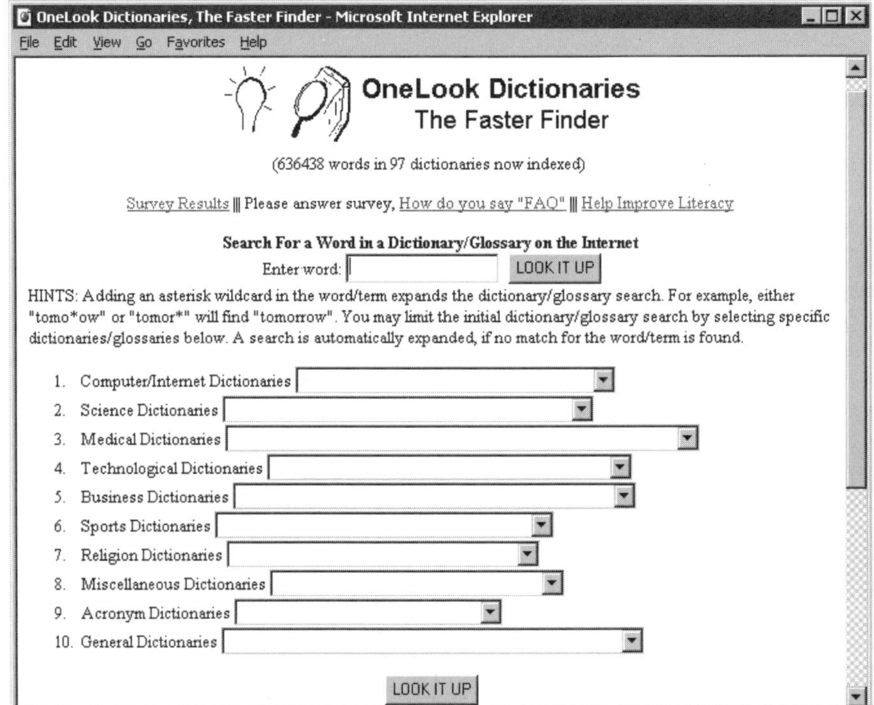

▶ OneLook Dictionaries contain 636,438 different words. It almost makes you feel guilty asking for just one, doesn't it?

handy resource can search through 97 dictionaries simultaneously, or you can restrict your search to a particular area such as medical or religious dictionaries. Both WWWebster's and OneLook support the use of wildcards, allowing you to find multiple words or hedge your bets on the spelling. Of course, neither of these sites can help you when you receive an email from your Algerian penpal. For that you need a dual-language dictionary, and

Wildcards

Wildcards are characters that are used to represent unknown characters in a word. The asterisk replaces multiple letters (so you could enter **demo*** to find 'democracy' or 'demographic'); while the questionmark replaces a single letter (so **te?t?** would find 'tests' or 'teeth').

Dictionaries On The Web (**http://www.ling.helsinki.fi/~hkantola/dict.html**) is the place to find one. This has links to a huge number of translation dictionaries including Russian, Estonian, Czech, Latin and German, most of which translate to or from English.

For a less demanding look at languages, try these oddball sites. The Aussie Slang & Phrase Dictionary (**http://www.uq.edu.au/%7Ezzlreid/slang.html**) is a real ripper worth a burl! BritSpeak is a site that has English as a second language for Americans (although it also has an American-English version). It's intended to be tongue-in-cheek, but some of its humour is quite unintentional, though they'll probably call me a bounder for saying so. You can find BritSpeak at **http://pages.prodigy.com/NY/NYC/britspk/main.html**.

Still no rhyme for 'orange'

The word 'orange' continues to look an unlikely candidate for your latest love-poem, as confirmed by the Rhyming Dictionary at http://www.cs.cmu.edu/~dougb/rhyme.html. This keyword search lets you choose between perfect and partial rhymes, or homophones (such as there/their/they're).

Thesauruses

The most pristine book in my collection is Roget's Thesaurus. To look at it, you'd think I care for it deeply. I don't – I find it very unfriendly (hostile, antagonistic and, indeed, adverse). Fortunately, Roget's online version, at **http://web.cs.city.ac.uk/text/roget/thesaurus.html**, uses the now-traditional keyword search. Just type in a word, and then choose the desired meaning from the resulting list to see its synonyms.

Quotations

'The Internet is a great way to get on the Net.' So sayeth US Senator Bob Dole, and it takes a brave man to disagree. Another good way is to say something sufficiently wise, amusing or obtuse that people will include it in their online quotation pages. Everyone from Shakespeare to Stallone has said something quotable, and the best place to find it is **http://www.lexmark.com/data/quote-21.html**. This page gives an immense hypertext list of words from 'Ability' to 'Zest' – just click a likely word to open a page of related quotes.

Alternatively, visit Project Bartleby at **http://www.columbia.edu/acis/bartleby/bartlett** to read quotes by choosing an author from the list, or by running a keyword search. The quotes are limited to classical literature (no Oscar Wildes or George Bernard Shaws here), and the search engine responds best to a single-word entry.

BY THE WAY

Sling 'em a zinger

Looking for something a little snappier to use in your speeches, or something to add an extra fillip to your email signature files, and so on? Zingers boasts a large collection of more than five hundred such one-liners located at http://users.aol.com/sallee/html/zingers.html.

If you're in the market for the cringe-making 'foot-in-mouth' type of quotation, try the Comedy Break quotes page at **http://www.comedybreak.com/quotes**, or the unwittingly ironic Supermodel Quotes (wickedly subtitled 'From The Mouths Of Babes') at **http://www.sils.umich.edu/~sooty/thoughts.html**.

And Lots More Besides...

Need to find the meaning of some of those irritating acronyms and abbreviations that seem to crop up so often in modern life? Head off to the Acronym Lookup at **http://www.ucc.ie/cgi-bin/acronym**. This simple service consists of just a textbox (nope, no button!). Type in your acronym, and press Enter to see the results.

Another often-needed reference is a weights and measures converter. For a straightforward list of units and their conversion factors, visit **http://www.soton.ac.uk/~scp93ch/refer/convfact.html**. The list is comprehensive, and appears on a single page, so you could even save the page to your own disk for easy use. But if you'd prefer to avoid the brain-exercise of doing the maths yourself, the Measurement Converter at **http://www.mplik.ru/~sg/transl** has the answer. Choose one of the nine categories (such as Weight, Speed, Pressure or Area), type a figure in the appropriate box, and press the Tab key to see the equivalent value instantly displayed for all the other unit types.

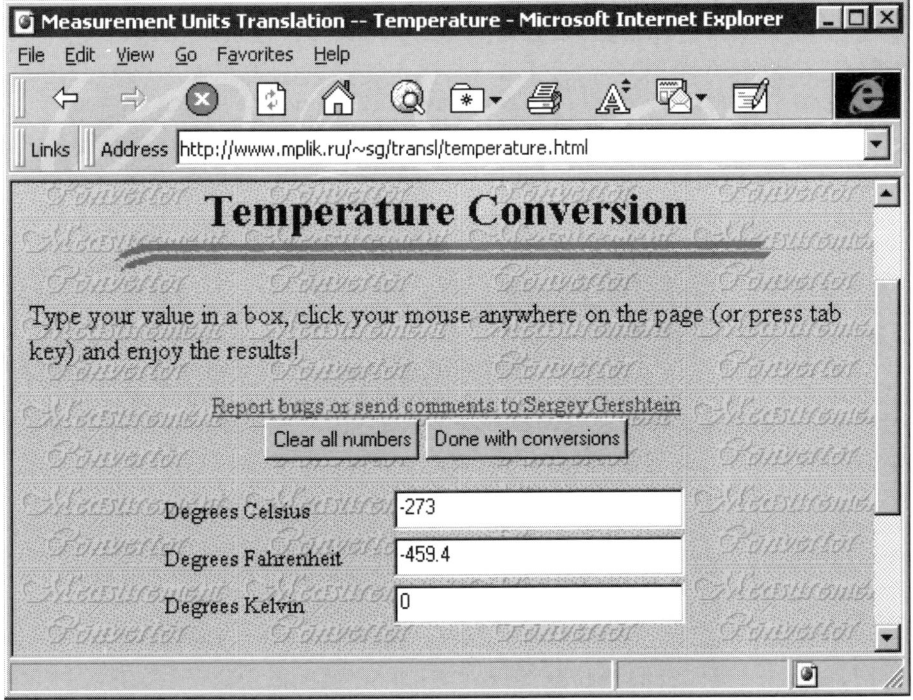

◀ The Measurement Converter gives nine categories of unit type, and immediate results.

Along similar lines, you'll find a useful currency converter at **http://www.xe.net/currency**. Type an amount into the textbox, select your Convert From and Convert To currencies from the drop-down lists, and click the button to see the result based on the latest exchange rates.

BY THE WAY

The writer's bible

Confused by the comma? Perplexed by the apostrophe? You need The Elements of Style by Strunk and White. In fact, if you write anything more adventurous than a shopping-list, this captivating little book is a must-have. But don't take my word for it – read it online at **http://www.columbia.edu/acis/bartleby/strunk**.

Finally, here's an unusual cross between a search engine and a reference lookup. Wired Source (at **http://www.wiredsource.com/wiredsource**) gives a list of categories such as Business, Companies, Politics, Science and Film.

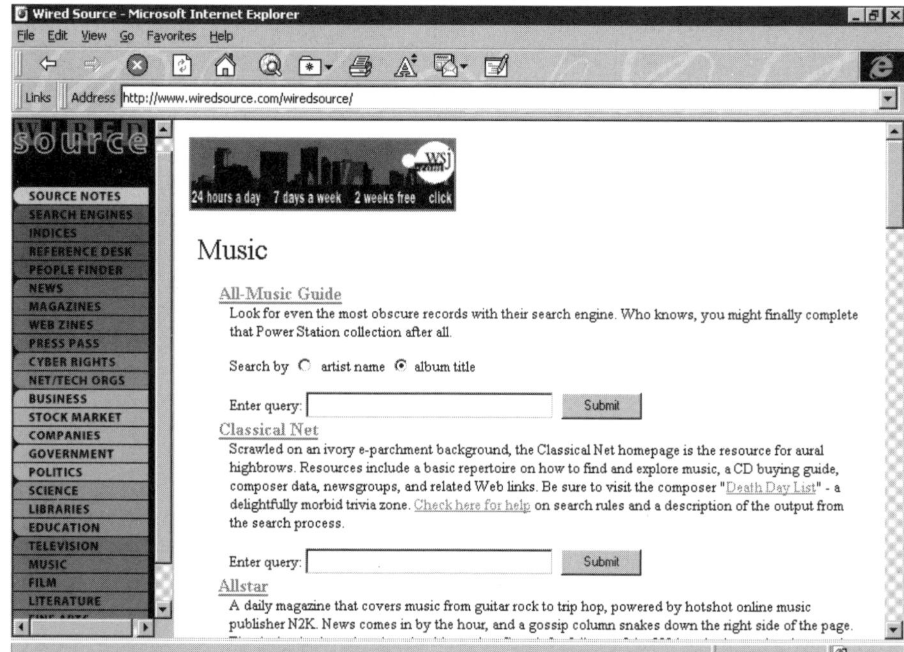

▶ Wired Source gathers hundreds of search facilities into one easy-to-use site.

Choose one of these, and a page will open displaying a list of specialist search engines, sites and links, as shown in the previous screenshot. Just pick the most likely looking candidate on the page and submit a keyword search. Although it's a US site, so some categories may not be helpful to UK users, this is one of the surest ways to find anything from details of a patent application to the complete David Bowie discography.

The Earth Unearthed

The world is generally accepted to be a pretty big place, and most calculations indicate that the universe is bigger still, so the potential for acquiring knowledge is inexhaustible. Whether you're looking for fact, conjecture or opinion, the Internet can help you find a street-map of Dallas, the best restaurant in Prague, a video of a lunar eclipse, or several answers to the mystery of crop-circles.

Discover the World

There's no single, comprehensive site for maps and atlases, so if you want something particular you'll have to be prepared for a bit of traipsing around. A good place to start is Encyberpedia's map links at **http://www.encyberpedia.com/maps.htm**. Although the USA is disproportionately well served, you'll also find maps of cities elsewhere in the world, atlases and historical maps, plus a few links to interactive and virtual reality map-sites.

If you want some local information to go with your maps, try visiting the Excite search engine's CityNet site at **http://city.net**. You can type the name of a country, region or city to run a keyword search, or (more enjoyably) click your way through the interactive maps to home in on the area you want. Once again, US cities are plotted and detailed to the last manhole cover at the expense of other countries, but nevertheless it manages to be a smart and informative site.

If you like these clickable maps, you'll enjoy a visit to Magellan Geographix (**http://www.magellangeo.com/HTML/atlas.html**) – you'll find a few extra UK cities here, plus superb graphics. Maps are sorted by Region, Country and City, and you'll also find links to a search facility, atlases, and Maps in the News. There's even an online store selling posters, T-shirts and yes, more maps!

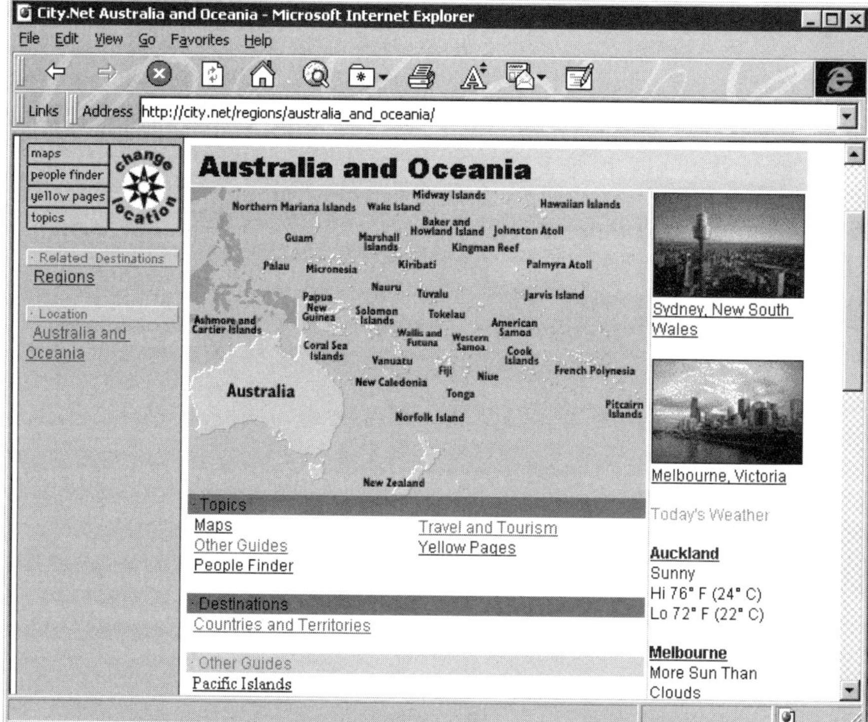

▶ CityNet's interactive maps lead to photos, local maps and background information.

For historical maps, check out the Oxford University Map Room at **http://rsl.ox.ac.uk/nnj**. Of course you'll get an even better selection by visiting the room itself, but the snag is that that entails a trip to Oxford! You can also find the Ordnance Survey online at two sites: **http://www.ordsvy.gov.uk** is the official Government site and **http://www.campus.bt.com/CampusWorld/pub/OS/mainmenu.html** is an educational site giving examples, a key to OS symbols and a UK gazetteer.

BY THE WAY

Flying colours

Looking for information on the flags of the world? Visit **http://flags.cesi.it/flags/allpaget.html** and click the flag you want from the list. The flags can be downloaded as GIF image files, and each one is accompanied by a page of fascinating historical background.

Zooming out for a global view, there's a mass of information available. If you need to check up on a time zone in a hurry, head along to **http://tycho.usno.navy.mil/tzones.html**, a US Navy site, and click the initial letter of the country you're interested in. For a slower but stylishly interactive way of reaching similar information, the WorldTime site at **http://www.worldtime.com/cgi-bin/user/hb1005/wt.cgi** will keep you clicking around in fascination for ages as you zoom in and out, and switch between night and day.

For more general information about the world, stop off at the Planet Earth Home Page (**http://www.nosc.mil/planet_earth/numbers.html**). Among the mine of data on this page you'll find links to world clocks, world and country populations, calendars, a World Factbook, the amusing US National Debt Clock, and the FBI Most Wanted List.

The world in pictures

For the best images and films of the Earth, visit the Earth Image Index at **http://bang.lanl.gov/solarsys/raw/earth**. This is a plain list of files (some quite large) in four categories: Animations, Earth Images, Earth Cloud Images and Earth Impact Craters. Many files have accompanying text documents providing background information.

Change the World

There are a number of pressure groups and organisations dedicated to educating and improving the world, and you'll find many of them online. If you know the name of a particular organisation or society, try entering it into your favourite search engine; if you don't, enter descriptive keywords such as **wildlife protection**. Here are a few organisations you may want to visit:

Organization	Web site URL
Amnesty International	http://www.oneworld.org/amnesty/index.html
Crime Prevention Initiative	http://www.crime-prevention.org.uk
Friends Of The Earth	http://www.foe.co.uk
Greenpeace International	http://www.greenpeace.org
Save The Children	http://www.oneworld.org/scf

The Universe... & Beyond!

If you need information about the rest of our solar system, the obvious starting point is NASA. In fact, the primary NASA site at **http://www.nasa.gov** is so immense it's hard to believe you'll ever need another site! Alongside image and movie galleries, there are sound files, details of new and current missions, information about the types of technology involved, the history of space travel, and the NASA organisation itself.

If you want to find undiluted Shuttle information, go to **http://www.100hot.com/framed/shuttle.nasa.gov.html.** This is an in-depth but friendly NASA site about Shuttle life, with videos of the craft taken from both inside and out, latest news about the Shuttle programme, and a wealth of fascinating background information that you won't find anywhere else.

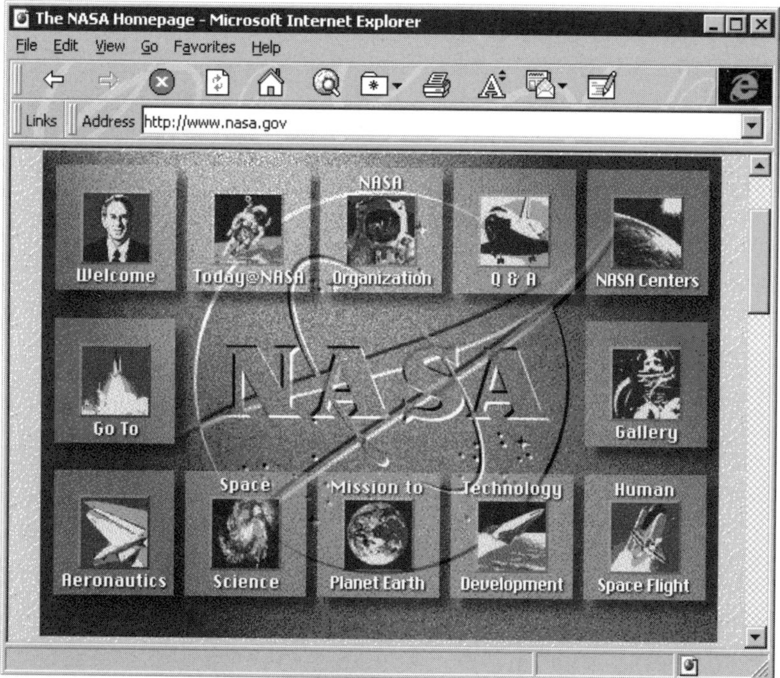

▶ Visit NASA and you'll probably never be seen again!

To boldly go where no man has gone before, head for the Royal Greenwich Observatory at **http://www.ast.cam.ac.uk**. The site is uninspiring, but its links can lead you to pictures from the Hubble Space Telescope, and many other observatories (and some of them provide live camera feeds to the Web).

More solar system links

Real astronomy addicts, can find a wealth of facts and figures about our solar system by visiting **http://www.rahul.net/resource/hotlinks/solar.htm**. The page is a simple list of links to all manner of resources – eclipses, meteors, a Mars atlas, moon maps, you name it.

A popular topic of discussion on the Internet, as elsewhere, concerns the existence of 'little green men' (and women, presumably) from outer space, and many web sites and newsgroups have sprung up to present, discuss and dispute the evidence for UFOs. The best of these is The Quest, at **http://www.netfeed.com/pstevens/quest2.htm**, which also covers crop-circles, ancient civilisations, paranormal phenomena, and many more mysteries and unanswered questions. Confirmed UFO addicts will also want to check out these sites:

- Bufora, the British UFO Research Organization, at **http://bufora.org.uk**.
- UFO Magazine at **http://www.ufomag.co.uk**.
- UFO Reality at **http://www.ufo-reality.co.uk**.
- SETI Institute at **http://www.seti-inst.edu**.

Usenet can put you in touch with other people around the world interested in the known and unknown universe. Take a look at the **sci.space** and **sci.astro** hierarchies, or drop in at **alt.sci.planetary**. You'll also find an **alt.paranormal** hierarchy, and there's a scattering of UFO-related groups that you can track down by filtering the list with **ufo**.

Education on the Internet

Education is at an interesting stage in its online development. Although universities and colleges were among the first sites to appear on the Net, online classes are still few and far between. The technology is there: conferencing programs like NetMeeting (see page 145) can link students to classes using video and sound; coursework can be sent back and forth by email; reference materials can be downloaded by FTP, or read from the World Wide Web.

One of the few UK organisations that can provide courses over the Internet, unsurprisingly, is the Open University. Its site, at **http://www.open.ac.uk**, explains how the system works, and it will even provide you with the software you need (you'll have to find your own computer though!). There are details of all the available courses here, and you can apply for a place on a course by email.

BY THE WAY

Schools on the Web

A site dedicated to UK schools on the Internet, with national curriculum information, a noticeboard, and a penpals page, is ifl@school (at **http://www.rmplc.co.uk**). It also features EduWeb – a list of email addresses and web-page links to thousands of schools nationwide.

Elsewhere on the UK Net, practical education sites are still a bit thin on the ground. One site that appeared recently is GCSE Answers at **http://www.zoo.co.uk/~gcse**, which gives exam information, tips for success, and summaries of syllabuses. At the time of writing, only English language and literature are covered, but Maths syllabuses should be online soon.

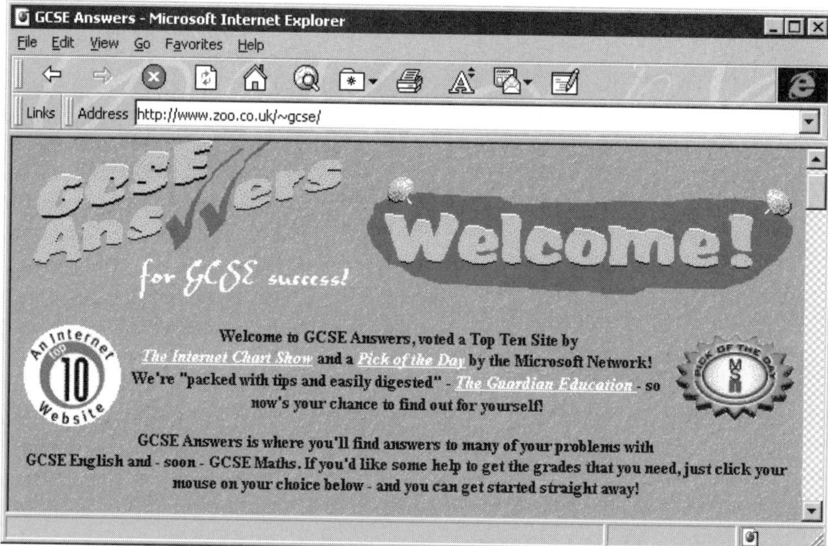

▶ Not the actual answers of course, but a useful step towards them.

The tradition for universities and colleges to have a presence on the Internet hasn't abated, and you can track them all down easily from the clickable maps at **http://scitsc.wlv.ac.uk/ukinfo/uk.map.html**. This page shows universities, and two links at the top of the page open similar maps for UK colleges and research establishments – click on any location and you'll be whisked straight to its web page. The links to research venues, especially, are many and varied, including museums, libraries and observatories, and make excellent resources for your own online research. The university sites have an extra value – many of them include a fund of local information such as bus and train timetables, maps, and places of interest.

Find a Job Online

We all get involved in the employment market at some time or other in our lives, and it's usually a frustrating, hit-and-miss ordeal. Although the Internet can't give you any firm guarantees, it can give you access to resources that your 'unwired' competitors don't have, and it puts all these right on your computer desktop to take some of the drudgery out of job-searching and self-promotion.

GOOD QUESTION

Where can I learn to write a CV?

Go to **http://www.yahoo.co.uk** and run a keyword search for **resume**. You'll see a list of Yahoo employment categories that have a Resumes subcategory (click on **Next 20** to view more of the list). Pick a link that matches the type of work you're involved in, and browse through some of the CVs written by others to pick up a few ideas.

If you're looking for (or offering) full- or part-time work, there are two UK sites that are head and shoulders above the rest. Between them they offer many thousands of vacancies. The first is PeopleBank, at **http://www.peoplebank.com**, which gives its services free to jobseekers. Just fill in the online registration form, and you can then submit your CV or browse through the database of job vacancies. The second is WorkWeb at (**http://www.workweb.co.uk**). This site splits its vacancies into 25 searchable categories, and also provides support services for jobseekers, and information about employment agencies.

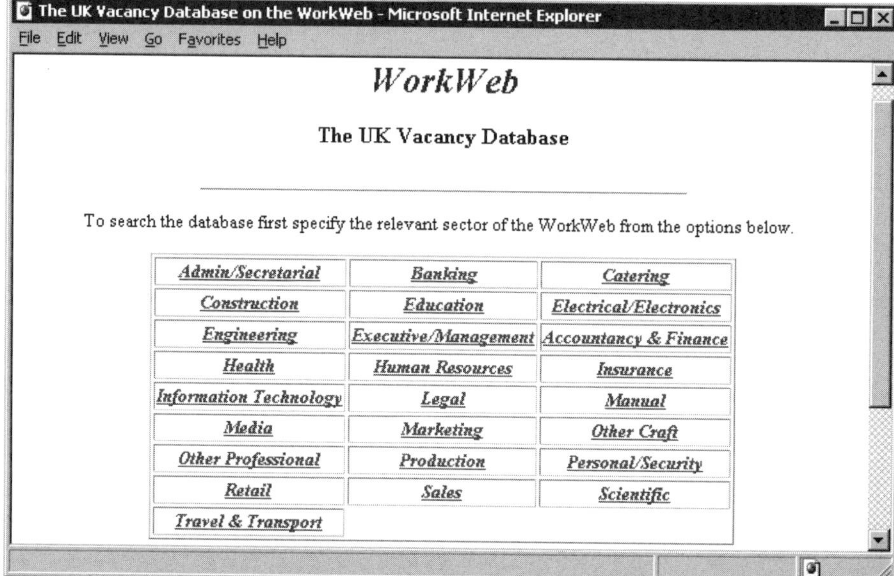

▶ Pick an employment category and then search WorkWeb's database.

If there's a particular company you'd like to work for, it's worth visiting their web site. Many companies list their job vacancies online (although it sometimes takes a bit of clicking around to find the right page), and you can usually submit an application and CV by email. If you don't know the company's web address, use your favourite search engine to search for the company name, or try **www.*company-name*.co.uk** or **www.*company-name*.com**.

BY THE WAY

Scan the professional journals

Another way of looking for vacancies on the Web is to peruse the trade journals. Yahoo lists 15 categories of trade and professional journals such as Science, Culture, Computers and Arts. Visit **http://www.yahoo.co.uk/Reference/Journals**, pick a suitable category and choose a journal to read online.

If you want to be even more enterprising, why not publish your CV on the World Wide Web for all to see? If your line of work involves something that can be demonstrated on a computer, such as graphic design, journalism or music, you could even include examples on your web site. Most IAPs and online services provide free web-space, and in chapters 23 to 25 you'll learn how to go about creating and publicising your pages.

Newsgroups provide valuable methods of 'meeting' potential employers, employees, collaborators and customers. If you filter your newsgroup list with the word **job** you'll see a number of useful groups, including **alt.jobs, alt.jobs.overseas**, and an entire **uk.jobs** hierarchy that includes **uk.jobs.offered** and **uk.jobs.wanted**. It's worth looking for newsgroups catering for your particular profession or vocation too: sometimes the only way to learn of a job opportunity is to be on 'speaking terms' with the type of people who can point you in the right direction.

Jobs by mail

It doesn't get much easier than having job vacancies automatically delivered to your mailbox, does it? Head for **http://www.neosoft.com/internet/paml/bysubj.html**, click on **Employment** and look for a promising mailing list. Clicking the list-name will give you details about subscribing to the list.

20

PURSUE YOUR HOBBIES & INTERESTS

In This Chapter...

- Read magazines online
- Find other Internet users who share your hobbies
- Where to seek advice
- Find friendship (or even love!) in cyberspace
- Follow your favourite sports online
- See the sights of the world without leaving home

However solitary a pursuit your hobby is, it probably isn't something you like to follow completely alone. Whether you like gardening, fishing, stamp collecting or origami, part of the enjoyment is being able to talk about it with other enthusiasts and share knowledge and skills. The Internet can help here, but far from just being a place to air your origami anecdotes, it can teach you more about your hobby, give you advice and support on a range of issues, and help you to organise your own clubs and societies.

Read Your Favourite Magazines Online

The chances are good (and getting better all the time) that your favourite magazine has an online edition in the form of a web site. If so, the URL will probably be listed somewhere in the magazine itself, but it's worth visiting a search engine and typing its name into a keyword search. If that doesn't work, it's a racing certainty that there's an online magazine somewhere that fits the bill, so try a search in the form **magazine *your hobby***.

BY THE WAY

Pros and cons of online magazines

Online versions of magazines are usually free, but there is a price to pay. Often the online version will be 'published' a week or two later than the paper version, and it may not be a complete copy. In their favour, though, you can save a small fortune if you normally buy several magazines every month, and you can store interesting articles on disk rather than snipping out pages!

To point you in the right direction, two of the UK's biggest magazine publishers have sites containing all their magazines in online form. Head along to MAG.net (home of VNU Publications) at **http://www.vnu.co.uk**, or FutureNet (Future Publishing's site) at **http://www.futurenet.co.uk**, and fill in the registration forms to get free access to dozens of major magazines.

Still not found the magazine you're looking for? The trusty Yahoo lists a full 20 categories of magazine at **http://www.yahoo.co.uk/Regional/Countries/United_Kingdom/News_and_Media/Magazines**. If the magazine exists you'll almost certainly find it there, but here's a few popular publications to get you started:

Magazine	Web site URL
Cosmopolitan	http://www.designercity.com/cosmopolitan
Esquire	http://www.designercity.com/esquire/index.htm
Exchange and Mart	http://www.exchangeandmart.co.uk
Horse and Rider	http://www.equestrian.co.uk
Loaded	http://www.uploaded.com
Q Magazine	http://www.erack.com/qweb
Reader's Digest	http://www.readersdigest.co.uk
Select	http://www.erack.com/select
Top Gear Magazine	http://www.topgear.com

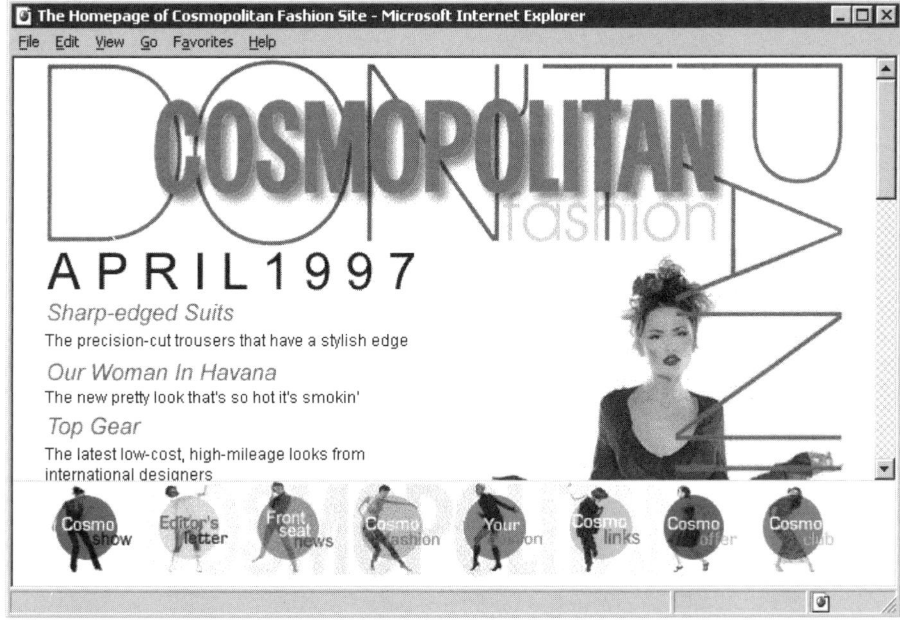

◀ Cosmopolitan online – at last Internet geeks can wear designer anoraks!

Get in Touch with Other Enthusiasts

The most obvious way to make contact with other enthusiasts who share your hobby is through Usenet. The **rec.** and **talk.** hierarchies cover a vast and varied range of interests between them, but if yours isn't there, use your newsreader's filter option to find it – after all, if a group as obscure as **alt.macdonalds.ketchup** can exist, there must be something out there about your own pet subject!

A better method still may be to subscribe to a related mailing list. Mailing lists greatly outnumber newsgroups, but there's no sure-fire way to find out what's available. You'll find a good selection of lists at the Publicly Accessible Mailing Lists site (see page 122), but a more reliable method could be to join a newsgroup and find out which mailing lists the other subscribers belong to.

BY THE WAY

Share it on the Web

The majority of web sites are created by personal users like you and me who want to share their interests, so why not join them? As well as being a satisfying achievement, it adds another opportunity for meeting people (as long as you give them an email link to click).

There are bound to be sites on the World Wide Web relating to your hobby, and a keyword search in your favourite search engine should find them. It's a safe bet that anyone creating a web site on a particular topic is an enthusiast, so why not check the site for an email address and get in touch?

Support & Advice at Your Fingertips

The Internet is the ideal place to find advice and support groups. In some cases, the Net is the only way you could ever access these services – if they exist in the 'real world' at all, they may be based on a different continent! If you know the name of an established organisation or group, you may be able to find it on the Web using a search engine. Otherwise, use a descriptive keyword-search such as **advice legal** or **support disability**.

BY THE WAY

Laugh away your problems

It's not always easy to smile through adversity. Unless it's someone else's adversity, of course – then you can laugh like a drain. Visit Other People's Problems at **http://www2.paramount.com/opp/index.html**, chortle sympathetically, and offer your own advice.

Here's a brief taste of some of the help available – as usual, you'll find links to many more sites on the free CD accompanying this book.

- Law Lounge is a complete one-stop free legal advice centre that can also point you to UK solicitors and barristers, law schools, and a range of other services. Visit **http://www.lawlounge.com**.
- For consumer advice, go to **http://www.open.gov.uk/oft/frames/consumer.htm** at the Office of Fair Trading. The site is split into categories including Credit & Debt, Holiday Problems, How To Complain, and General Consumer Rights.

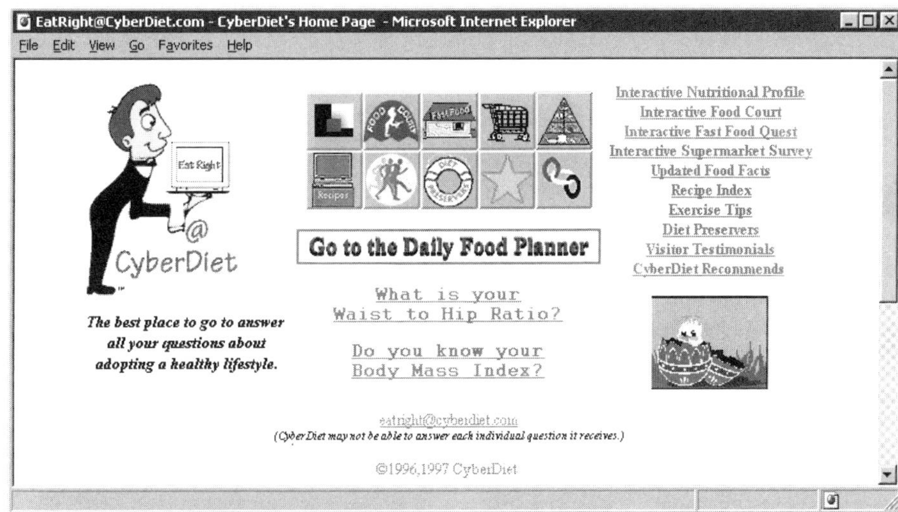

◀ Let CyberDiet tell you if you've exceeded your cheeseburger ration today.

- If you're looking for some straightforward health tips, head for CyberDiet at **http://www.cyberdiet.com**. Despite its name, the site covers all aspects of healthy living and provides copious tips.

Passively reading a web page may give you the information you need, but in some cases you'll want to draw on the experiences of others. In one recent case, after being told that nothing could be done for her child, a mother appealed for help in a support newsgroup and learned of a potentially life-saving operation in South America. There are many such newsgroups available; either filter your list with the word **support**, or take a look at the extensive **alt.support** hierarchy.

Share Your Interests with a Penpal

This is really one for the kids. There's a range of sites that can put you in touch with an email penpal, and you can find a good selection of them at **http://www.yahoo.co.uk/Society_and_Culture/Friendship/Pen_Pals/Kids**. The best, though, is KeyPals at **http://www.kidpub.org/kidpub/keypals**, shown in the next screenshot. As with most penpal search sites, you can enter an age (from 6 to 16) and location for your perfect penpal, but the bonus at KeyPals is that you can specify an interest too. The search results appear as a list of people's names, locations, and ages. Clicking one of these should start your email program and open a blank message window with the penpal's email address already inserted.

For a wider choice of penpals, and some casual online chat into the bargain, take a look at the newsgroups. By far the most popular is **soc.penpals**, but you'll also find plenty going on in **alt.kids-talk.penpals** and **alt.teens.penpals**.

A common parental concern is: "How do my kids know that their penpals really are other kids?" The answer is they don't, necessarily, so a little parental involvement would be wise in the early stages. However, if an adult

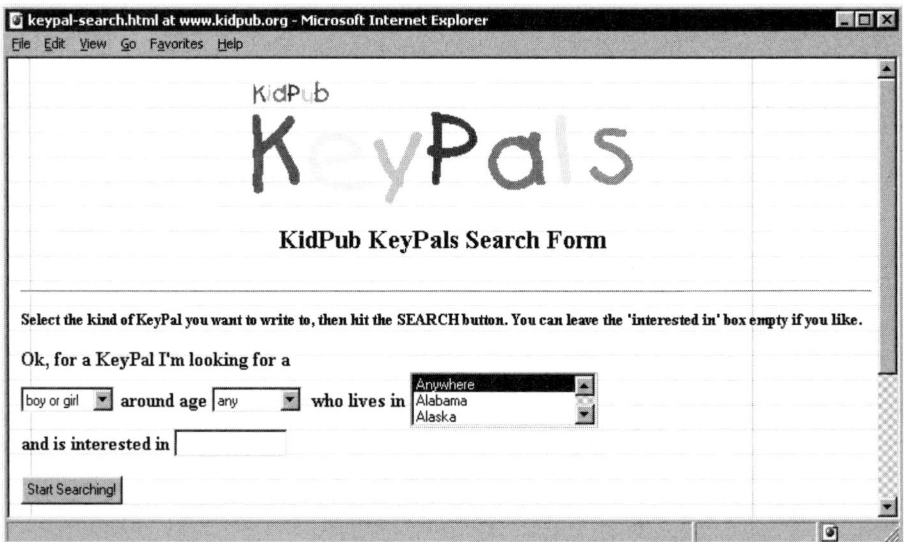

▶ Find penpals from all over the world at KeyPals.

were up to no good he'd be more likely to initiate contact himself than register at KidPals and wait for kids to contact him. A little extra caution is advisable when your kids receive unsolicited email.

Try Some Real Computer Dating!

No, I'm not suggesting you should take your Pentium out to dinner. By *real* computer dating, I mean that you can finally use your own computer to search an extensive database of people anxiously waiting to meet you. Visit Dateline at **http://www.dateline.uk.com** and give the service a trial-run by checking off the attributes your perfect partner should possess and then searching the database.

However, before you can even think of meeting anyone, you'll have to register with the service and part with some cash. After you've spent a little time on the Net, the idea of actually paying for a service starts to seem like an unnecessary extravagance – why not just search a little harder for a free service instead? Unfortunately, in the dating game there's very little option: although free dating-services do exist, most seem to have databases of about five people, all of whom live in a different hemisphere from you.

Keep Up with Your Favourite Sport

You'll find any sport in abundance on the Net – team web sites, sporting facts and figures, fan pages, fantasy games, and much more. The search engines are your key to finding these sites, as usual, by entering the name of your sport, team or player. Here's a mixed bag of links to get you started, and you'll find another bundle on the free CD accompanying this book.

Sports Site	Web Address
Adidas Webzine	http://www.adidas.com
Athletics World Records	http://www.hkkk.fi/~niininen/athl.html
Formula 1	http://www.siii.pt/f1
GolfWeb Europe	http://www.golfweb.com/europe
Ladbrokes Super Sports Service	http://www.sports.ladbrokes.co.uk
Paralympic Games	http://www.paralympic.org/sports/sports.htm
Rugby Leaguer	http://www.rugbyleaguer.co.uk
Tennis	http://www.tennis.com

If you're a football fan, don't waste your time tracking down a team-page with the search engines: instead head for the Soccer City site at **http://nettvik.no/sportsholmen/soccercity/eng1.htm**. Here you'll find links to more than three thousand web pages of UK soccer clubs, covering both official team sites and fan pages. And if you're tired of arguing about who's the best soccer player, visit Opta Interactive (**http://www.i-way.net.uk/opta**): using a painstaking scoring system for every league player, this site has it scientifically nailed down.

For almost any sports fan, the *Sporting Life*'s online edition (**http://www.sporting-life.com**) is a good candidate for your Favorites

BY THE WAY

A pain in the neck?

If you've suffered a sporting injury, visit Medisport at **http://www.medisport.co.uk** for a spot of self-diagnosis and suggested exercises and treatments. A common treatment is to wear a Medisport product, and the site can also help you locate your nearest stockist so that you don't have to limp too far.

▶ The Sporting Life site should be a regular port of call for all sports fans.

menu, covering Soccer, Rugby, Racing, Golf, Cricket, and more, together with the latest sports news and a messages centre. You'll also find some of the most popular sporting magazines such as *Total Football, Cycling Plus, Mountain Bike Pro,* and *Sailing Today* at Future Publishing's site (see page 276).

Track Down Your Favourite Celebrity

Every avid fan wants to know what their favourite film star, band or singer is up to, and you'll find at least one web site devoted to every celebrity you've ever heard of (and quite a few that you haven't!). Visits to some of these sites can turn up biographies, interviews, photos, film clips, and the latest reviews and news. You can use a search engine to track down these pages by entering the celebrity's name, but it's helpful to know how your chosen engine works before you do so. If it allows you to, enclose the name in quote signs (such as **"Jennifer Aniston"**) so that you'll only see pages in which both names appear. Alternatively, prefix each name with a plus sign (**+Jennifer +Aniston**).

The sounds of the stars

If you're looking for interviews with the stars, visit BiteSite at **http://www.bitesite.com**. This site features hundreds of interviews and plays them using streaming RealAudio sound (see page 291), although you can read text transcripts if you prefer.

If all that seems a little complicated, start by visiting Yahoo. You'll find a massive list of links to filmstar pages at **http://www.yahoo.co.uk/Entertainment/Movies_and_Films/Actors_and_Actresses**. The list of musical artists is longer still, and has had to be split alphabetically: visit **http://www.yahoo.co.uk/Entertainment/Music/Artists** and click an initial letter at the top of the page corresponding to the name of the band or the surname of the artist you're looking for. Most fan pages contain links to other fan pages.

For news and chat, celebrities have a similar level of coverage in the newsgroups as they do on the Web. There are large **alt.fan** and **alt.music** hierarchies with groups dedicated to specific artists such as **alt.music.paul-simon** and **alt.fan.jen-aniston** (OK, I admit it, I'm a fan), plus more general groups like **alt.music.midi** and **alt.music.bluegrass**.

▶ *Want to find your favourite celebrity's email address? Take a look at the By The Way Box on page 172 for a method that could turn up trumps.*

Take a Cyber-sightseeing Tour

One interest that most of us share is an ambition to 'see the world' – that vague term that encompasses natural and architectural wonders, famous works of art, and the ruins of ancient kingdoms. The trouble is, unless you have oodles of time and money, it's a difficult ambition to realise.

Sight	Web Address
Golden Gate Bridge	http://www.mcn.org/goldengate/index.html
Grand Canyon	http://www.kaibab.org
Great Barrier Reef	http://werple.mira.net.au/~margaret/frames1.htm
Leaning Tower of Pisa	http://www.cibernet.it/thebox/pisa/tower.html
Le Louvre	http://mistral.culture.fr/louvre/louvrea.htm
Mount Rushmore	http://www.state.sd.us/tourism/rushmore/rushmore.html
Niagara Falls	http://www.moran.com/falls/nfhome.html
Seven Wonders of the Ancient World	http://pharos.bu.edu/Egypt/Wonders
Yellowstone National Park	http://www.yellowstone-natl-park.com

Fortunately, the sights that we'd happily travel for days to see are only a few clicks away and can usually be found with a keyword search. Many of these web sites include background information too, but if you need more information you may be able to find a 'travelogue' site created by someone who's actually visited that country – try a search for **travelogue** ***country***. To save you a little time, here's a few of the sights you're probably itching to see:

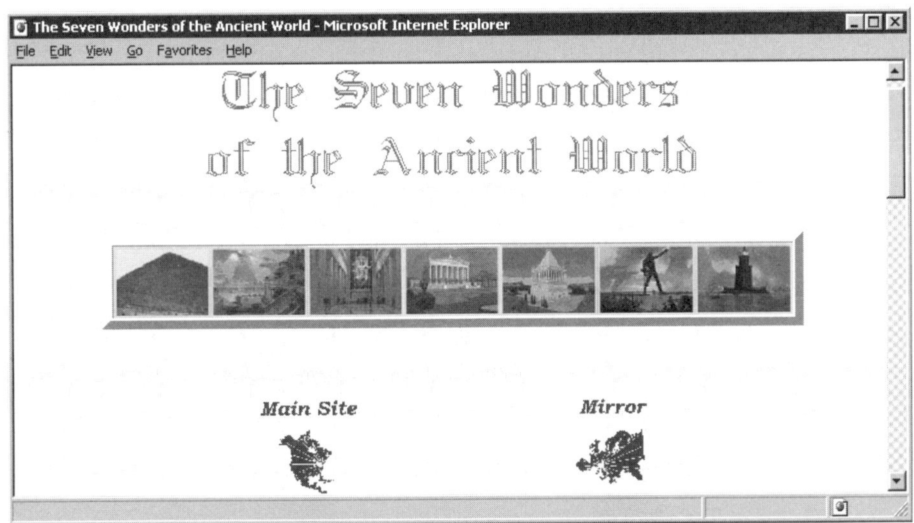

◀ The Seven Wonders of the Ancient World site features original artwork and plenty of information.

4

THE WEB – ACTIVE & INTERACTIVE

In This Part...

21

THE MULTIMEDIA EXPERIENCE

In This Chapter...

- Getting the best out of the Web's multimedia elements
- Listen to music & live radio with RealAudio
- View & download clips of your favourite movies
- Visit animated multimedia-intense Web Pages
- Virtual Reality – fly through 3D online worlds

If you've trundled through Part 3, you've got a pretty good idea of how much you can accomplish using your Internet connection. Without a doubt, the sheer scope of its content, together with its convenience, helps to explain the Net's popularity. But that's not all of it. After all, the Net has been reasonably convenient and varied for thirty-something years. No, the main reason for its popularity surge is that it's now fun to use – today's World Wide Web launches an all-out assault on your senses with animation, sound and video to give you a true multimedia experience.

In this chapter, you'll learn about the different multimedia elements used on the Web, the necessary software to make the most of them, and some of the unashamedly cool sites you can visit to chew some of this cyber-bubblegum. But first, a more pressing question…

Do I Need a Better Computer for Multimedia?

Multimedia is a sort of ex-buzzword. In 1996, a 'multimedia computer' had all the trimmings, cost a great deal more, and was a real 'must have' machine. However, in 1997 the word is rarely attached to computers – almost all new computers have a soundcard, CD-ROM drive, and a capable graphics card, which are the essentials of multimedia. But here's a quick hardware rundown for *good* multimedia:

- If your graphics card has 2Mb or more of memory fitted, letting you display more than 256 colours, visual elements like videos and virtual-reality worlds will be clearer, smoother, and generally more appealing.
- Some of the larger virtual worlds take their toll on both processor and memory: ideally, you should have at least a Pentium 120MHz processor and a minimum 16Mb RAM.
- The modem matters most. If you connect at less than 28.8Kbps, you'll just find the whole experience frustratingly slow. Movies and virtual worlds in particular can be huge files, so buy the fastest modem your service provider supports.

Do I Need a Lot of Extra Software?

There are literally hundreds of plug-ins and viewers out there for different types of multimedia file, and you certainly don't want them all! Of course, some cover the same types of file as others and you can simply choose the one you like best. Others are proprietary programs that let you view a type of file created by one particular company – if this format isn't in wide use on the Web you may prefer not to bother installing the software for it.

> BY THE WAY
>
> **The difference between a plug-in & a viewer**
>
> A plug-in is a program that displays a file in your browser's own window by adding capabilities to your browser that it doesn't have already. A viewer is an entirely separate program that opens its own window to display or play a file you've downloaded.

Let me make two suggestions to simplify things. First, start with the software I've included on the free CD accompanying this book – not only are these some of the best programs of their kind, but you don't have to download them either! Second, go and buy an 'uninstall' utility such as Quarterdeck's CleanSweep: these utilities monitor every change and addition made to your system when a new program is installed so that you can remove all trace of it later if you decide you don't like it.

RealAudio – the Sound of Cyberspace

You won't travel far on the Web before arriving at a site that uses RealAudio for music, speech, or a mixture of the two. RealAudio is a streaming format that plays as the file is being transferred, with none of that tedious waiting around for the sound file to download first. As soon as you click a RealAudio link, your RealAudio Player opens (as in the next screenshot), grabs the first few seconds of the transmission to help it to stay one jump ahead and ensure smooth playback, and then starts to play. You can pause or stop playback by clicking the appropriate buttons, or (if you were playing a single short sound-clip) replay the entire clip, which will now be residing in Internet Explorer's cache directory (see page 81). If you've installed Internet Explorer from the CD-ROM, you don't need to do anything more – the RealAudio plug-in is bundled with it. If you're using a different browser, you'll have to visit **http://www.realaudio.com** to download and install the player software.

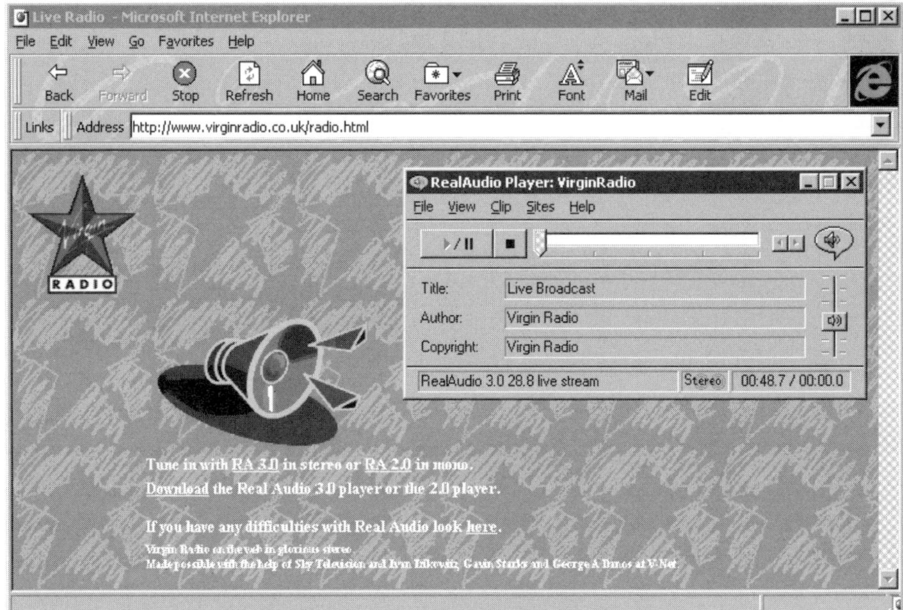

▶ A live RealAudio broadcast from Virgin Radio.

Getting the Action

So, where do you have to go to get some RealAudio action? As with all multimedia plug-ins and viewers, your first stop should be the web site of the people who wrote the program – you'll always find plenty of samples and links to let you play with your new toy once you've installed it. In this case, skip off to **http://www.realaudio.com**.
Below are a few more suggestions:

- Why not tune in to Virgin Radio at **http://www.virginradio.co.uk** to hear the wireless come down the wires?
- Want to hear the Top 40? Visit London's Capital Radio at **http://www.capital-fm.co.uk**, click the Top 40 link and click the RealAudio icon beside the chart hit you'd like to hear – you can even buy your CD singles here! Or click On Air to hear the live broadcast.
- Check out BiteSite at **http://www.bitesite.com** for RealAudio interviews with the stars.
- Visit Radio 1's Listening Booth at **http://www.bbc.co.uk/radio1/index.html** to mix your own radio show.

Other sound formats

RealAudio doesn't offer great sound quality – some sacrifices have to be made for the files to transfer this fast. Top-quality sound comes in the form of **.wav** files, which Internet Explorer can play without any extra help, and these weigh in at up to 10 megabytes for a top-quality one-minute file! A .wav file has to be downloaded in its entirety before it will play.

More Music with MIDI

MIDI is a different type of sound format from RealAudio and .wav files. Instead of being a recording of sounds, a MIDI file uses the sounds already built into your soundcard and just contains enough information to tell your soundcard what notes to play and when, making them much smaller by comparison. A MIDI file will usually have the extension **.mid** (although you may occasionally see the **.rmi** extension used).

The best plug-in for MIDI files is Crescendo from **http://www.liveupdate.com**, which comes in two flavours. The free plug-in (included on the free CD accompanying this book) will play the MIDI file when it's finished downloading. Crescendo Plus, which can be yours for a few dollars, will begin to stream playback almost as soon as you click the link to the MIDI file, just as the RealAudio player does with its own brand of audio.

There are two shortcomings with playback of MIDI. First, the Crescendo console replaces the page you were viewing, so you'll need to hit the Back button after listening to the file. Second, the file repeats endlessly, so if you chose to open a second browser window and continue surfing with a musical backing, it would very quickly drive you up the wall! Fortunately, many MIDI sites embed a Crescendo console into their pages to prevent this irritating quirk from happening. (Your other option is to right-click the link to the MIDI file, choose **Save As...** and play the file later using Windows' own Media Player.) Some web authors bypass the Crescendo console completely and embed a background MIDI file into their pages. This can be very irritating when you're trying to read what's on the page: your only escape is to leave the site or turn off your speakers!

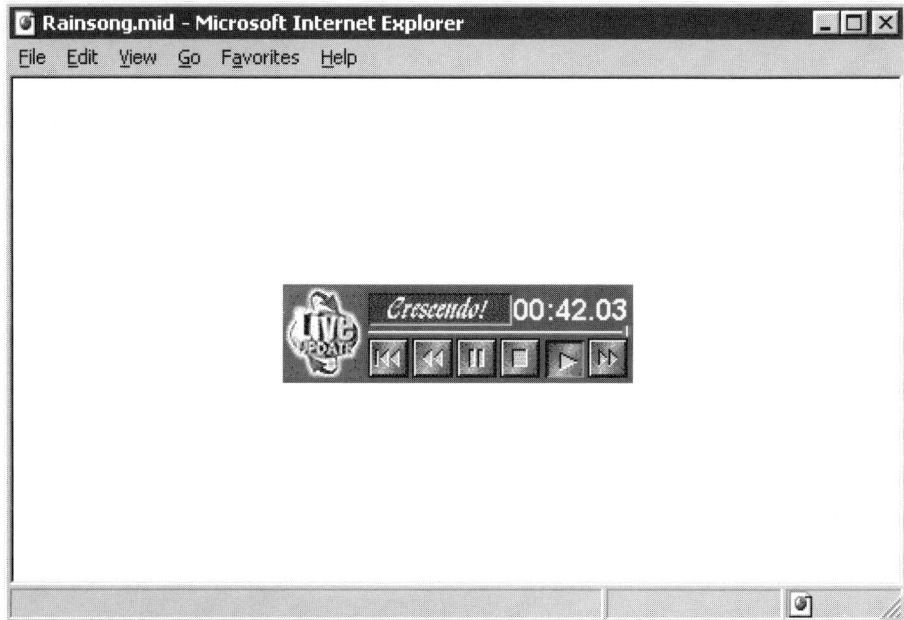

▶ The Crescendo console playing a MIDI file.

Duly armed with your Crescendo plug-in, here's a few of the sites that are worth visiting:

- The makers of Crescendo, Live Update, list some of the best MIDI pages at **http://www.liveupdate.com/streamsites.html**.
- MIDI File Central at **http://www.tst-medhat.com/midi/frame.htm** has a well organised site with MIDI songs listed by artist, and a mass of useful links too.
- Check out the MIDI Farm at **http://www.midifarm.com** for MIDI files, the best MIDI links, and yet more plug-ins.

BY THE WAY

The good, the bad and the ugly

Anyone with an ounce of musical talent and a MIDI sequencing program can create a MIDI file. The trouble is, many do, and an ounce isn't really enough. You'll find that some MIDI files sound absolutely superb while others sound as if a rebellious five-year-old just sat on a piano.

If you don't have a good wavetable soundcard, don't despair! You can still sample the delights of crystal clear MIDI sound on the Web using a sort of software soundcard. Head off to **http://www.edirol.com/vsc/index.html** to download Roland's Virtual SoundCanvas, or **http://www.yamaha.co.uk/html/h_midplg.htm** for Yamaha's MidPlug. Sadly you'll have to register and pay up if you want to make full use of these. And talking of paying for stuff, if you want to learn more about MIDI as a method of making music, check out my book, *The MIDI Files*, also published by Prentice Hall.

It's Movie Time... Soon!

First things first. Video files are big! A 1-minute movie will be roughly 2.5 megabytes, and in most cases you'll have to wait for the whole thing to download before you can watch it. With a 28.8Kbps modem, you're looking at 10 to 15 minutes' boredom for your minute of entertainment. All the same, as with most multimedia elements, it pays to have the software installed just in case you come across something that really seems worth the wait!

The three most common types of movie file on the Web are MPEG (which will have **.mpeg**, **.mpg** or **.mpe** extensions), QuickTime (**.mov** or **.qt**), and Video For Windows (**.avi**). If you've installed Internet Explorer, you should already have a program called ActiveMovie, which can play each of these types. ActiveMovie works as both a browser plug-in and a separate viewer that you can use to playback movies offline.

BY THE WAY

Deactivate ActiveMovie

If you have other movie viewers that you prefer, you can use those to open your MPEG and QuickTime movies instead of ActiveMovie. All you need to do is run the ActiveMovie File Types program (ActiveMovie.exe), click the Options tab, and clear the checkboxes.

Although ActiveMovie is a useful program, it doesn't always handle MPEG videos correctly, and it isn't completely compatible with QuickTime. Here are two other programs well worth adding to your collection:

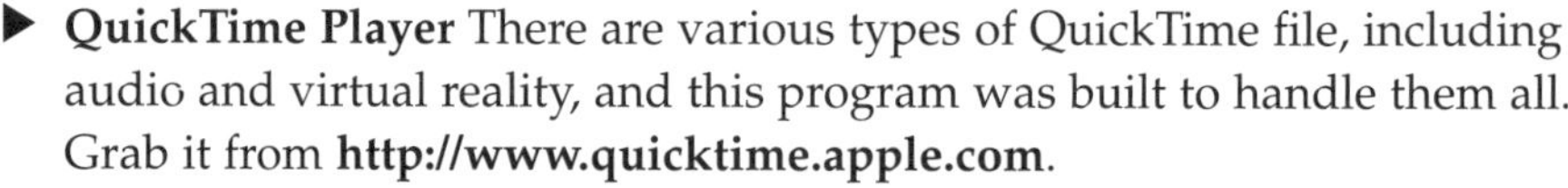

- **QuickTime Player** There are various types of QuickTime file, including audio and virtual reality, and this program was built to handle them all. Grab it from **http://www.quicktime.apple.com**.

- **Net Toob** An all-purpose plug-in that handles just about every video and audio file you'll come across. It can also stream some types of MPEG movie to prevent that agonising wait. You can install Net Toob straight from the free CD accompanying this book, and visit its web site at **http://www.nettoob.com** to register your copy.

Ready to watch some videos? For more than thirteen hundred QuickTime clips from cinema films, head for the QuickTime Archive at **http://www.film.softcenter.se/flics** and browse the alphabetical list for the name of the film you want. One of the best starting points for MPEG movies is the MPEG Monster List at **http://www.islandnet.com/~carleton/monster/monster.html**, which lists MPEG resources and information, links to more plug-ins, and a truly monster list of movie sites on the Web. Or try Bryan's cute animations at **http://www.oas.omron.com/bryan/anims.html**. Finally, don't forget to visit the QuickTime web site mentioned above – you'll find a Samples page with links to some very cool sites. Follow the link to BMW's site to try out QuickTime Virtual Reality!

▶ Saturday Night at the Movies. (But I started downloading on Tuesday!)

The Hot Topic – Cool Animation

The word 'animation' doesn't sound cool – it probably reminds you of Bugs Bunny – but it's a major multimedia craze on the Internet. Where images and text have always been fixed on the page, they can now move around and react to the mouse passing over them. Part of this popularity lies in the fact that animations are easier for the average user to create than videos, and they take no more time to download than an image.

It gets better! The two hottest types of animation are Macromedia's ShockWave and Flash, both of which you can view in Internet Explorer without adding anything else to your software mountain. However, if you're not using Explorer you'll have to head off to **http://www.macromedia.com** to download the necessary plug-ins.

How can I add animations to my Web page?

Flash animations are reasonably simple to create using Macromedia's Flash software. You can download a trial version from **http://www.macromedia.com**, but you'll have to be prepared to spend some serious money if you decide to continue using it!

The list of good animation sites is seemingly endless – you'll keep bumping into them wherever you go on the Web. Unless, of course, you're actually looking for one. So here's a few to let you see what all the fuss is about:

- Visit Macromedia's Flash Gallery at **http://www.macromedia.com/shockzone/edge/flas**h for links to some of the Flash-iest sites on the Web.
- Try the Cool ShockWave Site Of The Week at **http://www.shocker.com/shocker/cool.htm**.
- You'll find a nice ShockWave site, with links to more, at The Shockade (**http://www.expanse.com/shockade/index.htm**).
- For a bit of overkill in the Flash department, visit the Microsoft Network at **http://www.msn.com**.

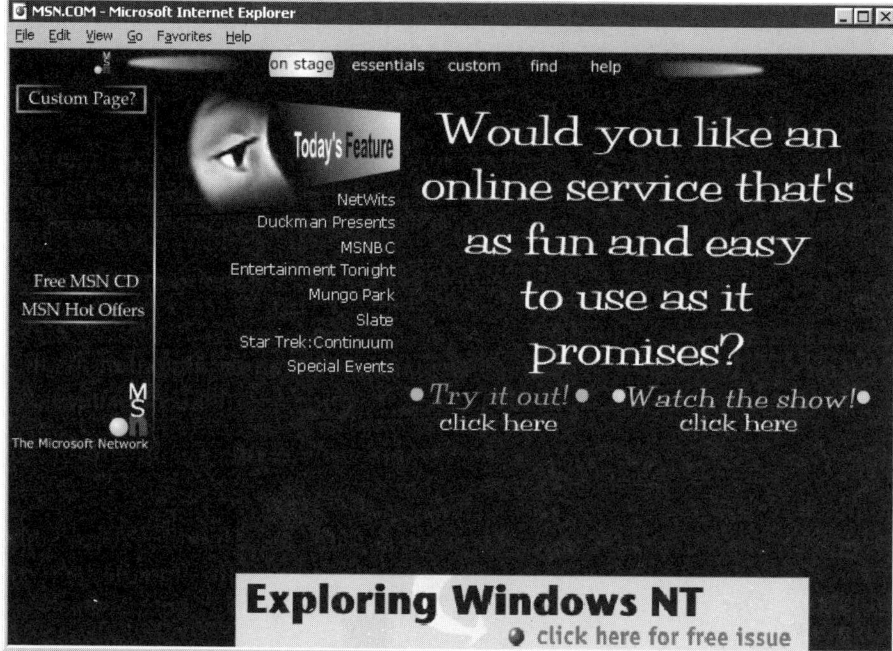

▶ The MSN home page – if it holds still, click it!

Explore Virtual 3D Worlds

Virtual reality is something that's either going to grab you immediately, or leave you cold. Using on-screen controls (often combined with right mouse-button menus), you can select angles from which to view the scene, walk or fly through it, zoom in and out, and in the more recent VRML 2.0 format, interact with objects you find. True VRML files have the extension **.wrl** (although they're often accompanied by a collection of GIF images that form various elements of the world), and you'll need to install a plug-in first.

JARGON BUSTER

VRML

An abbreviation of Virtual Reality Modelling Language, the programming language used to build these graphical 'worlds'. The original version of the language was 1.0; the latest version, 2.0, adds new features such as the ability to pick up and move virtual objects.

In fact, there are many companies also producing proprietary plug-ins for their own brands of 3D worlds, but I suggest you pause a while and see if virtual reality is your cup of tea. Most plug-ins are pretty big programs, and the worlds themselves can be tiresomely slow to download and slow-moving once you start to explore – you'll definitely benefit from a fast Internet connection and a fast processor! All these words of warning aside, VRML is a whole new experience you've got to try at least once, so grab one of these **.wrl** plug-ins:

- **Superscape Viscape** from **http://www.superscape.com**. You'll find a world full of more virtual worlds hosted by Superscape at **http://www.com**.

- **Cosmo Player** from **http://vrml.sgi.com/cosmoplayer**, which also has links to more sites that make great use of VRML.
- **WIRL** from **http://www.vream.com**. A large plug-in, which adds a few extra facilities to ordinary VRML. These come into their own when you start exploring the unusually fast and interactive worlds you'll find at the same site.

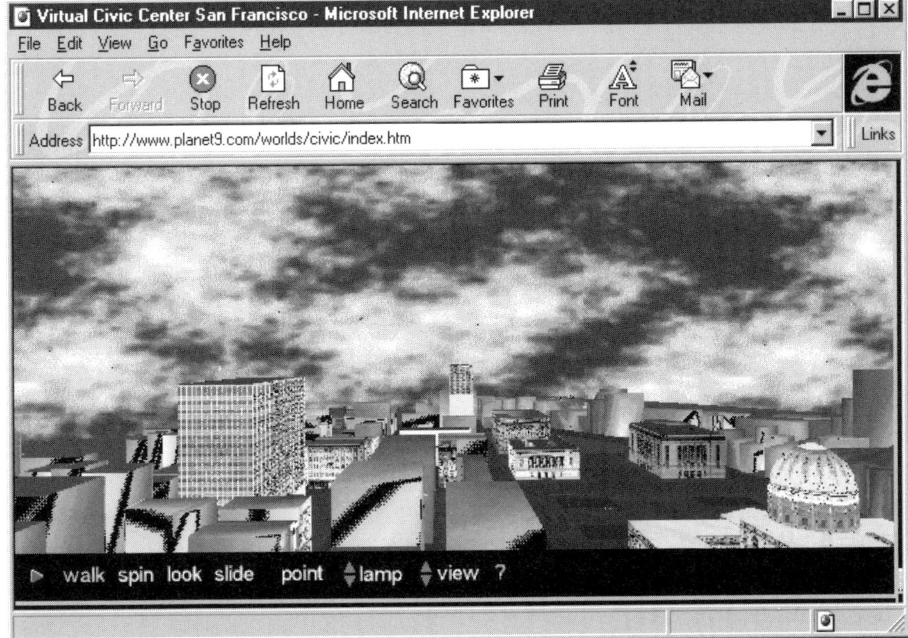

◀ A virtual flight through San Francisco.

If you've followed the links from these sites and you still need more, visit Planet 9 at **http://www.planet9.com** to cruise through virtual American cities, or **http://nowtv.com/vrml/index.htm** to play 3D online games with other visitors to the site. If you fancy something that loads a little quicker, Protozoa's weird collection of 3D interactive creatures at **http://protozoa.protozoa.com/vrml_scenes** fit the bill nicely, and download in not much more than 30 seconds.

GOOD QUESTION

Where can I find other plug-ins?

You'll find the best selection at Tucows, a particularly good site for Internet-related software. Head for **http://tucows.cableinet.net/window95.html** and click the **Browser Plug-ins** heading. While you're there, take a look at **ActiveX Plug-ins** for Internet Explorer.

22

ROBOTS, CAMERAS & OTHER ODDITIES

In This Chapter...

- ▶ Watch live camera feeds from all over the world
- ▶ Command Internet-linked robots by remote control
- ▶ Watch world TV channels (rather slowly)
- ▶ Bizarre, pointless, but amusing, interactive Web sites
- ▶ Say hello to JavaScript, Java & ActiveX programs

People are weird – and if you need proof of that, the Web is the perfect place to look. After all, it's built by people, and very few constraints are placed upon them. At one end of the weirdness spectrum is the page that says: 'Hi. My name's Nigel. I like Cluedo. Here's a picture of my cat.' You'll find a lot of pages built by people who have nothing of interest to offer, but feel the need to demonstrate that in public. (OK, psychologists, perhaps that's interesting in itself?)

Fortunately, this chapter focuses on the other end of the Weirdometer – people who are brimming with unusual ideas, and put vast amounts of time, effort, and even money into getting them on to the Web for the rest of us to share. These sites may be as absurd, pointless, and unnecessary as anything created by Nigel and his cat, but it's this special brand of unabashed, entertaining weirdness that makes the Web the unique place it's become.

Catch the Action with Live Cam

I still find this one hard to believe. People who probably seem outwardly quite sane spend their hard-earned money on a special type of camera, rig it up to the Web via some complicated programming and a (usually) permanent Internet connection, and then point it at a street corner, or their desk, or a fish-bowl…

But what's really hard to believe is the reaction of someone visiting those sites, and I'm as guilty of this as anyone else. Try it, and you'll see what I mean. Point your browser at the corner of Hollywood and Vine (**http://hollywood.bhi.hollywood.ca.us:8000/pictures/image01.gif**), and refresh the image every few seconds. You'll see the traffic lights changing,

BY THE WAY

Push or pull?

We met 'push technology' on page 236, where it was being used to send news stories down the wires to your computer. Some live-cam sites use the same system to send an updated camera view every few seconds or minutes. At many sites, though, you'll have to 'pull' – in other words, to view a newer picture, click Internet Explorer's **Refresh** button, or press F5.

vehicles passing, people moving in and out of shot… and it's entertaining! The longer you have to wait for something to actually move, the more rewarding it is when it happens.

OK, maybe I'm just too weird, but I can't be alone – there are thousands of web cameras running all over the world, and they can't all be there just for my amusement! Here's a taste of a few more:

- Visit **http://www.netlinkservices.com/cam.htm** to see if Lee is working at his computers.
- Check out the Manhattan skyline from the top of the Empire State Building at **http://www.realtech.com/webcam**.
- Take a look inside Jason's office at **http://george.lbl.gov/cgi-bin /jason/cave-cam**.
- See what Cujo the parrot is doing today (although he's not what you'd call a busy parrot), at **http://www.spies.com/arubin/cujo.gif**.
- Find a huge collection of links to more informative or entertaining web-cams on Tommy's List at **http://www.rt66.com/~ozone/cam.htm**.

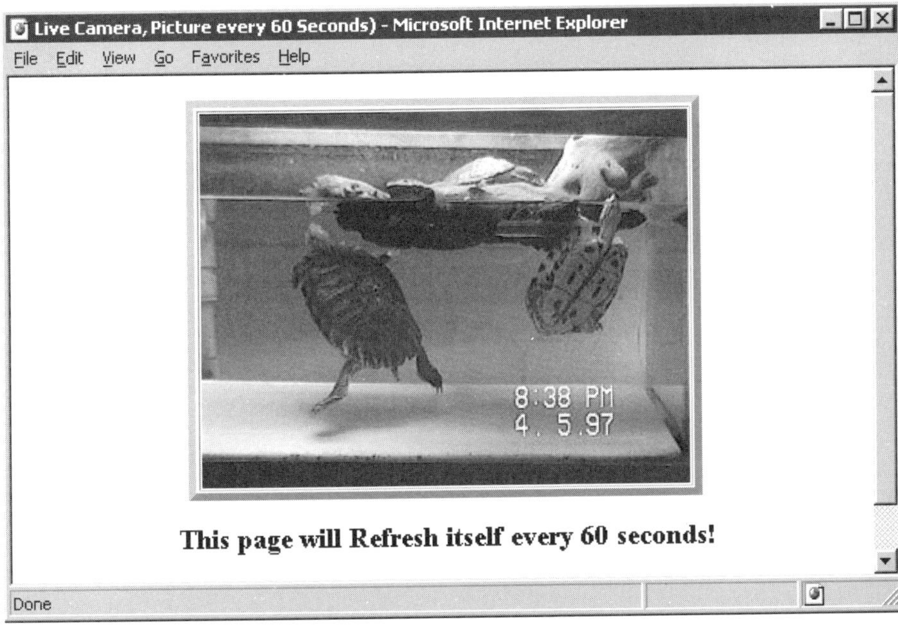

◀ The mesmerising TurtleCam at http://www.campusware.com/turtles.

BY THE WAY

Pan about the house

If you like a bit of snooping, point your browser at **http://atlantis.austin.apple.com/html/gan2/house.html** and explore Ganyard's house by clicking appropriate parts of the photographs. An interesting example of what one web-fan can produce with just a camera and a little too much time on his hands!

Robots in Cyberspace

Venturing even deeper into Weirdsville, you'll also find robots hooked up to the Web. Some have cameras trained on them so that you can see what they're doing; others are actually mobile, with cameras attached to act as 'eyes'. The technology involved here is pretty staggering, so there are relatively few robot sites, and you may have to wait some time before you can take a turn controlling a robot yourself. At most sites you'll be assigned control for only a few minutes – make sure you read the instructions while you're waiting so that you'll know how the controls work when your turn comes around.

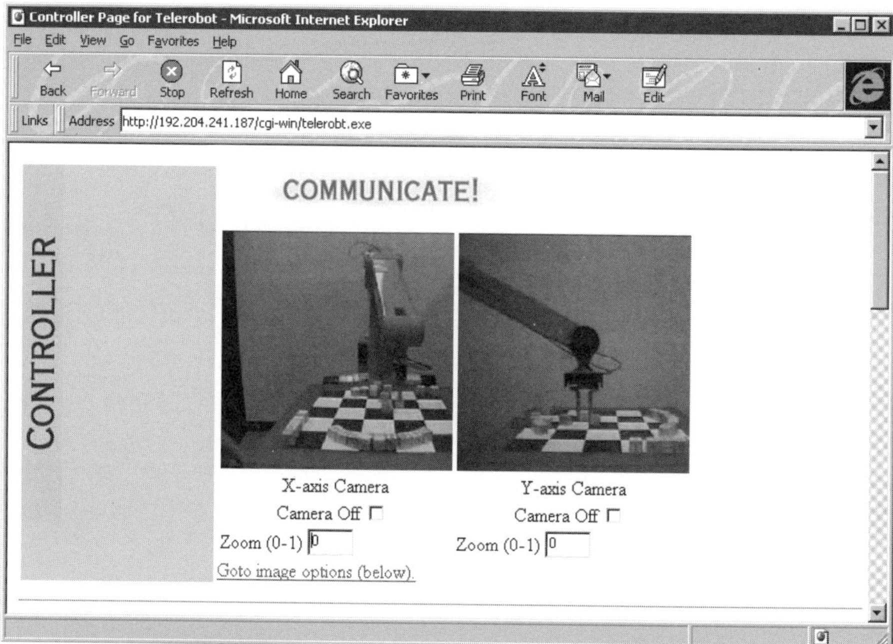

▶ Tell Telerobot where to put its building-blocks.

A great place to start is Telerobot at **http://192.204.241.187 /cgi-win/telerobt.exe**, where your task is to arrange building blocks. The controls are simple and the images are unusually clear and in colour. Another enjoyable robot is Xavier (**http://www.cs.cmu.edu/People/Xavier**) who roams through an office at your command. Xavier's a popular guy, though, and he keeps US business hours, so he can be hard to reach.

For a more calming use of cyber-robotics, visit the Telegarden at **http://telegarden.aec.at/index.html**. By clicking **Guest Entrance** (followed by **Enter Garden**) on the next page, you can watch this horticultural robot at work. Alternatively, if you register as a member, you can water the garden and plant seeds by remote control, and leave messages for other members.

Live TV – Almost

Another innovation brings you television over the Internet, provided by TV Live at **http://www.users.interport.net/~mnw/tvlive.htm**. Choose from 16 cable and US local channels, or follow the **Click here for Live Views** link for access to channels from all over the world. Sadly, the pictures update only once every 3 minutes, but if you've got the RealAudio player installed (see page 291), you will get streaming sound from some of these channels.

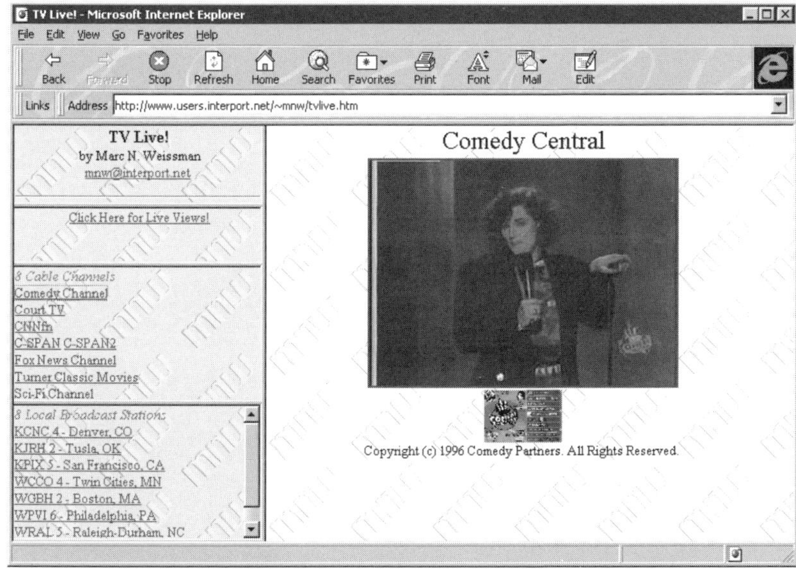

◀ Tune into channels all over the world at TV Live.

And There's More...

Perhaps there are exceptions to the 'weirdness rule'. After all – there are many web-authors out there providing a much needed service from a sense of civic duty. Keep these URLs handy, you never know when you'll need them next:

- Is the Chez Oxford Hot Tub a cold tub? Visit **http://mckusick.com:451** for the vital statistics.
- Check the status of Brian's phone at **http://www.arl.wustl.edu/~brian/Office/Phone**.
- Any news from Paul's refrigerator? Find out at **http://hamjudo.com /cgi-bin/refrigerator**.
- I suppose all the laundry machines at **http://spleen.mit.edu/LAUNDRY/laundry_java.html** are still busy?
- Sample the wonders of UCC's online Coke machine at **http://www.ucc.gu.uwa.edu.au/drink.**

If you're in the mood to send a few messages of your own, and you want a change from email, why not try out a few of these sites instead. Visit **http://www.yikes.com/printer**, type a message to Eric, and it'll be printed out on his trusty ImageWriter printer. Or will it? For a more immediate result, send a message to the folk who work on the Netscape browser. Head for **http://home.netscape.com/people/mtoy/sign** and type a message into the box. The message will appear on the wall above their heads, and by clicking the link beside the textbox you can see it happening via a live-cam link. (Click on **Refresh**, or press F5 every few seconds to update the image).

BY THE WAY

Got a minute? Write an opera!

Visit **http://brainop.media.mit.edu** and take part in an interactive opera by playing graphical portrayals of real instruments. There are many different instruments to choose from, and plenty of other weird and wonderful places to explore on this site.

Try Some Interactive Graphics

While some people rush around connecting cameras, robots and hot tubs to the Internet, others take a more sophisticated approach. They build challenging, constructive programs that people really want – programs like the Mr Showbiz Plastic Surgery Lab! You'll find this indispensable resource at **http://www.mrshowbiz.com/features/games/surgery**. Pick a set of celebrities to work with, choose features to combine from each, and then click the button to carry out the 'operation'.

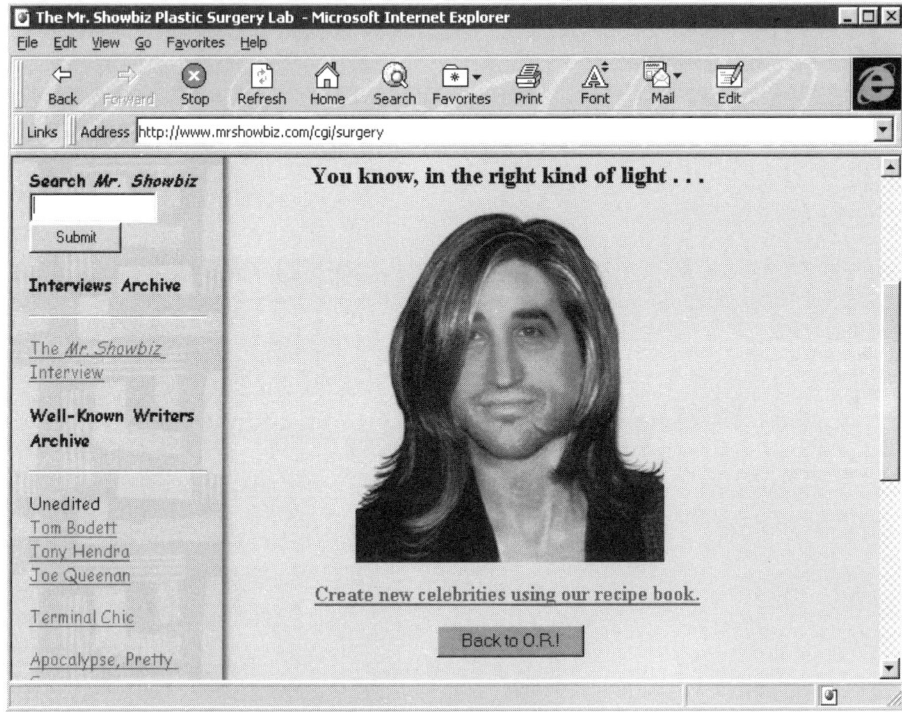

◀ Jennifer Aniston (and a few of her Friends) after plastic surgery from Mr Showbiz!

Food is one of the things that doesn't travel well on the Internet. Modern telephone lines are too narrow even for spaghetti! But all is not lost as pizza is available – visit the Pizza Server at **http://www2.ecst.csuchico.edu/~pizza**. Click on **Order and view a pizza over the Web**, then choose your toppings (salami, red pepper and golfball is good). Finally, click the button to place your order – you'll see it displayed on the screen. Although you can download the result, it'll be in the rather chewy GIF format.

Shocked fish

Here's a neat Shockwave program to try. Visit the Amazing Fishtank at **http://morganmedia.com/m2/shock.html**, release a few fish into the tank, and watch what happens! (If you don't see anything on this page, you'll need to visit **http://www.macromedia.com** to install the small Shockwave plug-in.)

For more artistic interactivity, check out The Fractory at **http://tqd.advanced.org/3288/myo.html**. By choosing zoom ratios and colour palettes, and clicking on various points of an image, you can create and explore the infinite variations of fractal art. And if you produce a result that's too good to leave behind, fill in the form to send it to any email address.

Visit Web Pages that Talk Back!

Some of the weirdest stuff on the Net – the pages that make you ask 'Why bother?' – are also the simplest. None will keep you entertained for hours at a stretch, but you'll get a few minutes' amusement from each of them. Here's about 20 minutes' worth to get you started:

- The Random Recipe Generator at **http://bobo.link.cs.cmu.edu /cgi-bin/dougb/recipe**. This produces daft recipes such as '51-Minute Water' (which has a list of ingredients as long as your arm). Click on **Refresh** or press F5 to see another one.
- Kevin's Fridge Magnets at **http://www.northcoast.com/savetz/fridge/fridge.cgi** (shown in the next screenshot). Click the link to put your own message on the page, and you'll be returned to this main page to see it displayed. The next visitor to the page will also see it, and it will be added to the list of previous messages further down the page.
- The Surrealist Compliment Generator at **http://pharmdec.wustl.edu/cgi-bin/jardin_scripts/SCG** does just what it says: you'll receive a random compliment such as 'Your mother once had eyes that shone like the legs of Mae West'. If that made your heart skip a beat, click **Refresh** or press F5 for another.
- As an antidote to all those compliments, your next port of call should be

the Abuse-A-Tron at **http://www.xe.net/upstart/abuse**. You may like to scribble these down for use in casual conversation – there's no arguing with: 'You chase cars and bark at them, you hairy, pustule-licking, lewd harbinger of an itinerant somnambulist.'

- Finally, check out the Mood Detector at **http://www.chrysalis.org/oeno/testmood.htm**. Make sure you firmly press your thumb onto the screen for the full 5 seconds or the results could be inaccurate.

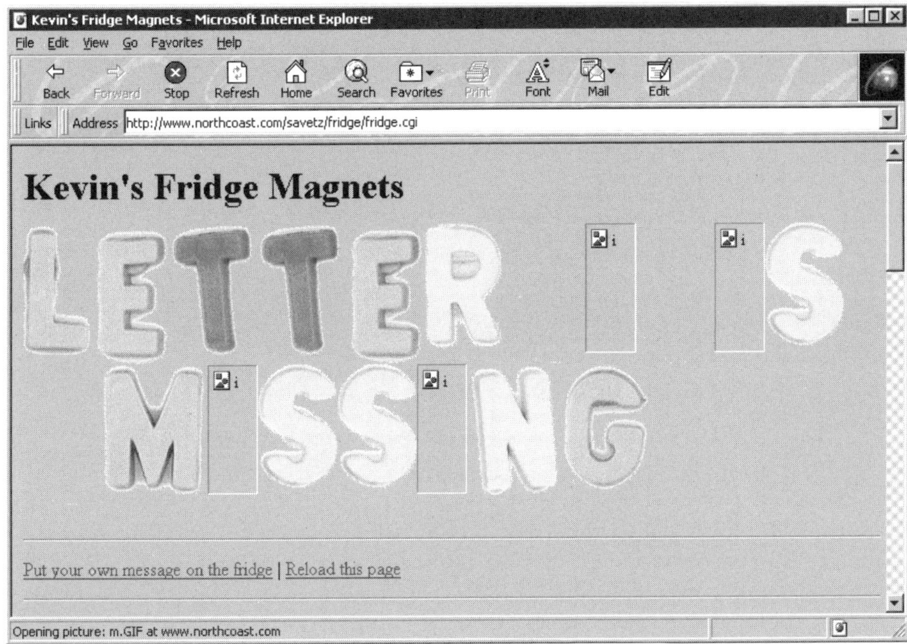

◀ Add your own heading to Kevin's 'fridge' for all to see.

GOOD QUESTION

Where can I find more of this weird stuff?

Try Curious Sites On The Web at **http://www.cfanet.com/glasgurl/curious/curious.htm**, the Internet Directory UK's Weird section at **http://main.emap.com/id/uk/category/Weird!.htm**, or Weird, Bizarre, Funny & Engrossing at **http://www.now2000.com/bigkidnetwork/weirdsites.html**.

Meet the Multilingual Web

After visiting some of the sites I've mentioned in this chapter, you may have realised that there's something rather strange going on – web pages aren't supposed to do this! A web page is just plain text with a few extra little codes added to set colours, fonts, and layouts, insert pictures, and other simple stuff. (More about that in the coming chapters.) Surely there's more happening here than just plain text? After all, nothing like this ever happens in Notepad!

This is yet another example of how much the World Wide Web has changed in the last couple of years: there are now several different languages that can be used to write programs that will run on (or from) a web page – any program that you can run on your computer's own operating system can now be inserted into a page. Sounds dead useful, doesn't it? And it is, except that to date the main use of these languages has been in the creation of web-based entertainments and page-enhancements. True usefulness probably won't appear widely for another year or two. I'm not going to try to teach you how to use these languages, but here's a brief introduction to the three that are used the most.

JavaScript

The simplest of the three to learn and use, constructed specifically for use on the Web. This is a scripting language – it's written in plain text (although it looks very technical), and slots straight into the page with no extra files needed. This way, the script can run as soon as the page arrives at your browser, making it an ideal language for flashy effects (one of its main uses). To see some JavaScript pages in action, head for **http://home.netscape.com/people/jamie/jwd_javascript_qs.html** and follow the links you find there.

Java

This is related to JavaScript, but Java programs can run on any computer and aren't restricted to the Web. Java can be used to write full-blown applications such as word processors and databases, though its main use is still in creating interesting ornaments for web pages, which are referred to as 'applets'. Java programs have to download to your computer before they can run, which they do automatically when you arrive at the page. The program files have the extension **.class**.

Check out some Java games at **http://www.favorites.com/javapage/java.html**, or look at some of the applets created by Sun, the designer of Java, at **http://www.javasoft.com/applets/js-applets.html**.

BY THE WAY

Strange but true

Java? Strange name you may be thinking. The basics of this complex programming language were thrashed out between hard-working programmers during many long sessions in a coffee house in Silicon Valley, so the language was christened Java – the US slang for coffee.

ActiveX

This is a Microsoft language known, until recently, as OLE. ActiveX programs are known as 'controls', and are normally downloaded to your system when you visit pages that contain them. Once there, they remain in place so that any other pages you visit containing the same control can be viewed instantly without waiting for the same components to be installed again. To see some of these controls in action, visit Microsoft's ActiveX Gallery at **http://www.microsoft.com/activex/gallery**.

23

YOUR OWN WEB SITE – THE BASICS

In This Chapter...

- The Web page language – it's all tags
- Helpful software you can use (if you really want to)
- A simple Web page: title, heading & paragraphs
- Formatting text with bold & italic type
- Inserting links to other pages & Web sites

Up to this point in the book, you've learnt how to use just about every area of the Internet – the major (and not-so-major) services, the search engines, plug-ins and multimedia, interactive pages, shopping, the whole shebang – but it's still everyone else's Internet you're using! Sooner or later you'll want to grab a little corner of it and make it your own.

The mechanics of creating a web site are simple enough, and over the next three chapters I'll show you how to do it. Of course, whole books have been written on this subject so this isn't an exhaustive reference, but you'll find many more examples, tips and links to more information on the free CD accompanying this book, plus a HTML quick-reference glossary in Appendix E. For best results, treat these chapters as a tutorial – work through them and experiment with the examples yourself, and in a few days this will all seem very simple stuff!

HTML – the Language of the Web

Pages on the World Wide Web are written in a language called HTML (HyperText Markup Language). So what's that all about? Well, we've met hypertext already – those underlined, clickable links that make the Web so easy to navigate. A markup language is a set of codes or signs added to plain text to indicate how it should be presented to the reader, noting bold or italic text, typefaces to be used, paragraph breaks, and so on. When you type any document into your word processor, it adds these codes for you, but tactfully hides them from view: for example, if you wanted bold text, it shows you bold text instead of those codes. However, in HTML you have to type in the codes yourself along with the text, and your browser puts the whole lot together before displaying it.

These codes are known as **tags**, and they consist of ordinary text placed between less-than and greater-than signs. Let's take an example:

```
<B>Welcome to my homepage.</B> Glad you could make it!
```

The first tag, `<B>`, means 'turn on bold type'. Halfway through the line, the same tag is used again, but with a forward-slash inserted straight after the less-than sign: this means 'turn off bold type'. If you displayed a page containing this line in your browser, it would look like this:

Welcome to my homepage. Glad you could make it!

Of course, there's more to a web page than bold text, so clearly there must be many more of these tags. But you don't have to learn all of them! There's a small bundle that you'll use a lot, and you'll get to know those very quickly. For the rest, just turn to page 384 to look them up!

Do I Need Special Software?

Believe it or not, creating a web site is something you can do for free (once you've started paying for an Internet connection, that is). Because HTML is entirely text-based, you can write your pages in Windows' Notepad, and throughout these chapters I'm going to assume that's what you're doing. You can use any other word processor, but you'll have to remember to save your files as plain text when you've finished. However, there are other options:

WYSIWYG

A delightful acronym (pronounced 'wizzywig') for 'What you see is what you get'. This is used to describe many different types of software that can show you on the screen exactly what something will look like when you print it on paper or view it in your web browser.

WYSIWYG Editors

In theory, WYSIWYG editors are the perfect way of working: instead of looking at plain text with HTML tags dotted around it, you see your web page itself gradually taking shape, with images, colours and formatting displayed. But there are a couple of drawbacks. First, WYSIWYG editors cost serious money compared to most of the other types of Internet software. Second, they probably won't help you avoid learning about HTML. Once in a while the editor won't do what you want it to do, and you'll have to switch to its text-editing mode to juggle the tags yourself. More often, you'll see something clever on someone else's page and want to find out how it was done: if you don't understand the language, you might remain ignorant forever! If you want to see how someone else's page was put together and you're in Internet Explorer either click on the **View** menu and choose **Source**, or right-click on the page and choose **View Source**. Notepad will open the HTML code for that page.

My early experience with HTML was that it's far easier to learn the language itself than it is to learn how the WYSIWYG software works, but if you'd like to give the WYSIWYG method a shot, here are two of the most popular:

- **Microsoft FrontPage** You can find out more about this at **http://www.microsoft.com/frontpage**, but you'll have to take a trip into town to buy a copy.
- **Adobe PageMill** Visit **http://www.adobe.com/prodindex/pagemill/main.html** for details, downloads and online payment.

Markup Editors

Using a markup editor is rather like using Notepad – you see all the HTML codes on the page in front of you. But instead of having to type in tags yourself, a markup editor will insert them for you at the click of a button or the press of a hotkey, in the same way that you use your word processor. You may still choose to type in some of the simple tags yourself, such as the tag for bold text mentioned earlier, but for more complicated elements such as a table with a lot of cells, this automation is a great time- and sanity-saver.

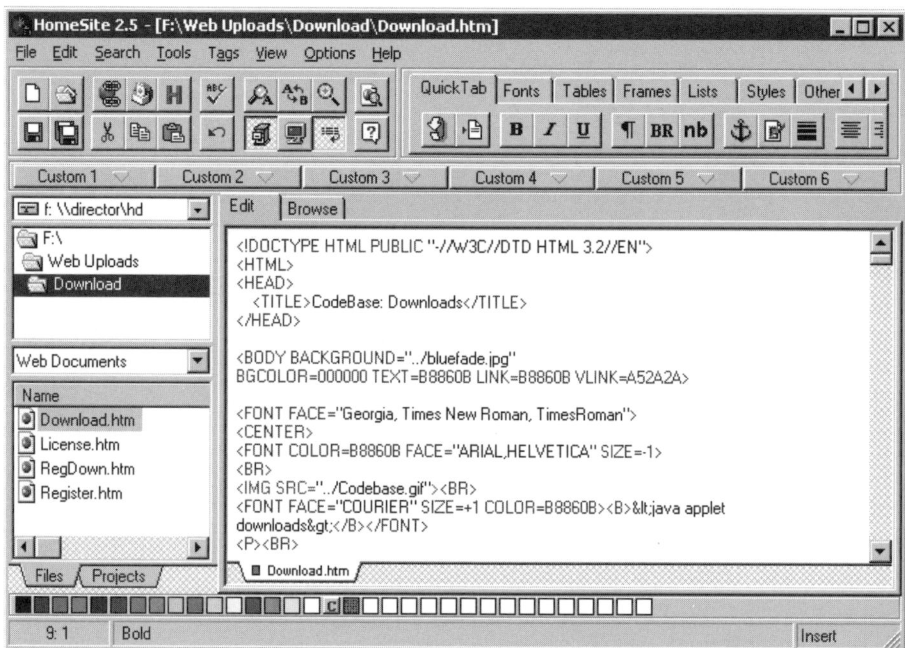

▶ Colour-coding and one-click tag insertion in HomeSite.

Markup editors are also ideal for newcomers to HTML. If you don't know one tag from another, just click the appropriate buttons on the toolbar to insert them: once you've seen them appear on the page a few times, you'll soon start to remember what's what!

Here are three of the most popular and feature-packed markup editors. You'll need to register these if you want to use them beyond the trial period, but I wholeheartedly recommend picking one of these to start you off:

- **HomeSite** from **http://www.dexnet.com/homesite**
- **WebEdit PRO** from **http://www.luckman.com**
- **HTMLed** from **http://www.ist.ca**.

Text Converters

Some modern word-processors like Lotus WordPro and Microsoft Word have begun to include features to turn your documents into web pages. At their simplest, they'll let you create an ordinary word-processed document and then choose a **Save as HTML** option from the File menu to convert it into a web page. The result won't be as effective as other pages on the Web, but it's an ideal way to convert a long document when the only other option is to add all the tags yourself!

BY THE WAY

If you use Microsoft Office 97, the web-authoring features don't stop at Word. Excel allows you to save a worksheet in HTML format, and PowerPoint helps you create multimedia pages by converting slides to web format. You'll also find a library of pictures, sounds and animations that you can use to spice up your pages.

You can also create web pages from scratch in these programs. For example, Microsoft Word has its own Web Page Wizard that can set you up with a ready-to-edit template like the one shown in the screenshot overleaf. To start it up, go to **File | New...**, then click the **Web Pages** tab and double-click **Web Page Wizard**. You can add and delete elements on the page, and use the standard drawing and editing toolbars to slot in anything else you need.

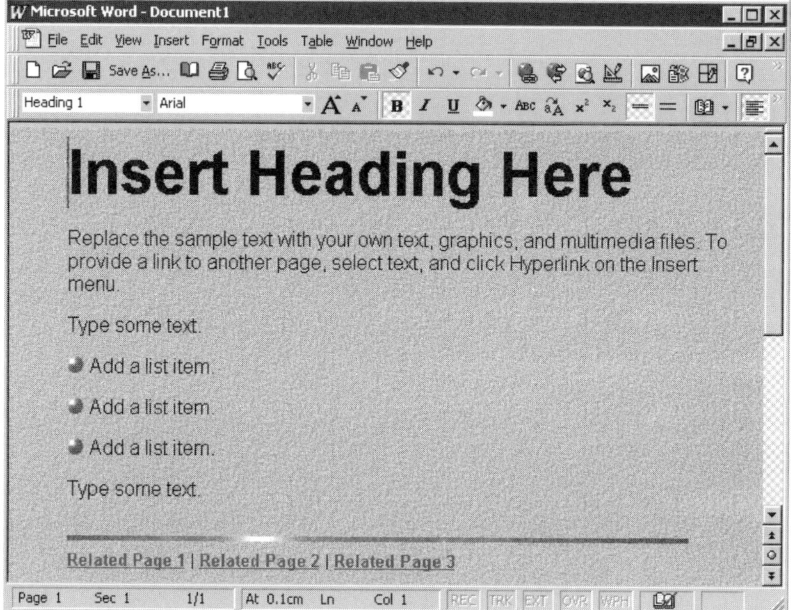

▶ Creating a web page from a Microsoft Word template.

Let's Get Started

There are some things that will appear in almost every HTML document you write, so let's start by making a template file you can use every time you want to create a new page. Start Notepad, and type the text below. Save this file using any name you like, but make sure you give it the extension **.htm** or **.html**. Every web page you write must be saved with one of these extensions – it doesn't matter which you choose, but you'll find life a lot easier if you stick to the same one each time!

```
<!DOCTYPE HTML PUBLIC "-//W3C//DTD HTML 3.2//EN">

<HTML>
<HEAD>
  <TITLE>Untitled</TITLE>
</HEAD>

<BODY>


</BODY>
</HTML>
```

None of those tags do anything exciting by themselves, but it's worth knowing what they're for. The first line is a piece of technical nonsense that tells a browser that the document is written in the latest version of the HTML language. The rest of the document is placed between the <HTML> and </HTML> tags, and falls into two separate chunks: the **head** (the section between <HEAD> and </HEAD>) and the **body** (between <BODY> and </BODY>).

The document's head is pretty dull: all it contains is the title of the document, inserted between the <TITLE> and </TITLE> tags. There are other bits and pieces that can be slotted in here, and you'll meet some of those in Chapter 25, but the title is the only element that must be there.

Do I have to type these tags in capitals?

No, browsers are not particular about the case of the tags. If you prefer <title>, or <Title>, or even <tItLe>, it's all the same to your browser. But typing tags in capitals makes them stand out from the rest of your text, which can be useful at times.

The body section is the one that matters. Between these two tags you'll type all the text that should appear on your page, and put in the tags you need to display images, set colours, insert hyperlinks to other pages and sites, and anything else you want your page to contain.

Now that you've created a basic template, let's start adding to it to build up a respectable-looking page.

Add a Title & Text

The first thing to do is to replace the word **Untitled** with a sensible title for the document, such as **Links To The Best Multimedia Sites** or **My EastEnders HomePage**. Pick something that describes what the page will be about, but keep it fairly short: the text between the <TITLE> and </TITLE> tags will appear in the title-bar at the very top of most browsers, and if you're entry is too long to fit, it'll just get chopped off!

BY THE WAY

Choose your title carefully

The title of your document is more important than it might seem. First, some search engines will list the title of your page (see Chapter 25). Second, if someone likes your page enough to add it to their Favorites or Bookmarks list, this is the title they'll see in their list when they open it.

Now we'll add some text to the page. Either type the same as I've entered below, or replace my first and second paragraph entries with whole paragraphs if you prefer. When you've done that, save the file as **links.htm** or **links.html**, but don't close Notepad yet.

```
<!DOCTYPE HTML PUBLIC "-//W3C//DTD HTML 3.2//EN">

<HTML>
<HEAD>
  <TITLE>Links To The Best Multimedia Sites</TITLE>
</HEAD>

<BODY>
<H1>Welcome To My Homepage!</H1>
Here's the first paragraph.
<P>And here's the second paragraph.

</BODY>
</HTML>
```

Now you're ready to take a look at your masterpiece in your browser. There are several ways you can do this: find the file you just saved and double-click it, or open your browser and type the path to the file in the address bar, or choose **File | Open** and click on **Browse**. When your browser displays it, it should look just like this screenshot.

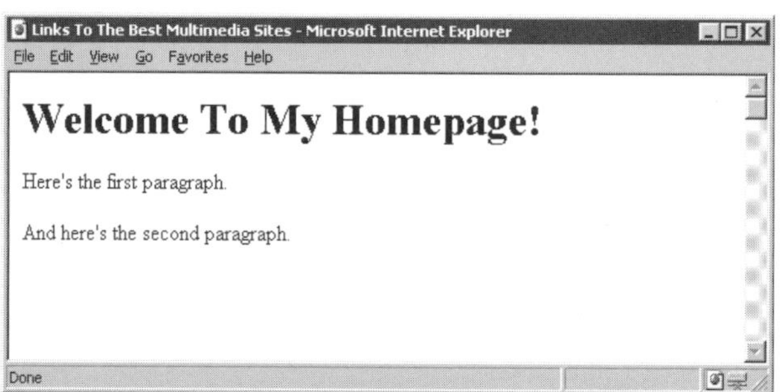

So what are those new tags all about? Let's take the <P> tag first. This tells your browser to present the following text as a new paragraph, which automatically inserts a blank line before it. And this raises an important point about HTML: you can't insert blank lines just by pressing Enter or Return. Although you can see blank lines in Notepad when you do that, your browser will just ignore them, which is why you need to start a new paragraph by entering <P>. (Notice that you don't have to put in a closing </P> at the end of a paragraph – the act of starting a new paragraph isn't an ongoing effect that has to be turned off again.)

So how do you start a new line without starting a new paragraph? Another tag, <BR>, will give you a 'line break'. In other words, the text that follows that tag will start at the beginning of the next line with no empty line inserted before it.

The other pair of tags that cropped up was <H1> and </H1>, which formats a line of text as a heading. You can choose from six sizes: H1 is the largest, followed by <H2> and </H2>, down to the smallest, <H6> and </H6>. In one nifty little manoeuvre, these tags change the size of the text you place between them and make it bold. They also automatically start a new paragraph for the heading (so you don't need to place a <P> tag at the start of the line) and start a new paragraph for whatever follows the heading. Try changing the size of the heading by altering those tags to see the different effects, re-saving the file, and clicking your browser's **Refresh** button to update it.

Be Bold (or Be Italic...)

The tags for bold and italic text are logical and thus easy to remember: <B> for bold, and <I> for italic. As both of these are ongoing effects, you'll have to enter closing tags (</B> or </I>) when you want the effect to stop. And, just as in your word processor, you can combine these tags, so if your document contained this:

```
This is <I>italic</I>. This is <B>bold</B>. This is
<B><I>bold & italic</I></B>.
```

the result would look like this in your browser:

This is *italic*. This is **bold**. This is ***bold & italic***.

Lesser-used text-formatting tags that may come in handy one day are superscript (`<SUP>` and `</SUP>`) and subscript (`<SUB>` and `</SUB>`). If you really feel the urge, you can underline text using another memorable pair of tags, `<U>` and `</U>`, but be careful how you use underlining: most people surfing the Web expect underlined text to be a hyperlink, and may find your gratuitous use of these tags confusing.

BY THE WAY

Spaces in HTML

Just as browsers ignore your use of the Enter or Return key when you create your web pages, they have a similar attitude to the Spacebar. However many spaces you enter in a row, only the first will be recognised. If you really need more than one space, either type in the code ** ** for each space you need (so **   ** would give you three spaces), or better still, use the <PRE> tag explained on page 340.

Insert Links to Other Sites

It's an unwritten rule of the Internet that a web site should contain links to other web sites. After all, the entire Web works by being interconnected, and if people surf their way to your site and have to retrace their steps before they can continue surfing, they'll steer clear in future! So let's put in another `<P>` tag to start a new paragraph, and add that sorely needed link as shown below:

```
<P>Visit Macromedia's snazzy <A
HREF="http://www.macromedia.com/shockzone">Shockzone</A> site.
```

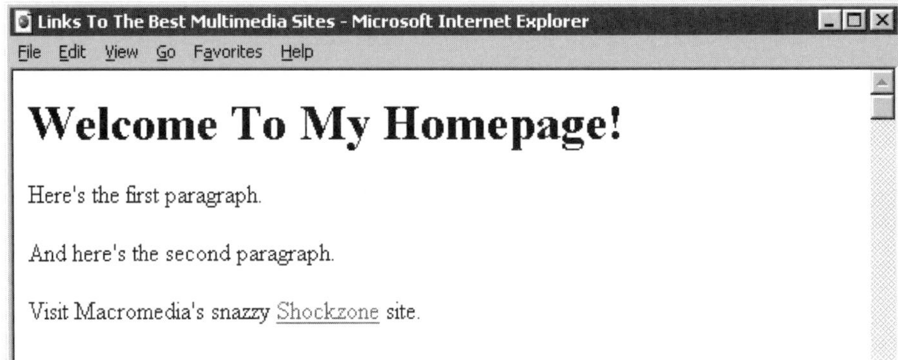

This is a more complicated tag, so let's look at it bit by bit. Although we call these 'links', in HTML they're called **anchors**, and that's where the `A` comes from after the first < sign. An anchor usually begins with the `<A HREF=` tag. Following that comes the URL of the page you want to link to, always enclosed in double-quotes, and the > sign to finish the opening anchor tag.

Immediately after the opening anchor tag, type in the text that you want visitors to your page to click on. This could be a single word, a sentence, or even a whole paragraph, but don't forget to put something in here, or there'll be nothing to click on to reach that site! Finally, type in the closing anchor tag, `</A>`.

BY THE WAY

Get it central

You can place elements centrally on the page by placing them between `<CENTER>` and `</CENTER>` tags (HTML is an American language, so make sure you use the US spelling!). This applies to headings, paragraphs of text, images, and almost anything else you may want to include.

Links to Other Pages on Your Own Site

The link we just added used something called an **absolute URL**. An absolute URL gives the whole path to the page you want to open, including the http:// bit and the name of the computer. When you want to create links to other pages on your own site you can use a different, more simple method.

Create a new HTML document, and save it to the directory where the other is stored. Let's assume you've called it **morelinks.html**. Now, in your first document, you can create a link to this new page by typing this anchor:

```
<A HREF="morelinks.html">Here's a few more links.</A>
```

Yes, it's just a filename. This is called a **relative URL**. It tells your browser to look for a file called **morelinks.html** and display it. Since a browser doesn't know where else to look, it searches the directory containing the document it's displaying at that moment. As long as **morelinks.html** really is in that same directory, the browser will find it and open it.

What's so great about relative URLs?

First, you have less typing to do – and that also lessens the chances of making mistakes. But best of all, you can click these links in your browser to check that they work. If you click a link to an absolute URL, your browser will have to connect to your IAP first to find that computer.

You can make a browser look somewhere different for a file in a similar way. Open the directory containing these two documents, create a subdirectory called **pages**, and move the **morelinks.html** file into it. The link we just added now needs to be changed to the following:

```
<A HREF="pages/morelinks.html">Here's a few more links.</A>
```

The browser now looks in the current directory for another directory called **pages**, and looks inside that for **morelinks.html**.

Finally, let's open **morelinks.html** and create a link back to our original document (which we called **links.html**) so that you can click your way to and fro between the two. To do this, we need to tell the browser to look in the parent directory of **pages** to find this file. If you're familiar with using MS-DOS, you'll recognise this straight away: to move up one level in the directory tree, just type two dots:

```
<A HREF="../links.html">Here's my first links page.</A>
```

So far we've looked at linking to other web pages, but a hyperlink needn't necessarily point to a **.html** document. If you have a movie file, a text file, a

BY THE WAY

Case-sensitive filenames

When you refer to a page or file in your document, the case is absolutely vital. If you type in a link to **Index.html** and the file is actually called **index.html** or **Index.HTML**, the page won't be found. Most web authors save all their files with lower-case names to remove any uncertainty. Similarly, although you can use long filenames, they mustn't include any spaces.

sound file, or whatever, create the link in exactly the same way entering the location and name of this file between the double-quotes. However, if the file is particularly large, it's good practice to mention its size somewhere nearby so that people can choose whether or not to click that link.

Email Links

Another type of anchor allows a visitor to your page to click a link that opens their email message window, with your email address already inserted, ready for them to send you a message. This is a lot like any other anchor, with the URL replaced by your email address. The only difference is that the word **mailto:** must be inserted immediately after that first quote sign. Here's an example – just replace my email address with your own:

```
<A HREF="mailto:rob.young@btinternet.com">Click here to
send me an email</A>
```

24

COLOURS, IMAGES & WEB PAGE LAYOUT

In This Chapter...

- Choose page & text colours, & add a wallpaper image
- Select & change fonts, sizes & colours
- Divide the page into sections with horizontal rules
- Use images to add sparkle or act as links
- Create your own animations for your pages

In the last chapter you created a basic web page consisting of headlines, text (with a little style and paragraph formatting), and hyperlinks. It won't win any awards, but what matters is that you've worked with a few HTML tags and seen the effect they have on a page. Armed with this experience, let's improve the look of the page by adding colours, choosing images and fonts, and applying a few more formatting and design touches.

You Too Can Have a <BODY> Like Mine!

So far, in our example web page, everything looks a bit dull. The background is white, the text is black, the hyperlinks are blue – these are the default colours set up by Internet Explorer, and it's using them because we haven't told it to use anything different. However, all of this is easily changed by typing our preferences into that opening `<BODY>` tag.

This brings us to a new area of HTML. A tag like `<B>` is self-contained – it simply turns on bold text, with no complications. Other tags need to contain a little more information about what you want to do. A good example is the `<FONT>` tag, which we'll look at more closely later in this chapter. By itself, it isn't saying anything useful: which font? what size? what colour? You provide this information by adding **attributes** to the tag such as `SIZE=3`, `FACE=Arial`, and so on, so a complete font tag may be: `<FONT SIZE=3 FACE=Arial>`.
The `<BODY>` tag doesn't have to contain attributes, but browsers will use

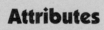

Attributes

These are additional pieces of information slotted into a tag. Each attribute is separated by a space, and needs an equals sign between the attribute itself and the setting to be used for it. It doesn't matter what order the attributes appear in, and you don't need to include a particular attribute if you don't want to change its setting.

their own default settings for anything you haven't specified, and different browsers use different defaults. Most web authors like to keep as much control as possible over how their pages will be displayed, and make their own settings for the body attributes.

The following chart shows you the six most useful attributes you can use in the <BODY> tag:

This Attribute	Has This Effect
BGCOLOR=	Sets the background colour of the web page
TEXT=	Sets the colour of text on the page
LINK=	Sets the colour of the clickable hyperlinks
VLINK=	Sets the colour of a link to a previously visited page
ALINK=	Sets the colour of a link between the time it's clicked and the new page opening
BACKGROUND=	Specifies an image to use as the page's 'wallpaper'

Without further ado, open the original **links.html** document you created in the last chapter, and change the <BODY> tag so that it looks like this:

```
<BODY BGCOLOR=MAROON TEXT=WHITE LINK=YELLOW
VLINK=OLIVE ALINK=LIME>
```

Save the file, and take a look at it in your browser. OK, the colour scheme may not be to your taste, but it's starting to resemble a 'real' web page! Try swapping colours around to find a scheme you prefer. There are 140 colours to choose from, so skip ahead to Appendix F and pick a few from the list, or take a look at the Colour Chart on the free CD accompanying this book.

The other attribute is BACKGROUND=, which places a GIF or JPEG image on the web page, and tiles it to fill the entire area. Let's assume you want to use an image file called **hoops.gif**, which is in the same directory as the current document. Inside the body tag, add: BACKGROUND="hoops.gif" (not forgetting the double-quotes). Your whole <BODY> tag may now look like this:

```
<BODY BACKGROUND="hoops.gif" BGCOLOR=MAROON TEXT=WHITE
LINK=YELLOW VLINK=OLIVE ALINK=LIME>
```

There are a few things worth bearing in mind if you choose to use a background image. First, make sure the image file isn't too large. If someone arrives at your page and sees a 50Kb background image starting to download, they'll probably rush away again without waiting to find out what else is on your page! Second, make sure you choose a text colour that will be easy to read over the background image (or an image that isn't too garish). Third, pick a BGCOLOR= colour that will allow your text to show up clearly – that way, if the background image is taking a while to download, visitors will still be able to read your page comfortably.

Set Up Your Font Options

At the moment you're also stuck with a single font (probably Times New Roman). Once again, this is set up by your browser by default and, of course, different browsers may use different default fonts. Fortunately, the <FONT> tag allows you to choose and change the font face, size and colour whenever you need to. Here's an example of a <FONT> tag using all three attributes:

```
<FONT FACE="Verdana,Arial,Helvetica" SIZE=4
COLOR=RED>...</FONT>
```

Let's take these one at a time. The FACE attribute is the name of the font you want to use. Obviously this must be a font on your own system, but the same font needs to be on the system of anyone visiting your page too: if it isn't, their browser will revert to their default font. You can keep a bit of control by listing more than one font (separated by commas) as in the example above. If the first font isn't available, the browser will try the second, and so on.

GOOD QUESTION

Which font faces should I use?

Most visitors to your site will have TimesRoman, Helvetica, Courier and Dialog on their systems. TrueType fonts are better, and the safest are Arial and Times New Roman. Microsoft supplies a pack of fonts for the Web, which includes Comic Sans MS, Verdana, Impact and Georgia, and is now used by many web authors. You can download any of these you don't already have from **http://www.microsoft.com/truetype/fontpack/win.htm**.

Font sizes in HTML work differently than in your word processor. There are seven sizes numbered (unsurprisingly) from 1 to 7, where 1 is smallest. The default size for text is 3, so if you want to make your text slightly larger, use SIZE=4. The SIZE attribute doesn't affect the headings we covered in the previous chapter, so if you've used one of these somewhere between your <FONT> and </FONT> tags, it will still be formatted as a heading.

The colour of the text has already been set in the <BODY> tag, but you may want to slip in an occasional <FONT COLOR=PURPLE>...</FONT> to change the colour of a certain word, paragraph, or heading. After the closing </FONT> tag, the colour will revert to that set in the <BODY> tag.

Big text, small text

If you find it hard to keep track of the font size you're currently using, don't waste time worrying about it! Instead, you can use the simple, easy-to-remember commands <BIG> and </BIG> to make text one step larger, or <SMALL> and </SMALL> to make it one step smaller.

With the earlier changes to the <BODY> tag, and the addition of a couple of </FONT> tags, here's what the body of our document may look like now:

```
<BODY BGCOLOR=MAROON TEXT=WHITE LINK=YELLOW
VLINK=OLIVE ALINK=LIME>

<FONT FACE="Comic Sans MS" COLOR=YELLOW>
<H1>Welcome To My Homepage!</H1>
</FONT>

<FONT FACE="Arial">

Here's the first paragraph.
<P>And here's the second paragraph.
<P>Visit Macromedia's snazzy <A
HREF="http://www.macromedia.com/shockzone">Shockzone<
/A> site.

</FONT>
</BODY>
</HTML>
```

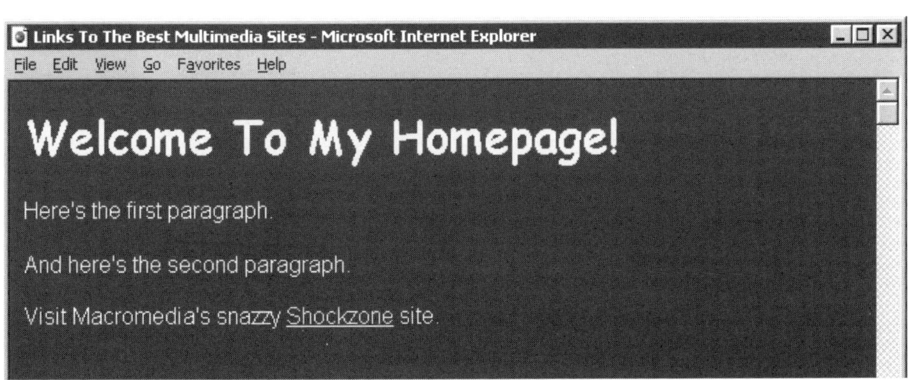

Horizontal Rules (OK!)

Horizontal rules are straight lines that divide a page into sections. For the simplest type of rule, the only tag you need is <HR>. This automatically puts a horizontal rule across the full width of the page, on a new line, and any text that follows it will form a new paragraph. Because the rule isn't something that needs to be turned off again, there's no closing tag.
If you want to, you can get clever with rules by adding some (or all!) of the following attributes:

Use this attribute	for this result
`ALIGN=`	Use `LEFT` or `RIGHT` to place the rule on the left or right of the page. If you leave this out, the rule will be centred.
`SIZE=`	Enter any number to set the height of the rule in pixels. The default setting is 2.
`WIDTH=`	Enter a number to specify the width of the line in pixels, or as a percentage of the page (such as `WIDTH=70%`).
`NOSHADE`	This removes the 3D effect from the rule. There's no equals sign, and nothing more to add.
`COLOR=`	Enter the name of a colour. The default setting depends on the background colour. Only Internet Explorer supports this attribute – other browsers will ignore it.

It's worth playing with the `<HR>` tag and its attributes to see what unusual effects you can create. For example, the following piece of code places a square bullet in the centre of the page, which makes an effective and smart, 'minimalist' divider:

```
<HR SIZE=10 WIDTH=10 COLOR=LIME NOSHADE>
```

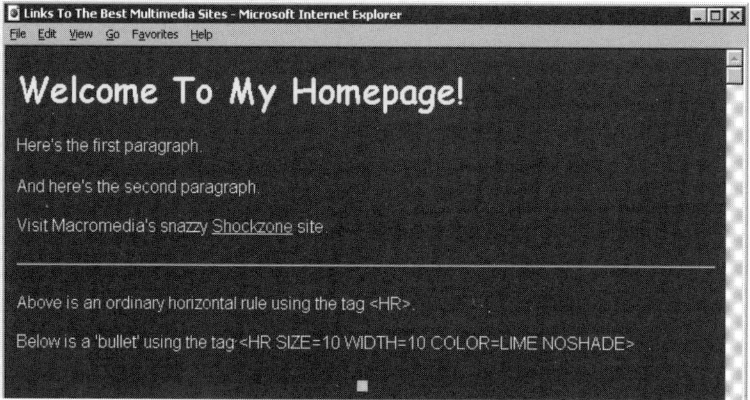

Add Spice with an Image

The horizontal rule is the simplest type of graphical content you can include on a page, but it's hardly exciting. To liven up a dull page, you can't go far wrong with a well-chosen image. Images on the Web are usually in either of two formats:

- **JPEG** This format usually has a **.jpg** or **.jpeg** extension. The images are saved with 16 million colours, making them ideal for photographs but unnecessarily large for pictures you create yourself.
- **GIF** These images have a **.gif** extension, and save images in up to 256 colours. This gives pretty lousy results for photographs, but it's the ideal format for anything else. Using the latest version of the GIF format (GIF89a), you can opt to make one of the colours in the image transparent, so that when it appears on your page you'll be able to see the page's background colour (or `BACKGROUND=` image) in place of that colour.

BY THE WAY

Make your GIFs smaller

When you create a GIF image, try reducing its number of colours to 16 before you save it. In most cases you won't notice any loss of picture quality, but the size of the file will be considerably smaller, so visitors to your page won't have to wait as long for the image to download.

Once you've chosen the image you want to use, the `<IMG>` tag will slot it on to the page. This tag works rather like the `<FONT>` tag – by itself it's meaningless, with all the information being supplied by adding attributes. Let's assume you want to insert an image called **splash.gif**, and the image file is in the same directory as your current HTML document:

```
<IMG SRC="splash.gif">
```

This is the `<IMG>` tag at its most basic: the SRC attribute (which is short for 'source') tells the browser where to find the image file you want to display, following exactly the same rules as those for relative URLs, which we looked at in the previous chapter. Unless you preceded this tag with `<P>` or `<BR>`, the image will be placed immediately after the last piece of text you entered.

If you enclose the entire tag between <CENTER> and </CENTER> tags, the image will be placed below the previous line of text, centred on the page. However, you get a little more choice than that about where the image should be by adding the ALIGN attribute:

This Attribute	Does This
ALIGN=TOP	Aligns the top of the image with the top of the text on the same line.
ALIGN=MIDDLE	Aligns the middle of the image with the text on that line.
ALIGN=BOTTOM	Aligns the bottom of the image with the bottom of the line of text.
ALIGN=LEFT	Places the image on a new line, and against the left margin.
ALIGN=RIGHT	Places the image on a new line, and against the right margin.

Using these attributes, you can place the image roughly where you want it on the page. What's still needed is a bit of fine tuning: after all, if you use ALIGN=MIDDLE, the image will be butted right up against the text on the same line. The answer comes in the form of two more attributes that add some blank space around an image: HSPACE= inserts space either side of the image (horizontally), and VSPACE= adds space above and below it (vertically). Just enter a number in pixels after the equals sign. As usual with attributes, if you only need to use one of these, there's no need to include the other. So far, then, an image may be inserted with a tag that looks like this:

```
<IMG SRC="splash.gif" ALIGN=MIDDLE HSPACE=30 VSPACE=6>
```

GOOD QUESTION

How do I create a GIF or JPEG image?

There are many good graphics programs around that can handle these formats, but the most popular by far is Paint Shop Pro. You can download a trial version from **http://www.jasc.com**. The latest versions also have built-in effects and filters that help the artistically challenged create some very arty images

Enter the Image's Width & Height

Two of the most important <IMG> attributes are WIDTH= and HEIGHT=, with which you specify the size of the image. If you've experimented with the tags above, you'll have noticed that your browser displays the image properly without these tags, so you're probably wondering why on earth you'd bother to do this. At the moment, you're looking at pages and images that are already on your own system – there's no downloading involved yet. When your page is on the Web and someone visits it, things work a little differently. When the browser arrives at an `<IMG>` tag, it has to download the image and display it before it can work out where to put the other parts of the page, such as text. However, if the browser already knows how much space is needed for the image, it can hold it in reserve and just display an empty box until the image downloads, with the text correctly positioned around it. Another reason is that some people surf the Web with the option to display images turned off: if you don't enter the dimensions of your images, they'll simply see a tiny placeholder icon instead of a full-size box, which could upset your carefully planned layout!

BY THE WAY

Enter an alternative

It's common practice to enter some alternative text in place of an image. This is displayed in the placeholder box until the image is downloaded and displayed, and also appears in a 'tooltip' when the mouse moves on to the image. Add the attribute `ALT=""` and place a description of the image between the quotes, such as `ALT="A picture of my cat"`.

You can find the image's dimensions easily by loading it into almost any graphics program. For example, in Paint Shop Pro you'll see the width and height displayed in the bottom left-hand corner. Make a mental note of them, and add them to your tag like this:

```
<IMG SRC="splash.gif" ALIGN=MIDDLE HSPACE=30 VSPACE=6
WIDTH=84 HEIGHT=81>
```

Bear in mind that if you enter the dimensions of an image in this way, the browser will take your word for it! In other words, the browser will scale the image to these proportions regardless of what the original image looked like. This can be useful to increase or decrease the size of an image without having to create a completely new version of it (alternatively it can be used if you want to create weird effects), but if you get the dimensions wrong, it's also a prime opportunity to screw things up!

Reuse Your Images!

Try to reuse images on different pages if you can. After an image has been displayed once, it will be reloaded from the browser's cache rather than downloaded, making your site a more immediate and pleasing experience for your visitors.

Use an Image as an Anchor

In the last chapter you learnt how to create hypertext links, or anchors, to a web page or file using the tag **<A HREF="URL"> *clickable text*</A>**. But the clickable section that appears on the page doesn't have to be text: you can use an image instead, or both image and text. For example, if you slot the whole image tag given above into the anchor tag, the image will appear exactly as it did before, but will now act as a clickable link:

```
<A HREF="morelinks.html"><IMG SRC="splash.gif"
ALIGN=MIDDLE HSPACE=30 VSPACE=6 WIDTH=84 HEIGHT=81
BORDER=0></A>Click this image to open my other links page.
```

If you want to make both the text and the image clickable, add some text before or after the `<IMG>` tag like this:

```
<A HREF="morelinks.html">Click this image to open my
other links page.<IMG SRC="splash.gif" ALIGN=MIDDLE
HSPACE=30 VSPACE=6 WIDTH=84 HEIGHT=81 BORDER=0></A>
```

The screenshot shows what those two methods look like when displayed in your browser:

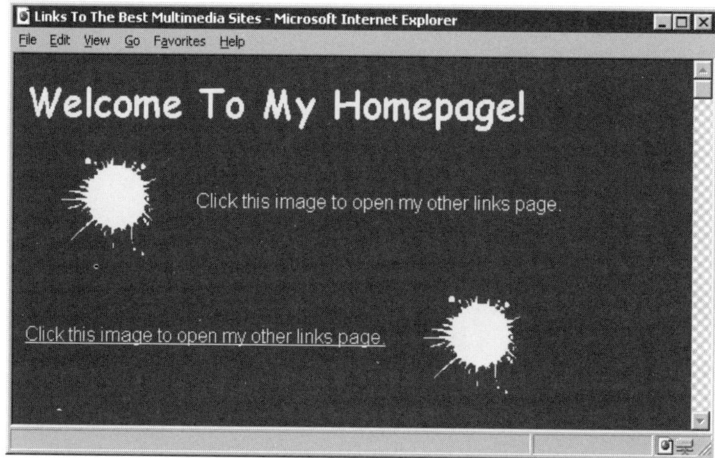

Turn off the image border

When you use an image as a link, a border will appear around it. You can alter the thickness of the border by adding `BORDER=` to the `<IMG>` tag followed by a number in pixels. If you'd prefer to have no border, enter `BORDER=0`, but make sure it's obvious that the image is clickable to avoid confusing visitors to your page. The border attribute can be added to any image, whether it's acting as a link or not.

How About a Little Animation?

The GIF image format has another little trick up its sleeve that can add sparkle to a page – you can use it to create animations. These are known by the simple enough name of 'animated GIFs', but you'll need special software to build the finished article. First, though, you need to create a series of images, each one slightly different from the others, like a cartoon, and save each with a different name and the **.gif** extension. Then you need to load these into the special software that can string them together in the order you choose, set the length of time that each frame of the animation should remain on the screen, and save them as a single animation (still with the extension **.gif**). The animation is placed on your page using exactly the same `<IMG>` tag and attributes as we looked at earlier. Two good, easy-to-use animators are:

- **PhotoImpact GIF Animator** from **http://www.ulead.com**.
- **Microsoft GIF Animator** from **http://www.microsoft.com/imagecomposer/gifanimator/gifanin.htm**

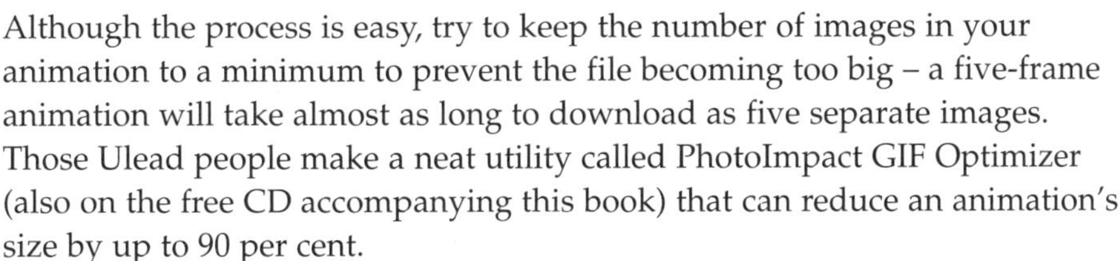

Although the process is easy, try to keep the number of images in your animation to a minimum to prevent the file becoming too big – a five-frame animation will take almost as long to download as five separate images. Those Ulead people make a neat utility called PhotoImpact GIF Optimizer (also on the free CD accompanying this book) that can reduce an animation's size by up to 90 per cent.

Useful HTML Extras

We haven't by any means exhausted the supply of HTML tags, but we have covered most of those you'll be using regularly, and you should have enough ammunition here to make a good start on your own site. You'll find plenty

more in Appendix E, and examples on the free CD with this book, but let's shift into quickfire mode to look at a last little bundle of tags to keep handy.

Comments

You can enclose anything on your page between `<!--` and `-->` tags, and your browser will ignore them. The intention of these comment tags is that you can put little notes in your document to help you edit it later, such as `<!--The next bit of code inserts the image-->`, but they can be usefully inserted around a piece of code that you want to remove from the page, but don't want to actually delete completely in case you need to reinstate it sometime.

Marquee

A marquee is a piece of text that scrolls across the page. Only Internet Explorer supports this tag at the moment, so it's best not to use it for any text that is really important, but it makes a neat effect. Begin by adding the following code:

```
<MARQUEE ALIGN=Middle HEIGHT=10 WIDTH=80%
BGCOLOR=Maroon SCROLLAMOUNT=3 BEHAVIOR=Scroll
SCROLLDELAY=3 DIRECTION=Left HSPACE=0 VSPACE=0
LOOP=INFINITE>This text is scrolling</MARQUEE>
```

All the possible attributes are included above, and you'll recognise some of them, such as HSPACE and VSPACE. Height can be specified as a percentage of the page or (more usefully) as a number in pixels. Width is best set as a percentage. You can choose a BGCOLOR setting to blend the marquee into your page, or make it stand out, and the text will be displayed according to your last use of the <FONT> tag (or the TEXT attribute in the <BODY> tag). You can experiment with the SCROLLAMOUNT and SCROLLDELAY settings to achieve a comfortable speed, and change the BEHAVIOR setting to Slide or Alternate.

Paragraph Alignment

We met the <P> tag in the previous chapter. By itself, it inserts a blank line and places the following text on the next line. But the <P> tag also has an optional attribute, ALIGN=, that can be used with the settings LEFT, CENTER or RIGHT. The first two aren't particularly useful: by default, all paragraphs are left-aligned anyway, and it's easier to use the plain old <CENTER>...</CENTER> tags to centre elements on a page.

But if you ever want to align a paragraph of text with the right margin, surround it with these tags:

```
<P ALIGN=RIGHT>This text is right-aligned.</P>
```

Note that you have to use a closing </P> tag if you add an attribute to this tag, otherwise all the remaining text on your page will be aligned the same way!

Lists

HTML gives you built-in easy ways of making bulleted or numbered lists with the addition of just a couple of tags. To create a list, just insert the tag <LI> at the beginning of each line. No paragraph or line-break tags are needed, so the following code would create a list containing three items:

```
<LI>Here's item one.<LI>Here's a second item.<LI>And
here's a third.
```

Now decide whether you want a bulleted or a numbered list. For a numbered list, enclose the entire code between <OL> and </OL> tags (which stands for 'ordered list'); for a bulleted list, use <UL> and </UL> tags (meaning 'unordered list), as shown in the next screenshot.

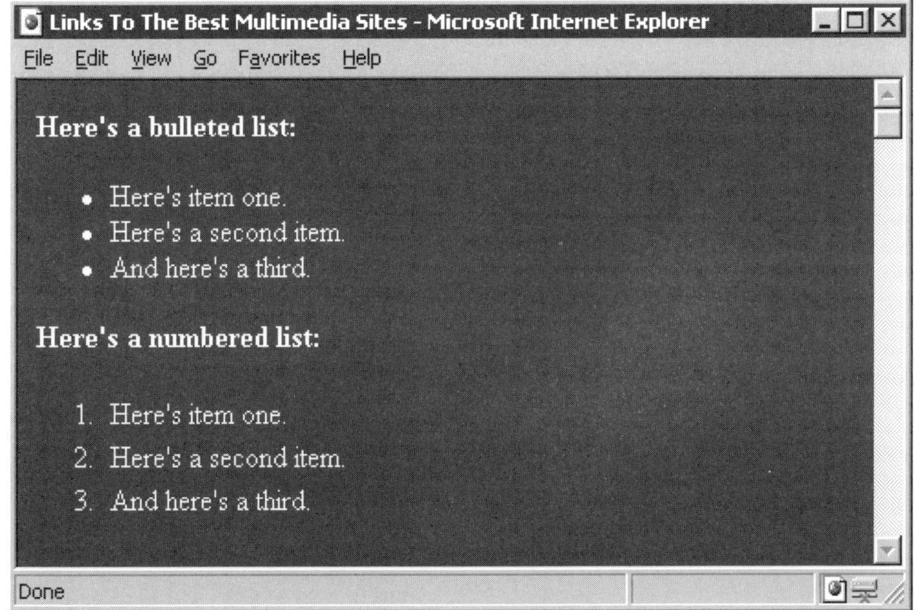

BY THE WAY

Make the editing easier

Since browsers ignore the use of carriage-returns, use them liberally to space out your code. For example, although you can choose to enter list entries all on one line, your code will be easier to understand and edit at a later stage if you place each on its own line.

If you use a numbered list, you can add the `TYPE=` attribute to the `<OL>` tag to choose which numbering system you'd like to apply. The default is arabic numbers. To use capital letters, enter `TYPE=A`, for small letters `TYPE=a`. You can also use large roman numerals (`TYPE=I`) or small Roman numerals (`TYPE=i`). So your complete tag may look like this:

```
<OL TYPE=I><LI>Here's item one.<LI>Here's a second
item.<LI>And here's a third.</OL>
```

Pre-formatted Text

If you're having trouble laying out a piece of text exactly as you want it, enclose it between `<PRE>` and `</PRE>` tags. This way, all the spaces and carriage-returns you type into that portion of your document will be displayed in exactly the same way in the browser with no need to muck about with <P> or <BR> tags. The ability to use the space bar also gives you an easy way to indent a line of text.

Make This Your Internet Explorer Start Page

In Chapter 6 you learnt how to change your Start Page in Internet Explorer. Your choices were to use a blank document (so that Explorer didn't try to dial up every time you started it) or to use any other page on the Web. But now you know how to build your own pages, why not create your own start page instead, perhaps containing links to some of your favourite sites?

When the page looks OK loaded into Explorer, click your way to **View | Options | Navigation**, make sure the upper textbox shows **Start Page**, and click the button marked **Use Current**. Provided you don't move, rename or delete the HTML document you created (or any other files linked to it, such as images) this page will be displayed every time you run Internet Explorer, or click its **Home** toolbar button.

25

FROM DRAWING-BOARD TO WEB

In This Chapter...

- ▶ Planning & preparing to build your site
- ▶ Find free Web space, graphics, animations & much more
- ▶ Upload & test your Web site
- ▶ Publicise your site for maximum exposure
- ▶ Add a 'hit counter' & submit your site to be judged

Now that you know something about HTML, it's time to put on your hard hat and start building. But there's more to constructing a good web site than a knowledge of HTML. How should the site be laid out? What about page design? Where do you find graphics files? How does your site get on to the Web? And how will everyone else know it's there? Looks like you've come to the right chapter...

Think First, Write Later!

A little planning never goes amiss, so try to do all your thinking before you start designing anything – especially graphics. I once spent ages designing a fabulous set of textual buttons for a page, and realised when I'd finished that no one but me would understand where they were linking to unless I put an explanatory paragraph beside each one! I had to junk the lot and start again. Remember that you'll know how to navigate your site, but your visitors won't, and they'll usually expect it to be obvious.

Decide what topics your site will cover, and how you can split them up into different pages rather than one long page. Make sure your first page contains links to all the others, and that those links really do explain what visitors will find there. On arrival at any other page, visitors should be able to switch back to the home page with a single click and (if at all possible) to all of your other pages too.

BY THE WAY

Grrr, I hate it when they do that!

When you plan your own site, consider what you like and dislike about other sites you've visited. For example, most people hate to find large graphics on a page before they know what the site is even about. Other pet-hates are repetitive music, large unnecessary background WAV files, links that don't tell you what they're linking to, and text that's exactly the wrong colour for the background.

Of course, if you're going to have a web site, you want people to visit it. Consider why they'd visit your site and make sure you deliver what you promise. Popular sites are those that give something away (we all love freebies don't we?) – it may be software, useful information, or entertainment, but a couple of paragraphs about your hobbies and a picture of your cat is unlikely to leave people panting for more. If you want to take this seriously, add a 'What's New' page to keep regular visitors informed about the latest changes and additions, and make sure it contains the dates of those changes and links to the relevant pages.

Finally, bear in mind that most visitors to your page are using a screen resolution of 800 x 600 on a 15-inch monitor. Although some sites ask visitors to switch screen resolutions to view their pages, no one is likely to do that – they expect you to design a site that looks good on any screen size. Try adjusting your own resolution, and the size of your browser window, every so often to see your pages as others may see them.

BY THE WAY

Don't trust the download times!

If you use a program that tells you the download time of a page as you build it (such as Microsoft FrontPage), don't rely on its being totally accurate. Not everyone uses the faster 28.8Kbps modem, not everyone will have a good connection to your site, and a download time can't include the hugely variable connection times. Think in terms of at least doubling the figure.

Talk to Your Service Provider

Before you begin the creation process, check a few details with your service provider. First you want to know how much web space is available to you. (If your provider doesn't give you web space for free, don't pay yet – you may be able to find free space elsewhere, as you'll find out in the next section.) Here are three more things to find out:

- Ask if you can upload your files by FTP. A few IAPs have their own methods of handling this, but most will tell you the address to connect to using your FTP program. You'll log on using your normal username and password and start copying the files across.
- Find out if you can create your own directory structure. Most IAPs will let you upload whole directories, but a few insist that only files can be uploaded. If all your links refer to files in subdirectories and you later find

out that everything has to be in the same directory, you'll have a lot of editing to do!

- The URL to your site will normally be **http://www.*serviceprovider*/~*username*** with all the files (and subdirectories) in this directory making up your site. When somebody arrives at this directory an index file should be automatically displayed, and this would usually be your first, welcoming page. In most cases this will be called **index.htm** or **index.html**, but check this with your service provider in case its system uses something different.

The Quest for Free Web-space

There is such a thing as a free lunch, (well, free web space anyway!) Believe it or not, there are several companies out there on the Internet that actually provide web space entirely free of charge – you don't have to pay, or buy anything else from them, you don't have to carry any advertising (other than perhaps a small logo with their name on it), and you don't have to make any commitments. Just go to the relevant sites, check out the details, and grab with both hands.

▶ GeoCities, one of the major providers of free space on the Web.

The only negative aspect to these 'free space' companies is that if they delete all your files, or their computers go down for 6 months, you're not in a strong position to complain. If that doesn't bother you, try some of these sites:

- GeoCities at **http://www.geocities.com**
- Netline Corporation at **http://www.netline.com**
- Phrantic at **http://www.phrantic.com**
- InterMedia Software at **http://intermid.com/html/weboffer.htm**.

Buttons, Backgrounds, Bullets, Applets...

Armed with a good graphics program, there's not much you can't do. But why bother? You can find everything you need on the Web and download it. There are many sites handing out the bits and pieces that you'll want to use on your pages, but let me unreservedly recommend one of my own sites, WebSight, at **http://www.btinternet.com/~ry/WebSight**. Here you'll find dozens of wallpaper backgrounds for your pages, graphical horizontal rule replacements, animated GIFs, Java applets and JavaScripts with easy download and setup instructions, and links to lots more useful stuff.

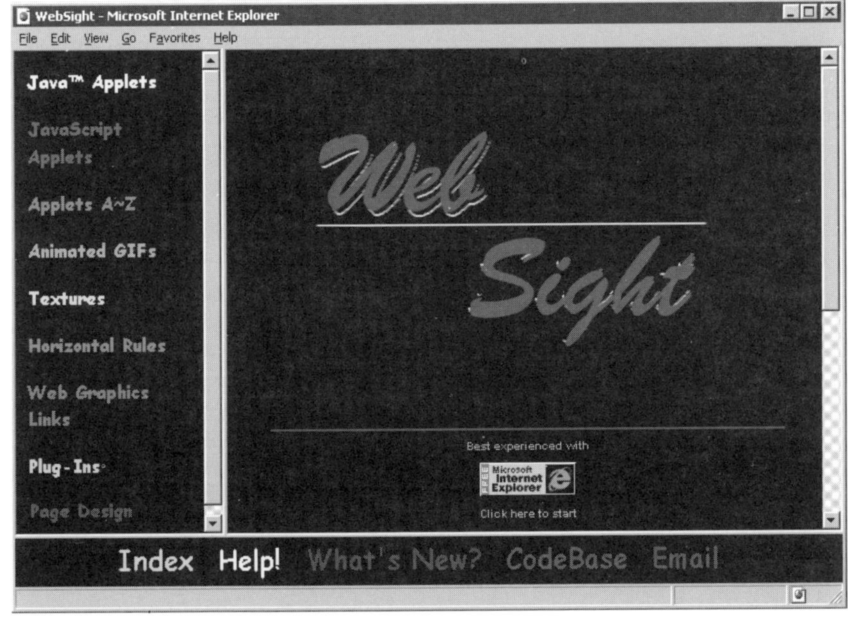

◀ Make WebSight your first stop for all those irresistible add-on goodies.

If that's not enough for you, head for the Microsoft Site Builder Gallery at **http://www.microsoft.com/gallery/default.asp**, which will provide you with a bit of everything, including complete 'theme' sets of backgrounds, images and icons. For a little help on the art of page design itself, visit one of these:

- Creating Killer Sites at **http://www.killersites.com**.
- Jeffrey Zeldman Presents… at **http://www.zeldman.com**.
- HTML Authoring at **http://www.asiweb.com/htmlauth.htm**.

Or, if you learn more easily by discovering how *not* to do it, visit Web Pages That Suck at **http://www.webpagesthatsuck.com**.

BY THE WAY

Of course it's under construction!

There's a trend on the Web to add 'Under Construction' graphics to indicate that a web site isn't finished. Don't fall into that trap! The entire Web is under construction, and a good site should always be evolving. If, by Under Construction, you mean that the links don't work, either remove them or fix them!

You're Ready to Upload!

Or are you? Before you do so, load all your pages into your browser one by one and check them. Test all your internal links (links to other pages from your own site) by clicking them to make sure they work. If your HTML software has a built-in spellchecker, use it. If it doesn't, consider loading the documents into a word processor to spellcheck – you'll have to remember to save as plain text when you've finished, and put up with the spellchecker disagreeing with all of your HTML tags.

Now follow the instructions you were given by your service provider to upload the files to the web server. At the risk of being obvious (not everyone realises this straight off), every file that forms a part of your site must be uploaded – images, documents, ZIP files, sound files and so on; if it's supposed to be a part of your web site, it must be on the web server and not just on your own computer. As you upload, make sure you keep the directory structure the same. For instance, if all your graphics files are in a subdirectory called images (and your links to them look something like `<IMG SRC="images/mypicture.gif">`), you must have a directory on the web server called **images**, in the same relative location to your HTML documents, that contains the same graphics files.

BY THE WAY

Easy site upload with FTP

When you upload using an FTP program such as WS_FTP, you don't have to transfer the files one by one. Make sure the left-hand pane is displaying the contents of the directory containing your whole web site, click the file or directory at the top of the list, then hold Shift and click the one at the bottom. With the entire contents now selected, click the right-pointing arrow to transfer the lot in one go.

When your site is uploaded to the server, start your browser, type your URL into the address bar and check each page to make sure that everything is as it should be (including all your links to other web sites). If you need to change a file, make the change on your own system and then upload the file again – provided you don't change its name, it should replace the original. Depending on your service provider's system, you should be able to see all your files and subdirectories in your FTP program's right pane, and delete or rename them as necessary.

Hit the Publicity Trail

So you have a web site, and it works. You want people to come and visit it, so you need to let them know it exists. One method is to contact the authors of sites covering similar subjects and ask if they'd like to exchange links – you add a link to their sites in return for links to yours. The other, more useful way to publicise your site is to get it listed with as many search engines as you can. There are two ways to do this, which should capture almost every search engine going.

Feed the Robots

The first thing to do is to adjust your home page in such a way that the search engines using roving robot-programs will find your site and describe it correctly. First, make sure that the title of your page (which appears between the <TITLE></TITLE> tags) is as meaningful as possible. Second, add the <META> tag to the header of your page. This tag has two attributes: NAME= (which can be "keywords" or "description") and CONTENT=. Let's say your site is about camels:

```
<!DOCTYPE HTML PUBLIC "-//W3C//DTD HTML 3.2//EN">

<HTML>
<HEAD>

<TITLE>The Ultimate Camel Reference</TITLE>

<META NAME="keywords" CONTENT="camels, dromedaries,
quadrupeds">
<META NAME="description" CONTENT="The ultimate
database of camel information, plus our fabulous
Spot The Hump competition!">

</HEAD>

<BODY>


</BODY>
</HTML>
```

In the keywords tag, list the words that people may type into a search engine to find sites like yours. In the description tag, type a short paragraph that explains what your page is about, to whet the appetite of intrepid web-surfers. Most search engines will display this description below the link to your site. It also helps if the first paragraph of text on your page sounds reasonably descriptive and appetising: some search engines will quote from this instead of using your meta description.

What happens if I don't add a META tag?

Either a large bundle of search engines won't be able to add your site to their database, or they'll index it wrongly. For example, if you leave out the description, the index will probably consist of the first few lines from your page, which may contain no useful information at all.

Submit to the Directories

Some search engines and directories don't use robots, so you'll need to submit details of your site to them manually. One way to do this is to visit each search site, one by one, and look for a link marked **Submit Your Site** or something similar, and then follow the instructions.

A better method is to visit a service that can submit your details to many different search sites at once. There are several hundred different search sites, and these services will want some money from you to submit to the whole lot, but their free services cover several dozen of the major search engines and directories. Choose one of these services and nip along to fill in the details:

- Add Me! at **http://www.addme.com**
- Submit It! at **http://www.submit-it.com**
- Submit.net at **http://www.submit.net/announce/index.html**.

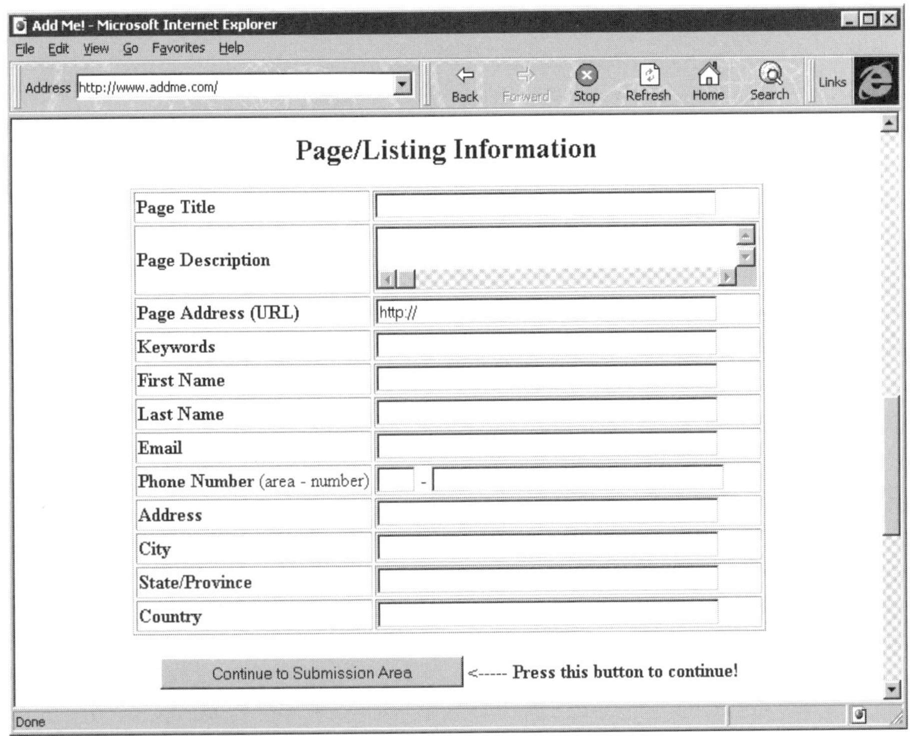

◀ Enter your details at Add Me! to register your site with the major search engines.

You may even choose to visit all three – keep a note of the search engines your details were submitted to using the first service, and then see if the remaining services cover any others. Take your time filling in the information, and make sure it's correct. When the form appears on the screen, you may want to disconnect from the Internet while you fill it in so that you don't feel rushed.

Gauge Audience Reaction

The only way to get true feedback about your site is to include email links on your pages, as we covered in Chapter 23, and to encourage visitors to tell you what they liked, what they didn't, and what they were hoping to see. Another interesting device is to place a counter on your page that tells you (roughly) how many visits your site has received. (You may even want to put a counter on every page to get a rough idea of which links from your home page most visitors find interesting.) One of the most informative and reliable counter-services can be found at ICount (**http://www.icount.com/register.html**). Fill in the simple details, choose a password, and the service will then display a HTML code. Swipe it with the mouse, copy it to the clipboard, and then paste it into one of your pages. You'll need to repeat this for each counter you want.

BY THE WAY

Ask your IAP about counters

Some service providers have their own special program (called a CGI program) running on their web server that you can use to put counters on your pages. This is likely to give you a more realistic count than one of the free counter-services. Get in touch with your IAP to see if they can offer this service.

The highest compliment anyone can pay to your site in Net jargon is to say it's cool. If you think you've got a cool site, why not submit it to be judged by one of the site-review organisations on the Web? If you're successful, you'll be able to display a sort of 'I've got a cool site' logo, and you should get many more visitors tramping around your pages as a result. Here are some of those organisations' sites (well worth a visit, even if you don't yet have a cool site of your own to submit):

Judging Site	URL
Coolynx Of The Day	http://www.virtualynx.com/coolynx
I.Way 500 Best Sites	http://www.cciweb.com/iway.html
Magellan Internet Guide	http://www.mckinley.com
Point Top 5% Sites	http://www.pointcom.com
Riddler	http://www.riddler.com
Wow! Web Wonders	http://www.bergen.gov/AAST/Wow

And if you're not yet cool enough? Perhaps that's something to celebrate, but if you really want to be cool, examine as many sites as you can that are sufficiently cool to win awards for it and try to discover what makes them that way. You'll also find tips, tricks and effects to increase your 'cool quotient' on the free CD accompanying this book.

APPENDICES

In These Appendices...

A **Getting Connected with Windows 95**

B **Getting Connected with Windows 3.1**

C **Using Netscape Navigator**

D **JargonBuster Super Reference**

E **HTML Tag Glossary**

F **HTML Colour Names**

GETTING CONNECTED WITH WINDOWS 95

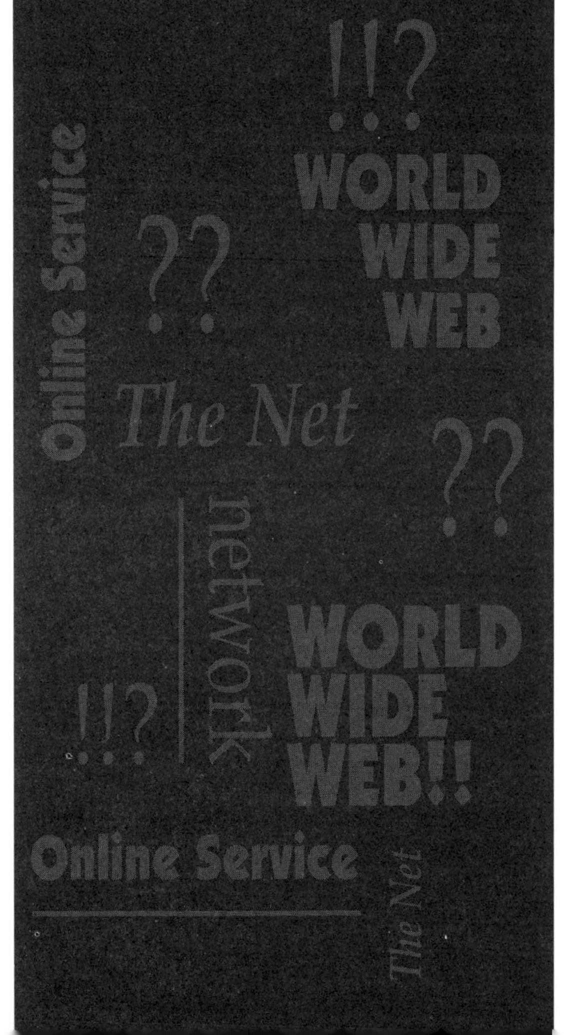

Windows 95 includes support for Internet connections that its predecessor didn't, making it easier to set up and a lot cleaner to use. There are three tasks to take care of: first you'll need to install the **TCP/IP** protocols that let your computer talk in 'Internet language'; second you'll install the **Dial-Up Adapter** that lets your computer make calls through your modem; and finally you'll create a **Dial-Up Networking connection** that you can double-click when you want to go online.

Installing TCP/IP

1 Open Control Panel and double-click the **Network** icon.
2 Click the **Add...** button.
3 In the left pane of the next dialog choose **Microsoft**, and in the right pane choose **TCP/IP**.
4 Click **OK**. You'll be prompted to restart your computer, but you may prefer to delay doing that until you've finished all the installations.

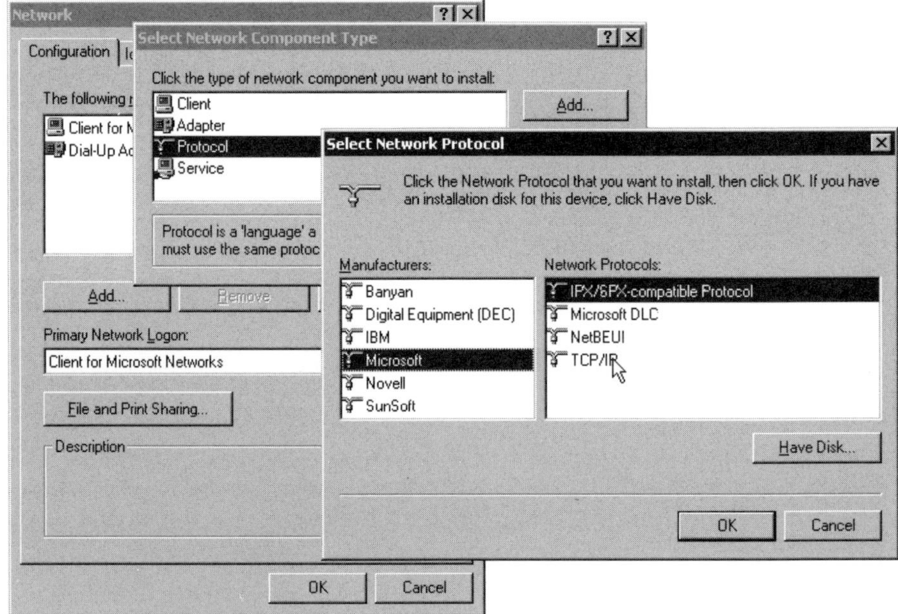

▶ The sequence of dialogs you'll see when installing the TCP/IP protocols.

Installing the Dial-Up Adapter

1 Check to see if you have **Dial-Up Networking** installed already. Double-click the My Computer icon and look for a folder-like icon labelled Dial-Up Networking. If it's there, skip straight to step 5. If you don't have

that icon, you'll need to install it as follows (making sure you've got your Windows 95 installation disks at the ready).

2 Open Control Panel and double-click **Add/Remove Programs**.
3 Click the **Windows Setup** tab, then select **Communications** and click the **Details...** button.
4 Check the box beside **Dial-Up Networking**, click **OK**, then click **OK** again to install it.
5 With Dial-Up Networking installed, go back to Control Panel, double-click **Network**, and then double-click on **Dial-Up Adapter**.
6 Click the tab marked **Bindings** and make sure there's a checkmark in the box beside **TCP/IP**. (If there isn't, click the box until the checkmark appears.) Click **OK**.

Creating a Dial-Up Networking Connection

1 Open My Computer and double-click the **Dial-Up Networking** icon.
2 Double-click the **Make New Connection** icon.
3 On the first page enter a name for your connection (any name you like). Click **Next**, and type the area code and telephone number you were given to dial in to your provider's computer. Select the **United Kingdom** entry from the drop-down list of country codes. Click **Next**, then click **Finish**.
4 Now right-click this new connection's icon and select **Properties**. If you are dialling a local number to your access provider, remove the checkmark beside **Use country code and area code**. (If you were given an 0345 or 0845 number, which is charged at local rate, you'll need to leave this box checked.)
5 Click the **Server Type** button or tabbed page. Select **PPP: Windows 95, Windows NT 3.5, Internet** from the drop-down list, and make sure the only boxes that are checked on this page are **Enable software compression** and **TCP/IP**, as shown in the next screenshot.
6 Next, click the **TCP/IP Settings...** button and grab the list of details your service provider gave you.
7 If your service provider gave you your own IP address (which is very unlikely), select the **Specify an IP address** button and then enter the address in the box beneath. Otherwise, make sure **Server assigned IP address** is selected.
8 Make sure **Specify name server addresses** is selected, and type the DNS address you were given into the **Primary DNS** box. If you were also given an alternative DNS address, type this into the **Secondary DNS** box.
9 Click **OK**, and **OK** again, and your connection is ready to roll!

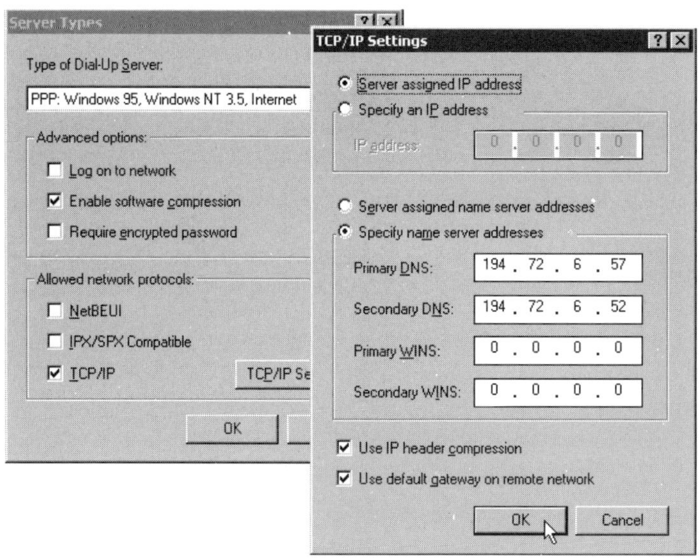

▶ Following steps 7 and 8, this is how those dialogs should look once you've entered your settings into them.

Using Your Connection

To start your connection, open your Dial-Up Networking folder and double-click the icon you just created. A dialog will appear, like the one shown in the next screenshot, into which you'll need to enter your username and the logon password you were given. To save your doing this every time, check the box marked **Save password**, then click **OK**.

BY THE WAY

Get a fast connection

To get to that all-important connection icon more quickly, drag it on to your desktop or Start Menu to create a shortcut within easy reach. By editing the shortcut's properties, you could even add a shortcut-key for ultra-quick access when you need it.

This box will be replaced by a smaller one that will keep you informed about what's happening with messages like **Dialling** and **Verifying username and password**. Soon you should see the magic word **Connected**. If so, you can now turn to Part 2 of this book, start one of your client programs, and get well and truly Netted!

When you've finished surfing and you're ready to log off, you need to click the **Disconnect** button. Where you find this will depend on your version of Windows 95. If the connection dialog minimised to a button on the Taskbar when you connected successfully, click that Taskbar button and you'll see the Disconnect button and the length of time you've been online. If the dialog vanished entirely when you connected, double-click the little icon in the tray that shows two tiny green computers: as well as the Disconnect button, you'll see your total online time together with the amount of data sent and received so far.

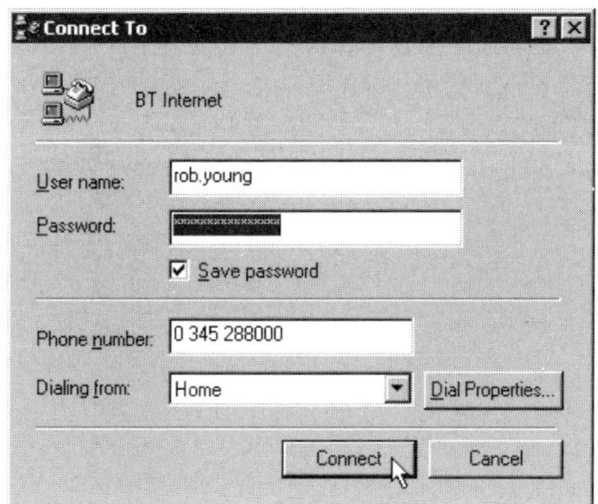

◀ Double-click your new connection, enter your username and password, and click the Connect button.

What Did I Do Wrong?

With some IAPs you've done everything necessary, and your connection will purr sweetly into life. However, with others you'll get as far as the **Verifying username and password** message and then see a message telling you that Dial-Up Networking couldn't 'negotiate a compatible set of network protocols'. What this means is that your logon details couldn't be passed to the IAP's computer from the dialog shown in the previous screenshot.

To overcome this problem, you'll need to create a logon script that sends these details the way your IAP's computer expects to receive them. Once again, the method of doing this depends upon your Windows 95 version. Start by right-clicking your Dial-Up Networking connection and selecting **Properties**. If you see a tab labelled **Scripting**, follow steps 5 and 6 below to create a script file, then click that **Scripting** tab and enter the path and name of your script file in the box (or use the **Browse** button to locate it) and click **OK**. If you don't have that **Scripting** tab, you'll need to grab your Windows 95 installation disk(s) and follow each of these steps:

1 Open Control Panel, double-click **Add/Remove Programs** and click the **Windows Setup** tab. Click the **Have Disk** button.
2 Click the **Browse** button and navigate to the CD's Admin\Apptools\Dscript directory.

3 With this directory selected you'll see the filename called **Rnaplus.inf** in the File Name box. Click on **OK**, and on **OK** a second time.
4 In the next dialog you'll see a single item, **SLIP and Scripting for Dial-Up Networking**. Check the box beside this entry and click on **Install**. After the program has been installed it's time to create the script.
5 Ideally your access provider will have provided a script (or will provide one if you ask nicely). If not, here's an all-purpose script that may do the trick. Open Notepad and type the following, replacing the italic text with your own username and password:

proc main
  waitfor "login:"
  transmit "*username*"
  transmit "^M"
  waitfor "password:"
  transmit "*password*"
  transmit "^M"
  waitfor "protocol:"
  transmit "PPP^M"
endproc

6 Save this file to anywhere you like, and give it any name, but make sure you give it the extension **.scp**. Close Notepad.
7 Click the Start button and go to Programs | Accessories | Dial-Up Scripting Tool (the program you installed in the earlier steps).
8 In the left pane of this program, click the name of your dial-up connection. Click on Browse, locate the script file you just created and double-click it. Click OK to confirm and close the scripting tool, and try your connection again.

B

GETTING CONNECTED WITH WINDOWS 3.1

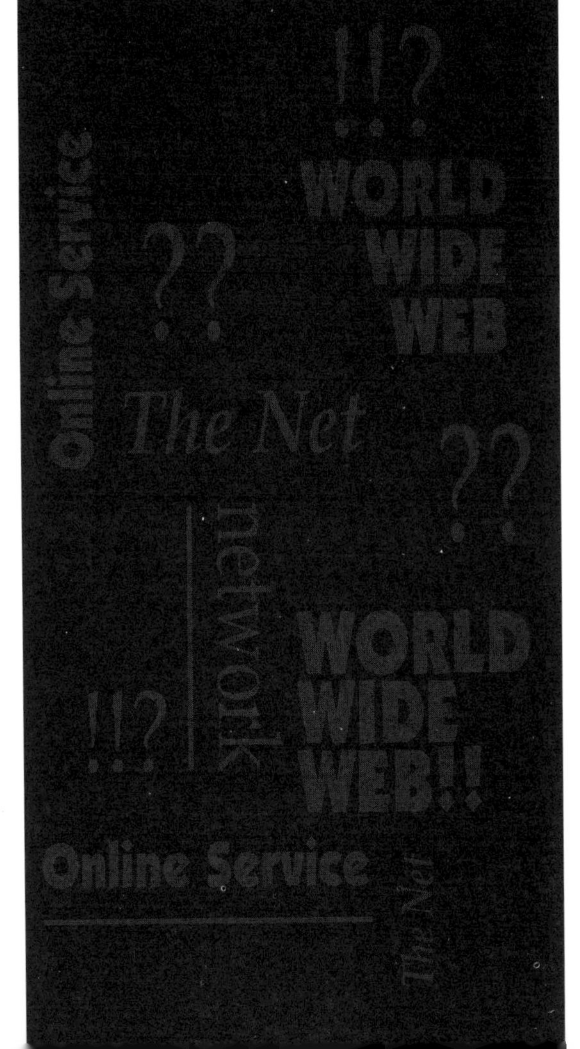

Although Windows 95 has built-in support for Internet connections, Windows 3x isn't at all difficult to configure. When you subscribed to your access provider you probably received a disk that includes a program called **Trumpet Winsock**. If you didn't, phone up and ask for it!

There are two steps to connecting: the first task is to install Trumpet Winsock and to edit your AUTOEXEC.BAT file so that Windows knows where to find this program. The second is to configure the program itself using the list of technical details you were given. (If you get into difficulties, Trumpet includes plenty of useful documentation to help you on your way.)

Installing Trumpet Winsock

1 Create a directory on your hard-disk called C:\TRUMPET.
2 Copy all the Trumpet Winsock files from your IAP's disk into this directory (unzipping them if they were supplied in a ZIP archive).
3 Create a new program item in Program Manager with the command line **C:\TRUMPET\TCPMAN.EXE** so that you can start this program easily when you're ready to connect.
4 Now you need to edit your AUTOEXEC.BAT file using System Editor or Notepad to add this new directory to your path statement. After you've done so, it may look like this:

   SET PATH=C:\;C:\DOS;C:\WINDOWS;C:\TRUMPET;

4 Shut down Windows and reboot your computer to force Windows to read this newly edited AUTOEXEC.BAT file.

What is a Winsock anyway?

Winsock stands for Windows Sockets, and it's the software that Windows needs to be able to talk 'Internet language', using the TCP/IP protocols we met earlier. It doesn't do anything exciting, but it's the vital link that lets all your Internet programs talk to your IAP's computer.

Configuring Trumpet Winsock

1 Start Trumpet Winsock by double-clicking TCPMAN.EXE in your new TRUMPET directory (or by double-clicking its Program Manager icon.

2 As the program opens you'll see a dialog containing several fields into which you'll need to enter the details you were given by your IAP. (This dialog only appears the first time you run the program, and these settings will be saved the first time you close it.)

3 Type the **IP address, Netmask, Name server** (DNS) and **Default Gateway** IP addresses and the **Domain Suffix** into the correct fields (remembering to type the dots between each number). If you were given two DNS addresses, type both into the **Name server** field leaving a single space between them.

4 Check the **Internet SLIP** or **Internal PPP** box according to the type of connection you were given by your IAP, and make sure that the port setting matches the port to which your modem is connected and its correct speed is entered.

5 Click **OK** and you'll see the main Trumpet window – you're now ready to dial up and connect.

6 Open the **Dialer** menu and click **Login**. In the three dialogs that appear one at a time, enter the telephone number you were given to dial in, your username, and your password.

7 If all goes according to plan, Trumpet will connect to your IAP and you'll see a message like **CONNECT 38400** appear (it's the word 'Connect' that matters – the speed will depend on your own modem). Press the ESC key on your keyboard, and you're ready to start one of your Internet programs, turn back to Part 2 and start surfing!

If instead you see a message like **Script Aborted**, you have two options:

- Go back to the Dialer menu and choose Manual Login. Type **ATDT** followed by the telephone number of your IAP's computer. As Trumpet tries to connect you, prompts will appear on the screen such as **Username**: and **Password**:. Type these details as you're prompted for them, pressing Enter after each. When you see the **CONNECT** message press ESC and you're officially online.

- Contact your IAP's support line to ask for a login script – the chances are that they'll have been asked for this many times before. Failing that, try editing the file LOGIN.CMD in your TRUMPET directory, according to the details included in Trumpet's own documentation.

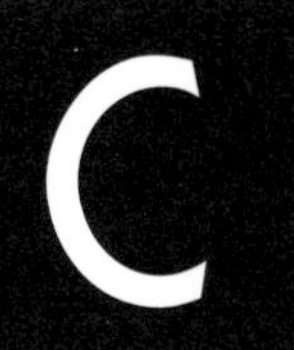

USING NETSCAPE NAVIGATOR

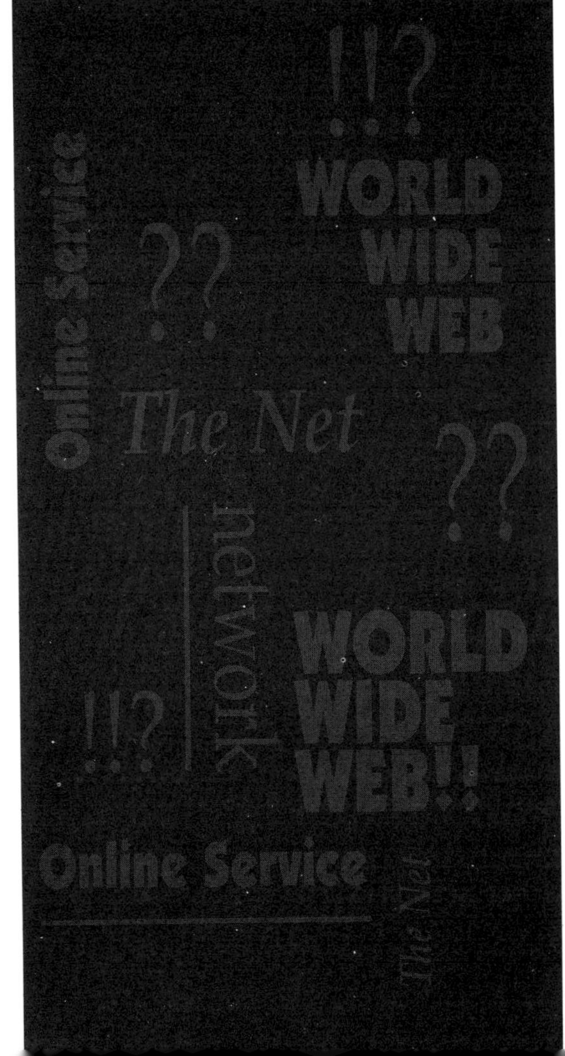

In the sections of this book that deal with the World Wide Web and browsers, I've assumed that you're using Microsoft's Internet Explorer. If you're not, you're probably using the other major contender for the crown, Netscape Navigator. Fortunately, most of the facilities available in Explorer are also available in Navigator, and many of them can be accessed by similar toolbar buttons, menu options or keystrokes, so you'll probably find it quite easy to steer Navigator around the Web from reading the earlier chapters. Nevertheless, to prevent confusion, the list opposite gives the main browser features that are found in different places or have different names to the Explorer counterparts.

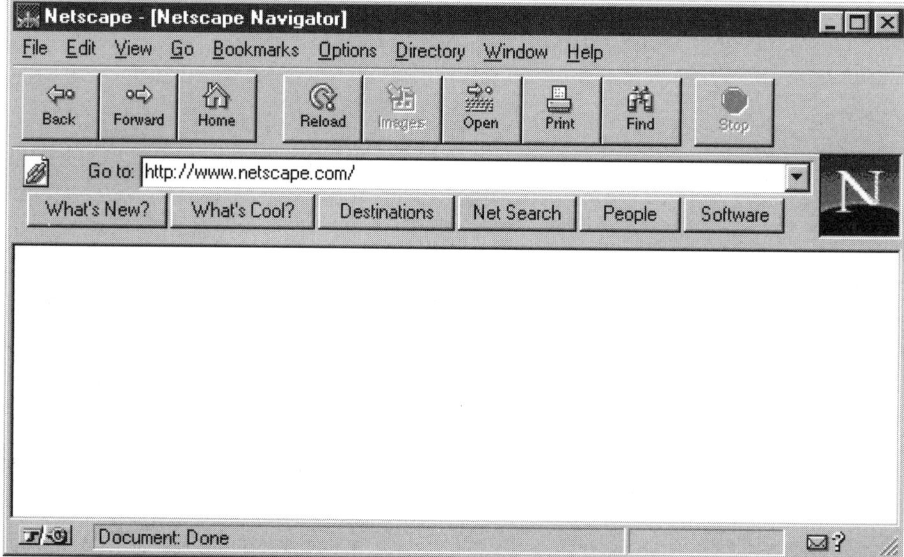

▶ Netscape Navigator.

To Do This	Select This Netscape Option
Reload the current page	Click the **Reload** button, or press Ctrl+R.
View the document's HTML source	Go to **View | Document Source**.
Open a second browser window	Press Ctrl+N, or select **File | New Web Browser**. The new window will display your start page, which Netscape calls a 'home page'.
View the History list	Press Ctrl+H, or select **Window | History**.
Save a link to a site to visit again	Select **Bookmarks | Add Bookmark**, or press Ctrl+D. Bookmarks are the equivalent of Explorer's 'Favorites'.
Organise your bookmarks	Press Ctrl+B, or select **Window | Go to Bookmarks**.
Visit a bookmarked site	Select **Bookmarks** and click the site to visit on the menu.
Switch off automatic display of images	Open the **Options** menu and click on **Auto Load Images** to remove the checkmark.
Switch off Navigator's toolbar	Remove the checkmark from **Options | Show Toolbar**.
Switch off the address bar	Remove the checkmark from **Options | Show Location**.
Switch off the lower button-bar	Remove the checkmark from **Options | Show Directory Buttons**.
View a list of installed plug-ins	Go to **Help | About Plug-ins**.
Open the default search engine site	Click the **Net Search** button.
Choose a different home page	Go to **Options | General Preferences...** and choose the **Appearance** tab. Either select **Blank Page**, or type the URL of the page or file you'd like to use in the textbox below.
Edit settings for plug-ins and viewers	Go to **Options | General Preferences...** and click the **Helpers** tab.
Turn on/off support for active content	Go to **Options | Network Preferences...** and click the **Languages** tab. Add or remove the checkmarks in the two boxes.
Change the size of the cache	Go to **Options | Network Preferences... | Cache** and type a new figure into the **Disk Cache** box.
Empty the cache directory	Go to **Options | Network Preferences... | Cache** and click the **Clear Disk Cache Now** button.
Find cool sites to visit	Click the buttons on the lower button-bar.

JARGONBUSTER SUPER REFERENCE

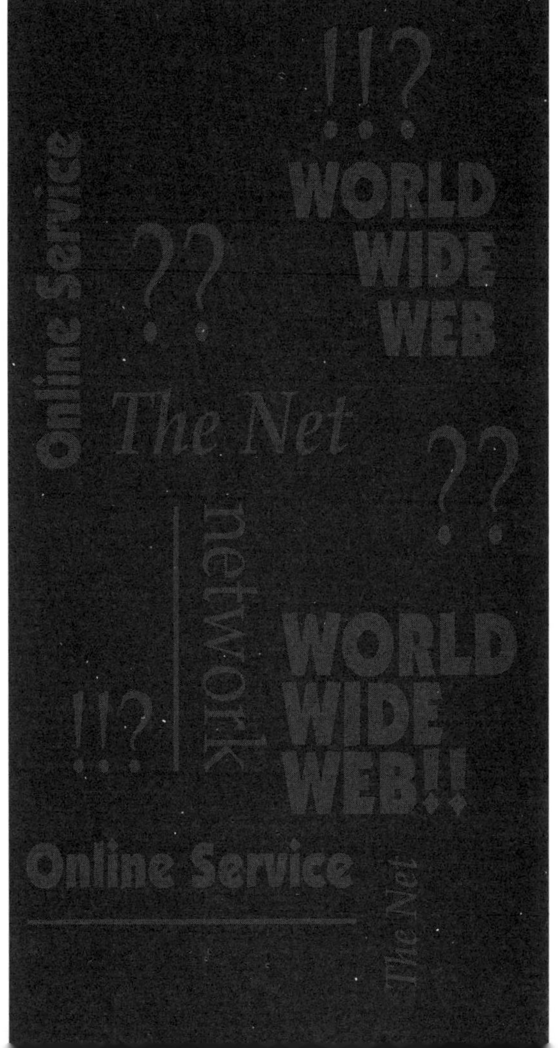

Arriving on the Internet is a bit like arriving in a foreign country – suddenly everyone around you seems to be talking a different language. This is the part of the book that helps you to find out what they're going on about, or even to learn to speak like a native yourself. Yes, it's all the technical stuff, but we'll keep it as painless as possible.

Keep a look out for words and phrases in *italic* text – they indicate a related entry. The figures you'll find in square brackets (such as [252]) at the end of some of the definitions are the page numbers on which you'll find the subject covered in more depth.

access provider A general term for a company that lets you connect to the *Internet* by dialling in to its computer in return for money. This may be an *Internet Access Provider* or an *online service*.

ActiveX A new multimedia programming system developed by Microsoft for use on the *World Wide Web*. [311]

alias A nifty short name for something whose real name is much longer. For example, your *email* software will usually let you refer to yourself as Joe Bloggs instead of joe_bloggs@somewhere.co.uk.

animated GIF A type of animation created by loading two or more *GIF* images into an animation program, setting an order and delay times, and resaving as a single file. [337]

anonymous FTP A method of getting access to files on an *FTP* site without needing special permission or a logon name. Instead you enter **anonymous** as your *logon* name, and your email address as your password. [126]

anonymous remailers Services that will forward your *email* messages or newsgroup *articles* after stripping out your personal details, so that no one can tell who sent them. [211]

Archie A system that lets you track down files on *FTP* sites by entering the name of the file (or part of it) into a program that can search through indexes of files on these computers. [154]

archive A single file which usually contains several (or many) other files to make for quicker and easier *downloading*. Most archives also compress these files into a smaller space than they'd ordinarily take up, speeding up downloads still further. [184]

article This is the name for a message sent to a *newsgroup*. [116]

ASCII Pronounced 'ass-key', and often referred to as **plain text**. This is a text system that allows ordinary numbers and letters, punctuation marks such as spaces, tabs and carriage-returns, plus a few special characters, but no formatting or font information. ASCII text can be recognised by almost any type of computer and read in any word processor.

attachments Files included with a message to be sent by *email* or to a *newsgroup*. Messages that contain attachments are indicated by a paper-clip icon in most software.

attributes In *HTML*, these are additions to *tags* that let you specify or change what the tag should do. For example, `<HR>` creates a rule across the page. Adding the `WIDTH=` and `ALIGN=` attributes lets you create a short rule placed on the left or right side of the page. [328]

bandwidth A general term for the amount of information that can be transferred over an Internet connection. Often used in terms of 'wasting bandwidth' by, for example, sending the same *article* to 30 different *newsgroups* when it was only relevant to one.

BBS (Bulletin Board System) A computer which provides an *email* service and file archives (and perhaps more), which members can connect to via modem. Some online services such as CompuServe started life as BBSs before becoming connected to the *Internet*.

binaries or **binary files** The term for a file that contains anything but plain *ASCII* text (such as a program, movie or formatted document). Also appears in *newsgroup* names to indicate that non-text files can be attached to *articles*.

bookmarks The Netscape Navigator name for *Favorites*.

bounced email *Email* messages that come back to you instead of being delivered, usually because you typed the *email address* wrongly.

browser The vital piece of *Internet* software, ostensibly designed for viewing pages from the *World Wide Web*, but capable of handling almost all of your Internet activities. The two most popular browsers are Microsoft's Internet Explorer and Netscape's Navigator. [59]

cache A directory on your own system into which your *browser* stores all the files it *downloads* from the *World Wide Web* in case you want to view those pages again – it can then load them quickly from this directory instead of downloading them all over again. [81]

chat A type of conversation which takes place by typing messages back and forth instead of speaking (other than to swear at the chat software). A popular chat system is *IRC*, but online services have their own chat rooms, and other software allows one-to-one chatting by 'dialling-up' an *email address* rather like using a telephone. [134]

client The name for something (usually a software program) that makes use of a service. For example, your email program is a client that makes use of the *email* service. The opposite term is *server*. [26]

compressed files see *archive*

containers The name for the type of *tags* used in *HTML* that must have a closing tag (such as `<B>...</B>` for bold text). The text to which the tags are being applied is contained within them.

cookies Small text-files that some *web sites* store on your computer so that they know who you are next time you visit. [202]

cyberspace A word coined by William Gibson in his novel *Necromancer*. It's used as a generalised term for the Internet and everything that comes with it.

Dial-Up Networking The *TCP/IP stack* built into Microsoft Windows 95, Window NT 4.0, and later operating systems, that makes setting up an *Internet* connection a relatively pain-free task.

DNS see *Domain Name System*

domain name The name given to a computer on the *Internet* that's (vaguely) recognisable to human beings, such as **www.royalnetwork.com**. Every computer on the Net has its own unique name. [24]

Domain Name System (DNS) Also defined as Domain Name Server. This system translates the friendly *domain names* that we humans like to work with into *IP addresses* that computers like to work with. [25]

dot address Another name for *IP address*.

downloading The act of copying files (of any type) to your own computer from some other computer. The opposite term is *uploading*.

email or **e-mail** Short for 'electronic mail', a system that lets you send text messages over a *network* from one computer to another. [86]

email address An address consisting of your *username* and the *host* name of your service provider's computer, in the form **username@host**. Because this host name is unique, and you're the only subscriber with that username, the address is as personal to you as your telephone number. [87]

emoticons Little pictures (usually faces) made out of typed characters and viewed sideways-on, such as :-) meaning 'happy'. [100]

encryption The term for altering data or text to turn it into meaningless gobbledegook. Only someone with the correct decoding information (or 'key') can read and use it. [203]

FAQ (Frequently Asked Questions) A list of questions and answers on a particular subject. These are frequently placed in *newsgroups* so that the group doesn't become bogged down with new users asking the same questions all the time. You'll also find FAQs on web sites, and almost anywhere else in the computing world.

Favorites A menu in Microsoft's Internet Explorer *browser* (and a corresponding directory on your hard-disk) containing shortcuts to sites that you visit regularly. You can easily revisit a site by clicking its name on the menu, and add new sites to the menu with a couple of clicks. [64]

Finger A command (or a software program that sends the command), which returns information about someone whose *email address* you entered. Also used as a verb, so this is one instance in which you can 'finger' someone and get away with it. [157]

flame A negative or abusive response to a *newsgroup article* or an *email* message. [119]

follow-up A reply to an *email* or *newsgroup* message that contains the same subject line (prefixed with RE) and continues the same *thread*.

freeware Software that you don't have to pay for. [180]

FTP (File Transfer Protocol) One of the many *protocols* used to copy files from one computer to another on the Internet. Also used in terms like 'an FTP site' (a site that lets you grab files from it using this protocol), and as a verb, as in 'You can ftp to this site'. [124]

gateway A program or device that acts as a kind of translator between two *networks* that wouldn't otherwise be able to communicate with each other.

GIF One of the two major graphics formats used on the *Internet* (along with *JPEG*). GIF images can be saved with between 2 and 256 colours, so they contain less information than the 16-million-colour JPEG format, and therefore make smaller files. They're suitable for anything but photographs and the most lifelike art. See also *animated GIFs*. [333]

Gopher A menu-based system for storing, searching for and retrieving documents, which was the precursor to the *World Wide Web*. [150]

history list A list of recently visited sites stored by your *browser* so that you can see where you've been, get back there easily, or find out what someone else has been using your browser for. [65]

home page Two definitions for this one: 1. The page displayed in your *browser* when you first run it, or when you click the Home button; 2. The first page (or main contents page) of a *web site*.

host A computer connected directly (and usually permanently) to the *Internet* that allows other computers to connect to it (like your service provider's computer). This also leads to the expression 'host name', which means the same as *domain name*.

HTML see *Hypertext Markup Language*

HTTP (HyperText Transfer Protocol) The *protocol* used to transfer web pages around the *Internet*, with the images and other ingredients that go with them.

hypertext A system of clickable text used on the *World Wide Web*, as well as in older Windows help files and CD-ROM-based encyclopaedias. A hypertext *link* can be inserted wherever a cross-reference to another part of the document (or an entirely different document) is needed. [58]

Hypertext Markup Language (HTML) A fairly simple system of textual codes that can be added to an ASCII text-file to turn it into a web page. [58]

IAP see *Internet Access Provider*

Internet Often shortened to 'the Net'. The Internet is a gigantic *network* of computers, all linked together and able to exchange information. No one owns or controls it, and anyone can connect to it. Without the capital 'I', an internet is a more general term for networks connected to each other.

Internet Access Provider (IAP) A company that allows anyone to connect to the *Internet* by dialling into their *host* computer. All they ask in return is that you give them money. Also sometimes referred to as an Internet Service Provider, or ISP. [34 and 40]

Internet Protocol (IP) see *TCP/IP*

IP address (Internet Protocol Address) Every computer on the Internet has its own unique address, which can appear in two forms: the friendlier *domain name*, or as an IP address that computers themselves use. This consists of four numbers separated by dots, such as 148.159.6.26. Also known as a 'dot address'. [24]

IRC (Internet Relay Chat) An *Internet* service that provides one of the most popular *chat* systems, which can be accessed using many different IRC programs. Chat rooms in IRC are referred to as 'channels'. [137]

ISDN An abbreviation for Integrated Services Digital Network. An ISDN line allows faster access to the *Internet* than current modems allow, and can simultaneously handle voice and data. [37]

ISP (Internet Service Provider) see *Internet Access Provider*

Java A software-programming language developed by Sun MicroSystems Inc. The language is often used to write small programs called 'applets' that can be inserted in a web page.

JavaScript A similar language to *Java*, except that it's written in plain text and can be inserted 'as is' into a *HTML* document to place effects or small programs on a web page.

JPEG Along with *GIF*, this is one of the two most used formats for images on the Net. This format saves information for 16.7 million colours, making it ideal for photographs but creating unnecessarily large files for most forms of artwork.

leased line A line leased from the telephone company that provides a permanent, dedicated connection to an *Internet Access Provider*. Leased lines are lightning fast and cost a small fortune. (Also known as a 'T1 connection'.) [37]

link As a noun, a link is a piece of clickable *hypertext*, identifiable by being underlined and a different colour from the ordinary text around it. As a verb, to link to a site or page means the same as to open or *download* it.

log off A synonym for 'disconnect' – logging off means telling the computer you're connected to that you've finished for this session.

log on/logon Either of these can be used as a noun or a verb. When you log on to a service or computer you are identifying yourself, usually by entering a *username* and password. This act may be referred to as 'a logon', or 'logging on'. Your username may be termed a 'logon name'.

lurking A cute term for observing something without taking an active role. This may refer to visiting *chat* rooms and just following conversations rather than chatting, or reading *newsgroups* without posting any *articles* yourself.

mailing list This can mean two things: 1. A list of *email addresses* to which you can send the same message without making endless copies of it, all with different addresses inserted; 2. A discussion group similar to *newsgroups*, but all the messages sent to the group are forwarded to its members by email. [120]

mail server A computer (or program) dedicated to transferring *email* messages around the *Internet*. This may be referred to as an *SMTP* server or a *POP3* server.

MIME (Multipurpose Internet Mail Extensions) A method of organising different types of file by assigning each its own 'MIME type'. Most of the *Internet* software you use can recognise these types and determine what to do with a file it receives (or ask you how you want to treat it). MIME is used to handle *attachments* in *email* and *newsgroup* messages, as well as files found on web pages.

mirror site An exact copy of a site located on a different computer. Many popular sites have one or more mirrors around the world so that users can connect to the site nearest to them, thus easing the load on the main computer.

modem An acronym formed from the words 'modulator' and 'demodulator'. A modem converts data back and forth between the format recognised by computers and the format needed to send it down telephone lines. [32]

MPEG Along with *QuickTime*, one of the two most popular formats for movie files on the *Internet*, requiring an MPEG player and (ideally) special hardware for playback. [295]

MUD (Multi User Dungeon) A type of text-based adventure game that can be played by a single user, or by multiple users adopting characters and 'chatting' by typing messages. [153]

netiquette An amalgamation of the words 'Internet' and 'etiquette' that refers to good behaviour on the Net. Netiquette essentially boils down to two rules: avoid offensive comments and actions, and don't waste Internet resources (or *bandwidth*). [103 and 118]

network Two or more computers that are connected (or can be connected via telephone lines and *modems*) and can pass information back and forth.

newbie A colloquial name for someone new to the *Internet*, or to a particular area of it, who is perhaps prone to a bit of fumbling around. Although a slightly derogatory term, it's not meant to be offensive – you may describe yourself as a newbie when appealing for help.

newsgroups A discussion group with a particular topic in which users leave messages for others to read and reply to. There are almost thirty thousand such groups, and many more *mailing lists* which follow similar methods. Newsgroups are sometimes referred to as *Usenet* groups. [106]

newsreader The software program you use to access *newsgroups*, and to read, send, and reply to *articles*.

news server A computer (or program) dedicated to transferring the contents of *newsgroups* around the Net, and to and from your computer. This may be referred to as an *NNTP* server.

NNTP (Network News Transfer Protocol) One of many *protocols* used on the Net to transfer information around. This particular protocol handles messages from *newsgroups*.

offline A synonym for 'not connected'. In Net terms, being offline is generally a good thing (unless you're trying and failing to get *online*): the ability to compose messages offline and send them all in a bunch later, or view *downloaded* files offline, can save you money in connection charges.

online A synonym for 'connected'. Anything connected to your computer and ready for action can be said to be online. In *Internet* terms, it means that you've successfully dialled in to your service provider's computer and are now connected to the Net. The opposite term is *offline*.

online service A members-only service that allows users to join discussion groups (or 'forums'), exchange *email* messages with other members, download files, and a fair bit more besides. Most popular online services (such as America Online and CompuServe) are now connected to the *Internet* as well. [33 and 46]

packet The name for a unit of data being sent across the Net. A system called 'packet switching' breaks a file up into packets, marks each with the addresses of the sending and receiving computers, and sends each packet off individually. These packets may arrive at your computer via different routes and in the wrong order, but your computer uses the extra information they contain to piece the file back together.

PGP (Pretty Good Privacy) A popular, but rather complicated, system of *encryption*. [203]

PING (Packet InterNet Groper) The name of a command (or a program that sends a command) that tests a connection between two computers. It does this by sending a tiny amount of data to a specified computer and noting how long it takes to reply. (The reply, incidentally, is called a PONG.) [157]

plug-in An add-on program for a *browser* that can play or display a particular type of file in the browser's own window. [290]

PoP (Point of Presence) An unnecessarily technical name for a telephone number you can dial to connect to your service provider's computer. Many service providers have PoPs all over the country; others cater just for the major cities or a single small area.

POP3 (Post Office Protocol) One of two *protocols* (along with *SMTP*) used to transfer *email* messages around the Net. POP is used for receiving email, and lets you collect your messages from any computer you happen to be using. The '3' refers to the latest version of the protocol. [89]

posting When you send an *email* message, the word 'sending' is quite good enough. When you send a message to a *newsgroup*, it isn't. Instead, for no adequately explained reason, the word 'posting' is used.

PPP (Point to Point Protocol) A *protocol* used to connect computers to the Internet via a telephone line and a modem. It's similar to *SLIP*, but more recent and easier to set up.

protocol A type of 'language' that two computers agree to speak when they need to communicate and don't speak each other's native language. In other words, a sort of Esperanto for computers, but networking and *Internet* connections use a great many different protocols to do different things.

QuickTime Along with *MPEG*, this is one of the most popular movie file formats on the Net, developed by Apple. To view these files you'll need the QuickTime Viewer. There is also a virtual reality version (QuickTime VR) which is gaining in popularity. [295]

RealAudio The most popular format for *streaming* audio on the Net, requiring the RealAudio Player (included with Internet Explorer) for playback. [291]

refresh (or **reload**) Forcing the *browser* to *download* a web page again by clicking a toolbar button labelled Refresh (in Internet Explorer) or Reload (in Netscape Navigator). You may do this to make sure you're looking at the latest version of a page, or as an attempt to get things moving again if the page began to download and everything ground to a halt.

rot13 (rotated 13) A simple method used to *encrypt email* and *newsgroup* messages so that you won't accidentally read something that may offend you. [115]

search engine A web site that maintains an index of other web pages and sites, allowing you to search for pages on a particular subject by entering keywords. Because these engines gather their information in different ways, you can get markedly varying results from using different search sites. [164]

server A computer or program that provides a service to a *client*. For example, your *email* client (the program that lets you work with email messages) connects to your service provider's mail server when you decide to send or receive your email.

service provider A general term for a company that gives you access to the *Internet* by letting you dial in to its computer. This may be an *Internet Access Provider* or an *online service*.

shareware A system for selling software that lets you try before you buy. If you like the program, you pay for it. If you don't, you stop using it and delete it from your system. [180]

signature A short piece of text you can create that gets appended to your *email* and *newsgroup* messages when you send them. This may give contact information (perhaps your name, email address, company name, etc), a neat little phrase or quote, or perhaps an elaborate piece of *ASCII* art (rather like an *emoticon*, but bigger).

SLIP (Serial Line Internet Protocol) A similar *protocol* to *PPP*, but older and best avoided (especially if you use Windows 95, Windows NT 4.0, or later).

smiley see *emoticon*

SMTP (Simple Mail Transfer Protocol) Along with *POP3*, one of the two *protocols* that are used to transfer *email* messages around the Net. SMTP can be used to both send and receive messages, but POP3 has more flexibility for receiving. When POP3 is being used, SMTP simply handles the sending of messages. [89]

source The name for the *HTML* document that forms a web page, containing all the *tags* that determine what your *browser* should display, and how. You can look at the source for a web page in Internet Explorer by clicking the View menu and selecting Source.

spamming A Net jargon term for sending the same message to multiple *newsgroups* or *email* recipients regardless of their interest (or lack of it). Most spamming consists of unsolicited advertisements. Apart from the personal aggravation it causes, spamming is also a massive waste of *bandwidth.* [119]

streaming Some of the latest formats for video and audio on the Net allow the file to play while it's being downloaded, rather than forcing you to wait for the entire file to *download* first.

tags The name for the *HTML* codes added to a plain *ASCII* document, which transform it into a web page with full formatting and *links* to other files and pages. [314]

talk A talk program lets you speak to someone elsewhere in the world using your *modem* and *Internet* connection instead of your telephone. You need a soundcard and microphone, and the other person must be using the same program you are. Also known as Voice On the Net (VON). The term 'talk' is also used to describe the kind of typed chat that takes place between two people rather than a group in a *chat* room. [143]

TCP/IP (Transmission Control Protocol/Internet Protocol) Two vital *protocols* that work together to handle communications between your computer and the rest of the *Internet.*

TCP/IP stack For a computer to connect to the *Internet,* it must have a TCP/IP stack, which consists of *TCP/IP* software, *packet* driver software, and sockets software. Windows 95 and later Windows operating systems come with their own TCP/IP stack called *Dial-Up Networking.* In Windows 3x, the TCP/IP stack has to be installed separately: one of the best stacks is Trumpet *Winsock.* (See also *Winsock.*)

Telnet A program that allows *Internet* users to connect to a distant computer and control it through their own computer. Nowadays the main use of Telnet is in playing games like *MUDs.* [152]

thread An ongoing topic of conversation in a *newsgroup* or *mailing list.* When someone posts a message with a new Subject line they're starting a new thread. Any replies to this message (and replies to replies, and so on) will have the same Subject line and continue the thread. [113]

TLAs (Three Letter Acronyms) Not necessarily acronyms, and not necessarily three letters either, but TLAs are a type of shorthand for common phrases used in conversation and messages on the Net, such as BTW for 'By the way'. [101]

Transmission Control Protocol (TCP) see *TCP/IP*

uploading The term for copying files from your own computer to a distant computer, usually by using *FTP*. The opposite term is *downloading*.

URL (Uniform Resource Locator) (Pronounced 'earl'.) The unique 'address' of a file on the *Internet* consisting of a *protocol* (such as http://), a computer name (such as www.computer.co.uk) and a path to the file on that computer (such as /public/files/program.zip).

Usenet A large network that distributes many of the Net's *newsgroups*. [106]

username A unique name you're assigned by a service that enables you to *log on* to it and identify yourself, demonstrating that you're entitled to access it. When you set up your *Internet* access account, your username will usually form part of your *email address* too. [41 and 88]

uuencode/uudecode To send computer files in *email* or *newsgroup* messages, they have to be converted to plain *ASCII* text first. Uuencoding is a system for converting files this way; uudecoding converts the text back into a file at the other end. Special software may be needed to do this, but many email and newsgroup programs have built-in automatic uuencode/uudecode facilities. [96]

VBScript A scripting language developed by Microsoft. It is similar to *JavaScript*.

Veronica An acronym for 'Very Easy Rodent-Oriented Net-wide Index to Computerised Archives'. Veronica is a facility built into *Gopher* that allows searching for files on gopher sites.

viewer A program used to view, play or display files that you find on the Net. Unlike a *plug-in*, a viewer will open the file in its own separate window. Because it's a stand-alone program, you can also use it *offline* to view files already on your own system. [290]

virus A small program created by a warped mind that can use various methods to attach itself to programs. When the program is run, so is the virus. A virus may do no more harm to your system than making it go beep occasionally, or it may trash all your data and even make your computer unusable. The main risk of 'catching' a virus comes from using programs on a floppy-disk of unknown origin or *downloaded* from the *Internet* without first running them through virus-checker software. [188]

Voice On the Net (VON) see *talk*

VRML (Virtual Reality Modelling Language) A language used to build 3D models and 'worlds' that you can view using special software. [298]

WAIS (Wide Area Information Server) A little-used service for searching databases of information on the Net.

Web see *World Wide Web*

web page A single document (usually having the extension .htm or .html) forming a tiny part of the *World Wide Web*, often containing text, images, and *links* to other pages and files on the Web. To view web pages you need a *browser*. [57]

web server A computer or program dedicated to storing *web pages* and transmitting them to your computer to be viewed in your *browser*.

web site A collection of related *web pages* and files, usually created by or belonging to a single individual or company, and located on the same *web server*.

web space Usually refers to space on a *web server* provided to *Internet* users so that they can create and publish their own *web sites*. This space may be provided free, or for a monthly charge. [343]

Whois A command (or a program which can send the command) that can find someone's email address and other information about them based on the name you enter. [159]

Winsock An abbreviation of Windows Sockets, the sockets software program for Windows operating systems called Winsock.dll that forms the basis of a *TCP/IP stack*.

World Wide Web A vast collection of documents and files stored on *web servers*. The documents are known as *web pages* and are created using a language called *HTML*. All these pages and files are linked together using a system of *hypertext*. [57]

HTML TAG GLOSSARY

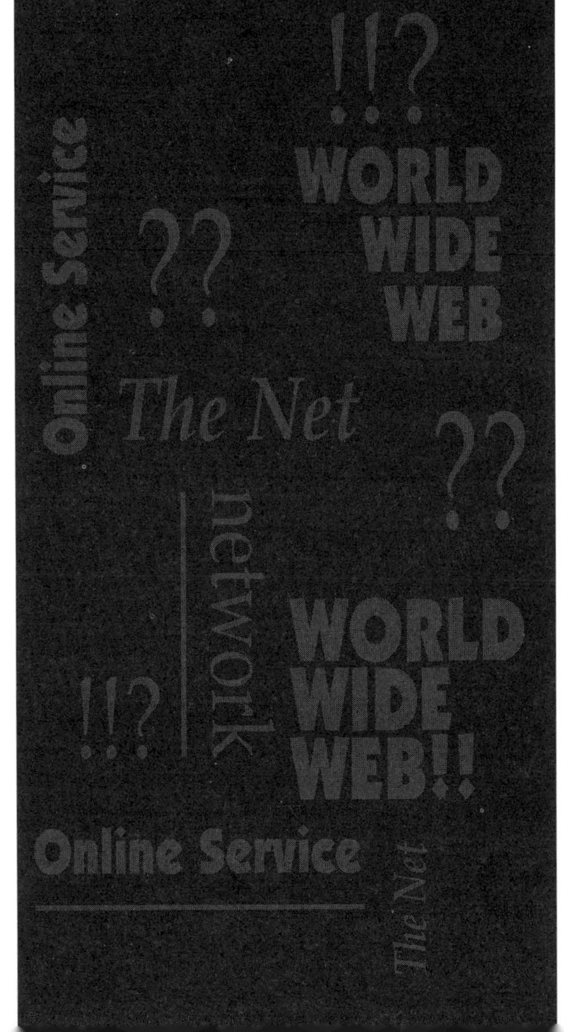

The following appendix is intended as a quick-reference guide to the most useful HTML tags (including those already covered in Chapters 23 and 24) together with their attributes. You'll find examples of these and more on the free CD-ROM accompanying this book if you'd like to see what they look like in use (and, perhaps, just copy the code instead of trying to understand it!).

This section has been set out as follows:

- For HTML elements that must have a closing tag, both the opening and closing tags are included, separated by an ellipsis which is where your own text will go.
- Where information must be placed between double-quotes, they have been included.
- As usual, any text in bold-italics will be substituted with your own settings.
- Where only fixed alternatives are available (as in the case of alignment options) they are separated by pipe symbols, such as **left** | **right** | **center**.

Comments

<!-- ... -->
Turns all the text between these elements into a comment, ignored by browsers.

Document Structure

<HTML>...</HTML>
Encloses the whole document, containing the <HEAD> and <BODY> sections.

<HEAD>...</HEAD>
The header portion of the document, containing the <TITLE> and, optionally, the <META> elements.

<BODY>...</BODY>
Encloses the body portion of the document, including all text to be displayed and tags used for formatting, links, images, etc.

Optional attributes are:

BGCOLOR=*colour*	Colour of the page background
TEXT=*colour*	Default colour of the page's text
LINK=*colour*	Colour of hypertext links
VLINK=*colour*	Colour of visited links
ALINK=*colour*	Colour of active (just-clicked) links
BACKGROUND=*"file"*	Image file to be tiled as page wallpaper

<BASE>
Specifies a URL from which all relative links in a document will be resolved, or a default frame- or window-name into which all links will be opened. One or both of these attributes must be used:

HREF=*"url"*	The base URL to resolve links
TARGET=*"frame"*	The default frame- or window-name

<META>
Provides information about the document itself, such as providing descriptions and keywords for use by search engines, or author and expiry details. Either or both of the first two attributes may be used; the CONTENT attribute must be present.

HTTP-EQUIV=*http header*	Recognised HTTP header such as **Expires**
NAME=*meta name*	Name of META information, such as **Author**
CONTENT=*value*	The value to be associated with the given name

Title & Headings

<TITLE>…</TITLE>
Encloses the title of the document. This must be included in the header.

<H1>...</H1>
Encloses text to be formatted as a heading. <H1> defines the largest possible heading, <H2> is slightly smaller, and so on down to <H6>, the smallest. Any of these can take the optional attribute:

ALIGN=center | left | right	Aligns the heading on the page. The default is **left**

Character Formatting

<FONT>...</FONT>
Specifies or alters the type and style of font to be used for the enclosed text. Takes one or more of these attributes:

FACE=*"font1, font2, ..."*	Name of font to be used, plus alternatives
SIZE=1 | 2 | 3 | 4 | 5 | 6 | 7	Size of the font to use. The default size is 3
COLOR=*colour*	Colour in which the text should be displayed

<B>...</B>
Formats the enclosed text in bold type.

<I>...</I>
Formats the enclosed text in italic type.

<U>...</U>
Underlines the enclosed text.

<S>...</S>
Strikes through (crosses out) the enclosed text.

<EM>...</EM>
Emphasises the enclosed text; most browsers will format this as italic type.

<STRONG>...</STRONG>
Strong emphasis of the enclosed text; most browsers will format this as bold type.

<TT>...</TT>
Formats the enclosed text using a typewriter-style font.

<BIG>...</BIG>
Makes the enclosed text one size larger.

<SMALL>...</SMALL>
Makes the enclosed text one size smaller. Both `<BIG>` and `<SMALL>` adjust the text size in relation to your last selected `<FONT>` size setting.

^{...}
Formats the enclosed text as superscript.

_{...}
Formats the enclosed text as subscript.

<BLOCKQUOTE>...</BLOCKQUOTE>
Formats the enclosed text as a quotation, usually by indenting it on the left and right.

<PRE>...</PRE>
Displays the enclosed text exactly as typed, observing carriage-returns, styles, spaces, etc.

Paragraphs & Layout

<P>
Indicates the start of a new paragraph, inserting a blank line before the text that follows this tag, and aligning it with the left margin by default.

<P ALIGN=center | left | right>...</P>
Works in the same way as <P> by itself, but aligns the enclosed text centrally or with the left or right margins.

**
**
Inserts a line break at the point where the tag appears. You can use this repeatedly to insert blank lines as well. Optionally takes the following attribute:

CLEAR=left | right | all	The following text will be placed at the next point where there is a clear position at the left or right margin, or a clear position at both margins

<NOBR>...</NOBR>
Prevents the enclosed text from breaking at the right margin.

<WBR>
Marks a point where the text may be wrapped to the next line if a break is necessary in a line. Usually used within <NOBR> tags to prevent a line of text stretching off the edge of the browser window.

<HR>
Places a horizontal rule across the width of the page with a blank line above and below it. Optional attributes are:

WIDTH=*number(%)*	Width of the line in pixels or as a percentage of page width
SIZE=*number*	Height of the line in pixels. The default is 2
COLOR=*colour*	Colour of the line (automatically made solid)
NOSHADE	Removes 3D shading to make a solid line
ALIGN=center | left | right	Sets alignment of the line. The default is **center**

<CENTER>...</CENTER>
Places all the enclosed text, images and other content centrally on the page.

Lists

<LI>
Creates a list entry when used with <UL>, <OL> or <DIR>. Automatically places the entry on a new line. <LI> can also be used by itself to place a bullet at the start of a new line.

<UL>...</UL>
Creates an unordered (or bulleted) list, using entries placed after <LI> tags.

<OL>...</OL>
Creates an ordered (numbered) list, using entries placed after <LI> tags, and taking the following optional attributes:

START=*number*	The number from which the list should count
TYPE=1 | A | a | I | i	The numbering system to use: numerical | capital letters | small letters | roman numerals | small roman numerals. The default is numerical.

<DIR>...</DIR>
Creates a directory list of entries by indenting the <LI> entries that follow. Can also be used as a 'cheat' to indent text from the left margin of the page; each use will indent the text a little more.

<DL>...</DL>
Creates a definition list, using <DT> and <DD> to create the list entries within the <DL> tags.

<DT>
Creates an entry in a definition list. The entry is automatically placed on a new line and aligned with the left margin.

<DD>
Creates a definition for a <DT> entry. The text following the <DD> tag is automatically placed on a new line and indented.

Images & Multimedia

<IMG>
Inserts an image at that point on the web page. The SRC= attribute is required, the others are optional.

SRC="*filename*"	The URL, or name and location, of the image file
ALIGN=top | middle | bottom | left | right	Alignment of the image. The default is **left**
WIDTH=*number*	The width of the image
HEIGHT=*number*	The height of the image
VSPACE=*number*	The space in pixels to leave clear above and below
HSPACE=*number*	The space in pixels to leave clear to either side
ALT="*text*"	Alternative text to be displayed
BORDER=*number*	0 means no border. Higher numbers give thicker borders.
USEMAP=*map name*	Indicates that this is an image map, and gives the name of the map to be used.

<MAP>
Used with client-side image maps to specify the name of the map, and to plot the coordinates of areas of the image and assign URLs to them. Takes the attribute:

NAME=*map name*	Specifies the name of the map which should correspond with the USEMAP= attribute of one of your images.

<SCRIPT>...</SCRIPT>
Inserts a script into an HTML document, usually in the header. Needs the attribute:

LANGUAGE=JavaScript | VBScript	The name of the scripting language used

<MARQUEE>...</MARQUEE>
Places a scrolling marquee on the web page using the text enclosed within these tags. The text will be the colour last specified (either in the <BODY> tag or by enclosing the entire marquee code within <FONT> tags.) The available attributes are:

WIDTH=*number(%)*	Width of the marquee in pixels or as a percentage of page width
HEIGHT=*number*	The height of the marquee
VSPACE=*number*	The space in pixels to leave clear above and below
HSPACE=*number*	The space in pixels to leave clear to either side
ALIGN=top | middle | bottom	Aligns the marquee with any text on the same line
BGCOLOR=*colour*	The colour of the marquee's background
DIRECTION=left | right	The direction in which the text should move. The default is **left**
BEHAVIOR=scroll | slide | alternate	Determines how the text should move. The default is **scroll**
LOOP=*number* | infinite	The number of times the marquee should repeat, or an endless repetition
SCROLLAMOUNT=*number*	How many pixels the text should scroll at a time
SCROLLDELAY=*number*	Length of pause between each movement of the text

<BGSOUND>
Automatically plays a WAV or MIDI file when the page loads.

SRC="*filename*"	The URL, or name and location, of the sound file
LOOP=*number* | infinite	The number of times to repeat, or endless repetition

<APPLET>…</APPLET>
Inserts a Java applet on the web page, taking these attributes:

CODE=*"class file"*	The name of the Java class to be run
CODEBASE=*location*	The location of the class file if not in the same directory as the HTML document
WIDTH=*number*	The required width of the applet
HEIGHT=*number*	The required height of the applet
VSPACE=*number*	The space in pixels to leave clear above and below
HSPACE=*number*	The space in pixels to leave clear to either side
ALIGN=center | left | right | middle | texttop | textbottom | textmiddle | baseline	The alignment of the applet
ALT=*"text"*	Alternative text to be displayed if the browser doesn't support Java applets
NAME=*name*	Assigns a name to the applet

<PARAM>
A tag used with Java applets to specify optional settings that may have been built into the applet by its author. Takes the following two attributes:

NAME=*name*	The specified parameter name
VALUE=*"value"*	The chosen value for that parameter

Links

<A>…</A>
Creates a link to the web document or file named in the HREF= attribute, or creates an anchor which can be linked to by using the NAME= attribute.

HREF=*"url | name"*	Formats the enclosed text as a link to the URL or named anchor. The value may also be **"mailto:*emailaddress*"**.
TARGET=*"frame"*	Specifies the name of a frame or window in which the linked document should be opened.
NAME=*"name"*	Creates an anchor at the point where the enclosed text occurs that can be linked to by adding ***#name*** to the end of the HREF= value.

Tables

<TABLE>...</TABLE>
Formats the enclosed text (including the rest of the tags in this category) as a table. The following optional attributes can be added:

Attribute	Description
ALIGN=center | left | right	Sets the alignment of the table. The default is **left**
BORDER=*number*	Thickness of border. The default is no border
WIDTH=*number(%)*	Width of the table in pixels or as a percentage of page width
CELLPADDING=*number*	Space between the sides of a cell and its contents, in pixels
CELLSPACING=*number*	Space between the table's border and its cells, in pixels
BGCOLOR=*colour*	Background colour of the table (recognised only by Internet Explorer)
BACKGROUND=*"file"*	Image file to be used as a table's background (Explorer only)
BORDERCOLOR=*colour*	The colour of the table border (Explorer only)

<TR>...</TR>
Short for 'table row'. The enclosed text and `<TD>` tags will form a new row of cells in a table. (The closing `</TR>` tag can be left out with no harmful effects.) This tag can take the `ALIGN`, `BGCOLOR`, `BACKGROUND` and `BORDERCOLOR` attributes exactly as used by the `<TABLE>` tag, plus the following:

Attribute	Description
VALIGN=top | middle | bottom | baseline	Sets the vertical alignment of all text in this row
CHAR=*"character"*	Sets a particular character that will be aligned according to the `ALIGN=` setting
CHAROFF=*"number%"*	Sets a percentage offset for the first alignment character

<TD>...</TD>
Short for 'table data'. This tag creates a new cell in the current row and encloses the text (or other content) to be placed in that cell, although the

closing tag may be left out. <TD> can take the ALIGN, BGCOLOR, BACKGROUND, BORDERCOLOR, VALIGN, CHAR and CHAROFF attributes mentioned above, as well as the following:

COLSPAN=*number*	The number of columns that this cell will span
ROWSPAN=*number*	The number of rows that this cell will span
NOWRAP	Prevents the text from wrapping in a cell

<CAPTION>…</CAPTION>
Can be used within the <TABLE> element to create a caption above the table using the enclosed text. The available attribute is:

ALIGN=top | bottom | left | right	Sets the alignment of the caption

HTML COLOUR NAMES

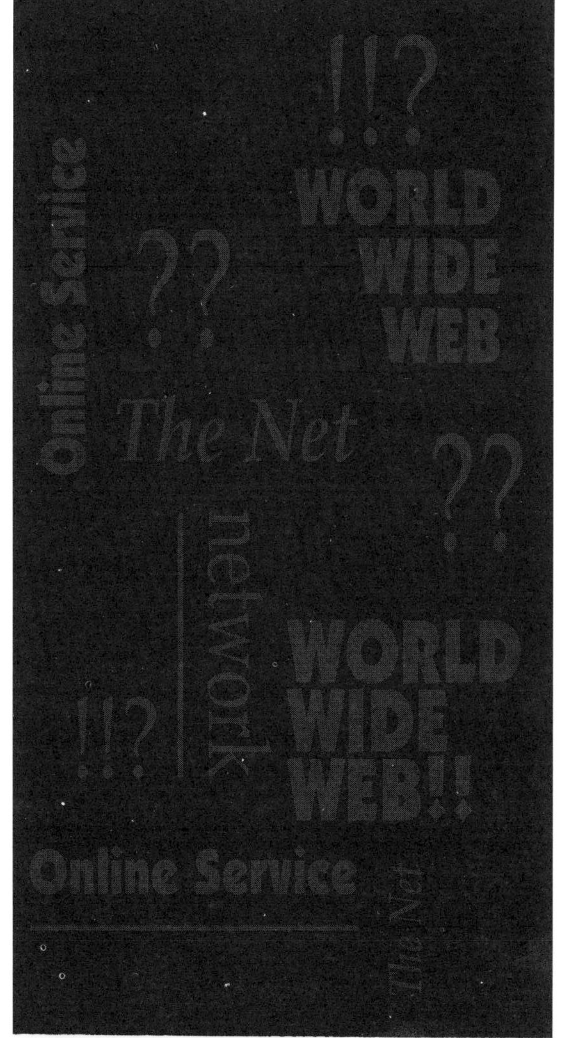

Colours in HTML come in two flavours: named colours and hex numbers representing colours. The hex system is explained in greater detail on the CD-ROM with this book, but in brief, any colour you want to use is made up of varying proportions of red, green and blue. Each of these three colours can have a value of anything from 0 to 255, which gives a total of 16.7 million available shades.

However, not all browsers can display all these colours. To ensure that your pages look the way they're supposed to on almost any system, it's preferable to stick with the 140 colours listed below. The corresponding hex numbers are also given here, and you can enter either into your HTML documents – the tag `<FONT COLOR=FF0000>` means just the same as `<FONT COLOR=RED>`. For want of a better system, the colours are simply presented in alphabetical order by name; you'll also find a colour-chart with swatches on the free CD-ROM accompanying this book.

Name	Hex
AliceBlue	F0F8FF
AntiqueWhite	FAEBD7
Aqua	00FFFF
Aquamarine	7FFFD4
Azure	F0FFFF
Beige	F5F5DC
Bisque	FFE4C4
Black	000000
BlanchedAlmond	FFEBCD
Blue	0000FF
BlueViolet	8A2BE2
Brown	A52A2A
Burlywood	DEB887
CadetBlue	5F9EA0
Chartreuse	7FFF00
Chocolate	D2691E
Coral	FF7F50
CornflowerBlue	6495ED
Cornsilk	FFF8DC
Crimson	DC143C
Cyan	00FFFF
DarkBlue	00008B

Name	Hex
DarkCyan	008B8B
DarkGoldenrod	B8860B
DarkGray	A9A9A9
DarkGreen	006400
DarkKhaki	BDB76B
DarkMagenta	8B008B
DarkOliveGreen	556B2F
DarkOrange	FF8C00
DarkOrchid	9932CC
DarkRed	8B0000
DarkSalmon	E9967A
DarkSeaGreen	8FBC8F
DarkSlateBlue	483D8B
DarkSlateGray	2F4F4F
DarkTurquoise	00CED1
DarkViolet	9400D3
DeepPink	FF1493
DeepSkyBlue	00BFBF
DimGray	696969
DodgerBlue	1E90FF
Firebrick	B22222
FloralWhite	FFFAF0

Name	Hex
ForestGreen	228B22
Fuchsia	FF00FF
Gainsboro	DCDCDC
GhostWhite	F8F8FF
Gold	FFD700
Goldenrod	DAA520
Gray	808080
Green	008000
GreenYellow	ADFF2F
Honeydew	F0FFF0
HotPink	FF69B4
IndianRed	CD5C5C
Indigo	4B0082
Ivory	FFFFF0
Khaki	F0E68C
Lavender	E6E6FA
LavenderBlush	FFF0F5
LawnGreen	7CFC00
LemonChiffon	FFFACD
LightBlue	ADD8E6
LightCoral	F08080
LightCyan	E0FFFF
LightGoldenrodYellow	FAFAD2
LightGray	D3D3D3
LightGreen	90EE90
LightPink	FFB6C1
LightSalmon	FFA07A
LightSeaGreen	20B2AA
LightSkyBlue	87CEFA
LightSlateGray	778899
LightSteelBlue	B0C4DE
LightYellow	FFFFE0
Lime	00FF00
LimeGreen	32CD32
Linen	FAF0E6
Magenta	FF00FF
Maroon	800000
MediumAquamarine	66CDAA

Name	Hex
MediumBlue	0000CD
MediumOrchid	BA55D3
MediumPurple	9370DB
MediumSeaGreen	3CB371
MediumSlateBlue	7B68EE
MediumSpringGreen	00FA9A
MediumTurquoise	48D1CC
MediumVioletRed	C71585
MidnightBlue	191970
MintCream	F5FFFA
MistyRose	FFE4E1
Moccasin	FFE4B5
NavajoWhite	FFDEAD
Navy	000080
OldLace	FDF5E6
Olive	808000
OliveDrab	6B8E23
Orange	FFA500
OrangeRed	FF4500
Orchid	DA70D6
PaleGoldenrod	EEE8AA
PaleGreen	98FB98
PaleTurquoise	AFEEEE
PaleVioletRed	DB7093
PapayaWhip	FFEFD5
PeachPuff	FFDAB9
Peru	CD853F
Pink	FFC0CB
Plum	DDA0DD
PowderBlue	B0E0E6
Purple	800080
Red	FF0000
RosyBrown	BC8F8F
RoyalBlue	4169E1
SaddleBrown	8B4513
Salmon	FA8072
SandyBrown	F4A460
SeaGreen	2E8B57

Name	Hex
Seashell	FFF5EE
Sienna	A0522D
Silver	C0C0C0
SkyBlue	87CEEB
SlateBlue	6A5ACD
SlateGray	708090
Snow	FFFAFA
SpringGreen	00FF7F
SteelBlue	4682B4
Tan	D2B48C

Name	Hex
Teal	008080
Thistle	D8BFD8
Tomato	FF6347
Turquoise	40E0D0
Violet	EE82EE
Wheat	F5DEB3
White	FFFFFF
WhiteSmoke	F5F5F5
Yellow	FFFF00
YellowGreen	9ACD32

DIRECTORY

!!?
WORLD
WIDE
WEB
??
Online Service
The Net
??
WORLD
WIDE
WEB
!!?
Online Service

1: UK Internet Access Providers

Use the list below to find an IAP with a local POP and the services you're looking for, then give them a ring, ask about pricing, and check some of the other details mentioned in Chapter 3. All the IAPs noted here offer the basic services of email, World Wide Web, FTP, Telnet, Gopher, IRC and newsgroup access. Extra details are included under 'Notes'.

Bear in mind that this isn't an exhaustive list, and these details change regularly – for example, more and more IAPs are starting to offer free web-space – so it doesn't hurt to ask if the details don't exactly match what you want. Most IAPs have special packages for business users and other connection options available.

Company	Telephone	Email	WWW Site	POPs
ACE	(01670) 528204	info@ace.co.uk	www.ace.co.uk	UK coverage
Notes: Free web-space				
Aladdin	(01489) 782221	info@aladdin.co.uk	www.aladdin.co.uk	15 UK towns and cities
Notes: Free web-space; POP3 email; FTP archive				
Almac	(01324) 666336	info@almac.co.uk	www.almac.co.uk	UK coverage
Notes: Free web-space; FTP archive; free demo service				
AngliaNet	(01473) 211922	tony@anglianet.co.uk	www.anglianet.co.uk	Ipswich
Notes: Web space available; POP3 email				
Aspen Internet	(01672) 511290	admin@aspen-internet.net	www.aspen-internet.net	UK coverage
Notes: PPP; POP3 email; domain registration				
Avel PiP	(01872) 262236	info@avel.net	www.avel.com	Southwest only
Notes: PPP; free web-space				
Bournemouth Internet	(01202) 292900	sales@bournemouth-net.co.uk	www.bournemouth-net.co.uk	Bournemouth
Notes: Multiple POP3 email accounts				
Brunel Internet	(01922) 59890	sales@brunel.co.uk	www.brunel.co.uk	Aldridge
Notes: PPP; FTP archive				
BT Internet (British Telecom)	(0800) 800001	info@bt.net	www.btinternet.com	UK coverage
Notes: Free web-space; POP3 email				
Cable Internet	(0500) 541542	info@cableinet.co.uk	www.cableinet.co.uk	36 UK towns and cities
Notes: PPP; free web-space; multiple email addresses				
Cerbernet	0171-360 8010	sales@styx.cerbernet.co.uk	www.cerbernet.co.uk	London
Notes: Free web-space; FTP archive				
City NetGates	(0117) 907 4000	info@netgates.co.uk	www.netgates.co.uk	Bristol
Notes: Email forwarding; web space				
CityScape	(01223) 566950	sales@cityscape.co.uk	www.cityscape.co.uk	UK coverage
Notes: Free web-space; POP3 email; FTP archive				
Connect Ireland	00 353 1 670 6701	info@connect.ie	www.connect.ie	Dublin
Notes: Free web-space				
Cygnet Internet Services	0181-880 4650	sales@cygnet.co.uk	www.cygnet.co.uk	London
Notes: Web space; FTP archive				
Dean Software	(01878) 311044	info@deansoft.com	www.deansoft.com	North only
Notes: Web space; FTP archive				

Company	Telephone	Email	WWW Site	POPs
Demon Internet	0181-371 1234	sales@demon.net	www.demon.net	UK coverage
Notes: PPP; POP3 email; FTP archive; free demo available				
Direct Connection	0181-297 2200	sales@dircon.co.uk	www.dircon.co.uk	Almost full UK coverage
Notes: PPP; POP3 email; free demo available				
Direct Net @ccess	(01232) 330311	info@d-n-a.net	www.d-n-a.net	UK coverage
Notes: 3 email addresses; free web-space				
Dorset Internet	(01202) 659991	sales@lds.co.uk	www.lds.co.uk	almost full UK coverage
Notes: PPP; FTP archive				
Dungeon Network Systems	(01638) 711550	info@dungeon.com	www.dungeon.com	Ipswich, Mildenhall
Notes: Web space available				
Easynet	0171-209 0990	admin@easynet.co.uk	www.easynet.co.uk	UK coverage
Notes: Free web-space				
Eclipse Networking	(01392) 424440	eclipse@eclipse.co.uk	www.eclipse.co.uk	Exeter
Notes: PPP; POP3 email; web and FTP space				
edNET	0131-466 7003	info@ednet.co.uk	www.ednet.co.uk	Edinburgh
Notes: PPP; free web-space; FTP archive				
Electric Mail	(01223) 501333	info@elmail.co.uk	www.elmail.co.uk	12 UK towns and cities
Notes: PPP; web space				
Enterprise	(01624) 677666	sales@enterprise.net	www.enterprise.net	UK coverage
Notes: PPP; web and FTP space				
FastNet International	(01273) 675314	sales@fastnet.co.uk	www.fastnet.co.uk	Brighton
Notes: Web space; 15-day free trial				
Frontier Internet Services	0171-242 3383	info@ftech.net	www.ftech.net	UK coverage
Notes: PPP; POP3 email; web space				
Garden CityNet	(01462 485624)	colinb@gardencitynet.co.uk	www.gardencitynet.co.uk	7 Herefordshire towns
Notes: Web space available; POP3 email				
Gifford Internet	(0117) 939 7722	admin@gifford.co.uk	www.gifford.co.uk	Bristol
Notes: PPP; web space available				
Global Internet	0181-957 1005	info@globalnet.co.uk	www.globalnet.co.uk	UK coverage
Notes: PPP; web space available				
GMTnet	(01509) 269999	sales@gmtnet.co.uk	www.gmtnet.co.uk	Derby, Leicester, London, Loughborough, Maidenhead, Nottingham, Slough
Notes: PPP; web space				
GreenNet	(01509) 269999	support@gn.apc.org	www.gn.apc.org	London
Notes: PPP; POP3 email; free demo available				
Griffin Internet	(01332) 606160	info@griffin.co.uk	www.griffin.co.uk	Derby
Notes: PPP; web space; 7-day trial				
Hiway	(01635) 550660	info@inform.hiway.co.uk	www.hiway.co.uk	UK coverage
Notes: POP3 email; free web-space; FTP archive and space				
IBM Global Network	(0800) 973000	internet_europe @vnet.ibm.com	regsvr01.fl.us.ibm.net /cgi-bin/fees?ISO=gb	Bristol, Edinburgh, Glasgow, Leeds, London, Manchester, Nottingham, Portsmouth, Warwick
Notes: Various subscription options available				
IntoNet	0181-942 9214	info@intonet.co.uk	www.intonet.co.uk	UK coverage
Notes: PPP; web space				
KENTnet Internet Services	(01580) 890089	sales@kentnet.co.uk	www.kentnet.co.uk	Ashford, Hastings, Heathfield, Maidstone, Rye, Staplehurst, Tunbridge Wells
Notes: Free web-space; FTP archive; domain registration; conferencing				
London Web Communications	0181-349 4500	contact@londonweb.net	www.londonweb.net	London
Notes: PPP; FTP and web space				

Company	Telephone	Email	WWW Site	POPs
MANNET	(01624) 623841	postmaster@mcb.net	www.mcb.net/mannet	Isle Of Man
Notes: PPP; FTP and web space available				
MBC Internet Services	(01902) 651111	info@mbcis.co.uk	www.mbcis.co.uk	Birmingham, Wolverhampton
Notes: PPP; web space available				
Meganet Internet Services	(01483) 31119	info@meganet.co.uk	www.meganet.co.uk	Guildford
Notes: PPP; web space; FTP archive				
Mercia Internet	(01827) 69166	sales@mercia.net	www.mercia.net	UK coverage
Notes: FTP and web space				
NetDirect Internet	0171-732 3000	info@ndirect.co.uk	www.ndirect.co.uk	London
Notes: PPP; FTP and web space; domain registration				
Netforce Group	(01245) 257788	sales@netforce.net	www.netforce.net	UK coverage
Notes: PPP; Web and FTP space available; FTP archive				
.netKonect	(01420) 542777	info@netkonect.net	www.netkonect.net	UK coverage
Notes: Web space available				
Nildram	(0800) 072 0400	info@nildram.co.uk	www.nildram.co.uk	UK coverage
Notes: PPP; FTP and web-space				
North West Net	0161-950 7777	info@nwnet.co.uk	www.nwnet.co.uk	Liverpool, Manchester
Notes: Free web-space				
Onyx Internet	(0345) 715715	sales@onyxnet.co.uk	www.onyxnet.co.uk	UK coverage
Notes: Web space available				
Oxford CommUnity Internet	(01865) 856000	info@community.co.uk	www.community.co.uk	UK coverage
Notes: PPP; POP3 email; web space				
Paradise Internet Network Services	(01256) 414863	sales@pins.co.uk	www.pins.co.uk	Basingstoke
Notes: PPP; web space available				
Paston Chase	(01603) 502061	info@paston.co.uk	www.paston.co.uk	Norwich
Notes: PPP; web space				
Pavilion Internet	(01273) 607072	info@pavilion.co.uk	www.pavilion.co.uk	Brighton
Notes: Web space				
Power Internet	(01908) 503126	info@powernet.co.uk	www.powernet.co.uk	Birmingham, Milton Keynes
Notes: PPP; free-trial offers; free web-space				
Primex Information Services	(07000) 774639	info@alpha.primex.co.uk	www.primex.co.uk	UK coverage
Notes: PPP; web space; various subscriptions available				
Rednet	(01494) 513333	info@rednet.co.uk	www.rednet.co.uk	UK coverage
Notes: PPP; free web-space; POP3 email				
Sonnet Internet	0171-891 2000	enquire@sonnet.co.uk	www.sonnet.co.uk	UK coverage
Notes: PPP; web space				
Spud's Xanadu	(01268) 515441	sweh@spuddy.mew.co.uk	www.spuddy.org	Canvey Island
Notes: Free service; PPP; POP3 email				
Talk-101	(01925) 245145	sales@talk-101.com	www.talk-101.com	UK coverage
Notes: PPP; FTP and web space				
Taynet	(01382) 561296	admin@taynet.co.uk	www.taynet.co.uk	Dundee
Notes: PPP; POP3 email; web space				
Technocom	(01753) 730400	sales@technocom.co.uk	www.technocom.co.uk	London. Maidenhead, Slough
Notes: PPP; free web-space; free trial available				
The Internet In Nottingham		(0115) 956 2222	info@innotts.co.uk	www.innotts.co.uk Nottingham
Notes: Web space				
The Web Factory	(0116) 223 0070	sales@webleicester.co.uk	www.webleicester.co.uk	Leicester
Notes: Web space available				

Company	Telephone	Email	WWW Site	POPs
Total Connectivity Providers	(01703) 393392	sales@tcp.co.uk	www.tcp.co.uk	UK coverage
Notes: PPP; POP3 email; web space; free trial				
U-NET	(01925) 484444	hi@u-net.com	www.u-net.com	UK coverage
Notes: PPP; POP3 email; web space				
Unipalm Pipex	(01223) 250100	sales@pipex.net	www.unipalm.pipex.com	Almost full UK coverage
Notes: PPP; free web-space				
Voss Net	(01753) 737800	staff@vossnet.co.uk	www.vossnet.co.uk	London, Slough
Notes: PPP; 7-day free trial				
Wave Rider Internet	(01564) 795888	info@waverider.co.uk	www.waverider.co.uk	Birmingham
Notes: PPP; free web-space; FTP archive				
Web 13	0131-229 8883	queries@presence.co.uk	www.presence.co.uk	Edinburgh
Notes: Web space available				
WildNET	(01604) 36560	stuartj@wildnet.co.uk	www.wildnet.co.uk	Bristol, Hereford, Milton Keynes, Northampton
Notes: PPP; web and FTP space				
WSS Internet	(01793) 420764	info@WSkiSoft.co.uk	www.WSkiSoft.co.uk/ISPUser	Swindon
Notes: Free trial; PPP; web space				
Zetnet Services	(01595) 696667	info@zetnet.co.uk	www.zetnet.co.uk	UK coverage
Notes: Free web-space; free trial				

2: UK Online Services

The following is a list of the online services available. If you don't have the free software required to subscribe, give them a call and ask for it. Most services offer several different subscription schemes that include varying amounts of 'free' online time per month, or unlimited access for a higher monthly fee. Don't forget to find out what your options are or your online time could end up costing you far more than it needs to!

Company	Telephone	Email	WWW Site	POPs
America Online (AOL)	(0800) 279 1234	queryuk@aol.com	www.aol.com	UK coverage
CIX	0181-296 9666	sales@compulink.co.uk	www.compulink.co.uk	UK coverage
ClaraNET	0171-647 1000	sales@clara.net	www.clara.net	UK coverage
CompuServe Information Service	(0800) 289378	70006.101@compuserve.com	www.compuserve.com	UK coverage
Delphi Internet	0171-757 7080	ukservice@delphi.com	www.delphi.co.uk	London. (UK coverage via GNS Network.)
Microsoft Network (MSN)	(0345) 002000		www.msn.com	UK coverage
Virgin Net	(0500) 558800		www.virgin.net	UK coverage

3: UK Cyber Cafés

Name	Address	Telephone	Email	WWW Site
3W Café	4 Market Place, Bracknell, Berkshire	(01344) 862445	dave@3w.co.uk	http://www.3w.co.uk
Beiderbeckes Internet Café/Restaurant	30-32 Bondgate, Darlington, Co. Durham	(01325) 282675.	wired@beiderbeckes.co.uk	http://www.users.dircon.co.uk/~beider3

Name	Address	Telephone	Email	WWW Site
Cable CyberBar	Molineux Stadium, Waterloo Road, Wolverhampton	(01902) 651111	info@mbcis.co.uk	http://www.mbcis.co.uk/Bar
CaféNet	2-3 Phoenix Court, Guildford, Surrey	(01483) 451945	internet@cafénet.co.uk	http://www.cafénet.co.uk
Chaucer Cyberspace	Chaucer Tech. School, Spring Lane, Canterbury, Kent	(01227) 763636	isocts@mail.chaucer.ac.uk	http://www.chaucer.ac.uk /~cyberspace/cyberspc.htm
Cyberia Café	39 Whitfield Street, London		cyberia@easynet.co.uk	http://www.cyberiacafé.net/cyberia
Cyberia Café	48 High Street, Kingston Upon Thames, Surrey	0181-255 4440		http://www.indus.co.uk /cyberia/index.htm
Cyberia Café	73 New Broadway, Ealing	0181-840 3131	ealing@cyberiacafé.net	http://cyberiaeal9.cyberiacafé.net /CYBERIA-ealing
Café Internet	22-24 Buckingham Palace Road, Victoria, London	0171-233 5786	café@caféinternet.co.uk	http://www.caféinternet.co.uk
Café Internet	28 North John Street, Liverpool	0151-255-1112	info@caféliv.u-net.com	http://www.caféliv.com
CyberZone	1 Dingwall Road, Croydon, Surrey	0181-681 6500	zone1@cyberzone.co.uk	http://www.cyberzone.co.uk
Electric Frog	42-44 Cockburn Street, Edinburgh	0131-226 1505	admin@electricfrog.co.uk	http://www.electricfrog.co.uk
Get Surfed!	4-6 Peterborough Road, Harrow, Middlesex	0181-426 4446	info@getsurfed.co.uk	http://www.getsurfed.co.uk
Hard Drive Café	16 King Street, Luton, Bedfordshire	(01582) 485621	jw@hardcafé.co.uk	http://www.hardcafé.co.uk
Internet@Brubakers	Blossom Street, York		tony@brubakers.theplanet.co.uk	http://www.brubakers.theplanet.co.uk /brubakers
NetPlay Café	8 Fletchers Walk, Paradise Circus, Birmingham	0121-248 2228	info@netplaycafé.co.uk	http://www.netplaycafé.co.uk
Netscafé	9 Bennington Street, Cheltenham, Gloucestershire	(01242) 232121	info@netscafé.co.uk	http://www.netscafé.co.uk
Planet 13	25 High Cross Street, St. Austell, Cornwall			http://www.planet13.co.uk
Punters Cyber Café	111 Arundel Street, Sheffield	(0114) 276 2668		http://www.punters.co.uk
Reality Bites	95 Kings Road, Reading, Berkshire	(0118) 9591000	smiley@reality.technocafés.co.uk	http://www.reality.technocafés.co.uk
Reality-X	54 Broughton Street, Edinburgh	0131-478-7099		http://www.reality-x.co.uk
Revelations	Shaftesbury Square, Belfast			http://www.revelations.co.uk
Spiderz Web	Carlisle Business Centre, Carlisle Road, Bradford	(01274) 223 300	webmaster@spiderzweb.co.uk	http://www.spiderzweb.co.uk
Southport Internet Café	10 Princes Street, off Eastbank Street, Southport	(01704) 534109	info@mail.café.uk.com	http://www.café.uk.com
Surf.net Café	13 Deptford Church Street, London	0181-488 1200		http://www.dircon.co.uk/surfnet
The Edge	St George's Centre, St Ann's Road, Harrow, Middlesex	0181-4242427		http://the-edge.ha1.com
The Holodeck Cybercafé	42 Railway Road, Coleraine, County Londonderry		info@holodeck.org	http://www.holodeck.org

Name	Address	Telephone	Email	WWW Site
The Six Bells	32 Mill Road, Cambridge	(01223) 576306	sixbells@cityscape.co.uk	http://www.gold.net/sixbells
Window on the World Cyber Bar	Kirklees Media Centre, 7 Northumberland Street, Huddersfield, West Yorkshire		WoW_Café@architechs.com	http://www.architechs.com/mediacentre/wow_café

4: UK Software Companies

Company	Telephone
Adobe Systems	0181-606 4000
Aldus	0131-451 6888
Andromeda Interactive	(01235) 529595
Attica Cybernetics	(01865) 200892
Autodesk	(01483) 303322
Avalon	(01624) 627227
Borland	(01734) 320022
Broderbund	(01753) 620909
Brooklyn North Software Works	(0500) 284177
Central Point International	(01628) 788580
Claris	0181-756 0101
Corel	(0800) 581028
Delrina	0181-207 7033
Digital Workshop	(01295) 258335
Dorling Kindersley	0171-753 3488
Electronic Arts	(01753) 549442
Gold Disk	(01753) 832383
Gremlin Games	(0114) 275 3423
GSP	(01480) 496789
Guildsoft	(01752) 895100
Health Perfect	0181-200 8897
IBM Software Enquiries	(01329) 242728
Interplay	(01235) 821666

Company	Telephone
Intuit	0181-990 5500
Lotus Development	(01784) 455455
Macromedia	0181-358 5857
Micrografx	(0800) 626009
MicroProse	(01454) 329510
Microsoft	(01734) 270001
Mirage	(01260) 299909
MoneyBox Software	(01392) 429424
Ocean	0161-839 0999
Pegasus Software	(01536) 495000
Psygnosis	0151-282 3000
Quark Systems	(01483) 454397
Quarterdeck UK	(01245) 494940
Sage	0191-255 3000
S&S International	(01296) 318700
Serif	(0800) 924925
Softkey	0181-789 2000
SoftQuad	0181-236 1001
Starfish Software	0181-875 4455
Symantec	(01628) 592222
TopLevel Computing	(01453) 753944
Wang UK	0181-568 9200

5: UK Hardware Companies

Company	Telephone	Product
AMD	(01256) 603121	Processors
Apricot Computers	0121-717 7171	PCs
Brother UK	0161-330 6531	Printers
Compaq	0181-332 3888	PCs, Notebook PCs
Conner	(01294) 315333	Hard-drives
Creative Labs	(01734) 344322	Soundcards, multimedia peripherals
Cyrix	(0800) 137305	Processors
Diamond Multimedia	(01753) 501400	Display adapters, multimedia peripherals
Epson UK	(01442) 227478	Printers
Fujitsu	0181-573 4444	Hard-drives, printers, scanners
Hayes	(01252) 775533	Modems

Company	Telephone	Product
Hercules	(01635) 861122	Display adapters
Hewlett-Packard	(01344) 369369	Printers
Hitachi	0181-849 2087	CD-ROM drives, monitors
IBM	(0345) 500900	PCs, Notebook PCs
Iiyama	(01438) 745482	Monitors
Intel	(01793) 431144	Processors
Iomega	(0800) 898563	Archive and backup drives
IPC Corp UK	(01282) 618866	PCs, Notebook PCs, peripherals
JVC	0181-896 6000	CD-ROM drives
Kodak	(01734) 311500	Printers
Lexmark International	(01628) 488200	Printers
Logitech	(01344) 891313	Mice, trackballs, scanners
Matrox	(01793) 614002	Display adapters
Microsoft	(01734) 271000	Mice, trackballs, keyboards
Microvitec	(01274) 390011	Monitors
Mitsumi	(01276) 29029	CD-ROM drives
NEC Computer Products	0181-993 8111	PCs, CD-ROM drives
Nikon	0181-541 4440	Scanners
Olivetti	(0800) 447799	PCs, Notebook PCs, printers
Orchid Europe	(01256) 844899	Display adapters
Packard Bell	(0800) 314314	PCs
Panasonic	(01344) 853508	Monitors, printers, CD-ROM drives
Pioneer	(01753) 789731	CD-ROM drives
Plasmon Data	(01763) 262963	Recordable CD drives
Primax	(01235) 536374	Scanners
Psion	0171-258 7376	Palmtop computers
Roland UK	(01792) 702701	Soundcards, MIDI hardware
Seagate	(01628) 474532	Hard-drives
Sony UK	0181-784 1144	CD-ROM drives, monitors
Star Micronics	(01494) 471111	Printers
Toshiba	(01932) 785666	CD-ROM drives, printers, Notebook PCs
Trust Peripherals	(01376) 500770	Scanners, modems, multimedia peripherals
US Robotics	(01734) 228200	Modems
VideoLogic	(01923) 271300	Display adapters
Visioneer	0181-358 5850	Scanners
Western Digital UK	(01372) 360055	Hard-drives

6: UK Retailers

Company	Telephone	Product
Byte Direct	0121-766 2565	PCs/peripherals
Choice Peripherals	(01909) 530242	Peripherals/components/software
Currys	(01442) 888000	PCs/peripherals
Dabs Direct	(0800) 558866	PCs/peripherals/software/components/consumables
Dan Technology	0181-830 1100	PCs
Dart Computers	(01794) 511505	PCs
Dell	(0500) 500111	PCs
Dixons	(01442) 888000	PCs/peripherals/software/consumables

Company	Telephone	Product
Elonex	0181-452 6666	PCs, Notebook PCs
Fox Computers	(01621) 744500	PCs/peripherals/components
Gateway 2000	(0800) 342000	PCs, Notebook PCs
Memory Bank	0181-956 7000	Memory/peripherals/software/components
Mesh Computers	0181-452 1111	PCs
MrPC	(01282) 777888	PCs/peripherals/software
Multimedia Direct	(01635) 873000	Multimedia hardware
Novatech	(0800) 777500	PCs/peripherals/software/consumables
PC World	(0990) 464464	PCs/peripherals/software/consumables
Pico Direct	(01483) 202022	Notebook PCs/Notebook peripherals
Plug & Play Technology	0181-341 3336	PC Cards/Notebook peripherals
Roldec	(01902) 456464	Peripherals/components
Silica Systems	0181-309 1111	PCs/peripherals/software
Simply Computers	0181-498 2130	PCs/peripherals/components
SMC Computers	(01753) 550333	PCs/peripherals/components
Software Warehouse	(01675) 466467	Software/peripherals/components/consumables
Stak Trading	(01788) 577497	PCs/peripherals/components
Taurus Component Shop	(01978) 312372	Components/peripherals
Tech Direct	0181-286 2222	Notebook PCs/printers/peripherals/consumables
Technomatic	0181-205 9558	PCs/peripherals/software/components
The Link	0541 5455400	Mobile phones/faxes/pagers/electronic organisers
Time Computer Systems	(01282) 777111	PCs
Tiny Computers	(01293) 821333	PCs
Virgin	0171-631 1234	Software

7: UK General Services

Company	Telephone
Data transfer, conversion, duplication	
AL Downloading Services	0181-994 5471
Mapej	(01691) 778659
Data recovery (disk failure, corruption, viruses)	
Authentic Data Recovery	(0800) 581263
Ontrack Data Recovery	(0800) 243996
Vogon International	(01734) 890042
PC rental	
MC Rentals	(01952) 604411
Micro-Rent	0171-700 4848
Skylake Rentals	(0800) 373118
PC security/anti-theft	
Datamark Security	(01494) 434757
Secure PC	0171-610 3646
PC memory	
AW Computer Memory Bargains	(01382) 643739

Company	Telephone
Click	(0800) 666500
Mem Com	0161-427 2222
Mr Memory	(01483) 799410
Offtek	0121-722 3993
Rightnight	0181-668 4199
Printer consumables	
Cartridge Express	(01765) 690790
Inkwell Direct	(01344) 843444
Jetica	(0800) 614153
Laser Printer Technologies	(01482) 656630
Mannink	(01462) 455651
Owl Associates	(01543) 250377
Squire International	0181-886 3078
Themis	(01883) 3330333
Vectorjet	(01763) 273115

Company	Telephone
Floppy-disks	
Owl Associates	(01543) 250377
Product Trade & Services	(0800) 136502
Squire International	0181-886 3078
Shareware	
AWH Computer Services	(01563) 850645
Demon Shareware	(01325) 301849
Ferrari Software	(01843) 865083
Hornesoft PD	(01142) 967825
MicroWorld	(01425) 610699
Telescan	(01253) 829292

Company	Telephone
Bulletin Board Services (Premium rate charges apply)	
BBS Elite	(0891) 518299
Café Net	(0891) 615010
Komputer Knowledge	(0891) 515066
Mainline BBS	(0891) 615795
MegaDownLoad	(0891) 516126
Microland Bulletin Board	(0891) 990505
Strangeways BBS	(0891) 408040

Company	Telephone	Product
Specialist suppliers		
BBD Dust Covers	(01257 425839)	Computer dust-covers
C&T	0171-637 1767	Storage hardware
Capital Litho	(01386) 40321	Personalised mouse-mats
Linefeed	0171-474 1765	CD writers and media
MJ Communications	(07000) 663367	Modems
Monitor Man	(01453) 885599	Monitors
Semaphore Systems	0171-625 7744	Components
The Keyboard Company	(07000) 102105	Keyboards
The Monitor Shop	(01159) 110366	Monitors

INDEX

Acknowledgements

Although only one name finds its way onto the front cover, it takes the efforts of a huge team of people to turn a few scribbles into a finished book. My warmest thanks go to the following people who steered this project, kept it on course, and made it so much fun to be a passenger:

Alison Stanford, the production editor: my scribbles go in, a book comes out. How does this happen?

Colin Hawes and Sophy Friend at Amber Books for lending us their superb design and editorial skills.

Maria Catt, Maggie Macleod, and the whole marketing team, without whom the rest of us would be a waste of space!

Caroline Ellerby, the copyeditor, for translating from Gibberish to English, and correcting all my speeling miskates.

And extra special thanks to two incredible people:
Jason Dunne, commissioning editor extraordinaire, for his unerring guidance, belief, and sense of what works… and for still taking my calls after four books together! Laura Miller, tireless editorial assistant, for her supreme patience and persistence (and for staying so cheerful while being patient and persistent!).

BECOMING A PRENTICE HALL AUTHOR

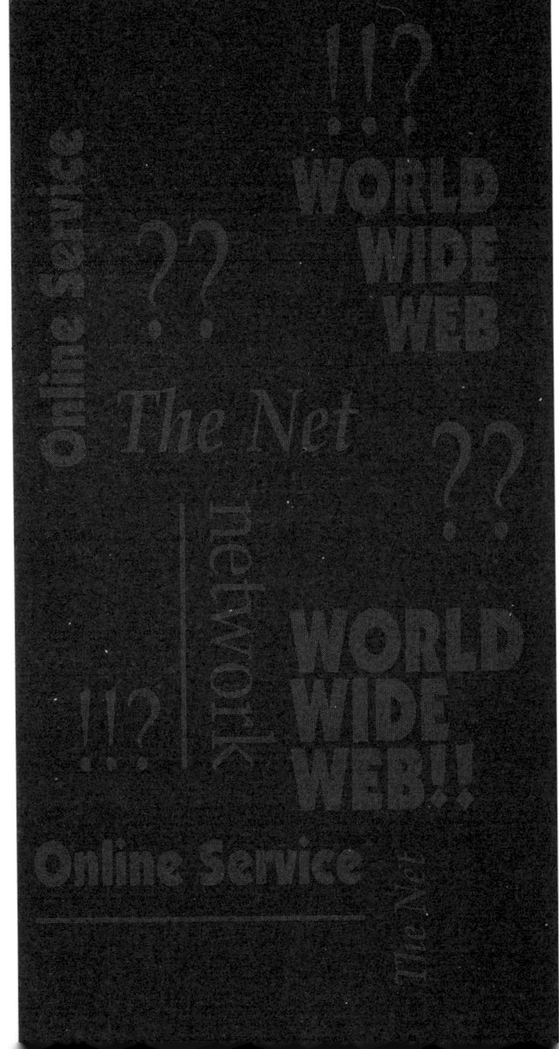

Getting Published with Prentice Hall

1. Can I Do It?

It is easy to think of the publishing process as a series of hurdles designed to weed out would-be authors. That may be true of some publishing houses, but not Prentice Hall.

- We do all we can to encourage new talent.
- We welcome unsolicited manuscripts.
- We carefully examine every proposal we receive, and we always write back to let the authors know what we think of it.

Although many of our authors have professional or educational experience, we look first for a passion for your chosen subject area. Some of our most successful books are written by first time authors. If you have built up expertise in any business, finance or computing topic, please get in touch. You'll be surprised how easy it is to get through to a commissioning editor.

2. Is Prentice Hall a Successful Company?

Prentice Hall is a highly respected brand in technical, financial and scientific publishing, a status reflected in our relationships with the book trade and various professional bodies. We're part of Simon & Schuster, a $2 billion dollar global publishing company. Simon and Schuster is host to Macmillan General Reference, The Free Press, Frommers, Macmillan Computer Publishing (home of renowned computer imprints such as Sams, Que, Waite Group Press, Ziff-Davis Publishing, Hayden and New Riders Press). Simon & Schuster is itself owned by Viacom Inc, one of the world's largest entertainment and publishing companies. Viacom owns film and tv studios (Paramount Pictures), world-wide cable networks (MTV, Nickelodeon) and retail outlets (Blockbuster Video).

3. What Sort of Books Does Prentice Hall Publish?

We are happy to consider book proposals on absolutely any topic, although we have a special interest in business, computing and finance. Our progressive editorial policy encourages new authors and gives us the flexibility necessary in a rapidly changing technological environment.

4. What are the Rewards of Writing a Book?

Prentice Hall royalty rates are among the most competitive in the industry, and many of our authors earn considerable sums through royalties.

Payments are calculated along industry-standard guidelines, i.e. the author receives a percentage of the publisher's net sales revenue. The amount you receive depends on the selling price of the book, so talk to your editor about your likely income. We always offer preferential royalty rates for senior figures within any industry, or for books on hot topics written by experts. For the right book at the right time, the financial reward to the author can be extremely generous.

If you are an academic or a member of a profession, your livelihood may depend upon your intellectual reputation. Successful Prentice Hall authors enjoy a constant stream of business and vocational opportunities as a direct result of getting published. A book works like a business card, advertising the author's talent across a vast network of potential contacts.

5. How Do I Know my Ideas are Good Enough to Publish?

In assessing the market-readiness of book proposals or finished manuscripts, Prentice Hall editors draw upon a huge database of technical advisors. All of our reviewers are senior figures within their field, and their role is to offer free advice to potential authors, highlighting both the strengths and weaknesses of proposals and manuscripts. The aim of the review process is to add value to your ideas, rather than just approving or rejecting them.

Many of our authors have not written a book before, so we are there to help them with advice on grammar and style.

6. How Much Control Would I Have Over My Book?

We understand that a book is a highly personal statement from the author, so we invite your participation at all stages of the publishing process, from the cover design through to the final marketing plans. A Prentice Hall book is a co-operative venture between author and publisher.

7. Will I Get any Help with the Technical Aspects of Book Production?

Our highly professional staff will ensure that the book you envisaged is the book that makes it to the shelves. Once you hand over your manuscript to us, we will take care of all the technical details of printing and binding. Beyond the advice and guidance from your own editor, our 64-page author guide is there to help you shape your manuscript into a first-class book. Our large and efficient production department is among the quickest in the industry.

We are experts at turning raw manuscripts into polished books, irrespective of the technical complexity of your work. Technical queries can be answered by your production contact, assigned, where relevant, to you at contract stage. Our production staff fully understand the individual requirements of every project, and will work with you to produce a manuscript format that best complements your skills - hard copy manuscripts, electronic files or camera-ready copy, where we pay the author to set the text out on the page.

8. How Quickly Can You Turn My Manuscript into a Book?

The production department at Prentice Hall is widely acknowledged to be among the quickest in the industry. Our turnaround times vary according to the nature of the manuscript supplied to us, but the average is about three months for camera-ready copy and four months for a manuscript delivered on disk. For time-sensitive topics, we can turn out books in under twelve weeks.

9. Where Would my Book be Sold?

Prentice Hall has one of the largest sales forces of any technical publisher. Our highly experienced sales staff have developed firm business partnerships with all the major retail bookstores in Europe, America, Asia, the Middle East and South Africa, ensuring that your book receives maximum retail exposure. Prentice Hall's marketing department is responsible for ensuring the widest possible review coverage in magazines and journals.

Our books are usually present at major trade shows and exhibitions, either on our own stands or those belonging to major retail bookshops. Our presence at trade shows ensures that your work can be inspected by the most senior figures within any given field. We also have a very successful corporate and institutional sales team, dedicated to selling our books into large companies, user groups, book clubs, training seminars and professional bodies.

Local language translations can provide not only a significant boost to an author's royalty income, but also will allow your research/findings to reach a wider audience, thus furthering your professional prospects. To maintain both the author's and Prentice Hall's reputation, we license foreign language deals only with publishing houses of the highest repute.

10. I Don't have Time to Write a Book!

To enjoy all the advantages of being a published author, it is not always necessary for you to write an entire book. Prentice Hall welcomes books written by multiple authors. If you feel that your skills lie in a very specific area, or that you do not have the time to write an entire book, please get in touch regardless. Prentice Hall may have a book in progress that would benefit from your ideas. You may know individuals or teams in your field who could act as co-author(s). If not, Prentice Hall can probably put you in touch with the right people. Royalties for shared-author books are distributed according to respective participation.

11. Could my Company Benefit?

Many Prentice Hall authors use their book to lever their commercial interests, and we like to do all we can to help. If a well-written book is an excellent marketing tool for an author, then it can also be an excellent marketing tool for the author's company. A book is its own highly focused marketing channel, a respected medium that takes your company name to all the right people. Previous examples of marketing opportunities with our books include:

- Free advertising in the back pages
- Packaging in suitable corporate livery (book covers, flyers etc.)
- Mounting software demos in the back page on disk or CD-ROM

Although Prentice Hall has to keep its publications free of undue corporate or institutional bias, in general the options for cross-marketing are varied and completely open to discussion.

12. I Have an Idea for a Book. What Next?

We invite you to submit a book proposal. We need proposals to be formatted in a specific way, so please contact us at the address below for our free proposal guidelines.

The Acquisition Editor
Professional and Consumer Publishing
Prentice Hall
Campus 400, Maylands Avenue
Hemel Hempstead, Hertfordshire
HP2 7EZ
England

Tel: +44 (0)1442 881900
Fax: +44 (0)1442 252544
e-mail: jdunne@prenhall.co.uk

Licensing Agreement

This book comes with a CD software package. By opening this package, you are agreeing to be bound by the following:

The software contained on this CD is, in many cases, copyrighted, and all rights are reserved by the individual licensing agreements associated with each piece of software contained on the CD. THIS SOFTWARE IS PROVIDED FREE OF CHARGE, AS IS, AND WITHOUT WARRANTY OF ANY KIND, EITHER EXPRESSED OR IMPLIED, INCLUDING, BUT NOT LIMITED TO, THE IMPLIED WARRANTIES OF MERCHANTABILITY AND FITNESS FOR A PARTICULAR PURPOSE. Neither the book publisher nor its dealers and its distributors assumes any liability for any alleged or actual damages arising from the use of this software.

What's on the CD-ROM?

The first thing you need to look at on this CD is Virgin Net's outstanding Internet service. See over the page for details on how to sign up for your one month online FREE, plus 10 megabytes of web space to build your own web site! Once you're up and running with Virgin Net, take a look at our CD. It's packed with goodies to help you get the most from your Internet connection.

CD-ROM Contents

Software

Dozens of the most popular Internet applications – email, newsreader and FTP programs, multimedia plug-ins & viewers, graphics and HTML utilities, indispensable 'gadgets & gizmos' ... In short, everything you need!

Chapter-by-Chapter

Every chapter in the book has a corresponding section on the CD with instant links to all the great web sites reviewed. Simply insert the CD into your PC and click on where you want to go.

Build Your Own Web Pages with our HTML Reference
This section offers a mass of examples and practical information, sorted into categories such as Images & Mulitmedia, Frames, Tables and Tips & Tricks. Whether you want to learn more, or just copy and paste the examples I've given you, the answers are all at your fingertips.

Web Directory
Hundreds more links to the best of the Web, this time sorted into 24 categories – and all just a click away.

How Do I Get to all This Stuff?

To use the CD-ROM, insert the disc into your CD-ROM and follow these steps:

In **Windows 95:** Double-click the My Computer icon on your desktop, then double-click the icon for your CD-ROM drive.

In **Windows 3.1:** Start File Manager and then click your CD-ROM drive's icon on the toolbar.

Begin by reading the text-file **readme .txt** that you"ll see in the root directory of the CD-ROM. This provides extra information about using the CD, installing the accompanying software titles and easy instructions for setting up Microsoft ® Internet Explorer. When you're ready to continue, double-click the file named **index.htm**, to open it in Internet Explorer. In true point-and-click web style, this will lead you through the complete contents of the CD-ROM.

Welcome to Virgin Net

We're here to give you the best Internet service there is. That's it. Once you've tried it we hope you will stay with us for a long time. Exploring the Internet can be a confusing experience at first. Virgin Net is here to provide a helping hand — we will guide you through the pitfalls and help you get the best from the Internet.

Once you get online you'll find that we've provided you with a guide to some of the best things on the Internet, and a number of features of our own. Please feel free to contact us if you have any comments on how we might improve our service or if there are any new things you would like to see included.

Millions of computers storing billions of files accessed by tens of millions of people. But don't panic: we'll show you around and give you a guide book before turning you loose. And we'll always be close at hand with help.

If you feel yourself getting into trouble, please call our 24-hour helpline: 0500 55 88 44.

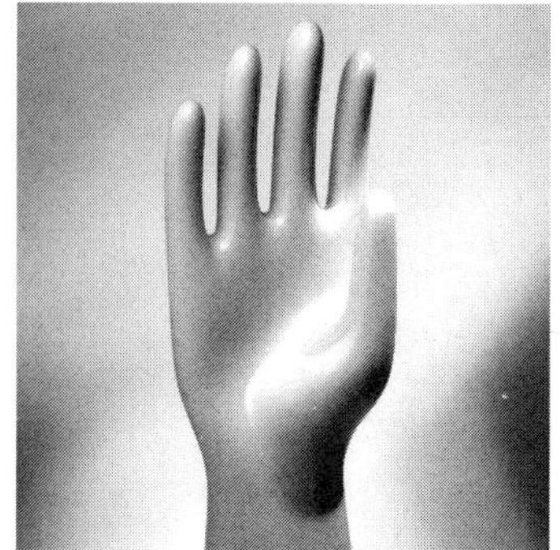

Virgin Net is simple to use. You don't need to know anything about the Internet

This booklet contains simple step-by-step instructions for getting onto the Internet, and will guide you through to a successful connection within a few minutes.

All you need is a personal computer, a modem, an ordinary telephone line and the installation CD, which you'll find on the inside back cover of this book. Within minutes, you'll have access to the world's biggest reference library, CD collection, department store and news-stand. You'll be able to search for information, communicate with people all over the world, discuss your interests and share ideas.

A box of electronics that allows your computer to communicate through a telephone line. It's like a TV aerial tuned to Virgin Net, receiving all the things that you see on your screen. But unlike an aerial, your modem also sends your commands back.

Your computer is connected to Virgin Net by telephone. No matter where your computer is getting information from, you only pay for a local call. Remember: while you're connected, you can't use that line to make or receive calls.

All for the price of a local phone call.

What you will need

An IBM compatible PC 486SX or better. If you have an Apple Mac, please call free on 0500 55 88 44 for information.

If you are running Windows 95, you may also need your original Windows 95 CD or diskettes.

This information will only be used if you choose to remain with us once your free trial period has expired.

Due to the amount of time it takes to set up a Direct Debit, we will need to have your first payment via Credit or Debit card.

1. A personal computer (PC), running Windows 3.1 or Windows 95.
2. A modem. Plug it's phone lead into a working telephone socket and, unless your computer has an internal modem, plug the other lead into the appropriate socket in your computer.
3. The CDs or floppy disks (diskettes) from this pack.
4. The following information:
   - Your name, address and postcode.
   - The code number in the plastic wallet on the inside back cover of this book.
   - The make and model of your modem.
   - Your payment details for your subscription (Credit card or Direct Debit).

All you have to do now is follow these three easy steps...

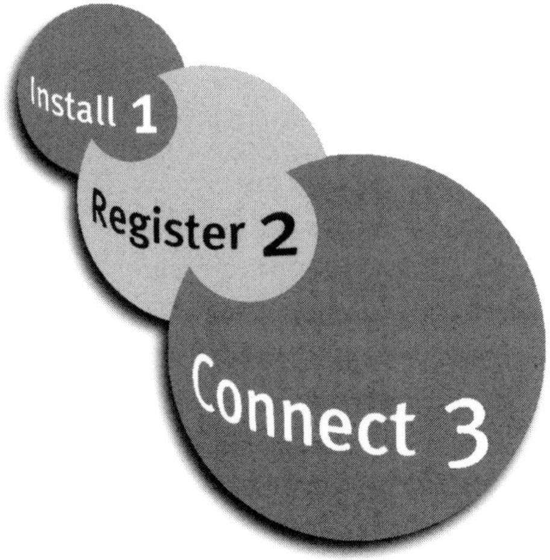

...and then you'll be ready.

The Virgin Net installation pack contains all the programs you need to connect to, and use, the Internet. Most of the information and entertainment you'll find on the Internet is linked by the World Wide Web. You navigate through the World Wide Web using a BROWSER. A browser is a program which knows how to play and display the many different types of pictures, sounds, movies or text files that you will find on the 'Web'. The browser is also your tool for moving around the Web, just using clicks of your mouse. It will also let you send and receive email, and read and send messages to newsgroups.

An easy way of finding most of the information on the Internet. The Web is made up of millions of linked pages of text and pictures, which you can display on your computer.

Keep in touch with your friends and colleagues by sending electronic messages. It's cheaper than a phone call.

Whatever your interest or hobby, you'll find people talking (in writing) about it in a newsgroup. Anyone can post messages to a newsgroup, and anyone can read them.

The browser included in the Virgin Net pack is called Netscape Navigator. We've also included Microsoft's Internet Explorer browser on the CD.

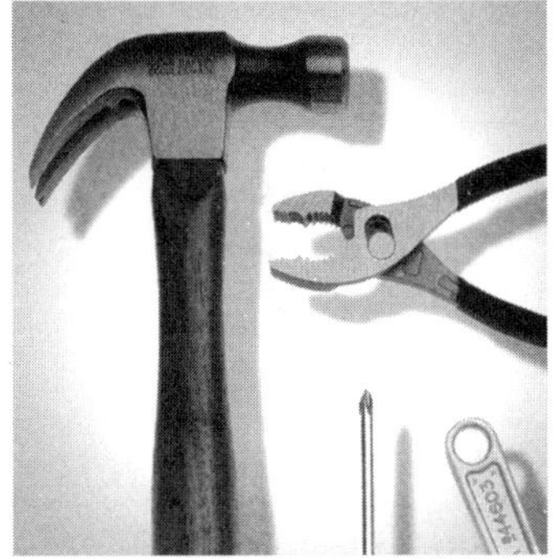

How to install Virgin Net

First of all, make sure that you have shut down any other programs and applications that are running on your computer, except for Windows 95 or Windows 3.1.

Next, put the CD into your CD-ROM drive. The Installation Program will do some tests on your computer, to see if you have disk space for the Virgin Net programs and if your machine can run them.

If there's a problem, the Installation Program will tell you exactly what it is. Some problems you can solve easily by following the on-screen instructions. If the problem is more serious, call our free 24-hour helpline on **0500 55 88 44**. Before you call, take a note of the problem message from the Installation program – it will help our team guide you through the solution.

During installation, you may be asked to insert your Windows 95 CD, so keep it handy. Virgin Net uses certain Windows 95 programs to connect your computer and modem to the Internet. These files may not have already been installed.

Windows 95 users only

(If you are using a CD and the installation starts automatically, you can skip straight to step 4.)

1. Select START on the Taskbar
2. Select RUN in the Start menu
3. Type D:\VIRGIN.NET\SETUP
4. Click OK and follow the on-screen instructions

Windows 3.1 users only

1. Open PROGRAM MANAGER
2. Select FILE from the Menubar
3. Select RUN
4. Type D:\VIRGIN.NET\SETUP
5. Click OK and follow the on-screen instructions

Once the browser installation is complete, you are ready to register with Virgin Net. To do this, your computer will dial and connect to Virgin Net for the first time. The Registration program makes a local rate telephone call to Virgin Net using your modem, and then asks for your personal and payment details. The information you provide is used to set up your account.

THIS INFORMATION IS CONFIDENTIAL AND COMPLETELY SECURE. YOUR DETAILS ARE SENT BY A DIRECT LINK TO OUR PRIVATE COMPUTER, WHICH IS NOT CONNECTED TO THE INTERNET. THERE IS NO WAY THAT THE INFORMATION YOU SEND CAN BE INTERCEPTED OR READ BY ANY OTHER INTERNET USER.

As soon as you have done this, Virgin Net will send you your unique Username and Password. Please make a note of these, as you will need them every time you want to connect to Virgin Net. Your Username is also the name you will use as your email address.

FROM NOW ON, YOUR UNIQUE VIRGIN NET USERNAME WILL TELL US WHO YOU ARE EVERY TIME YOU CONNECT, AND TYPING IN YOUR PASSWORD WILL CONFIRM IT.

Before you start, be sure to check that your modem, telephone line and computer are all properly linked up and the modem is switched on. Then, just follow the simple on-screen registration instructions.

Problems with registration

If the Installation procedure has been successful, it should have taken you directly to our on-line registration screen. But if it hasn't, don't worry. First try this:

1. Check that your modem is turned on and plugged in correctly.
2. Check that your telephone line is working properly. Do this by plugging in an ordinary telephone and dialling the special Virgin Net Registration number, **0645 50 54 40**. You should first hear the line ringing and then something that sounds a bit like a fax machine or static on the radio.

MAKE SURE THAT NO ONE IS ON THE PHONE BEFORE YOU TRY TO CONNECT TO VIRGIN NET. IT WON'T WORK AND THEY'RE LIKELY TO HEAR A HORRIBLE SCREECHING.

Finally, the registration process will install the remaining Virgin Net programs. These are:

- Global Chat: lets you talk live to other people on the Net by typing messages
- RealAudio: allows Netscape to play sound files without downloading them first
- Shockwave: allows Netscape to display interactive, animated graphics and movies

We also provide Cybersitter, which allows you to control your children's access to the Internet. Instructions for installing Cybersitter can be found by pressing the ONLINE HELP button on your browser.

THERE ARE MANY THINGS ON THE INTERNET YOU MIGHT NOT WANT YOUR KIDS TO SEE, ALTHOUGH THEY ARE FINE FOR CONSENTING ADULTS. CYBERSITTER LETS YOU BLOCK THESE SITES.

Once you've completed registration you will have everything you need to use Virgin Net and connect to the Internet any time you want.

Whenever you want to connect to Virgin Net, all you need to do is:

1. First, make sure that your modem, telephone line and computer are properly connected.
2. Then turn your modem and computer on and double-click the Virgin Net Netscape Navigator icon on your Windows 95 desktop or in the Virgin Net Program Group if you are using Windows 3.1.
3. Next you will be asked to enter your Virgin Net Username and Password.
4. Finally, click the connect button. Your modem will connect you to Virgin Net by making a local rate phone call.

TAP THE LEFT-HAND MOUSE BUTTON TWICE, QUICKLY. USUALLY USED TO START A PROGRAM. REMEMBER: ONCE YOU'RE USING NETSCAPE, YOU ONLY NEED TO CLICK ONCE TO JUMP TO A NEW LINK.

WHEREVER YOU ARE IN THE COUNTRY, YOUR TELEPHONE CONNECTION TO VIRGIN NET'S COMPUTERS IS ALWAYS CHARGED AS IF YOU WERE MAKING A LOCAL CALL.

Remember, your Virgin Net subscription does not include the price of this call, and all other connecting calls you make. The charges will appear on your phone bill.

Once the connection has successfully been made, the browser will download on to your screen the Virgin Net home page. Your home page is always the first thing you see each time you connect to the Internet, and the Virgin Net home page is designed clearly and simply to:

1. Help you to search for useful, entertaining or important information.
2. Give you direct links to the places we recommend.
3. Bring you up-to-the-minute news, sport and entertainment.
4. Let you download and play games or use your computer to connect to Web sites containing recorded and even live sounds, such as Virgin Radio.

GET INFORMATION OR FILES FROM A COMPUTER ON THE INTERNET AND COPY THEM ON TO YOUR OWN COMPUTER.

THE PLACE WHERE YOU'LL BEGIN YOUR EXPLORATION OF THE INTERNET. AND DON'T WORRY IF YOU EVER GET LOST – ONE CLICK OF THE HOME BUTTON ON YOUR BROWSER WILL TAKE YOU STRAIGHT BACK THERE.

WHAT A PROGRAMME IS TO TV AND A BOOK IS TO A LIBRARY, A WEB SITE IS TO THE INTERNET.

1215AM & 105.8FM. THE WORLD'S GREATEST RADIO STATION, OF COURSE.

That's it. The rest is up to you. Remember, you're in charge. From now on, we're just here to help.

Help – and where you can find it

We have made Virgin Net as simple and easy to use as possible. Even so, we know that for newcomers the Internet can be a strange and confusing place. That's why we've created an ONLINE HELP service that will answer the questions you're most likely to ask.

There are some questions that come up again and again. They're referred to as "Frequently Asked Questions" or FAQs. Before asking a question – either in Virgin Net or a news-group – it's a good idea to check to see if the answer is already in the relevant FAQ.

You can find the Virgin Net help service by pressing on the ONLINE HELP button on your browser. This will connect you to our advice centre where the answer to your problem should be quick and easy to find.

Electronic mail, better known as email, is so useful that many people get on to the Net just to use it.
It's that good. Unlike old-fashioned 'snail mail', you don't need a stamp and it travels at the speed of light.

Once you start using email, you will be able to send messages and documents quickly, cheaply and at any time of the day or night, to anyone in the world with an email address.

To start using email, press on the EMAIL button on the browser, and the email window will open.

To receive email, click on the GET MAIL button. Netscape will go to the Virgin Net computers, check to see if you have new mail waiting for you there and download any new messages on to your computer. New messages will appear in bold and you can read them by double-clicking on them.

Giant, mysterious black cabinets covered in thousands of flashing lights and quietly leaking white coolant fumes. No? Actually they look pretty much like your machine, except a bit faster. Probably.

We want to make using the Internet as easy as possible. And that means having the best help service you'll find anywhere. As well as our free 24-hour helpline, we've prepared an online tutorial to take you through the basics, step by step. We've written reference pages that answer the most commonly asked questions. You can find the Virgin Net help service by pressing on the ONLINE HELP button on your browser.

To send email, click on the TO MAIL button and an empty message window will appear. Type in the email address of the person you want to write to, and then type your message. Send it by clicking on the SEND button.

To reply directly to an email that you have received, the simplest way is by clicking on the RE:MAIL button. A window will open showing the original message with the sender's return email address already filled in. Just type your reply and press the SEND button.

To learn more about using email, use the Virgin Net online help service, where we have prepared a full guide to using and getting the best out of email.

Rave reviews for Virgin Net

“Of all the ISPs reviewed here, we feel that one stands out – Virgin Net... Virgin Net represents fantastic value for money”
What PC?

“★★★★★ For beginners who aren't sure”
Stuff Magazine

“This Internet Service Provider calls the shots”
The Independent

“Virgin Net, a competitively priced dial-up service... concentrating on making installation and the whole getting online experience easier and less technical”
Internet Magazine

“The masses are Web virgins, and therein lies the answer. It is none other than Virgin who will provide the breakthrough for the masses”
Computer Shopper